Kurds in Dark Times

Contemporary Issues in the Middle East
Mehran Kamrava, *Series Editor*

Select Titles in Contemporary Issues in the Middle East

Being There, Being Here: Palestinian Writings in the World
Maurice Ebileeni

*Generations of Dissent: Intellectuals, Cultural Production,
and the State in the Middle East and North Africa*
Alexa Firat and R. Shareah Taleghani, eds.

The Lost Orchard: The Palestinian-Arab Citrus Industry, 1850–1950
Mustafa Kabha and Nahum Karlinsky

Ottoman Children and Youth during World War I
Nazan Maksudyan

Readings in Syrian Prison Literature: The Poetics of Human Rights
R. Shareah Taleghani

Turkey's State Crisis: Institutions, Reform, and Conflict
Bülent Aras

Understanding Hezbollah: The Hegemony of Resistance
Abed T. Kanaaneh

*Victims of Commemoration: The Architecture
and Violence of Confronting the Past in Turkey*
Eray Çaylı

For a full list of titles in this series,
visit https://press.syr.edu/supressbook-series
/contemporary-issues-in-the-middle-east/.

Kurds in Dark Times

New Perspectives on Violence and Resistance in Turkey

Edited by Ayça Alemdaroğlu
and Fatma Müge Göçek

Copyright © 2023 by Syracuse University Press
Syracuse, New York 13244-5290

All Rights Reserved

First Edition 2023

23 24 25 26 27 28   6 5 4 3 2 1

∞ The paper used in this publication meets the minimum requirements of the American National Standard for Information Sciences—Permanence of Paper for Printed Library Materials, ANSI Z39.48-1992.

For a listing of books published and distributed by Syracuse University Press, visit https://press.syr.edu.

ISBN: 978-0-8156-3770-7 (hardcover)
978-0-8156-3780-6 (paperback)
978-0-8156-5564-0 (e-book)

LCCN: 2022023024

Manufactured in the United States of America

We dedicate this book to all academics who speak truth
to power throughout the world against all odds

To the Academics for Peace, who demand the state stop violence against
Kurdish civilians and create conditions for lasting peace in the country

To Mehmet Fatih Tıraş, a thirty-four-year-old academic who signed
the Peace Petition in 2016 as he was completing his PhD in economics
at Çukurova University, only to face so many obstacles in achieving that
goal and then in finding a job because of the government's stigmatization
of Peace Academics that he ended his life

And to İsmail Beşikçi, a Turkish sociologist who paid a large
price for his intellectual curiosity, courage, and resilience by being
not only excluded from Turkish academia but also imprisoned
for seventeen years for his views

Contents

List of Illustrations   *ix*
List of Tables   *xi*
Acknowledgments   *xiii*

Introduction
Ayça Alemdaroğlu and Fatma Müge Göçek   *1*

Part One. Alternative Perspectives on the Historical Origins of Ethnic/Racial Categories in Turkey

1. "Land of the Kurds" or "Land of the Rocks"?
Changing Perceptions of Kurdistan in Ottoman and European Sources
Metin Atmaca   *33*

2. Making Minorities in the Late Ottoman Period
Armenians and Kurds
Janet Klein   *63*

3. The Turkishness Contract and the Formation of Turkishness
Barış Ünlü   *90*

4. Kurds in the History of Displacement in Izmir, 1850–Present
Michael Ferguson   *119*

Part Two. Racialization and Violence

5. The Making of Coloniality in Turkey
Racialization of Kurds in a Working-Class District in Istanbul between 1950 and 1980
Güllistan Yarkın   *143*

6. "I Would Have Recognized You from Your Smell"
Racialization of Kurdish Migrant Farmworkers in Western Turkey
Deniz Duruiz   164

7. Anti-Kurdish Communal Violence in the Twenty-First Century
Origins, Patterns, Directions
Şefika Kumral   192

8. *Homo Sacer* at the Border
Turkish Narrative Violence in the Representation of the Roboskî Massacre
Ali Eşref Keleş   226

Part Three. Micropolitics of Resistance

9. Youth and Politics in Diyarbakır
Delal Aydın   255

10. Far from Separatist Violence
The Kurdish Political Prisoners' Hunger Strike of 2012 in Turkey
Amy Bartholomew and Ruşen Fırat Güllüoğlu   277

11. Silencing Historical Traumas versus Constructing Resistance Narratives
The Saturday Mothers and Peace Mothers in Turkey
Emine Rezzan Karaman   308

12. Institutionalizing Kurdish Women's Political Engagements
Party Politics and Affirmative-Action Measures
Hazal Atay   334

13. A Displaced, Unsettled Political Subject
Kurdish Women's Struggles in Europe
Nisa Göksel   356

Afterword
Hamit Bozarslan   389

Contributor Biographies   407
Index   413

Illustrations

1.1. Reversed map of Anatolia, 1732   *45*

1.2. European map showing "Curdistania," 1730   *55*

1.3. Drawing of Silêmanî, 1819   *57*

4.1. Building that housed the Mardin–Midyat Üçağıl (Kozê) Village Cooperation and Solidarity Association, 2013   *129*

7.1. Trends in communal versus extreme-right nationalist violence and military deaths, 1984–2011   *194*

7.2. Annual GDP per capita growth rate in Turkey, 1981–2011   *203*

7.3. Political Instability Index and military deaths in the Turkish state's armed conflict with the PKK, 1981–2011   *209*

7.4. Unified Democracy Score in Turkey, 1981–2011   *215*

7.5. Social movement mobilization of the Kurds, 1981–2011   *217*

8.1. Social construction of Turkish narrative violence against the Kurds   *235*

8.2. *Hürriyet* headline, 31 December 2011   *239*

Tables

7.1. Pearson Correlation Coefficients for Selected Variables   *197*

7.2 Coefficients of Negative Binomial Regression Analysis of Annual Frequency of Communal Violence against the Kurdish Population   *198*

7.3 Geography and Demographics of Interview Locations   *200*

7.4. Context and Targets of Collective-Violence Events   *218*

8.1. Ideological Affiliation and Ownership of Turkish Newspapers, 2009–2015   *228*

12.1 Women's Representation in the Turkish Parliament, 1935–2018   *338*

Acknowledgments

This book is built on a collaboration that began in 2016 at the Historical and Comparative Perspectives on Kurdish Politics Conference at Northwestern University. We are grateful to the Keyman Modern Turkish Studies Program and the Buffett Institute for Global Studies for sponsoring the conference and allowing us an invaluable institutional space for open discussion in North America at a time when such spaces have eroded in Turkey. In particular, we thank the Buffett Institute's former director Bruce Carruthers and especially Zeynep and Melih Keyman, the sponsors of the Keyman Program, for their ceaseless support for Ayça Alemdaroğlu in refashioning the Keyman Program from 2015 to 2020 as a hub for critical studies of Turkey. We also thank Metin Serbest, immigration/human rights lawyer and Northwestern alumnus, for his support for Northwestern University's Kurdish Studies Conferences in 2017 and 2018.

At these conferences, we developed a large network of scholars who, despite all the pressure and risk of persecution they face in Turkey, continue to think, research, and write on both past and present discrimination and violence in Turkey. Over the years, these conversations expanded to include scholars who study questions of ethnicity/race, violence, and resistance in other parts of the world, such as South Africa and Palestine. We thank all the conference participants and the authors who contributed to this volume for their intellectual fervor and inspiring work.

Kurds in Dark Times

Introduction

Ayça Alemdaroğlu and Fatma Müge Göçek

Thinking has recently and once again become very challenging in Turkey as the country became immersed in gross violations of human rights, repression, and violence in a repetition of the past. Such abuses and violence have a hefty cost for journalists, academics, students, and political dissidents. Yet, for most citizens, they remain unnoticed or marginal due to censorship, propaganda, and simply lies by the government. Hence, the systematic silencing obscures the extent and degree of rights violations and violence.

We argue here that the times we live in are akin to what Hannah Arendt describes in *Men in Dark Times* (1968). Reflecting on twentieth-century totalitarian regimes, Arendt contends that the darkness was not merely about physical destruction of Jews and others through genocides, purges, and hunger but also about the destruction of the truth by "bureaucratic rationalization" and "mere talk," which served to obscure the horrors conducted by drawing them into "incomprehensible triviality" (ix). Consequently, ordinary men and women, unable to think and judge for themselves, not only normalized terror and torture but also yielded their support to dictatorial regimes. Under such conditions, Arendt contends, the only possible defense of citizens against the totalitarian or bureaucratic tendencies toward "evil" would be "to think" because only thinking and judging for themselves would ultimately enable citizens to wrest their agency away from state propaganda and publicly call out evil (Berkowitz 2009).

Arendt further elaborates on the political implications of "thinking" when she critically analyzes the Nazi murderer Adolf Eichmann's trial in

Eichmann in Jerusalem (2006). She notes that Eichmann, notwithstanding his deeds' evilness, was strikingly "average"; his evil actions were motivated mainly by his ordinary bourgeois ambition of getting ahead by doing his job "well." Arendt draws parallels between Eichmann, bureaucrats, and ordinary citizens—which includes the colluding Jewish leaders—to argue that what emerged in Nazi Germany was a collective escape from "thinking" and making an ethical judgment. This mass evasion of accountability and collective responsibility for one's actions enabled the Nazi regime and its atrocities.

Arendt's analysis of "dark times" is pertinent to Turkey time and time again. Since 2013, the Turkish state has embarked on an intensified campaign against political dissent. The Kurds are once more the primary target of this campaign in addition to the unabated economic marginalization and political discrimination of them. Especially after the elections of June 2015 when the pro-Kurdish People's Democratic Party (Halkların Demokratik Partisi, HDP) won 13 percent of the vote in general elections, thereby becoming the third-largest party in the Turkish Parliament, the government's persecution of Kurds reached a new level. The state has also expanded censorship and propaganda, obstructing citizens' right to get informed and ability to think, judge, and call out human rights violations and state violence.

The HDP's electoral success had emerged on the coattails of the peace negotiations initiated by the ruling Justice and Development Party (Adalet ve Kalkınma Partisi, AKP) with Abdullah Öcalan, the imprisoned leader of the Kurdistan Workers' Party (Partîya Karkerên Kurdistanê, PKK). Yet that success caused the AKP to lose its majority vote, which is required to form the government. At that juncture, instead of attempting to form a coalition government, the AKP leadership instead plunged Turkey into violence and instability. A series of attacks—first, in Suruç the Islamic States of Iraq and Syria (ISIS) killed thirty-three members of the pro-Kurdish Socialist Youth group that had mobilized to help the Syrian Kurds' fight against ISIS in Kobane, and then the murder of two police officers in Ceylanpınar, for which the government held the PKK responsible, became a pretext for the government to end the Kurdish Peace Process and initiate an extensive military campaign in southeastern Turkey—known as Bakur

(Bakurê Kurdistanê), or Northern Kurdistan—and in the Kurdish regions across the border into Syria and Iraq.

The government under the AKP had initially searched for a peaceful solution to the Kurdish conflict mainly to meet the requirements for Turkey to join the European Union (EU). However, when the AKP's electoral support declined and the EU option proved to be improbable, the government restored the previous state-security approach, flaring the conflict. Hence, the AKP government chose violence over peace to stay in power. The government deployed thousands of military officers in massive security operations supported by heavy armaments to generate shock, awe, and fear. Concomitantly, it also declared blanket curfews in several Kurdish cities and towns where the PKK's youth affiliate—the Patriotic Revolutionary Youth Movement (Yurtsever Devrimci Gençlik Hareketi, YDGH) had become active in building barricades and digging trenches. The ensuing urban warfare in Turkey's Kurdistan escalated civilian deaths dramatically: between July 2015 and December 2016, some two thousand people, including about twelve hundred local Kurds, were reportedly killed in security operations. The extended curfews cut off entire Kurdish neighborhoods, confining residents in their homes for several days at a time. The brutal military campaign also razed several cities and towns to the ground in some parts of Kurdistan, displacing hundreds of thousands of citizens. The Office of the United Nations High Commissioner for Human Rights (2017) has documented many human rights violations in Kurdistan in the same period, including killings; excessive use of force; enforced disappearances; torture; destruction of housing and cultural heritage; prevention of access to food, water, emergency medical care, and livelihoods; and violence against women.

The Turkish state's retreat to military methods and violence against the Kurds since 2015 goes hand in hand with the deterioration of freedom of expression and academic freedoms. Scholars whose research makes a case against Turkey's state policy have always been at risk of persecution. Perhaps the most dramatic legal case of state violence against the Kurds has been the seventeen-year persecution of İsmail Beşikçi, a Turkish sociologist. He was the first intellectual in Turkey to define the Kurds as an "international colony" (Beşikçi 1990) and to vividly document Kurds' dire living conditions. Beşikçi then argued that the Turkish state and its governments legitimated the violence by alleging that the Kurds undermined "the Turkish nation's indivisibility." Even though he had not engaged in violence, his way of thinking about the Kurds deviated from the official narrative, so that was enough for the Turkish state to arrest and imprison him for seventeen years.

More recently, just as the faltering Kurdish Peace Process came to an end in 2015, Barış Ünlü, a fellow sociologist and a contributor to this volume, was taken to court for penning an exam question on Abdullah Öcalan at Ankara University. In the indictment, the Turkish prosecutor claimed that the exam question aimed to "legitimate" Öcalan's ideas and therefore amounted to "terror propaganda." Although the court acquitted Ünlü, his university continued to penalize him by censoring his academic activities: it forbade his participation in the Kurdish politics conference at Northwestern University in 2016, where initial conversations about this book took place. Ünlü was eventually dismissed from his university in the aftermath of the coup d'etat attempt on 15 July 2016.

In 2015, along with the end to the peace process and a rapid move back to the militarization of the conflict with the PKK, the government expanded the persecution of academia from an individual to a collective level in its reaction to more than a thousand academics' signing of a Peace Petition titled "We Will Not Be a Party to This Crime" ("Bu suça ortak olmayacağız") to protest the state's escalating violence against Kurdish civilians in the Kurdish region. The academics did so to raise public awareness and to request that the government take the initiative to end violence against the Kurds and resume the peace process. The government's response to the petition was too harsh: President Recep Tayyip Erdoğan led the charge by calling the petitioners "traitors." Within a day of his provocative speech identifying the academics as a target to be duly punished, several Turkish universities took punitive measures against faculty who had signed the petition, eventually expelling most of them from their positions. In addition to the universities, the judiciary also acted upon the Turkish president's provocation: the Istanbul Public Prosecutor's Office launched a criminal investigation against the petitioners under Article 7 of the Antiterror Law, charging academics with "engaging in terrorist propaganda." Initially, four academics suspected of penning the petition were arrested and remained imprisoned in pretrial detention for the full legal limit of forty days before they were released. In the meantime, engaged academics reopened the petition to additional signatures; more than a thousand more academics signed it to support their colleagues. Another petition, this time an international one, was circulated, asking the Turkish government to stop the persecution of the scholars, and was signed by hundreds of renowned scholars in the West, including Judith Butler, Noam Chomsky, Étienne Balibar, and several Nobel laureates.

Even though the government suspended the initial criminal investigation, it launched yet another one by exploiting the state of emergency declared following the coup attempt in July 2016. More than six thousand academics were dismissed: they were either legally stripped of the right to teach at the universities or became unemployed when their universities were closed down for alleged sedition. Also, hundreds of academics who signed the petition were prosecuted on antiterrorism charges, and many received prison sentences. The official stigma the president had pronounced against the Academics for Peace (Barış için Akademisyenler) drove a young academic, Mehmet Fatih Tıraş, to commit suicide. Many left their profession or fled Turkey entirely.

Eventually, in July 2019, after four nightmarish years in which the purges and trials had decimated the Peace Academics, the Constitutional Court finally ruled that penalizing them on charges of "terror propaganda" had violated their freedom of expression. By that time, however, hundreds had lost their jobs, even if they somehow managed to survive the persistent legal and political threats against their well-being.

In the process, Turkey's universities were cleared of a significant portion of critical academics who could speak truth to power. When the alleged threat the president concocted was thus eliminated, the Constitutional Court stepped in to change the initial verdict. However, the blackballed academics could not return to their positions. Nor was the country's president or university administrations held accountable for violating the academics' rights. Junior scholars who return to Turkey after completing their degrees abroad continue to counter several obstacles. A case in point is the experience of our contributor Güllistan Yarkın. After a two-year delay, the Inter-University Board (Yükseköğretim Kurulu) rejected her application to have her PhD from the State University of New York at Binghamton conferred in Turkey. The government uses an otherwise mundane bureaucratic procedure to facilitate universities' academic staff recruitment to punish critical scholars. The board's rejection letter stated that Yarkın had failed to identify the PKK as a terrorist organization in her dissertation, hence violating Turkey's Antiterror Law. In addition, the board found that her identification of Turkey as a colonial state violated Article 301 of the Criminal Law, which stipulates crimes against the nation, the state, and the government (Yarkın 2022). Yarkın is one among many who are criminalized in Turkey for refusing to use sanctioned official language in their study of social and political phenomenon such as the PKK.

Amid this official war against academics, we began our collaboration that eventually led to this book. We, the two editors of this volume, had signed the Peace Petition, but we were practically immune to its immediate punitive consequences because we live and work abroad. We wanted to utilize the relative freedoms and resources at our institutions in the United States to promote collective critical thinking, especially when spaces to do so are minimized under the widespread oppression by today's authoritarian regime in Turkey. In other words, when the Turkish state exerts violence against the Kurds to legitimate, consolidate, and sustain its authoritarian rule, we as social scientists feel that it is necessary now, more than ever, to think together and call out the past and present "wrongs" of the Turkish state's Kurdish policy.

Our initial conversation took place in Chicago in the fall of 2016 at the Historical and Comparative Perspectives on the Kurdish Politics Conference at Northwestern University. The conference program included talks by academics on the formation and evolution of Turkish state policy toward the Kurds, resistance and autonomy movements, political parties, and the everyday struggles of Kurdish citizens.

The Northwestern conference was one of the first of several Kurdish studies meetings in North America, followed successively by ensuing meetings at Northwestern and other major North American research universities such as Yale, the University of Toronto, and Brown. We intended to use the academic space available to us in the United States to call attention to the erosion of the already-restricted public space and academic freedom in Turkey as well as the escalating violence against the Kurds.

Turkey's authoritarian regime possesses a relentless capacity to operate an extensive security regime, violate citizens' fundamental rights and freedoms, and disseminate disinformation. We argue that the authoritarianism that we witness in Turkey and elsewhere in the world today poses no fewer challenges than those posed by early twentieth-century fascist dictatorships. That is why we began here within a framework inspired by Hannah Arendt: what she argued regarding collective violence in Nazi Germany is still very relevant today. What is needed in dark times, Arendt wrote, are people who think and who by engaging in thinking create a space within which they can take on the wrongs committed in society. So this book is the physical product of our collective effort to think, judge, and declare what is "wrong" in Turkey in relation to the treatment of Kurds. It is also a product of our commitment as social scientists to understand and explain the origins, forms, and lived experiences of discrimination, displacement, and violence that occur in the world. We believe that the democratization of Turkey and other states require acknowledging past injuries and responding to the present demands for justice.

We now turn to further contextualizing our work by first providing a historical overview of the Kurdish issue in Turkey. Then, we summarize the book's contribution to existing literature and how each chapter helps highlight the systematic discrimination and violence Kurds have faced in Turkey as well as their experiences and resistance in surviving these assaults.

Historical Background of Turkey's Kurdish Politics

Though the exact number of Kurds living in Turkey is unknown, the current estimates are between 13 to 20 percent of the total population (Kirişçi and Winrow 1997, 15; McDowall 2000, 3; Pultar 2011; van Bruinessen 1978, 1992). The term *Kurdish* applies to speakers of one of four closely related Indo-Iranian languages—Kurmanji, Sorani, Zaza, and Gurani— and to their descendants (McDowall 2000, 9–10). If the Turkish-speaking descendants of Kurds were also included in the population figures, the total number of Kurds in Turkey would undoubtedly be much higher, probably reaching at least a quarter of Turkey's present population. It is impossible to know the exact population of any ethnic group because the state does not officially collect population data about ethnicity in order not to undermine the unitary-nation myth on which Turkish nationalism depends. Moreover, over the past three decades the state has evacuated thousands of villages for posing a "security threat." Millions of Kurds have migrated to cities in western Turkey and western Europe, primarily Germany. Although we do not precisely know the Kurdish population size, economic and social indicators show that the southeastern region, predominantly populated by Kurds, is one of the least-developed areas in the country (Bildirici and Koç 2018; İçduygu, Romano, and Sirkeci 1999; Yadırgı 2018).

Yet underdevelopment is not a cause of what became known as Turkey's "Kurdish problem." It is at best an outcome of that problem, which has been generated largely by the oppression of and denial of rights to an ethnic minority (the Kurds) by a majority group (the Turks). The state discourse has blandly reduced the "Kurdish problem" to a mere socioeconomic issue—the underdevelopment of the country's Southeast region—hence denying the history of discrimination and oppression. Moreover, until recently, it has denied the existence of Kurdish ethnic identity and continues to punish Kurds' political demands for equality and justice. Furthermore, the Turkish discourse also dismisses Kurds' political actions and steals their agency by claiming that Kurds are gullible pawns in the hands of Western states that aim to weaken Turkey, as they tried to do in the past. Hence, the state in Turkey insists on identifying the Kurdish region solely according to its geographical parameters, "the Southeast," and assumes that the employment of the historically accurate proper name used by the Kurds, "Kurdistan," is an endorsement of their secessionist struggle.

Political unrest in Turkey's Kurdistan in the Republican Era was almost coeval with the republic's establishment in 1923. The Sheikh Said Rebellion of 1925 emerged in reaction to the increasingly secular and ethnic Turkish character of the emerging Turkish state and attempted to bring back the old Ottoman imperial social order in which the Kurds and

Turks, as members of the dominant Muslim community, were treated as equals. Other rebellions in Ağrı in 1927–30 and in Dêrsim (Tunceli) in 1937–38 followed this initial uprising. Because these rebellions risked the success of Turkish nationalism in building a nation-state with a homogenous community, the state reacted very harshly, decimating Kurds indiscriminately by the thousands as well as oppressing other religious and ethnic groups in Turkey. This suppression was accompanied by the literal disappearance of the word *Kurd* from the Turkish lexicon; the banning of spoken Kurdish and expressions of Kurdish cultural identity in spaces under state surveillance and control, such as schools; the replacement of almost all Kurdish village and town names with Turkish ones; and the denial of parents' right to give Kurdish names to their children (Barkey 2000; Jongerden 2009; Zeydanlıoğlu 2012). In response to these measures, although some Kurds did assimilate, many others either refused, left the country, or became silent.

Even though the Kurdish rebellions before World War II had a strong tribal and religious character rather than a national one, this pattern underwent significant change after Turkey's transition to multiparty system in 1946. In the following decades, Kurds who complied with the state's security regime were allowed to join Parliament and hold significant official posts provided that they publicly suppressed their identity as Kurds. Later, amid the political liberalization allowed with the 1961 constitution in the 1960s, Kurds gradually formed a separate political movement. The continuing migration to urban areas in western Turkey and increased access to higher education escalated public awareness of Turkey's vast economic and political disparities, contributing to pluralization and subsequently to radicalization of politics and state–society relations. Kurdish activists were initially absorbed into leftist organizations prominent among students attending universities in Istanbul and Ankara. It was in these organizations, such as the Worker's Party of Turkey (Türkiye İşçi Partisi, TİP), that they began to reconceptualize the Kurds as a colonized people and to demand recognition of their ethnic difference and national liberation. In the 1970s, a number of Kurdish political organizations emerged to challenge the Turkish state nationalism and its ethnic politics.

Out of these organizations, the Kurdistan Worker's Party, although characterized often by internal disunity and conflict, established its hegemony in the 1980s, superseding other left-wing and conservative Kurdish organizations, such as the Kurdistan Democratic Party of Turkey (Türkiye Kürdistan Demokrat Partisi, TKDP), which closely identified with Mustafa Barzani's party in Iraqi Kurdistan (Gunes 2013).

In its formation, the PKK described traditional Kurdistan as a colony where tribal leaders and the local bourgeoisie had colluded to help the Turkish state exploit the lower classes, thereby identifying the liberation of Kurdish tribal society as the primary target of the party's revolutionary struggle. The goal was both national liberation and socialist transformation through armed insurgency in Kurdistan (Jongerden and Akkaya 2016). The PKK's early and sporadic use of violence, mainly against Kurdish tribal leaders and other Kurdish organizations, turned into a protracted guerrilla war against the Turkish security forces and state personnel in 1984.

The military coup of 1980 had a deep impact on Turkey. As some scholars have argued, two separate regimes came into being with the coup: autocratic militarism in the eastern provinces populated predominantly by Kurds and their semiauthoritarian incorporation in the western part of the country (Jacoby 2005). The 1980s also witnessed the transformation of the state's ethnic politics. The Turkish Republic employed Turkishness as an umbrella identity under which all citizens of Turkey who spoke Turkish and shared "Turkish culture" were "Turks." This generalization did not stand the test of time, however. The many ethnic and religious groups eventually started to publicly identify themselves as separate from the Turks. Rather than including these groups in the national body politics on equitable terms, however, the Turkish state and especially the military started to persecute all social groups other than Muslim Sunni Turks as potential threats to the nation (Ataman 2002). As a consequence, the violence against the Kurds continued, with the Turkish military now openly taking the lead.

With the commencement of military operations in 1984, the Turkish state and the PKK became identified as the two opposite sides between which every citizen had to choose (Cornell 2001, 39). The state listed the

PKK as a "terrorist organization" and carried out a successful international campaign for the European Union and the United States, among other countries, to do the same. Furthermore, the state has insisted on equating virtually all expressions of Kurdish identity with "PKK terrorism," and the Turkish military has been especially adamant about pursuing only an armed solution to the Kurdish demands. How one refers to the PKK is a litmus test for the state to distinguish friend from foe, "patriot" from "traitor." The state continues to surveil public speech and written text to see how the PKK is referenced both inside and outside Turkey.[1]

Despite its designation as a terrorist organization, the PKK was able to mobilize necessary resources, thousands of active fighters, and ideological support from the civilian society. Several favorable conditions contributed to this outcome in the 1980s and early 1990s. First, the flight of the PKK leader Abdullah Öcalan and a small group of activists to Syria in 1979 before the military coup protected them from the military regime's obliteration of political dissent. Second, the torture that Kurdish political prisoners were subjected to under the military regime in places such as the notorious Diyarbakir Prison between 1980 and 1984 helped later fill the ranks of the post-1980 PKK (Marcus 2007). The PKK appealed to Kurds' hearts and minds by its articulation of already-existing local conflicts between landlords and peasants in favor of the latter, its initial military efficacy and resilience in fighting the Turkish military, and its discursive strategies to create and promote a homogenous Kurdish identity (Barkey and Fuller 1998; Gunes 2013; Jongerden and Akkaya 2016; Romano 2006). Moreover, the PKK's well-financed organization contributed to the sucess in spreading its ideology. The exact sources of its financing are elusive, but both voluntary and enforced support from Kurds in Turkey

---

1. Indeed, two Turkish diplomatic personnel from the Turkish consulate in Chicago followed our conference at Northwestern and penned an official letter to the president of Northwestern University, contending that the university should not support conferences where descriptions of the PKK beyond "terrorist" were given. Typical of the Turkish Republic's policy, the letter demonstrated the disregard for freedom of thought and expression and the extension of the state's surveillance and intimidation to academic institutions abroad.

and from Kurdish migrants and refugees in western Europe, extortion of funds from businesses and transborder smuggling, and, finally, indirect and direct backing from other states in the region, such as Syria, have helped sustain the PKK's fight (Barkey and Fuller 1998, 29–34).

The Gulf War of 1990–91 initially proved beneficial to the Kurds of Turkey when the US-led operation against Iraq released northern Iraq from the Iraqi state's control, creating the US-backed Kurdish Federated State. During this period, the Turkish state undertook an active role in working out the power-sharing agreement between two local Kurdish powers, Mustafa Barzani's Kurdistan Democratic Party (KDP, Partiya Demokrat a Kurdistanê) and Celal Talabani's Patriotic Union of Kurdistan (PUK, Yekîtiya Nîştimanî ya Kurdistanê), with the intent to prevent the PKK from joining this new federated state. The ensuing conflicts between the KDP and the PUK instead ended up fostering the PKK's growth, which based its operations thereafter in Iraq, wresting by 1994 large chunks of territory away from the control of the Turkish military.

The Turkish state countered the Kurdish resistance by adopting counterinsurgency tactics. One rural tactic entailed recruiting Kurdish tribesmen into a local militia known as "village guards" (*korucu*) (Işık 2021). Another tactic was to force Kurdish civilians to "evacuate" their villages, thereby disrupting guerrilla logistics by physically removing the population. Some three thousand Kurdish settlements were cleared in southeastern Turkey, forcibly displacing about a million Kurds (Ayata and Yükseker 2005; Human Rights Watch 2002; Jongerden 2010; Kurban 2012). The military brutally pushed the locals out of their villages with beatings, rapes, and extrajudicial killings and set many villages on fire to prevent the guerrillas and the residents from coming back (Ron 1995). Also, in the early to mid-1990s, to exhaust the ranks of Kurdish leaders, the state's secret paramilitary organizations assassinated prominent Kurdish intellectuals and leading members of Kurdish political parties (Göral 2021; Göral, Işık, and Kaya 2013).

In the meantime, the state also devised a massive infrastructure project as a complimentary way to deal with the conflict. The Southeastern Anatolia Dam Project (Güneydoğu Anadolu Projesi, GAP), originally planned in the 1970s, aimed to create a large network of dams and hydroelectric plants to channel the water from the Euphrates and Tigris Rivers into a vast reservoir to water large tracts of the arid southeastern Anatolia region (about 10 percent of Turkey's total land). In the 1990s, the project was revised into a more ambitious scheme to transform, integrate, and control the region and undermine the PKK's influence (Bilgen 2018; Jongerden 2010; Özok-Gündoğan 2005; Yörük and Özsoy 2013). Although the project remains incomplete even after many revisions of its completion date in the past thirty years, and although its development goal has proven to be a solution neither to high unemployment in the region nor to large regional disparities in Turkey, it has nevertheless expanded the state's administrative and service infrastructure in the region.

At the same time, the state adapted to Kurdish guerrilla warfare, forcefully driving large Kurdish populations out of the region to urban centers elsewhere in Turkey. These policies sapped the PKK's control in the region, so much so that by 1998 Syria remained the PKK's last remaining supporter. The Turkish state then exploited its alliance with Israel to threaten Syria with war unless it expelled Öcalan and the PKK bases in the Bekaa Valley. Damascus complied and Öcalan was captured in Kenya in 1999 with the help of US government intelligence. The PKK forces that had relocated from Syria to northern Iraq likewise received a severe blow from the Turkish military in 1999, effectively ending the war (Cornell 2001; Radu 2001).

Despite these setbacks, the capture of Öcalan in 1999 and Turkey's EU accession negotiations in the early 2000s facilitated the growing influence of legal Kurdish political parties in local and national politics, and a new state policy toward Kurdish demands favored political solution over violence. The election of Kurdish deputies as independents to the Parliament in July 2007, the AKP government's reforms recognizing the Kurdish language and cultural rights, and the peace process bolstered a brief period of hope for peace in Turkey.

The AKP's effort to distinguish itself from the state establishment and the Kemalist regime and its initial commitment to EU accession led to the passing of legal regulations that recognize Kurdish language and cultural rights. The AKP government also endeavored to replace the politics of forgetting with remembering, taking several steps to recognize past state violence. In that context, the government made an official "apology" for the Dêrsim Massacre of 1937–38, when tens of thousands of Kurdish Alevis were killed in a Turkish military campaign. State prosecutors also brought court cases against the military leaders of the coup in 1980 and against state security and paramilitary forces for gross human rights violations, including the killings, disappearances, and displacements of Kurds in the 1990s (Yıldız 2015). During one such legal case in 2009, *Temizöz and Others*, the former Gendarmerie commander, Colonel Cemal Temizöz (ret.), and eight other military officials were tried for killing twenty-one civilians between 1993 and 1995. Scholars initially hoped that this approach would create a platform for an informal and unofficial truth commission to be established and thus lead to reconciliation. However, against such hopeful expectations and amid the resumed Turkish military operations in Kurdish cities, this court case—like tens of thousands of similar cases—ended with the acquittal of all the defendants in November 2015 (Göral 2021). Moreover, the AKP's shift in state discourse from denial to reconciliation went hand in hand with the killing of thirty-four Kurdish civilians, most of whom were children and young men, in an airstrike in Şırnak province in 2011. Although the "Dêrsim apology" is applauded domestically and internationally for its democratic potential, the government's actions in Şırnak proved that the "apology" was merely a tool to score political points and far from any actual pursuit of reconciliation (Ayata and Hakyemez 2013).

Nevertheless, since the early 1990s Kurdish participation in national and local politics has successfully created a new institutional basis for political expression, distinct symbolic resources, and novel access to domestic and international audiences (Watts 2006). Although Turkey's Constitutional Court has banned a series of these Kurdish parties in the past three decades, their political cadres remain resilient and have simply continued their political journey in new parties. In 2015, the HDP, the latest iteration of a legal pro-Kurdish party, achieved unprecedented electoral success by getting 13 percent of the national vote. This success was made possible in part by the HDP's deliberate effort to voice the democratic demands of non-Kurdish groups in the country. However, as we mentioned earlier, the HDP's growing vote meant the AKP's loss of its parliamentary majority to form the government, which brought a de facto end to the Kurdish Peace

Process and an unleashing of a new cycle of persecution of Kurdish politicians and activists.

The retreat to a security framework in the state's approach to the Kurdish political movement went hand in hand with the deterioration of human rights in the country. Turkey's persecution of thought and expression reached a new extreme after the coup d'etat attempt in July 2016. Under the auspices of counterterrorism measures and the declaration of emergency rule, hundreds of media outlets, especially those operating in Kurdish, were shut down. Turkey became an open-air prison for journalists who did not toe the government line, surpassing China and other authoritarian states in the number of journalists it imprisoned. More than one hundred thousand civil servants were sacked from the military, state bureaucracy, and schools, and thousands more were arrested or detained. Many elected mayors, politicians, and HDP representatives, including the former HDP cochairs Selahattin Demirtaş and Figen Yüksekdağ, have been in prison since 2016 (Tepe and Alemdaroğlu 2021). The AKP government claims that it has the right to take these measures to "ensure national security." However, the court cases against the elected politicians are based on weak and vague evidence and frequently built upon the testimonies of "secret witnesses." The police employ this evidence to frame legal activities such as political meetings and protests, social media posting, and voluntary work in civil society organizations as "terrorist" activities. The government's growing use of the police and judiciary for political purposes indicates that judicial repression and securitization have become Turkey's primary strategies to contain political dissent and Kurdish politics today.

In the meantime, the war in Syria, the construction of Kurdish regional autonomy in Rojava, and the paramount role of Kurdish forces in the fight against ISIS boosted international recognition of Kurdish demands for autonomy while also intensifying the Turkish government's concerns about the political empowerment of the Kurds inside and outside the country. Also, since 2016 Turkey has organized a series of operations to constrain and defeat the Syrian Kurdish party, the Democratic Union Party, and its armed wing, the People's Protection Units, which the Turkish state identifies with the PKK. Turkey's refashioned aggressive nationalism seems to have so far stalled the expansion and consolidation of the autonomous Kurdish administration taking shape at its border. However, it is too soon to analyze the long-term effects of this heightened Turkish nationalism, widespread internal oppression, and costly expansionist militarism on Kurds.

The Volume's Contribution and Outline

Since at least the Sheikh Said Rebellion in Turkey in 1925, Kurds have continued to seize occasional headlines in North America and western Europe. However, before the Gulf War of 1991, there were not more than a dozen books on the Kurdish issue (e.g., Edmonds 1957; Kinnane 1964; van Bruinessen 1978, 1992). In the late 1990s, this dearth was changed to a flood as many new books and studies appeared in the English language, with studies on Kurds becoming more apparent especially in Middle East studies. As Nicole Watts (1998) argues, the integration of Kurds into Middle East studies was important because it allowed a move away from the state-centric approach, which dominated the analysis of countries in the region. In doing so, it also debunked official imaginaries regarding national homogeneity and state power. Although the newfound attention to Kurds in the region has challenged nationalist claims and state-centric narratives and perspectives, until very recently the Kurdish studies literature in English nevertheless focused largely on macropolitical analyses. For example, the vast majority of existing academic work on Turkey's Kurdish issue comprises four threads: the Turkish state's nationalism and ethnic politics, the origins and evolution of the PKK, the political ideology of Abdullah Öcalan, and Kurdish political parties (Barkey and Fuller 1998; Bilgin and Sarıhan 2013; Kirişçi and Winrow 1997). They all present top-down and macro perspectives, prioritizing sweeping historical narratives over temporally and spatially tuned alterations as well as preferring written documents by dominant agents over ordinary people's oral testimonies. In doing so, these studies privilege state and party perspectives over people's experiences and microstruggles for equality and justice.

In the 2010s, a new generation of scholars from prestigious North American and European universities began to take an interest in the Kurds' predicament in Turkey, leading to a surge not only in the quantity of the academic output in books, journal articles, and conference presentations but also in its quality. This new cohort of scholars possesses solid knowledge of social theory, linguistic skills, and methodological training; as such, they advance the field of Kurdish studies from the backwaters of area studies to the social sciences' frontiers. Among these scholars, many are indeed in the fields of sociology, anthropology, and geography and engage with cutting-edge theories of race, intersectionality, biopower, spatial and temporal dimensions on inequality as well as with new ways of thinking about representation, recognition, violence, displacement, and resistance (Biner 2020; Bozçalı 2020; Çaylı 2021; Darıcı 2013; Ergin 2014; Gambetti and Jongerden 2015; Günay 2019; Gunes and Zeydanlıoğlu 2014; Hakyemez 2017; Saraçoğlu 2011; Üstündağ 2019). Specifically, the most recent works on the Kurds in Turkey focus on violence, especially how political actors are involved in the conflict.

Current social science literature on violence and possible avenues toward peace often advocates that scholars need to expand beyond the political to fully capture the oppressed people's experience from their vantage point. Such an expansion first necessitates adopting a critical perspective (Cassano 2010) that approaches political crises not at the macro institutional level but rather through the inherent local power negotiations on the ground. Such a perspective moves away from the naturalized standpoint of the hegemonic Turkish state to civil society, from top-down state-centric descriptions to bottom-up society-centric analyses, and from the elites to ordinary people (Nickel 2012). Recent studies also focus on societal processes of meaning production (Malesevic 2010), the problematization of victimhood (Enns 2012), and the gendered negotiation of power (Ahall 2012). Finally, in line with new approaches, we acknowledge that the conflict resolution between the Turkish state–society and the Kurds is possible only if both sides are treated ontologically and discursively as equals (Cobb 2013).

This book is intended to be an illustration of the changing perspectives in Kurdish studies outlined here. It endeavors to bring together the theoretically grounded and meticulously researched work of young scholars. We editors are sociologists who work in political and comparative historical sociology, but the contributors come from many other disciplines in the social sciences and humanities. The chapters draw on a variety of methodological and theoretical approaches in their respective fields. Many of the contributors base their analyses on multiple methods of research and extended ethnographic fieldwork. They unequivocally exhibit the shifting scope and research questions surrounding Kurds in Turkey from conventional political science approaches to the analysis of politics defined more widely as a power struggle over meanings and resources. Overall, the chapters in this book capture the temporal, spatial, and affective construction of racial and ethnic categories, on the one side, and the negotiation and resistance strategies of laypersons, on the other. As such, this volume opens a very significant window into Kurds' lives in Turkey, generating meaningful insights into their formal political interaction with the Turkish state and society as well as into their more extensive, more amorphous nonpolitical and informal experience.

This volume comprises three parts. Part one delves into the social and historical construction of Kurdishness and Kurdistan; part two focuses on the Kurds' marginalization and racialization; and part three moves on to deciphering the elements of Kurdish mobilization, thereby, we hope, ending on an optimistic note.

Part one focuses on the historical and discursive construction of Kurdishness and Kurdistan, how Kurds are politically, spatially, and temporally situated in the making of ethnic/racial hierarchies in the Ottoman Empire and Republican Turkey vis-à-vis the core Muslim/Turkish community. The first three chapters analyze historical texts, but the fourth chapter also presents how the history of displacement and migration has influenced the treatment and experience of Kurds in one of Turkey's metropolitan cities.

In chapter 1, Metin Atmaca demonstrates how the geographic location of Kurdistan has shifted throughout the centuries in connection with Ottoman administrative needs and priorities, especially with respect to its regional power struggles with the Safavids. Until the nineteenth century, the area that the Kurds inhabited—along with Armenians, Assyrians, Turcomans, and others—remained mostly terra incognita. The Ottoman Empire then administratively structured the Kurds' habitat into two regions: (1) provinces (*eyalet*) and towns such as Bitlis, Diyarbekir,

Van, Muş, and Mardin that were integrated into the Ottoman land system as *tımars* (fiefs), and (2) provinces that remained autonomous, thus forming a buffer zone in the frequently changing borders between the Ottoman Empire and the Safavid Empire. These administrative units' boundaries and what was defined as the center of Kurdistan changed with each sultan's accession. Atmaca's chapter thus ably demonstrates how politics intersected with space and territory in defining the location of Kurdistan and its people through time.

In chapter 2, Janet Klein explores Kurds' identification as a minority group in the early twentieth century. Her work debunks the Ottoman Empire's official discourse, whereby the term *minority* was employed to refer only to non-Muslim imperial subjects, such as Christians and Jews. At the same time, the Ottoman state regarded the Kurds as part of the Sunni Muslim core of the empire. By drawing on Kurdish, Ottoman, and European sources and especially on the Kurdish-Ottoman press from 1898 to 1919, Klein shows, first, that the Armenians and then the Kurds became the target of imperial "minoritization" with the growth of nationalism in the Ottoman Empire from the mid-nineteenth century on. These groups moved from being officially regarded as loyal Ottoman subjects to being defined as internal "others" who threatened Ottoman imperial sovereignty and territorial integrity. When the Ottoman state specifically targeted its Armenian subjects, it initially regarded the Kurds tenuously as part of the dominant Muslim majority. Later, however, when the Ottoman state's interests conflicted with those of the Kurds, the latter were denigrated as "uncivilized and unreliable elements" that threatened the territorial integrity and unity of the empire. At the turn of the twentieth century, Kurds tried to resist this marginalization by emphasizing their loyalty and strategic geographical significance to the imperial borders in the East and their unique identity, history, and dominance on their own ancestral lands. They initially pushed for an imperial order stating that they did not have a minority designation, but they eventually had to accept regional states' assimilationist policies. Over time, the Kurds even adopted Orientalist discourses that portrayed Kurdish people as backward. By 1918, Klein argues, the Ottoman state's denialist discourses about the Kurds were already publicly palpable and continue to this day.

In chapter 3, Barış Ünlü moves on to the subject of the transition from empire to nation-state, analyzing the racial/ethnic formation of the Turkish Republic. Drawing on whiteness studies in the United States in general and on Charles Mills's (1999) concept of "racial contract" in particular, Ünlü argues that "the Turkishness contract"—the foundational contract of the Turkish Republic—has generated an ethnic/racial hierarchy in the distribution of power and valuable resources, thereby structuring everyday relations between the Turks and non-Turks. This contract has included punitive measures against those who do not adequately internalize or comply with the expectations of "Turkishness," which Ünlü defines as both a historical formation and everyday modes of thinking, feeling, and acting that transcend the social differences of class, gender, and ideological belonging. Ünlü's chapter is part of a larger book project that provides a critical reading of the construction of Turkish ethnicity vis-à-vis the Kurds and others (Ünlü 2018). Hence, his contribution turns the Turkish official narrative of the "Kurdish problem" on its head, arguing that the source of the problem here is not the Kurds, but the Turks, especially those who wittingly or unwittingly construct, impose, and monitor Turkishness.

In chapter 4, Michael Ferguson contextualizes the Kurds' experiences in Izmir since the 1850s, providing the long history of the displacement of migrants from all surrounding regions—such as the Balkans, Crete, the Crimea, Africa, and Syria—to that city. During the conflict between the state and the PKK in the 1980s and 1990s, forced displacement from their ancestral lands led Kurds to become the last community to settle on Kadifekale, the largest hill overlooking Izmir. Drawing on the literature on displacement, Ferguson focuses on Kurds' reception and experiences in the city, arguing that approaches to Kurds are predicated on the political stand taken by Turkish host groups. Whereas those who acknowledge the historical layers of forced displacement in turn recognize and welcome Kurds as yet another community of migrants, those who deny this historical precedent and embrace an imagined ethnoreligious unity in Turkey foster marginalization, exclusion, and violence against the Kurds.

Part two focuses on more recent forms of marginalization and racialization by examining both the mundane employment of symbols and emotions to differentiate, exclude, and control the Kurds as well as Kurdish reactions to these processes in different urban and rural settings. The contributors to this section employ multiple methods and extended ethnographic fieldwork, thereby shedding light on the cultural transformation in the country over time from the total official denial of Kurdish identity to its "unwelcomed recognition." They examine how the Kurds are stereotyped based on their physical characteristics and excluded as unworthy and dangerous others. They showcase how the Turkish state and societal violence against the Kurds has persisted before, during, and after the transformation.

In chapter 5, Güllistan Yarkın focuses on the earlier experiences of Kurds from the 1950s to the 1980s in the dominantly Turkish, working-class district of Zeytinburnu in Istanbul. She argues that Kurds in the district were stigmatized as "uncivilized, illiterate, unskillful, and dirty people." Such stigmas adversely affected not only the Kurds' own sense of self but also the perception and treatment of them by the broader society. Yarkın contends that such stigmas and wider ethnic and racial hierarchies have locked Kurdish workers to the very bottom of the labor market. Furthermore, she argues, Kurdish workers from Alevi families have experienced double stigmatization due to their religious beliefs, which deviate from the Turkish Sunni mainstream.

In chapter 6, Deniz Duruiz studies the more contemporary racialization of Kurdish laborers. Based on her extended ethnographic study of Kurdish seasonal workers, Duruiz demonstrates how racial categories inform labor relations on the Turkish-owned farms in the West, where Turkish locals employ affective and embodied registers to categorize workers according to their skin color, smell, and sexuality. The stigmas produced and reproduced by locals not only racialize Kurds but also end up defining the Turks as substantially different from and superior to Kurds. Duruiz argues that such racialized affective mechanisms also displace class antagonisms, thereby bypassing the formal structures of labor control. In addition, the seasonal labor regime in Turkey also indicates that the racial categories embedded in the economy turn Kurdistan into a repository of cheap labor.

In chapter 7, Şefika Kumral examines the emergence of a new form of violence against the Kurds in the 2000s. Significantly different from the state-perpetrated violence and large-scale armed conflict of the 1980s and 1990s in Kurdistan, this new communal form is enacted by local Turks who collectively engage in attempts to lynch or carry out joint raids against Kurdish citizens in predominantly Turkish cities and towns, geographically distant from the primary locations of the armed conflict. In an analysis based on the new Ethnic and Nationalist Violence in Turkey (ENViT) database, Kumral debunks conventional arguments that explain away this violence as the result of economic competition and security threat. Instead, she contends, the primary drivers are the electoral empowerment and increasing collective visibility and mobilization of Kurds in a period of what she refers to as "contested democratization." Kumral's piece competently demonstrates the violent reactions from within Turkish society to the new political visibility of Kurds.

In chapter 8, Ali Eşref Keleş focuses on the narrative violence committed against the Kurds by mainstream news media. He focuses on the Roboskî incident/massacre of 2011, when the Turkish military airbombed thirty-four villagers engaged in a routine and petty smuggling activity, well known to local officials and military personnel along the Turkey–Iraq border. This tragic event encapsulates a long history of state violence in Turkey, in which there is never an official apology, and no one responsible is brought to justice. Keleş specifically analyzes the coverage of the Roboskî incident in three Turkish newspapers from 2011 to 2015: the pro-Kemalist and central-right *Hürriyet*, the pro-government *Sabah*, and the leftist *Birgün*. All three, he shows, presented partial accounts of the incident, hence committing "narrative violence" by intentionally fragmenting and silencing part of the truth and thereby deceiving the public. Except for *Birgün*, the newspapers reflected the Turkish official discourse that denies state responsibility in the incident and blames the victims by associating them with the PKK. Although *Birgün* elaborated on the economic conditions that force Kurds to smuggle, thereby directly challenging the dominant Turkish narrative, it failed to account for and discuss the ethnic and racial dimension of the incident. After all, the victims were not only poor villagers but also Kurds, and it was this crucial ethnic fact that turned them into targets of such violence. In summary, then, the physical violence committed in the Roboskî incident was reproduced and extended through the public narrative violence that obscured the victims' identity and the exact conditions for their destruction.

Part three delves more deeply into the formation of Kurdish political subjectivities and mobilization in the context of historical and structural hierarchies of power, injustice, and repression. Youth, political prisoners, and women have been vital agents of this mobilization. The chapters in this section demonstrate the transformation of Kurdish political subjectivities and the intersection of Kurdish identity politics with democratization demands, whereby Kurds join ranks with Turkish progressives against inequalities and injustices in the country.

In chapter 9, Delal Aydın narrates the political mobilization of Kurdish youth through the formation of the Yurtsever (Patriotic) Youth Movement in the 1990s during a period of intensified clashes between the PKK and the Turkish military. Aydın demonstrates the development of political consciousness among Kurdish high school students in Diyarbakir in reaction to intensifying state repression. Most Kurdish youths mobilized around "patriotic identity," declaring their allegiance to the PKK. This new political subjectivity shattered and reconstituted previous popular and youthful meanings of differences about bodies and social practices, such as hairstyle, sports ability, and the like. The formation of such Kurdish youth dissidence ironically took place when the administrators and teachers of the youths' public high school actively worked to ensure they become compliant "citizens" assimilated into the Turkish majority.

In chapter 10, Amy Bartholomew and Ruşen Fırat Güllüoğlu examine another form of political mobilization and resistance—mass hunger strikes and death fasts—carried out by Kurdish prisoners. They focus specifically on the hunger strike launched in 2012 on the anniversary of the mass arrests of Kurdish mayors and political activists following the military coup of 1980 and the continuing isolation of the imprisoned PKK leader Abdullah Öcalan. The dominant Turkish official discourse has narrated the Kurdish hunger strikes as "separatist in aim and violent in means," thus as an inherently and fundamentally antidemocratic political action. Bartholomew and Güllüoğlu disagree. Based on interviews with a group of Kurdish hunger strikers and their defenders, they present the subjects' understanding of their actions not as an antidemocratic political action but rather as a response to their lived experiences of injustice. They argue that the hunger strikes were political acts undertaken by those who had no other formal political venues for expressing their demands.

The final three chapters focus on Kurdish women's pivotal role in mobilization and resistance against marginalization and violence. In chapter 11, Emine Rezzan Karaman turns to a critical instance of gendered mobilization and resistance: the Saturday Mothers' and Peace Mothers' activities. These groups were formed in the mid-1990s by the mothers of those Turks and Kurds who disappeared under Turkish police custody (Saturday Mothers) and by the mothers who lost their children (PKK fighters) in armed conflict (Peace Mothers). Karaman examines the mothers' collective struggle to find their loved ones in the short term and to attain justice and a peaceful resolution to the conflict in the long term. Mothers' narratives enable Karaman to provide a detailed account of the extreme violence exerted by Turkish security forces in the 1980s and 1990s, which not only murdered many but also destroyed or disappeared their bodies. Karaman observes how by sharing their stories of loss with the public, mothers foster empathy and form alliances in the broader society while also translating and transforming their individual traumas into collective memory. Finally, by bearing witness to the Turkish state's "unspoken violence," these mothers help form a crucial counternarrative to the Turkish state narrative.

In chapter 12, Hazal Atay studies the "feminization" of Kurdish politics within pro-Kurdish political parties in Turkey. She examines affirmative-action measures such as gender quotas, parity, women's assemblies, and copresidency. She discusses how and why these progressive gender measures have been incorporated into these parties' agenda. However, Atay argues that translating such measures into practice has not always been easy given the entrenched patriarchy in society. Nevertheless, the process has strengthened Kurdish women's footing in their fight against inequality at the intersection of gender, class, and ethnic hierarchies. Before stereotyped images of Kurdish female fighters warring against ISIS in Syria flooded the international media, Kurdish women had long been fighting for equality and justice at the local, national, and international levels. Atay's chapter tells us the story of their inspiring struggle to transform national politics.

In chapter 13, Nisa Göksel turns to Kurdish women's experiences in the diaspora in France and Germany, where the Kurdish movement has managed to form transnational solidarity. She pays special attention to the understudied social group of women political activists who once played an active role in Kurdish politics but then had to escape the persecution in Turkey and flee to Europe. Living abroad provides Kurdish women activists with new political opportunities, but, as Göksel illustrates, these women also encounter fundamental challenges. Kurdish women continue engaging in politics, but they do so in the diaspora while also struggling with multiple problems created by migration and displacement within a transnational context constantly reset by changing national and international security measures that target migrants, Muslims, and Kurdish political activists.

Finally, in the afterword, Hamit Bozarslan discusses each chapter's contribution to the understanding of the past and the present of the Kurds' struggle for rights and freedoms and how, for us as academics and laypeople, the insistence to think critically about silencing and repression ongoing around us is imperative to preserving our very capacity of making sense of the world.

In all, then, this volume presents a fresh approach to the study of Kurds in Turkey, one that moves away from a state-centric top-down macro analysis to a much more nuanced account that emphasizes the agency of local Kurds as they encounter, assimilate, or resist the attempts by Turkish state and society to colonize them in their ancestral lands.

References

Ahall, Linda. 2012. "Mother, Myth, and Gendered Societal Meaning Production." *International Feminist Journal of Politics* 14, no. 1: 103–20.
Arendt, Hannah. 1968. *Men in Dark Times*. New York: Harcourt, Brace.
———. 2006. *Eichmann in Jerusalem*. New York: Penguin Classics.

Ataman, Muhittin. 2002. "Özal Leadership and Restructuring of Turkish Ethnic Policy in the 1980s." *Middle Eastern Studies* 38, no. 4: 123–42.

Ayata, Bilgin, and Serra Hakyemez. 2013. "The AKP's Engagement with Turkey's Past Crimes: An Analysis of PM Erdoğan's 'Dersim Apology.'" *Dialectical Anthropology* 37, no. 1: 131–43.

Ayata, Bilgin, and Deniz Yükseker. 2005. "A Belated Awakening: National and International Responses to the Internal Displacement of Kurds in Turkey." *New Perspectives on Turkey* 32:5–42.

Barkey, Henri. 2000. "The Struggles of a Strong State." *Journal of International Affairs* 54, no. 1: 87–105.

Barkey, Henri J., and Graham E. Fuller. 1998. *Turkey's Kurdish Question*. Lanham, MD: Rowman & Littlefield.

Berkowitz, Roger. 2009. "Thinking in Dark Times." In *Thinking in Dark Times: Hannah Arendt on Ethics and Politics*, edited by Roger Berkowitz, Jeffrey Katz, and Thomas Keenan, 3–17. New York: Fordham Univ. Press.

Beşikçi, İsmail. 1990. *Devletlerarası sömürge, Kürdistan*. Istanbul: Alan.

Bildirici, Melike, and İlknur Koç. 2018. "Türkiye'de bölgeler arası gelişmişlik farklarının incelenmesi." In *Dünden bugüne ekonomi yazıları*, edited by Selçuk Koç, Sema Yılmaz Genç, and Kerem Çolak, 321–63. Kocaeli, Turkey: Kocaeli Üniv. Vakfı Yayınları.

Bilgen, Arda. 2018. "A Project of Destruction, Peace, or Techno-science? Untangling the Relationship between the Southeastern Anatolia Project (Gap) and the Kurdish Question in Turkey." *Middle Eastern Studies* 54, no. 1: 94–113.

Bilgin, Fevzi, and Ali Sarıhan, eds. 2013. *Understanding Turkey's Kurdish Question*. Plymouth, UK: Lexington Books.

Biner, Zerrin Özlem. 2020. *States of Dispossession: Violence and Precarious Coexistence in Southeast Turkey*. Philadelphia: Univ. of Pennsylvania Press.

Bozçalı, Fırat. 2020. "Probabilistic Borderwork: Oil Smuggling, Nonillegality, and Techno-legal Politics in the Kurdish Borderlands of Turkey." *American Ethnologist* 47, no. 1: 72–85.

Cassano, Frank. 2010. "South of Every North." In *Decolonizing European Sociology: Transdisciplinary Approaches*, edited by Encarnación Gutiérrez Rodríguez, Manuela Boatcă, and Sérgio Costa, 213–24. Surrey, UK: Ashgate.

Çaylı, Eray. 2021. *Victims of Commemoration: The Architecture and Violence of Confronting the Past in Turkey*. Syracuse, NY: Syracuse Univ. Press.

Cobb, Sara B. 2013. *Speaking of Violence: The Politics and Poetics of Narrative in Conflict Resolution*. New York: Oxford Univ. Press.

Cornell, Svante E. 2001. "The Kurdish Question in Turkish Politics." *Orbis* 45, no. 1: 31–47.

Darıcı, Haydar. 2013. "'Adults See Politics as a Game': Politics of Kurdish Children in Urban Turkey." *International Journal of Middle East Studies* 45, no. 4: 775–90. doi:10.1017/S0020743813000901.

Edmonds, Cecil John. 1957. *Kurds, Turks, and Arabs: Politics, Travel, and Research in North-eastern Iraq, 1919-1925*. Oxford: Oxford Univ. Press.

Enns, Diane. 2012. *The Violence of Victimhood*. University Park: Pennsylvania State Univ. Press.

Ergin, Murat. 2014. "The Racialization of Kurdish Identity in Turkey." *Ethnic and Racial Studies* 37:322–41.

Gambetti, Zeynep, and Joost Jongerden. 2009. *The Kurdish Issue in Turkey: A Spatial Perspective*. New York: Routledge.

Göral, Özgür Sevgi. 2021. "Waiting for the Disappeared: Waiting as a Form of Resilience and the Limits of Legal Space in Turkey." *Social Anthropology* 29, no. 3: 800–815.

Göral, Özgür Sevgi, Ayhan Işık, and Özlem Kaya. 2013. *The Unspoken Truth: Enforced Disappearances*. Istanbul: Truth Justice Memory Center.

Günay, Onur. 2019. "In War and Peace: Shifting Narratives of Violence in Kurdish Istanbul." *American Anthropologist* 121:554–67. doi:10.1111/aman.13244.

Gunes, Cengiz. 2013. "Explaining the PKK's Mobilization of the Kurds in Turkey: Hegemony, Myth, and Violence." *Ethnopolitics* 12, no. 3: 247–67.

Gunes, Cengiz, and Welat Zeydanlıoğlu, eds. 2014. *The Kurdish Question in Turkey: New Perspectives on Violence, Representation, and Reconciliation*. New York: Routledge.

Hakyemez, Serra. 2017. "Margins of the Archive: Torture, Heroism, and the Ordinary in Prison No. 5, Turkey." *Anthropological Quarterly* 90, no. 1: 107–38.

Human Rights Watch. 2002. *Displaced and Disregarded: Turkey's Failing Village Return Program*. New York: Human Rights Watch.

İçduygu, Ahmet, David Romano, and İbrahim Sirkeci. 1999. "The Ethnic Question in an Environment of Insecurity: The Kurds in Turkey." *Ethnic and Racial Studies* 22, no. 6: 991–1010.

Işık, Ayhan. 2021. "Types of Turkish Paramilitary Groups in the 1980s and 1990s." *Journal of Perpetrator Research* 3, no. 2: 42–65.

Jacoby, Tim. 2005. "Semi-authoritarian Incorporation and Autocratic Militarism in Turkey." *Development and Change* 36, no. 4: 641–65.

Jongerden, Joost. 2009. "Crafting Space, Making People: The Spatial Design of Nation in Modern Turkey." *European Journal of Turkish Studies* 10. http://ejts.revues.org/index4014.html.

———. 2010. "Village Evacuation and Reconstruction in Kurdistan (1993–2002)." *186 Etudes* 77:82–84.

Jongerden, Joost, and Ahmet H. Akkaya. 2016. "Kurds and the PKK." In *The Wiley Blackwell Encyclopedia of Race, Ethnicity, and Nationalism*, edited by John Stone, Rutledge M. Dennis, Polly S. Rizova, Anthony D. Smith, and Xiaoshuo Hou, 1–5. London: Routledge.

Kinnane, Derk. 1964. *The Kurds and Kurdistan*. Oxford: Oxford Univ. Press.

Kirişci, Kemal, and Gareth M. Winrow. 1997. *The Kurdish Question and Turkey: An Example of a Trans-state Ethnic Conflict*. Portland, OR: Frank Cass.

Kurban, Dilek. 2012. *Reparations and Displacement in Turkey: Lessons Learned from the Compensation Law*. Washington, DC: Brookings Institution.

Malesevic, Sinisa. 2010. *The Sociology of War and Violence*. Cambridge: Cambridge Univ. Press.

Marcus, Aliza. 2007. *Blood and Belief: The PKK and Kurdish Fight for Independence*. New York: New York Univ. Press.

McDowall, David. 2000. *A Modern History of the Kurds*. 3rd ed. New York: I. B. Tauris.

Mills, Charles. 1999. *The Racial Contract*. Ithaca, NY: Cornell Univ. Press.

Nickel, Patricia Mooney. 2012. "Sociology and the Future: Aspiration." *New Zealand Sociology* 27, no. 1: 70–74.

Office of the United Nations High Commissioner for Human Rights. 2017. *Report on the Human Rights Situation in South-East Turkey, July 2015 to December 2016*. Geneva: Office of the United Nations High Commissioner for Human Rights, Feb. At https://www.ohchr.org/Documents/Countries/TR/OHCHR_South-East_TurkeyReport_10March2017.pdf.

Özok-Gündoğan, Nilay. 2005. "'Social Development' as a Governmental Strategy in the Southeastern Anatolia Project." *New Perspectives on Turkey* 32 (Spring): 93–112.

Pultar, Eren. 2011. "Türkiye'de kaç kürt yaşıyor?" *T24 Online Journal*, 31 Jan. At https://t24.com.tr/haber/turkiyede-kac-kurt-yasiyor,124914.

Radu, Michael. 2001. "The Rise and Fall of PKK." *Orbis* 45, no. 1: 47–63.

Romano, David. 2006. *The Kurdish Nationalist Movement: Opportunity, Mobilization and Identity*. Cambridge: Cambridge Univ. Press.

Ron, James. 1995. *Weapons Transfers and Violations of the Laws of War in Turkey*. New York: Human Rights Watch.

Saraçoğlu, Cenk. 2011. *Kurds of Modern Turkey: Migration, Neoliberalism, and Exclusion in Turkish Society*. London: I. B. Tauris.

Tepe, Sultan, and Ayça Alemdaroğlu. 2021. "How Authoritarians Win When They Lose." *Journal of Democracy* 32, no. 4: 87–101.

Ünlü, Barış. 2018. *Türklük Sözleşmesi: Oluşumu, işleyişi ve krizi*. Ankara, Turkey: Dipnot Yayınları.

Üstündağ, Nazan. 2019. "Mother, Politician, and Guerilla: The Emergence of a New Political Imagination in Kurdistan through Women's Bodies and Speech." *differences* 30, no. 2: 115–45.

Van Bruinessen, Martin. 1978. "Agha, Sheikh, and State." PhD diss., Utrecht Univ.

———. 1992. *Agha, Sheikh, and State: The Social and Political Structures of Kurdistan*. London: Zed Books.

Watts, Nicole. 1998. "Expanding Kurdish Studies: A Review Essay." *Middle East Studies Association Bulletin* 32, no. 1: 19–24.

———. 2006. "Activists in Office: Pro-Kurdish Contentious Politics in Turkey." *Ethnopolitics* 5, no. 2: 125–44.

Yadırgı, Veli. 2018. *The Political Economy of the Kurds of Turkey: From the Ottoman Empire to the Turkish Republic*. Cambridge: Cambridge Univ. Press.

Yarkın, Güllistan. 2022. "Türkiye üniversite sisteminde Kürt çalışmalarının sınırları: Doktora diplomamın tanınmaması." *Kürt Araştırmaları*, 18 Feb.

Yıldız, Yeşim Yaprak. 2015. "Missing from Turkey's Peace Process." *Open Democracy*, 4 Apr.

Yörük, Erdem, and Hişyar Özsoy. 2013. "Shifting Forms of Turkish State Paternalism toward the Kurds: Social Assistance as 'Benevolent' Control." *Dialectical Anthropology* 37, no. 1: 153–58.

Zeydanlıoğlu, Welat. 2012. "Turkey's Kurdish Language Policy." *International Journal of the Sociology of Language* 217:99–125.

Part One

Alternative Perspectives on the Historical Origins of Ethnic/Racial Categories in Turkey

1

"Land of the Kurds" or "Land of the Rocks"?

Changing Perceptions of Kurdistan in Ottoman and European Sources

Metin Atmaca

Although the scholarship on Kurdish history discusses the boundaries of Kurdistan either in terms of its geographical limits or as a political frontier, it remains silent about the issue of the origins and transformation of Kurdistan over time. I argue here that throughout the centuries the boundaries and the core of Kurdistan changed dramatically, as did the name itself. I demonstrate this change through European and Ottoman[1] historical and literary sources. What I present here is a socially and historically constructed "political geography" that focuses on the changing perception of Kurdistan, including its boundaries, geographical features, urban centers, and inhabitants. I specifically employ historical maps and accounts, which provide sometimes vague yet oftentimes more specific descriptions of the Kurdish frontiers. My primary sources are the historical accounts of local geographers, statesmen, literary persons, and Kurdish emirs; I bring in other primary and secondary sources when necessary.

This chapter is a revised and expanded version of Metin Atmaca, "Change and Continuity in the Perception of the Kurdish Lands in European and Ottoman Sources," *Journal of Mesopotamian Studies* 3 (2018): 77–93.

1. I employ the name "Ottoman" rather than "Turk" because the Ottoman Empire consisted of many local ethnic groups in addition to the Kurds.

Before I turn to the political geography of Kurds in history, it is necessary to analyze how the Ottoman Empire, which bordered and contained the Kurds for centuries, perceived its own imperial boundaries: the Ottomans positioned their identities in relation to the Iranians (Acem) on the one side and the Europeans (Frenk) on the other. Adopting the Roman imaginary that they inherited through the Byzantine Empire, the Ottomans thus expanded this perception to portray themselves as Rum or Romans, especially in comparison with the images and portrayals of Iranians in literature, politics, and geography (Kafadar 2007, 2017). During times of conflict, however, the gentilics Rumi and Acem were paired together and used in binary opposition, often in poetry as well as in texts on religion and politics. Consequently, in the early Ottoman mindset there emerged two separate yet bordered worlds that were positioned not only geographically but also culturally. Yet a close reading of contemporaneous sources reveals that there was no agreement in relation to the exact geographical boundaries of these two worlds. This problem was compounded by the historical fact that most of the land between the Ottomans (Rum) and the Safavids (Acem) was populated primarily by the Kurds as well as by other ethnic and religious groups. Because of the discrepancy and subsequent ambiguity regarding the geographic frontier between these two powerful states, referred to literally as *serhadd* (frontier, borderland) by both the Ottomans and Iranians, this area remained terrae incognitae, "unknown lands," from the sixteenth to the nineteenth century. Hence, the imaginary of Kurdistan was historically mired due to its location on the borders of two powerful empires; this started to change only in the nineteenth century upon the redefinition of space and meaning with the arrival of modernity to the region.

Predicated on this historical context, this chapter comprises three parts. The first part discusses the depiction of Kurdish lands in medieval sources before the arrival of the Ottoman into the region. The second part, which is the most extensive, delineates the portrayal of Kurdish lands in Ottoman sources. The third part articulates the transformations in the spatial meaning of Kurdistan that occurred after the mid-eighteenth century when both Ottoman and European sources defined the core of

Kurdistan as "Silêmanî" (Ar. as-Sulaymaniyyah, Tr. Süleymaniye) or "Baban Sancak," as it was referred to in nineteenth-century literature.

Kurdish Lands in Medieval Times

Arabic medieval sources from the tenth to the twelfth centuries use three classifications as toponyms (place-names) for the lands the Kurds inhabited. One referred to them as "Land of the Kurds" (Bilad al-Akrad), where there were no precise boundaries or ethnic homogeneity implied, except by some scholars such as Imad al-din al-Isfahani, who specifically referred to the lands around Hasankeyf (1955, 421). The second classification was "Summer Pastures of the Kurds" (Zuzan al-Akrad), located around Jazirat Ibn 'Umar (Cizre), thereby combining two local ethnic groups, the Kurds and the Armenians, that claimed these regions as their ancestral lands. The third was "Mountains of the Kurds" (Jibal al-Akrad), where the land referred specifically to the mountainous space among Dinawar, Qazvin, Suhraward, and Hamadan.

The name "Kordestan" was first used around 1153, when Sanjar, the leader of the Seljuqid Empire (which preceded the Ottoman one) transformed the territory around Dinawar, Hamadan, Kermanshah, and Sinna into the administrative province of Kordestan, which stands for "the Land or Province of the Kurds" in Persian (James 2007).[2] As the Kurds moved farther west and north, the region denoting Kordestan also expanded, now including the lands around Lake Van. It should be noted, however, that alongside Kurds other ethnic and religious groups, specifically Armenians, Syriacs, and Arabs, also lived in these territories. Specifically, the Kurds were the majority only in Jibal al-Akrad, not in Zuzan al-Akrad or Bilad al-Akrad, during this period. If this was the case, why did Arab geographers name these regions after the Kurds rather than the Armenians or Syriacs? Some scholars suggest that religion played a significant

---

2. The medieval Arab sources referring to the Kurds and their land include Yahya Ibn Fadlallah al-'Umari (1988), Ibn Hawqal (1939), Ibn al-Athir (1998), Yaqut al-Hamawi (1957), and Ibn Khallikan (1968–72).

role. Kurds were Muslims who were active in defending the region first against the Christian Armenians and then against the shamanic Oğuz Turks and the Mongols. As a consequence, Arab scholars revealed in their choice of place-name their ideological desire to have this region transformed into an exclusively Muslim Kurdish political space (James 2014).

Even though more historical sources are available from the thirteenth and fourteenth centuries, the number of references in them to Kurds and Kurdistan declines. One exception is the fourteenth-century geographical source *Masalik al-absar fi mamalik al-amsar* (The Ways of Discernment into the Realms of the Capital Cities) by Ibn Fadlallah al-'Umari (1988, 3:124–35), who discusses "the Land of the Kurds" as the area between Hamadan and Cilicia. Hence, during this period this source locates the Kurds geographically as the inhabitants living mostly on the lands between western Iran and northern Iraq. In the fifteenth century, the use takes on an administrative meaning as regional conflict escalates. For instance, Nizam al-Din Shami's literary source *Zafarnama* (Book of Victory [Nizamüddin Şâmi 1987]) on Tamerlane's military campaigns in Anatolia and Iran refers to Kurdistan in both geographical and administrative terms. Geographically, the name "Kurdistan" alluded to the same exact geographical location between Hamadan and Cilicia as given in the fourteenth-century source. Tamerlane administratively granted this land to a certain emir as the "province of Kurdistan," which geographically covered the more northerly regions of Bitlis, Muş, Ahlat, and Van in eastern Anatolia (Nizamüddin Şâmi 1987, 125, 158, 332).[3] In the late fifteenth and sixteenth centuries, even Çemizgezek near central Anatolia was considered a part of Kurdistan (Chèref-ou'ddine 1873, 3; Scheref 1860, 163).

During the early sixteenth century, İdris-i Bidlisi (d. 1520), who was the architect of the political deal between the Kurdish emirs and the Ottoman Empire, referred to Bitlis as the "center of the government of Kurdistan." Yet the population at this administrative center was mainly non-Muslim and mostly Armenian. Baki Tezcan suggests that these regions were

---

3. Shami mentions Kurdistan in various places with reference to "emirs," "*vilayet*" (province), and "*derbend*" (passage) as well as to several other locations. One should note that Diyarbekir is mentioned here separately (Nizamüddin Şâmi 1987, 332).

named "Kurdistan" owing to the distribution of local power structure rather than to population composition because the Kurds administratively and politically ruled over the Armenians (2000, 542). Hence, the Kurdish emirs had already seized political power in the region before the arrival of the Ottomans in the region, with support from the local Muslim Seljuqid, Timurid, Aq Quyunlu, and Qara Quyunlu dynasties. Thus, it is especially important to note that unlike what the Turkish national historiography often claims, the concept of Kurdistan existed politically and geographically before the arrival of the Ottomans in the region.

Kurdish Lands in Ottoman Sources

The arrival of the Ottomans in the region locally led to an inherent tension with the other large empire, the Iranian Safavids, as for centuries both vied for power in what was to become the border between the two empires. The Kurdish emir İdris-i Bidlisi collaborated and developed local strategies with the Ottoman sultan Selim I (r. 1508–20) to impede the rise and expansion of the Iranian Safavid ruler Ismail I (r. 1501–24). Before setting on a military campaign against the Safavids, Selim specifically commissioned İdris-i Bidlisi to win over the local Kurdish emirs and beys and incorporate them into the Ottoman camp. It appears that Selim based his decision on detailed knowledge of the Kurdish lands; for years, agents of the sultan either living at or traveling through the empire's eastern frontier and Kurdistan carried over to Istanbul the local intelligence they gathered (Dehqan and Genç 2018, 205–6, 209–10). In line with the received intelligence, Selim I then placed his confidence in İdris-i Bidlisi, incorporating several Kurdish tribes into his army in the process.

Although Ottoman sources offer detailed information on these tribes, Safavid sources make only a few references, cursorily referring to them all as "Kurds" (Yamaguchi 2012, 111). In addition, the Iranians stereotyped the Kurds as "evil-natured, stubborn, morose and treacherous" (Matthee 2003, 167, citing Kaempfer 1977, 88, and Isfahani 1372/1993, 39, 77, 83). The difference between the Ottoman and Safavid dynasties' approach and perception of Kurds is due to the strategic importance of Kurdistan for the Ottomans. After all, during the sixteenth century, when the Safavid threat was at its height, the Ottomans maintained their interest in the Kurdish regions, collecting local information. Even after the incorporation of the Kurdish emirates into the empire during the same century, the Ottomans continued to diversify their regional policy toward each emirate, altering the local administrative rule based on the characteristics of each emirate. They classified the centers of Kurdish *eyalets* (province) and towns such as Diyarbekir, Bitlis, Van, Muş, Mardin, and the like near the eastern frontier as *yurtluk* (family estates), *ocaklık* (hereditary autonomous appanage or ancestral lands), or, more commonly, *yurtluk-ocaklık*, turning them into *timars* (fiefdoms) with some tax obligations. The Ottomans categorized the Kurdish emirates that were close to the Safavid territories, such as Hakkari, Behdinan, Baban, Botan, and Soran, into *hükûmets* (local governments with a high degree of autonomy) with no financial obligations. This Ottoman administrative division was very significant in terms of how these two zones of Kurdistan developed differently through time. The Kurdish lands turned into *timars* were literally included in the classical Ottoman land system, thereby becoming incorporated into the Ottoman body politic. In contrast, the Kurdish lands that became *hükûmets* remained autonomous, apart from the Ottoman land system and considered more like "buffer zones;" these lands were also strategically more vulnerable, frequently changing hands between the Ottomans and the Safavids either by force or by will.[4]

It is also significant to note that the Ottomans considered and treated their eastern Iranian (Muslim) frontier differently from their western European (Christian) frontier. They did not employ the ideology of *gaza* (holy war, fought by *gazi*s, holy warriors) when waging war on the Safavids. Nevertheless, the Safavids belonged to a different religious sect in Islam; they were Shi'i, whereas the Ottomans were Sunni. As a consequence, the Ottomans justified their war with the Safavids by a *fetva* (judicial opinion) granted by their *şeyhülislam* (the mufti of Istanbul and head of

---

4. The historiography on the Kurdish emirates tends to generalize the assumption of them as a "buffer zone," whereas mostly only the emirates on the frontier were seen as such, such as those with the status of *hükûmet*. For further discussion of Kurdistan's status as a "buffer zone," see Ateş 2013, 39; Fuccaro 2011; and O'Shea 2012, 71–72.

the Ottoman religious-legal hierarchy). For instance, the contemporaneous judicial opinions from the Ottoman *şeyhülislam*s Sarıgörez (d. 1522), Kemalpaşazade (d. 1534), and Ebussuud (d. 1574) declared Safavids and their Kızılbaş (Shi'i) supporters in Anatolia to be apostates, unbelievers, heretics, rebels, and brigands whose elimination by the Ottoman army was a religious duty (Atçıl 2017, 300–308). Such an adverse religious stand toward the Shi'i residing in Anatolia eventually led to the marginalization and oppression of this group under Ottoman rule.

After winning several wars against the Safavids in the sixteenth century, the Ottomans felt stronger and more militarily secure, leading them to become more lenient toward the Kurdish emirs as well. In 1521, a year after the Ottoman sultan Süleyman I (r. 1520–66) ascended the throne, he classified twenty-eight administrative units in Kurdistan as *cema'at-i Kürdân* (Kurdish communities), bestowing upon them the right to rule their own lands (Barkan 1953–54, 306–7). Sultan Süleyman even praised God for placing Kurdistan between the two Muslim dynasties, stating that "God made Kurdistan act in the protection of my imperial kingdom like a strong barrier and an iron fortress against the sedition of the demon Gog of Persia" (quoted in Aziz Efendi 1985, 14). In addition to being considered a buffer zone between the Ottoman and Safavid Empires extending over hundreds of miles, Kurdistan also acquired the imaginary of a strong "wall" and "fortress" that clearly marked the frontier between them.

The Kurdish administrative units in the Ottoman Empire did not always remain the same, however, and were transformed upon the accession of each Ottoman sultan, as did all the laws governing the land. Although succeeding sultans often rubberstamped the rulings of their predecessors, the *ferman* (imperial decree) renewing the status of the Kurdish emirates underwent specific changes literally in line with the current state of Ottoman political relations with the Safavids. Internal politics among the Kurdish emirs themselves also affected the current state of the Ottoman administrative units, especially when there were power struggles among the Kurdish ruling families. In the early seventeenth century, for instance, Ottoman official Ayn Ali presented a slightly different administrative structure of the Kurdish emirates, wherein their privileges were placed under the control of provincial administrations. To the province of Diyarbekir, which comprised eleven *sancak*s (banners or districts, an administrative subdivision of the *eyalet*) and five *hükûmet*s, the Ottoman officials created and added another eight districts of Kurdish beys (*ekrâd begi sancağı*) that also had tax obligations (Ayn Ali 1280/1863–64, 29–31). It is interesting to note the transformation in the Ottoman official perception of Kurds. Although the Kurds were initially viewed as a *cema'at* (community) at the beginning of their incorporation into the Ottoman body politic, this depiction changed almost a century later from being based on community to one predicated on Kurdish beys or leaders. Once the Kurds in Kurdistan were not viewed as a community, their co-optation into the Ottoman imperial structure as subjects became easier to achieve. Also, identifying the Kurds through their leaders alone eventually made it easier for Ottomans to remove them from power.[5]

Before the end of the sixteenth century, Şeref Xân (d. 1601), the Kurdish emir of Bitlis, decided to write in Persian, the literary language then used in the lands extending from India to Anatolia, an account of the history of the Kurdish dynasties and ruling families, which he titled *Şerefnâme* (Book of Honor, 1597). Because Şeref Xân intended his audience to comprise Ottoman and Kurdish rulers, his account contained a distinctly pro-Ottoman and Sunni bias.[6] In terms of his career on the ground, Şeref Xân's political life was also tremendously influenced by the Ottoman–Safavid rivalry, like the career of his father, Şemseddîn Beg (d. 1576), before him.

Şerefnâme traces the historical origins of Kurdish emirs to several regional dynasties, including the Ayyubids, the Abbasids, and the Umayyads, as well as to pre-Islamic rulers such as the Sassanid shahs and the Macedonian leader Alexander the Great. In the introduction, Şeref Xân also discusses several mythologies regarding Kurdish roots. In one myth, Kurds are traced to those people who ran away from the persecution of an Iranian king named Dahhak, taking refuge in the mountains. In another, the Kurds descend from a group of supernatural *cîns* (genies or

---

5. For more information on the Ottoman polity's incorporation of the Kurdish emirates, see Atmaca 2021.

6. This is the case especially with the text of the Ms. Dorn 306, located in the National Library of Russia (Alsancakli 2015, 139).

demons) that God then turned into human beings. A third myth states that the Kurds emerged from the marriage between a human and a giant. Description of some of the Kurds' typical characteristics ensues. They are extremely courageous and fearless yet also very argumentative in deciding who should be their leader. Also, they are good in the Islamic sciences but lack the literary talent for calligraphy and poetry (Scheref 1860, 1, 12–19).

In addition to his discussion of the origins of the Kurds, Şeref Xân also provided the geographic location of Kurdistan. According to him, the boundaries of Kurdistan started from Basra on the Persian Gulf and extended to Malatya and Maraş in central Anatolia, and it was surrounded by Persia (Fars), Iraq-i Ajam, Azerbaijan, and Armenia to the north and by Iraq-i Arab, Diyarbekir, and Mosul to the south. He concluded that no king had ever tried to occupy Kurdistan because of both the brave and querulous nature of the Kurds and their mountainous geography. Instead, such rulers symbolically pretended to be the overlords of the Kurds, treating the latter as suzerains who sent the rulers some "gifts" to demonstrate their loyalty, especially during military expeditions (Scheref 1860, 1, 12–19).

Kurds Caught between the Ottoman and Iranian Empires

Although Şeref Xân defined the boundaries of Kurdistan much more precisely than others did, the ambiguous terrae incognitae extended between Mosul and Aleppo on the one side and farther up northwest to Malatya on the other. Cemal Kafadar discusses the reason for this land ambiguity, stating that it was a "grey area or zone of transition where Turcoman tribes mixed freely with Arab and Kurdish tribes of northern Mesopotamia" (2007, 17). Hence, the boundaries between Turkish, Iranian, and Arab lands were fluid in practice because most of these boundaries were not only dominated by the Kurds but also contained Turcomans as well as non-Muslim groups such as the Armenians, Assyrians, Jews, and Chaldeans.

Several contemporaneous sources support these fluid boundaries. For instance, Fuzuli (d. 1556), a well-known poet of Ottoman and Azeri Turkish literature from Kirkuk, agreed with this portrayal as he imagined the vague boundary between "Baghdad and Rum" (or Arabs and Turks) as being somewhere between southeastern Anatolia and northern Iraq

(Kafadar 2007, 17). Yet Melayê Cizîrî (d. 1640), a well-known Kurdish poet and mystic, included Van and its surrounding region in the east within Kurdistan and then compared Kurdistan to Shiraz, Tabriz, Khorasan, and Isfahan (Shakely 1996, 245). He stated the following in a couplet:

> Not only Kurdistan, but also Shiraz, Jeng and Van give tax
> They happily pay their toll, and so [does] Isfahan. (Melayê Cizîrî 2012, 72)[7]

It is interesting to note that Cizîrî's perception of the boundaries of the Ottoman and Safavid Empires was shaped not by geographical markers but rather through particular political symbols, cultural differences, and characteristics. Cizîrî specifically built his perception of Kurdistan on the work of Yaqut al-Hamawi (d. 1229), a thirteenth-century Arab biographer and geographer. In his encyclopedic work on the Muslim world, *Mu'jam al-buldan* (Dictionary of Countries) (1957), al-Hamawi made many references to the Kurdish lands. He frequently referred to Mesopotamia and northwestern Iran as the land of the Kurds, classifying it as the *iqlim al-rabi'* (the fourth region). Both Cizîrî and the later seventeenth-century Kurdish poet Ehmedê Xanî (d. 1707) praised the Kurdish notables as rulers of this "fourth region." In couplets, Xanî places Kurdistan in the middle of the lands of the Rum, Acem, Arabs, and Georgians:

> Each lord of them is Hatam-like in munificence
> Each man of them is Rostam-like in combat
>
> Seen from the Arabs to Georgians
> The Kurdish lands have become like towers
>
> Those Turks and Iranians are surrounded by them
> The Kurds are scattered in all four corners

---

7. The original version of the couplet in Kurdish:
   Tenha ne Kurdistan didin Şîraz û Yeng û Wan didin
   Her yek li ser çavan didin hem ji Espehan têtin xerac.

On both sides the Kurdish tribes
Have become targets for the arrows of calamity. (Ehmedê Xanî 2010, 21)[8]

What is noteworthy in these couplets is the portrayal of the current position of the Kurds, caught between the Turks and the Iranians as dangerous targets coveted by both rival empires. Kurds cannot reach a solution that will remove them from this calamity because they are not united but occupied and divided among these groups. Indeed, in some other couplets, Xanî compares the Kurds with the surrounding ethnic groups that have built empires—namely, the Turks and Iranians; he explains why the Kurds could not become the Turks and Iranians' leader:

Had we set our unity
Had we relied on each other

The Turks, Arabs, and Iranians entirely
Would all be but serving us

We would have perfected the religion and state
We would have attained the sciences and wisdom. (Ehmedê Xanî 2010, 21–22)[9]

---

8. Here is the original of the couplets in Kurdish by Xanî:
   Her mîrekî wan bi bezlê Hatem
   Her mêrekî wan bi rezmê Ristem
   Bi'fkir ji Erab heta ve Gurcan
   Kurmancîye bûye şibhê bircan
   Ev Rûm û Ecem bi wan hesar in
   Kurmanc hemî li çar kenar in
   Herdu terefan qebîlê Kurmanc
   Bo tîrê qeza kirine amanc.
9. The original is as follows:
   Ger dê hebûya me ittifaqek
   Vêk ra bikira me inqiyadek
   Rûm û Ereb û Ecem temamî
   Hemiyan ji me ra dikir xulamî

Indeed, the Kurds' incapacity to unite starts to emerge as a significant theme as the other groups around them are able to coalesce into large empires that then start to oppress the Kurds to contain them.

Changing Relations: Ottomans and Kurds in the Seventeenth and Eighteenth Centuries

The ambiguity surrounding the borders and boundaries of Kurdish lands continued as late as the mid-nineteenth century. Then in 1847 with the Second Treaty of Erzurum, the Ottoman and Iranian Empires as well as the United Kingdom and Russia came together to attempt to negotiate the boundary disputes between the two empires; they did so "to produce a definitive and binding settlement of their territorial dispute and to narrow the frontier zone into a mappable line" (Schofield 2008, 152). To prove their claims to certain territories—particularly to the cities of Muhammarah (today's Khorramshahr), Zohab, and Silêmanî—the Iranian and Ottoman officials resorted to old *ferman*s, maps and travel accounts, such as Katib Çelebi's (d. 1657) seventeenth-century geographical account *Cihannüma* (Mirror of the World) (Aykun 1995, 117–18). Since Katib Çelebi's account bore the seal of the Ottoman sultan, Iranian delegates utilized it as evidence to claim sovereignty over the districts of Ahiska, Van, Kars, and Bayezid, also demanding the recognition of their rights over the district of Silêmanî (Ateş 2013, 97). In addition to Katib Çelebi's account, the Ottoman delegates presented copies of *Düstur'ul inşa* (Principals of Writing), which contained many documents from the previous correspondence and treaties collected by the Ottoman *reisü'l-küttâb* (chancery of the Imperial Divan, later secretary of state or chancellor) Sarı Abdullah Efendi in 1643. Also employed by the Ottoman side was the Ottoman official chronicler Mustafa Naima Efendi's *Tarih-i naima* (Naima's History) as well as Feraizi-zade's *Gülşen-i maarif* (Rose Garden of Wisdom), which were presented to the delegates in Erzurum as evidence that Silêmanî had

---

Tekmîl dikir me dîn û dewlet
Tehsîl dikir me 'ilm û hikmet

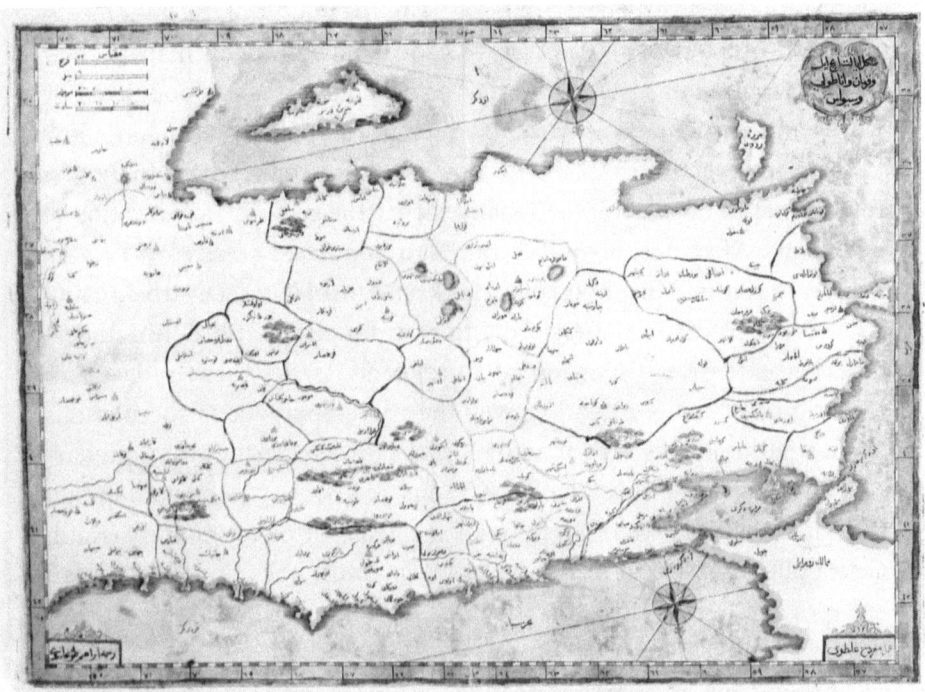

1.1. A reversed map of Anatolia produced by Ibrahim Müteferrika for Katib Çelebi's *Cihannüma*. From Kâtib Çelebi 1145/1732.

been a part of the Ottoman Empire for centuries (Aykun 1995, 118). It is interesting that Katib Çelebi's *Cihannüma* was used not only by the Ottomans and Iranians as testimony for their claims on territories but also widely by European scholars.[10]

10. Joseph von Hammer, an Austrian Orientalist of the nineteenth century, used Katib Çelebi's account extensively. In fact, before completing his ten-volume encyclopedia on Ottoman history in the 1830s, von Hammer translated *Cihannüma*'s sections on the Balkan regions of the Ottoman Empire (Katib Çelebi 1812). European historians and geographers later used Katib Çelebi's maps extensively until the late eighteenth and early nineteenth centuries, when the French and British diplomats, travelers, and cartographers visiting the region produced their own. However, the British and French maps continued to remain less detailed than Çelebi's own earlier versions. Although *Cihannüma* presented a mid-seventeenth-century account, its impact continued until much

Despite the level of detail in his work in the middle of the seventeenth century, Katib Çelebi does not label Kurdistan on any of his maps in their original copies but instead lists the region predominantly populated by Kurds and Armenians as "unknown territory," perhaps as a "no man's land."[11] However, the extensive detailed narration of the region in his text reveals that he does not intentionally silence the geographical location of Kurdistan. After describing several Kurd-populated areas such as Van, Adilcevaz, Bitlis, Muş, Erzurum, Hakkari, Mosul, Siirt, Diyarbekir, and a few other places in the eastern Ottoman Empire, Katib Çelebi undertakes an extensive discussion of Kurdistan. He first briefly describes the origins of the Kurds to convey the contemporaneous speculations about whether Kurds were actually Arabs. He then expands the boundaries of his Kurd-populated lands to Maraş and Malatya, concluding that the Kurdish lands were made up of eighteen Ottoman *vilayet*s (Katib Çelebi 2007, 448–50).[12] In Katib Çelebi's account, the core of Kurdistan emerges as Cizre because it is the place he treats as the most significant Kurdish town.

Around the same period that Katib Çelebi completed his magnum opus *Cihannüma*, Evliya Çelebi (d. 1684) also traveled through Diyarbekir, Mardin, Bitlis, Van, and some nearby cities that he referred to in sum as "Kurdistan." In comparison to Katib Çelebi, Evliya Çelebi is much more specific in outlining the Kurdish lands. He refers to Diyarbekir and all immediate surrounding lands as "the province of Diyarbekir of Kurdistan" (*eyalet-i Diyarbekr-i Kürdistan*) (Evliya Çelebi 2005, 199a). Evliya

---

later, shaping much of the geographical perception of Ottoman lands in the eighteenth and nineteenth centuries (Sezgin 2013).

11. Referring to Paul Wittek's characterization of early Ottoman western Anatolia, Nelida Fuccaro suggests that the Ottomans rendered rural Kurdistan a "no-man's land" or a zone of "cultural barbarism" (2011, 239). This might have been true in the seventeenth and eighteenth centuries, when the Ottomans put Kurdistan into oblivion, but it was not the case in the sixteenth and nineteenth centuries (Atmaca 2021, 51–57, 63–69).

12. After making some generalizations on the character of the Kurds, Katib Çelebi emphasizes that they are "Şafi'i" and "ehl-i Sünnet" (followers of the normative practice of the Prophet and his companions).

also employs the phrase "province of Kurdistan" (*eyalet-i Kürdistan*) when he specifically refers to Diyarbekir; he then uses the phrase "the land of Kurdistan" (*diyar-ı Kürdistan*) when referring to a much broader region extending as far as northern Iraq and northwestern Iran (Evliya Çelebi 2005, 217b). He includes the cities of Van (Kürdistan-ı Van), Soran (east and north of Erbil), and Bitlis in Kurdistan as well. It is also at this juncture that he differentiates the Kurdistan region within Safavid lands as "Kurdistan of Iran" (Kürdistan-ı Acemistan) (2005, 326b).

Specifically, Evliya describes what he believes are the broader geographical boundaries of Kurdistan:

> Named Kurdistan and land of rocks [*sengistan*], this is a great land, which includes seventy different settlements. One corner of it starts from the northern side of the land of Erzurum and Van to the land of Hakkari, Cizre, İmadiyye, Mosul, Şehrizul, Harir, Ardalan, Baghdad, Derne, Derteng, and Basra. Located in between Iraq and Anatolia [Irâk-ı Arab- ile Âl-i Osmân-mâbeyninde] six thousand Kurdish tribes and clans dwell on these highlands, where the nation of Acem would easily capture the Ottoman lands [Diyar-ı Rum] if they [the Kurds] had not become a stronghold [*sedd-i sedid*]. (2005, 219a)[13]

Evliya then ends his account by praying for the land to stay in between these two states forever.[14] Although he also notes that the majority of the Kurds belong to the Şafi'i school of law,[15] he nevertheless considers the Kurds as part of the Sunnis of the Ottoman Empire in practice. Yet Evliya captures the religious complexity of this area well when he refers to the unorthodox elements in Kurdistan, such as the mystics, gnostics, and miracle workers as well as the dervish lodges, shrines, and pilgrimage sites. In addition to these heterodox Sufi elements, Evliya also mentions

---

13. Fuccaro asserts that in using the term *sengistan*, Evliya referred to the "barbarian" character of Kurdistan (2011, 239).

14. "İnkırâzu'd-devrân Âl-i Osmân ile şâh-ı Acem mâbeyninde memâlik-i Kürdistân mü'ebbed ola, âmîn, yâ Mu'în" (Evliya Çelebi 2005, 200a).

15. "Kürdistân olup cümle halkı Şafi'îyyü'l-mezheb olmağile Şâfi'î müftîsi iştihardadır" (Evliya Çelebi 2005, 200a).

the "heretical" group the Yezidis[16] as part of the heterodox culture of Kurdistan.

Evliya also divides Kurdistan into its rural and urban components. While portraying rural Kurdistan as "the land of rocks," he depicts Bitlis and Diyarbekir as "havens of culture and civilization in contrast to their surroundings" (Fuccaro 2011, 245). According to Evliya, Bitlis has lush gardens, fountains, and public baths. Its cultured and multitalented ruler is like an Ottoman "renaissance" prince, and its notables own luxurious items such as sable furs (2005, 225b; see also Dankoff 2004, 76–77).

Almost half a century after Evliya penned his travelogue, Mustafa Naima (d. 1716), an Ottoman court chronicler, keeps referring to Kurdish lands as such. In one account, Naima mentions a Naqshbandi sheikh who was well received by all "the regions of Kurdistan" [*memalik-i Kürdistan*], specified as comprising Erzurum, Mosul, Ruha (Urfa), and Van (Mustafa Naima 2007, 899). He mentions Diyarbekir separately due to its different administrative identity; eight of the nineteen *sancak*s were administered by a Kurdish ruler residing there. Several of these *sancak*s are mentioned as being subject to taxes. Naima not only discusses the Kurds inhabiting the region referred to as Kurdistan but also describes in great detail those Kurds living outside Kurdistan, specifically in Sivas, Çorum, and Yozgat. For instance, he records that on one occasion in Sivas, many Turks, Kurds, Turcomans, and other ethnic groups that had gathered together from among Ottoman soldiers united to walk in protest against the leader of the region (Mustafa Naima 2007, 550).

Through time, then, particularly in the case of Evliya Çelebi's travelogue, Ottoman historians, bureaucrats, poets, and religious scholars became more publicly aware of the existence of the region of Kurdistan as well as of the Kurdish groups scattered across Anatolia, Iraq, and the Levant. It is therefore no accident that between the sixteenth and nineteenth

---

16. A Kurdish-speaking minority that emerged near Lališ in Iraqi Kurdistan during the twelfth century, the Yezidis follow a unique religious tradition that is traced back to ancient Mesopotamian religions such as Zoroastrianism as well as to the Abrahamic religions of Islam and Christianity.

centuries the number of references made to Kurds in Ottoman sources increased, with the general references becoming eventually replaced by more specific ones. Yet such references are still selective in that the Kurds are mentioned more frequently in relation to a conflict—that is, upon the emergence of a rebellion or an incident that the Ottoman government is interested in. As such, Kurds start to become associated in the Ottoman imaginary with violence rather than with a people living in particular locations in the empire.

Ottoman Kurdistan of the Nineteenth Century: Case of the Baban Emirate

In the first half of the nineteenth century, the way that Ottoman and European sources referred to Kurdistan by name changed once again.[17] Gaspard Drouville (d. 1856), for instance, emphasized the difference between "Kurdistan" and its Persian namesake "Kourdistan"; whereas the former was the "the country inhabited by the Kurds," including the lands in both Iran and the Ottoman Empire, the latter referred to "the government of Muhammad Ali Mirza"—namely, a specific political entity, or a province, located in western Iran (1825, 220, 223).[18]

In the social construction of the concept of Kurdistan through history, Turks and Iranians play major roles. After all, the first documented use of the name "Kurdistan" was by the Seljuq Turks in the twelfth century, continuing with the Iranians from the Safavid period until today. Under the Ottomans, however, the name "Kurdistan" referred to the geographical boundaries of those lands predominantly inhabited by the Kurds; for a short period between 1847 and 1867, however, the Ottoman Sublime Porte also created a province named "Kurdistan."[19] I therefore argue that the

---

17. For this section, I rely on my doctoral thesis (Atmaca 2013, 5–9).

18. Muhammad Ali Mirza was the eldest son of the shah of Iran, Fath Ali Shah, and was appointed to the western frontier region (Kermanshah, Zohab, and Sonqor to Hamadan, Lorestan, Bakhtiari, and Khuzestan) as governor-general from 1809 until his death in 1821 (Amanat 1994).

19. For a detailed study of the "Kürdistan Eyaleti" of this period, see Ülke 2014.

name "Kurdistan" refers to two separate social spaces: Ottoman Kurdistan and Iranian Kurdistan.

The boundaries of Ottoman Kurdistan correspond to Iraqi Kurdistan today yet also included the provinces of Hakkari and Şırnak in modern Turkey. From the beginning of the nineteenth century, these regions altogether denoted "Kurdistan" in Ottoman official sources. Yet the same sources also started to use the name "Kurdistan" far less frequently and instead referred to particular Kurdish emirates. Over time, the Ottoman official usage further narrowed in focus in relation to the relative power of different emirates; in the end, the name "Kurdistan" referred exclusively to the Baban territories. In most European sources, Kurdistan was defined as the geographical location of the emirates of Botan, Hakkari, Behdinan (Amêdî), Soran (Rewandiz), and Baban. Some sources added Bitlis to this list after the turn of the nineteenth century, however. For instance, the French traveler Adrien Dupre (d. 1831), who visited "Curdistan" between 1807 and 1809, listed "les principautés Curdes" (the Kurdish principalities), or the Kurdish emirates, as "Soran, Baban, Badinan, Tchambo [Hakkari], Bottan and Bitlisi" (1819, 91). He referred to the region of Kurdistan located in Iran largely as the "Erdelan Principality," occasionally including the territories of Mukris west of Lake Urumiya.

In the early nineteenth century, a growing number of Ottoman historians started to refer to the region known as "Kurdistan" in terms of Şehrezûr (Şehrizor, roughly corresponding to today's Kirkuk) and the Baban *sancak*. The Ottoman court historian Şanizade (d. 1826), for instance, discussed the beys of Kurdistan by referring to the Kurdish emirs in Koye (Koy Sancak), Baban, and Şehrezûr (Şanizade Mehmet Ataullah 2008, 754–55). He was probably the first Ottoman official who selectively emphasized southern Kurdistan as playing a more dominant role in regional politics than any other part of the empire. Indeed, during the early nineteenth century the Babans became the dominant emirate of the region, thereby drawing the attention of Ottoman scholars. For instance, Şanizade noted that the interaction between the Ottomans and the Iranians almost always concerned the Kurds. In this particular case, the Ottomans had two requests from Iran: to cease its occupation of Kurdistan and to return any fugitive Baban pashas (Şanizade Mehmet Ataullah

2008, 831). These interactions foreshadow the emergence of both the concept of southern Kurdistan and the significant role the Babans play in the process.

From the seventeenth century until 1784, the Babans were located in Qala Çolan (Karaçolan), a village-town in the north of Şehrezûr. After 1784, they moved their capital from Qala Çolan a few miles north to Milkhindî, naming the latter location "Silêmanî" in the process. The borders of the region ruled by the Baban dynasty were under constant change due to the repeated conflicts it had with its neighbors, including the Erdelan in the east on the Iranian side of Kurdistan and the Soran in the north. When not in a state of conflict with their neighbors, the Babans on occasion incorporated new lands onto their domain, including Kirkuk, Koye, Herîr, Şehribazar, and Pijder. As a consequence, the Babans were more frequently mentioned in a variety of sources. For instance, when Xane Pasha (d. 1732) occupied the Erdelani territories, the "influence of the [Baban] family stretched now with varying force from Kirkuk to Hamadan" (Longrigg 1925, 159). Again, when the Catholic father Giuseppe Campanile (d. 1835) visited the area around 1810, he noted that the Baban domains included "Karatcholan, Kara-Dar, Baziyan, Margu, Emar Menden, Hedjiler, Surdach, Kerabe, Korrok-Khoy, Serspi as well as Arbil, Kirkuk and Khoy-Sindjaq" (Campanile 2004, 40). At other times, the Baban domain remained strictly confined to Silêmanî. Particularly during the period from 1823 to 1851, upon the signing of the First Treaty of Erzurum, when the last Baban emir was removed from Silêmanî, the Babans were unable to expand their realm beyond their capital and some surrounding villages. This inability was due in part to the presence of Iranian and Turkish garrisons in their town as well as to the rise of the Mirê Kor ("the blind emir," d. 1838), emir of Soran emirate, in the northern neighborhood of Rewandiz (Longrigg 1925, 247, 249, 287).

The Ottoman official correspondence carefully distinguished Iranian Kurdistan from Ottoman Kurdistan when writing to the Iranian court. And when such official documents referred to Ottoman Kurdistan, they utilized the name "Kurdistan" without defining its boundaries or describing its geographical borders. Specifically, they used the name "Kurdistan" in reference to the Babans. On occasion, when the Ottomans referred to the matter of Kurdistan (*Kürdistan maddesi*) during disputes with the Iranians, it was evident that the region they had in mind was the Baban territories because they used *Kürdistan maddesi* interchangeably with the matter of Baban (*Baban maddesi*). For instance, a letter from the Ottoman governor of Baghdad, Davud Pasha, to the commander in chief (*serasker*), Rauf Pasha, dated 20 March 1824 (19 Receb 1239), states that "the matters related to the issue of Kurdistan have been sorted out" (*Kürdistan umurundan mâ'adâ olan mesâlih halledilmiş*), except for "the problem of the pashas of Kurdistan," who still allied with the Iranians. When discussing "the issue of Kurdistan," Davud Pasha was referring to the Baban *sancak*, and "the pashas of Kurdistan" specifically denoted the Baban leaders.[20]

Ottoman sources referred to the leaders of the Baban emirate interchangeably as the "Ottoman pashas" or *mutasarrıf*s (*sancak* governors) of Baban and later Silêmanî or as *Kürdistan mutasarrıfı* and *Kürdistan paşası*,[21] the pashas and leaders of Kurdistan. In terms of the concept of Ottoman Kurdistan, as more Kurdish regions were integrated into the Ottoman body politic, the titles of Kurdish political units changed from referencing a particular Kurdish dynasty to substituting the Ottoman administrative term instead, such as "Van *vilayeti*," "Hakkari *sancağı*," "Bayezid *sancağı*," and the like. Similarly, lands populated by the Kurds in the north of the Ottoman Empire, such as Erzurum, Van, Kars, Muş, and Bayezid, continued to be collectively referred to as *serhadd*, emphasizing their position in the Ottoman Empire as an imperial frontier; the Kurdish names and references were gradually silenced despite the Kurdish majority residing there. Cities in this region, such as Erzurum, were referred to as *serhad şehri*s ([Ottoman] frontier cities). Hence, it appears that the name "Kurdistan" gradually moved beyond the eastern boundaries of the

---

20. Cumhurbaşkanlığı Devlet Arşivleri Başkanlığı/Directorate of Presidential State Archives, Istanbul (BOA), Hatt-ı Humayun (HAT) #36617-A, 19.B.1239/20 Mar. 1824.

21. See the Ottoman document for "Kürdistan Mutasarrıfı," BOA, HAT #36750-I, 17.L.1239/15 June 1824.

Ottoman Empire and the Ottoman imaginary to refer to Kurds residing outside of the empire.

Despite the large number of references in Ottoman official correspondence to the Babans as the regional leaders of Kurdistan, when these sources mention Kurdistan, they hardly ever allude to other Kurdish leaders within the Ottoman Empire, such as Bedirxan. Rather, the Ottoman documents mention and discuss Bedirxan with the mere administrative title of "an Ottoman official," such as the "*kaimmakam* of Cizre, Bedirxan Beg" (*Cizre kaymakamı Bedirhan bey*)[22] in one document or "the *mütesellim* of Cizre, Bedirxan *Beg*" (*Cizre mütesellimi Bedirhan Bey*)[23] in another. Ottoman officials' diminution of the status of Kurdish leaders in Ottoman Kurdistan also applies to other significant Kurdish leaders, such as Mîrê Kor, or "Muhammed, *Beg* of Rewandiz" (Revanduz Beyi Mehmed Bey), who joined the Ottoman side during the war with Iran because of his particular religious beliefs adhering to the Şafi'i school of law, which had more in common with the Sunni Ottomans than with the Shi'i Iranians.[24] In another Ottoman document, Ali Pasha, who was responsible for removing the governor of Baghdad, recounts the help provided by Revanduzlu Mehmed Bey, who moved on Baghdad with his forces together with "the *mutasarrıf* of Baban."[25] In summary, then, while the Ottoman sources initially referred to Kurdistan without any reservations, the appellation changed as, first, Kurdistan was divided into Ottoman Kurdistan and Iranian Kurdistan, and then Ottoman Kurdistan was further articulated as different Kurdish regions started getting included in the Ottoman body politic either as administrative divisions or as frontier cities. Finally,

---

22. BOA, C.NF (Cevdet Nafia) #959, Folio: 20, 8.Ca.1259/7 June 1843.

23. BOA, A.MKT (Sadaret-Mektubi Kalemi Ervakı) #86, Folio: 9, 19.S.1260/9 Mar. 1844. Another document talks about the effect that the sheikhs of Khalidiyya had on the removal of threatening forces belonging to "Mütesellim of Cizre, Bedirxan Beg." See BOA, A.MKT.MHM (Sadaret Mektubi Kalemi Mühimme Kalemi Evrakı) #61, Folio: 2, 17.C.1263/1 June 1847.

24. BOA, HAT #36750-M, 07.L 1239/5 June 1824.

25. BOA, HAT #20815, 08.L.1246/23 Mar. 1831.

from the nineteenth century on, the Ottoman sources started to refer to the center of Kurdistan, if not Kurdistan itself, in reference to the Kurdish regions located outside of Anatolia, especially the Baban Emirate. Ultimately, then, it was political power that defined the region of Kurdistan through the centuries.

Kurdish Lands in European Sources

Moving beyond the Ottoman sources, many European—in particular British, Italian, and French—sources also refer to the Baban territories when discussing Kurdistan. For instance, two early Italian accounts pay special attention to the Babans. A Catholic father from the Vatican, Maurizio Garzoni (d. 1804), who was in Amêdî around the 1770s, counts the "five great Muslim principalities" of Kurdistan as "Bitlis," "Jazira" (Botan), "Amadia" (Behdinan), "Julamerg" (Hakkari), and "Karacholan" (Baban). After providing this information, Garzoni states that the Baban principality became the "the greatest and most powerful" one, especially after "it annexed the principality of Koi Sanjak [Soran]" (1787, 3-4). In addition to providing the names of the five Kurdish principalities, Garzoni estimates the overall size of Kurdistan at the time of his travels in the region by declaring that "this country in itself has an extent of around twenty-five days [of travel] by length and ten days by breadth" (3).

Another Catholic father, Giuseppe Campanile, who visited the Kurds thirty years after Garzoni, makes a similar observation about the Baban principality by stating that it is "the most extensive, most powerful, and most pleasant" emirate of all Kurdistan. Campanile adds two further Kurdish principalities to those already listed by Garzoni: "Soran" and "Baba[n]" (Campanile 2004, 12).[26] Whereas Garzoni does not name a capital for the entire Kurdistan region, Campanile contends that Bitlis is the center of Kurdistan because of its commercial importance and relative

---

26. Despite mentioning the Baban emirate, Father Campanile adds "Karatcholan" (Qala Çolan) to the list as well (2004, 11), perhaps relying on Garzoni's account.

1.2. A European map produced by the German map publisher G. Matthäus Seutter, showing "Curdistania." From Seutter 1730.

beauty. In any case, Campanile explicitly notes that "some like to name it [Bitlis] as the capital of all Kurdistan" (2004, 12).

Beyond the information presented by these two Italian fathers, the most comprehensive source written about the Babans is James C. Rich's *Narrative of a Residence in Koordistan* (1836). The "Koordistan" in Rich's title is the region located in the Southeast of the Ottoman Empire, today's northern Iraq, where the Baban territories were centered in Silêmanî. At the end of the first volume of his book, Rich gives details of a scroll titled "The Dates and Facts Connected with the History of Koordistan," which he received from the Baban pashas. The list recounts mostly facts about the Baban family but also refers to other Kurdish pashas as well as to Ottoman and Iranian rulers to the extent they are associated with the Babans (Rich 1836, 385–87). Rich also employs the names "Turkish Koordistan," "Bebbeh Koordistan," and "Southern Koordistan" when referring to Baban territories.

Next, in the periodical *Christian Secretary*, an article on the hostility of Iranians toward Baghdad notes that the Iranian governor Muhammad Ali Mirza "got possession of Sulimania, the residence of Pacha of Kurdistan" (7 December 1824). In these sources, then, even though the Baban territories are referred to as "Kurdistan," the cited capital of the region varies: Silêmanî in some but the "capital of lower Kurdistan"[27] in others. Likewise, underneath a drawing of Silêmanî at the beginning of his book *A Voyage up the Persian Gulf*, the British traveler William Heude (1819) also identifies it as "Sulimâney, the Capital of Kurdistan" (figure 1.3).

The gradual strengthening of the position of the Kurdish Baban Emirate to be eventually identified with Kurdistan is also reflected in the titles bestowed upon each of the Kurdish *mîr*s (Kurdish version of *emir*). For instance, whereas most Kurdish *mîr*s in the Ottoman Empire were given the title *beg/bey*, Baban leaders were referred to as *paşa*. After the Tanzimat in 1839, even though the Baban leaders as well as other Kurdish *mîr*s were now renamed *mutasarrıf*, many of the former preserved the title *paşa*, which had been bestowed upon them by the sultan or the governor of the province. In nineteenth-century Ottoman documents, the Baban emirs were also referred to as *mîr-i mîran*, "emir of all emirs," or *beglerbegi* because the Ottomans considered them to be the most powerful of the Kurdish *mîr*s. Indeed, the Baban leader Süleyman Pasha was officially given the title *mirmiran* in 1837. The sultan's decree accompanying the title deed states "Baban Mutasarrıfı Süleyman Paşa'ya mirmiran ve oğlu Ahmed Bey'e de kapıcıbaşı nişanlarının itası" (the bestowal upon the Baban leader Süleyman Pasha of the decoration 'emir of emirs' and the bestowal upon his son Ahmed Bey of the decoration keeper of the palace gate).[28] In addi-

---

27. See the entry "Solymania or Sherezur" in Brookes 1820.
28. BOA, HAT #23085, 29.Z.1252/5 Apr. 1837.

1.3. Drawing of Silêmanî with the subtitle *Sulimâney, the Capital of Kurdistan*. From Heude 1819.

tion, French sources referred to one of the most influential Baban pashas, Abdurrahman (r. 1788–1813), as *mirmiran*.[29] Hence, the region of Kurdistan acquired different symbolic valence in the nineteenth century as the Ottoman sources started to equate Kurdistan with the Baban Emirate outside the empire but to silence references to Ottoman Kurdistan.

Conclusion

I have argued in this chapter that the boundaries and capital of Kurdistan did not stay the same throughout the centuries. Whereas Bitlis was

---

29. Correspondance Consulaire et Commerciale (CCC), Bassorah (Basra), vol. 2 (1810–13), nr. 058, in Nieuwenhuis 1981, 42.

perceived as the center of the Kurdish culture, politics, and economics in the sixteenth century because of its literary and political power, Silêmanî replaced it in the nineteenth century (Chèref-ou'ddine 1873, 5). Interestingly, Şeref Xân also noted that Çemişgezek, located in Anatolia far away from Bitlis and Silêmanî, was "known by all especially with the name Kurdistan" and that the Ottoman official documents referred to "this province whenever this name ['Kurdistan'] is mentioned" (Scheref 1860, 163). Hence, the name "Kurdistan" came to denote a variety of geographical spaces throughout the centuries. I argue that what denoted Kurdistan was strongly connected with the local powers that ruled the regions where the Kurds lived because these local powers, such as the Ottomans, ultimately defined what constituted Kurdistan. From the nineteenth century on, when Kurds in the Ottoman Empire became incorporated into the empire as administrative units or frontier cities, the Ottomans as well as the Europeans started to refer to Kurdistan as a land distant from the center of the empire. As Kurds were thus symbolically removed from the Ottoman imaginary, their position within the empire kept worsening over time.

References

Al-Isfahani Imad al-din. 1955. *Kharidat alqasr wa jaridat al-'asr.* Vol. 4. Edited by M. B. al-Athari. Baghdad: MII (al-Iraq).
Alsancakli, Sacha. 2015. "From Bidlis to Ardabil via Aleppo and Isfahan." *Eurasian Studies* 13:133–52.
Amanat, Abbas. 1994. "Dawlatšāh, Moḥammad-'alī Mīrzā." In *Encyclopaedia Iranica*, vol. 7, 147–49. New York: Encyclopaedia Iranica Foundation.
Atçıl, Abdurrahman. 2017. "The Safavid Threat and Juristic Authority in the Ottoman Empire during the 16th Century." *International Journal of Middle East Studies* 49, no. 2: 295–314.
Ateş, Sabri. 2013. *Ottoman–Iranian Borderlands: Making a Boundary, 1843–1914.* New York: Cambridge Univ. Press.
Atmaca, Metin. 2013. "Politics of Alliance and Rivalry on the Ottoman–Iranian Frontier: The Babans (1500–1851)." PhD diss., Albert Ludwigs Univ. of Freiburg.

———. 2021. "Negotiating Political Power in the Early Modern Middle East Kurdish Emirates between the Ottoman Empire and Iranian Dynasties (Sixteenth to Nineteenth Centuries)." In *The Cambridge History of the Kurds*, edited by Hamit Bozarslan, Cengiz Gunes, and Veli Yadirgi, 45–72. Cambridge: Cambridge Univ. Press.

Aykun, İbrahim. 1995. "Erzurum konferansı (1843–1847) ve Osmanlı-İran hudut antlaşması." PhD diss., Atatürk Univ.

Ayn Ali. 1280/1863–64. *Kavânîn-i âl-i Osman der hulâsa-i mezâmîn-i defter-i dîvân*. Istanbul: Tasvir-i Efkar Gazetesi Matbaası.

Aziz Efendi. 1985. *Kanûn-nâme-i sultânî li 'Aziz Efendi: Aziz Efendi's Book of Sultanic Laws and Regulations: An Agenda for Reform by a Seventeenth-Century Ottoman Statesman*. Edited and translated by Rhoads Murphey. Cambridge, MA: Office of the Univ. Publisher, Harvard Univ.

Barkan, Ömer Lütfi. 1953–54. "H. 933–934 (M. 1527–1528) Malî yılına ait bir bütçe örneği." *İstanbul Üniversitesi İktisat Fakültesi mecmuası* 14, no. 5: 251–329.

Brookes, Richard. 1820. *The General Gazetteer or Compendious Geographical Dictionary*. London: Bumpus et al.

Campanile, R.P. Giuseppe. 2004. *Historie du Kurdistan*. Translated by R. P. Thomas Bois. Paris: L'Harmattan.

Chèref-ou'ddine. 1873. *Chèref-Nâmeh, Fastes de la nation Kourde*. Vol. 2, part 1. Translated and edited by François Bernard Charmoy. St. Petersburg, Russia: Commissionnaires de l'Académie impériale des sciences.

Christian Secretary. 1824. 7 Dec.

Dankoff, Robert. 2004. *An Ottoman Mentality: The World of Evliya Çelebi*. Leiden, Netherlands: Brill.

Dehqan, Mustafa, and Vural Genç. 2018. "Kurds as Spies: Information-Gathering on the 16th-Century Ottoman–Safavid Frontier." *Acta Orientalia* 71, no. 2: 197–230.

Drouville, Gaspard. 1825. *Voyage en Perse fait en 1812 et 1813*. Vol. 2. Paris: Librairie nationale et etrangére.

Dupré, Adrien. 1819. *Voyage en Perse fait dans les années 1807, 1808 et 1809*. Paris: J. G. Dentu.

Ehmedê Xanî. 2010. *Mem û Zîn*. Translated by Namık Açıkgöz. Edited by Ayhan Tek. Ankara, Turkey: Kültür ve Turizm Bakanlığı.

Evliya Çelebi. 2005. *Evliya Çelebi seyahatnamesi*. Vol. 4. Edited by Seyit Ali Kahraman and Yücel Dağlı. Istanbul: Yapı Kredi Yayınları.

Fuccaro, Nelida. 2011. "The Ottoman Frontier in Kurdistan in the Sixteenth and Seventeenth Centuries." In *The Ottoman World*, edited by Christine Woodhead, 237–50. London: Routledge.

Garzoni, P. Maurizio. 1787. *Grammatica e vocabolario della lingua kurda*. Rome: Stamperia della Sacria Congregazione de Propaganda Fide.

Heude, William. 1819. *A Voyage up the Persian Gulf and a Journey Overland from India to England in 1817*. London: Longman.

Ibn al-Athir. 1998. *Al-Kamil fi l-Ta'rikh*. Vols. 7 and 10. Beirut: Dar al-Kutub al-'İlmiyah.

Ibn Hawqal. 1939. *Kitab surat al-ard*. Vol. 1. Edited by J. H. Kramers. Leiden, Netherlands: Brill.

Ibn Khallikan. 1968–72. *Kitab wafayat al-a'yan wa anba'Abna' al-zaman*. Vols. 5 and 7. Beirut: Dar Sadir.

James, Boris. 2007. "Le territoire tribal des Kurdes et l'aire iraquienne (Xe–XIIIe siècles): Esquisse des recompositions spatiales." *Revue d'etudes sur les mondes Musulmans et Méditerranéens* 67–68:101–26.

———. 2014. "Arab Ethnonyms ('Ajam, 'Arab, Badu, and Turk): The Kurdish Case as a Paradigm for Thinking about Differences in the Middle Ages." *Iranian Studies* 47, no. 5: 683–712.

Kaempfer, Engelbert. 1977. *Am Hofe des persischen Grosskönigs 1684–1685*. Edited by Walter Hinz. Tübingen, Germany: Horst Erdmann.

Kafadar, Cemal. 2007. "A Rome of One's Own: Reflections on Cultural Geography and Identity in the Lands of Rum." *Muqarnas* 24:7–25.

———. 2017. *Kendine ait bir Roma*. Istanbul: Metis.

Katib Çelebi. 1145/1732. *Kitab-ı cihannüma*. Istanbul: Darü't- Tıbaatü'l-Amire.

———. 1812. *Rumeli und Bosna, geographisch Beschrieben von Mustafa Ben Abdalla Hadschi Chalfa*. Translated by Joseph Freiherr von Hammer-Purgstall. Vienna: Verlag des Kunst-und Industrie-Comptoits.

———. 2007. *Cihannüma*. Vol. 1. Edited by Fikri Sarıcaoğlu. Ankara: Türk Tarih Kurumu.

Longrigg, Stephen H. 1925. *Four Centuries of Modern Iraq*. Oxford: Oxford Univ. Press.

Matthee, Rudi. 2003. "The Safavid–Ottoman Frontier: Iraq-i Arab as Seen by the Safavids." In *Ottoman Borderlands: Issues, Personalities, and Political Changes*, edited by Kemal H. Karpat and Robert W. Zens, 157–74. Madison: Univ. of Wisconsin Press.

Melayê Cizîrî. 2012. *Dîwan*. Translated by Osman Tunç. Edited by Ayhan Tek. Ankara, Turkey: Kültür ve Turizm Bakanlığı Yayınları.
Muhammad Yusuf Valah Isfahani. 1372/1993. *Khuld-i barin (Iran dar ruzgar-i Safaviyan)*. Edited by Mir Hashim Muhaddis. Tehran: Bunyad-i Mawquufat-i Duktur Mahmud Afshar.
Mustafa Naima. 2007. *Tarih-i Naima*. Vol. 2. Edited by Mehmet İpşirli. Ankara: Türk Tarih Kurumu.
Nieuwenhuis, Tom. 1981. *Politics and Society in Early Modern Iraq: Mamluk Pashas Tribal Shayks and Local Rule between 1802 and 1831*. The Hague, Netherlands: Martinus Nijhoff.
Nizamüddin Şâmi. 1987. *Zafernâme*. Translated by Necati Lugal. Ankara: Türk Tarih Kurumu.
O'Shea, Maria Theresa. 2012. *Trapped between the Map and Reality: Geography and Perceptions of Kurdistan*. New York: Routledge.
Rich, James C. 1836. *Narrative of a Residence in Koordistan and on the Site of Ancient Nineveh*. Vol. 1. London: James Duncan.
Şanizade Mehmet Ataullah. 2008. *Tarih-i Şanizade*. Vol. 1. Edited by Ziya Yılmazer. Istanbul: Çamlıca.
Scheref, Prince de Bidlis. 1860. *Scherefnameh ou histoire des Kourdes*. Vol. 1. Edited by V. Véliaminof-Zernof. St. Petersburg, Russia: Académie impériale des sciences.
Schofield, Richard. 2008. "Narrowing the Frontier: Mid-Nineteenth Century Efforts to Delimit and Map the Perso-Ottoman Border." In *War and Peace in Qajar Persia: Implications Past and Present*, edited by Roxane Farmanfarmaian, 149–73. New York: Routledge.
Seutter, Georg Matthäus. 1730. *Atlas Novus Indicibus Instructus, oder Neuer mit Wort-Registern versehener Atlas*. Vienna: Johann Peter von Ghelen.
Sezgin, Fuat. 2013. Introduction to *Kâtip Çelebî'nin Esas Kitâb-ı Cihânnümâ'sı ve coğrafya tarihi'ndeki yeri / The Original Kitāb-i Cihānnumā of Ḥādjī Khalīfa and His Position in the History of Geography*, edited by Fuat Sezgin, 29–48. Istanbul: Boyut.
Shakely, Ferhad. 1996. "The Kurdish Qasida." In *Qasida Poetry in Islamic Asia and Africa*, edited by Stefan Sperl, C. Shackle, and Nicholas Awde, 244–51. Leiden, Netherlands: Brill.
Tezcan, Baki. 2000. "The Development of the Use of 'Kurdistan' as a Geographical Description and the Incorporation of This Region into the Ottoman

Empire in the 16th Century." In *The Great Ottoman-Turkish Civilisation*, vol. 3, edited by Kemal Çiçek, 540–53. Ankara: Yeni Türkiye.

Ülke, Cemal. 2014. "Kürdistan Eyaleti'nin idari yapısı (1847–1867)." Master's thesis, Mardin Artuklu Univ.

Yahya Ibn Fadlallah Al-'Umari. 1988. *Masalik al-absar fi mamalik al-amsar*. Vol. 3. Edited by Fuat Sezgin. Frankfurt, Germany: Institut für Geschichte der Arabisch-Islamischen Wissenschaften.

Yamaguchi, Akihiko. 2012. "Shāh Tahmāsp's Kurdish Policy." *Studia Iranica* 41, no. 1: 101–32.

Yaqut al-Hamawi. 1957. *Mu'jam al-Buldan*. Vol. 1. Beirut: Dar Sadir.

2

Making Minorities in the Late Ottoman Period

Armenians and Kurds

Janet Klein

Peppered generously throughout the pages of the Kurdish–Ottoman press from 1898 to 1919 are depictions by Kurdish writers of Kurds as loyal citizens of the empire and as long-standing faithful subjects of the Ottoman body. These descriptions, however, appear alongside proclamations of Kurdishness as a separate "national" identity. Why would a group that is elsewhere asserting its distinct identity (Kurdishness versus Turkishness, for example)—indeed, as a "nation"—also take great pains to emphasize the group's historic loyalty to the empire? The "loyalty" factor is critical here and needs further exploration.[1] I suggest that we read these texts alongside other contemporary accounts as witnesses to the larger process through which non-Turkish communities in the late Ottoman period were minoritized.

This chapter explores the construction of minorities in the late Ottoman period by focusing on the Armenian and Kurdish examples. It draws

---

1. In my earlier work, I interpreted these tensions differently. I have now come to appreciate their fuller significance as something that has mostly been recognized as "national" identity. Although I did recognize the troubled position of nondominant groups in new nation-states, I came to appreciate the significance of the minority status and to identify the minoritization process only over the course of the past decade. Although I began work on what eventually became this chapter earlier, I developed some of these ideas elsewhere: see Klein 2014, 2019a, 2019b, 2020a, 2020b.

on Kurdish, Ottoman, and European sources (in particular the Kurdish-Ottoman press) to highlight how foreigners, "the state," and locals (here, Kurds and their Armenian neighbors) perceived and participated in the construction of their communities as not just minorities but as "marked citizens" (Pandey 2006, chap. 6). Although, to the best of my knowledge, Ottoman (or even Turkish nationalist) official documents did not refer to non-Muslim groups—or even to Muslim groups—as "minorities" until 1920, when the National Pact (Misak-i Milli) discussed the rights of minorities (*akalliyetler*) (Bayır 2013, 68), following European treaties on minorities and minority rights after World War I, my focus is on the larger process through which the "minoritization" of certain groups occurred. I argue that this process was underway decades before the term *minority* came into play in official usage or even in popular parlance. I am attempting here to trace part of the story about how, in the words of Raymond Grew, when "formal, public distinctions are constructed[,] . . . [we see] the operation of an almost manic logic, whereby differences—once they have been socially or politically defined—take on a life of their own" (2001, 2).

Building upon some of my previous work, I am suggesting that these differences, which have been described and studied as national, ethnic, religious, or racial, become dangerous to certain communities when those communities come to be viewed through the lens of minorityhood and majorityhood. I argue that it is not just "difference"—even when acknowledged to be historically and socially constructed—that is on its own most significant when analyzing state-sponsored and grassroots movements against groups that have now come to be known as "minorities." Rather, the minority designation itself and the process through which these groups came to be constructed as minorities and minoritized are uniquely bound up in repression and mass violence. Violence is tied to minority designation when minorities—now conceived of as such—come to be regarded as threats to the territorial integrity and sovereignty of the "nation" and to the hegemony and imagined privilege of the dominant group, now envisioned as the "majority," or the legitimate citizens. Before exploring the Kurdish example, I flesh out some more general theoretical proposals about the historical construction of minorities and how this process played out in the late Ottoman period in particular. I emphasize the importance of the minoritization of the Armenians for the larger connection between minority designation and violence and then return to the Kurdish case.

Historiographical Problems with the "Minority" Designation

Recent literature has begun to recognize the construction of identities (instead of taking them as an age-old given) and has gone far in nuancing and historicizing strife between Muslim and non-Muslim communities; however, the very concept of "minority" remains ahistorical even in many of these recent and nuanced works. In the Ottoman context, non-Muslim groups are taken for granted as being minorities for periods long before the concept existed, and this has skewed our perception of the Ottoman past and identity construction even as scholars have offered important interventions.

"Minorities are not automatically minorities," as Gyanendra Pandey notes; "minorities, like communities, are historically constituted" (2006, 171). Indeed, the term *minority*—used in reference to a group "distinguished by common ties of descent, physical appearance, language, culture or religion, in virtue of which they feel or are regarded as different from the majority of the population in a society" (Bullock, Trombley, and Eadie 1988, s.v. "Minorities," quoted in White 2007, 65)—didn't emerge until the mid-nineteenth century and at this point was restricted to religious groups. Although the concept of "minority" quickly came to identify numerically inferior "national" and "ethnic" groups, as Benjamin White notes, "it is not surprising that *religious* minorities were identified first: before the emergence of secular nationalism, the politically salient form of identity was religious." "Nor," he continues, "is it surprising that religious minorities were not identified as *minorities* until quite recently (c. 1850). Previously, it was their status as subordinate *religious* groups that was important. Only when modern states appeared did the numerical inferiority of these groups become more salient than the religious cleavages separating them from the majority" (2007, 65–66, italics in original). Laura Robson adds that there were three contexts in which the concept of national "minorities" emerged in Europe: "Marxists proposing the formulation of some kind of Habsburg federalist system, international Jewish organizations advocating for specific collective Jewish rights and representation in eastern Europe, and new international organizations promoting pacifist and reformist agendas" (2017, 26). In the Ottoman context, religious communities were organized into the millet system, and although it is certainly true that non-Muslims were a subordinate group, they "were not subordinated because they were a minority (often they were not), but because they were non-Muslims" (White 2007, 66). As Derya Bayır emphasizes, "The millet order was not a minority protection system in the modern sense, but an organizational structure for dealing with non-Muslim diversity within a plural society. Thus, to picture Ottoman society along the lines of a Muslim versus non-Muslim or majority-minority dichotom[y] is too simplistic, and is in fact loaded with political agendas, which are a by-product of later developments in the nineteenth and twentieth centuries" (2013, 27–28).[2]

The literature on Christians and Jews in the Ottoman Empire has suffered from the ahistorical depiction of minorities, despite numerous other nuanced developments in this body of work. Two historiographical problems remain. The first is the tendency to treat the concept of "minority" ahistorically and without problematizing the term itself. As such, a plethora of works has emerged on "minorities" in the Ottoman Empire, and although some use the term rightly in their studies of the modern period when the concept of "minority" was in the process of being articulated, too many others employ the language of "minorityhood" when referring to Christians and Jews (or even ethnic groups) in earlier periods when the concept was rather meaningless. For those who do use the label for the appropriate historical era, most do not problematize it, much less trace how minorities were actually constructed as such, as in the late Ottoman period.[3]

---

2. Although it is not within the scope of this chapter to delve into the broader history of the millet system, it is worth noting Aron Rodrigue's (1995) point that the millet system we speak of was really invented in the nineteenth century.

3. Notable exceptions include Robson 2017 and White 2007 and 2011 for post-Ottoman constructions of minorities. The problem remains when it comes to Ottoman groups—a problem I'm attempting to tackle here.

Another problem lies in the treatment of intergroup relations. Scholars of late have found many flaws with previous mainstream portrayals of interreligious groups' interactions as inherently—even primordially—full of discord and have rightly opened our eyes to the complexities of these relationships and how they were often much more positive and fluid than mainstream literature has portrayed them. However, in their attempts to overturn ahistorical presentations of age-old religious hatreds or rigid group boundaries, some of these scholars have swung to the other extreme and have painted a much rosier picture of group relations than the historical record warrants. In other words, although it is good to recognize that these relations were much better and more nuanced than previous portraits showed them to be, the "kumbaya" approach leaves us without the means to consider conflict when it did arise, for indeed it did. Some recent research has brought us highly nuanced studies that capture the complexities of these relationships and the contingencies that converged to promote strife when it did occur (for example, Cora, Derderian, and Sipahi 2016; Klein 2011; Makdisi 2000; Philliou 2010; Yosmaoğlu 2014). What is important to point out here is that enmity between religious groups took on a dangerously different dimension with the evolution of the modern state and the development of a set of uneven power relations between European regimes and the Ottomans in which a discourse surrounding minorities and new concepts of rights became elements in a wider global discourse on modernity, civilization, sovereignty, identity, power, and citizenship.

For the remainder of the chapter, I continue to flesh out my theoretical proposals for viewing minorities in the late Ottoman period as the result of specific historical processes. Although the primary focus of this study is to explore this development through the Kurdish case, to do so it is necessary first to note the ways in which the Armenian example was central to the larger visions of peoplehood in the empire as well to the emergence of non-Turks as minorities and Turks as the majority. As I suggest later in this chapter, minoritizing the Armenians may have been central in defining the Turks as the "majority" in the late Ottoman period—for, indeed, majorities are constructed in tandem with minorities—and the minoritization of Kurds, which began in the late Ottoman period, played a central role in defining Turkishness-as-majority in the post-Ottoman period. Although it is not within the scope of this chapter to flesh out the "majoritization" of Turks, it is essential to acknowledge the ways in which the shifting notions of these three communities— increasingly reified as such—were connected and how the "Armenian question" played a key role in this process. Therefore, I begin with an analysis of the "Armenian question" and establish its centrality in the larger process of conceiving of minorities and majorities that played out in the late Ottoman period before I move on to the (related) Kurdish example.

The "Armenian Question"

The "Armenian question" and the question (indeed, the construction) of minorities arose in the context of European imperialism and the development of modern Ottoman statecraft and identities. As Benjamin White puts it, "The evolution of political thought leading to the establishment of the League [of Nations]," which ultimately finalized the division of the Ottoman Empire after World War I, "coincided with the evolution of the Ottoman communities into nations and minorities, a traumatic epistemological transformation which likewise afflicted much of Europe during that period" (2007, 64). Before the mid-nineteenth century, numerically inferior groups were not tainted with the kind of political mark that branded them in conjunction with the growth of nationalism and new concepts of peoplehood linked to the idea of representative government. With the Islahat Fermanı (Reform Edict) of 1856, "the millet order . . . changed from being part of a social contract for the peaceful coexistence of diverse groups to something closer to minority status" (Bayır 2013, 33–34). Twenty years later, with the first Ottoman Constitution, deputies were to commit to representing the entire Ottoman nation, not just their own individual ethnolinguistic or religious communities. However, it also became clear in the Ottoman Constitution that bills were to be reviewed with regard to "the territorial integrity of the country." The legal emphasis was shifting, with a sharpened focus on maintaining territorial and national unity (Bayır 2013, 34).

In this larger process, numerically inferior religious groups' lesser status shifted; they were previously subordinated because they did not share the religious (and later ethnic/"national") identity of the dominant group, but now their inferior status was also distinctly linked to their minority status (White 2007). Violence became bound up in minority designation when minorities came to be regarded as threats to the territorial integrity and sovereignty of the "nation" and to the hegemony of the dominant group. In other words, their "loyalty" as citizens was drawn into question. Armenians in the Ottoman Empire composed one group that came to be part of this wider shift in the second half of the nineteenth century. Indeed, as I suggest later, until the end of the empire, the Armenians were the "minority extraordinaire" for all of the reasons a group became minoritized.

As modern Ottoman statecraft developed, identities in the empire underwent the same type of transitions as they did elsewhere in the world. State builders began to subscribe to the idea that they needed to map and classify not only the geographic regions they sought to govern but also the people who lived within these areas. Because this process was intimately connected to the practice of defining, demarking, and defending borders as borderlands transitioned to bordered lands, the people who lived in these regions developed or were assigned new markers associated with their identities, and these markers were most often coupled with the perception of threat.

Armenians lived alongside Kurds in a region that not only was remote and difficult to govern but was also desired by foreign powers, so their new "minorityhood" arose concurrently with these perceived threats. Armenian minorityhood, more than that of any other Ottoman group in the late Ottoman period, came about as a result of both where they were *and* who they were (Mann 2005, 34)[4]—the product of internal Ottoman state-building dynamics and imperialist designs on Ottoman territory. The labeling of Armenians as a minority by Europeans and Russians and of eastern Anatolia as a region in which these foreign powers asserted they could intervene resulted in a series of "Armenian reforms" beginning in 1878; the last of these reform packages in 1914 would ultimately

---

4. Michael Mann (2005) discusses this in the context of the modernity of genocide.

play an instrumental role in the final demise of the Ottoman Armenian community (Akçam 2012, 129–36). I discuss these reform packages in more detail later.

Armenians embraced the wider package of Tanzimat reforms, but many grew disillusioned because they still were not regarded as equal citizens and saw a rise in repression. Feeling that their petitions to the central Ottoman government were falling on deaf ears and noting how Europeans were now carving out new spaces for themselves in the Ottoman Empire by invoking their "right" to "protect" Christians, some Armenians began to turn to Europe to press for reforms that would benefit their community specifically. The Treaty of San Stefano, which followed the Russo-Ottoman War of 1877–78, engaged the Sublime Porte "to carry into effect, without further delay, the improvements and reforms demanded by local requirements in the provinces inhabited by Armenians, and to guarantee their security from Kurds and Circassians" (quoted in Akçam 2006, 39). Owing to European fears that the Russians would gain too much control in Ottoman lands, the pressure to modify the treaty resulted in the transformation of Article 16 to a version that seemed weaker but specified that Europeans would oversee these reforms in Article 61 of the Berlin Treaty (Akçam 2006, 39).[5] When the empire's six eastern provinces received special designation by Europeans as the "Armenian provinces, the "loyal millet," as the Armenians had been called for a period, was now viewed with suspicion as traitors whose loyalty was in doubt. Increased repression led to more Armenian demands for foreign intervention and protection, and the Great Powers milked the Armenian plight as an opportunity to intervene.

We have numerous rich and nuanced accounts about how the central Ottoman government and local officials constructed Armenians as a (now "national") threat. It should also be noted, however, that not all officials

---

5. Article 61 of the Treaty of Berlin (1878) reads: "The Sublime Porte undertakes to carry out, without further delay, the improvements and reforms demanded by local requirements in the provinces inhabited by Armenians, and to guarantee their security against the Circassians and Kurds. It will periodically make known the steps taken to this effect to the powers, who will superintend their application" (quoted in Akçam 2006, 39).

were on the same page in viewing Armenians in this light. Regardless of how rich these accounts may be, none of them historicizes the process through which Armenians (then later Kurds) came to be constituted as minorities, a project I am setting out to do here. It is difficult to know exactly when state officials began to use the term *minority* (even unofficially), and that is still something I am working to tease out. In the meantime, however, I suggest that we focus on the process of *minoritization* because that process is clear in the still scant but growing literature on the historical construction of minorities if we submit these studies to scrutiny from a different angle. In addition, although there are powerful accounts that delineate the path through which Armenians came to be regarded as threats on an official level, much less attention has been paid to how Armenians' neighbors in eastern Anatolia regarded and/or participated in this set of developments that I see as a process of minoritization. Most of their neighbors were Kurds, the next major group to become the "minority extraordinaire."[6] The process through which Armenians were constructed as minorities and all that entailed merits study on its own, but here I consider it as part of the process through which Kurds also became a minority.

One source I have found to be especially helpful for unpacking the minoritization of Armenians and in particular how Armenians' Kurdish neighbors' views began to change accordingly, is the diary of an Ottoman official, Sadettin Pasha, who was sent to Van in January 1896 to convince Kurds to comply with the Armenian Reform Program of 1895. A growing number of Ottoman officials and local Kurds increasingly regarded the Armenians as threats to the empire's territorial integrity with the growth of Armenian revolutionary organizations in the 1880s and 1890s and their manipulation as tools by the Europeans, who used the pretext of Armenian oppression to meddle in the empire's internal affairs. The Armenian Reform Program of 1895 came in response to the violence unleashed

---

6. Although I do treat the initial, late Ottoman phase of the minoritization of the Kurds, it is not within the scope of this chapter to explore the multifaceted manners in which Kurds were minoritized (and at times embraced the language of minorityhood) in post-Ottoman states and Iran.

against Armenians in the Sasun rebellion, during which local Armenians rose up against changes in the implementation of tax collection that had resulted in increased taxes. The movement was mainly the outgrowth of mounting tensions between local Kurdish tribes and Armenian peasants, but Ottoman authorities sent troops to join the Kurdish tribes in applying "extraordinary terror" tactics against the "rebels" (Polatel 2016). News of the massacres began to spread widely, and Great Britain, France, and Russia sent a joint Inquiry Commission to conduct an investigation, after which these powers issued a memorandum in May 1895 urging the sultan to comply with reforms in what they now called the "Six Armenian Provinces." Owing to the tensions and continued violence that followed, these powers pressured the Porte to acquiesce to the Armenian Reform Program (Der Matossian 2014, 13).

Sadettin Pasha's diary introduces us to the ways in which the "Armenian question" affected the Kurds and their view of their Armenian neighbors as well as their own position and security in the empire. In his diary, Sadettin Pasha explains how his main agenda is to convey to the Kurds he met with that they should heed his advice so as not to attract the negative attention of the foreign audience that was closely watching the region. He reminds the Kurds that in these days of advanced communications, the world would be instantly aware of what is going on around the globe and that Christian countries simply would not tolerate Muslims oppressing Armenians (Sadettin Pasha [1896] 2003, 20–21).[7] Elsewhere he tells the Muslim notables and Kurdish chiefs gathered before him that they need to protect Armenians and that if there were any Armenians rebelling, it would be the government that would send forces (including the Hamidiye Light Cavalry) against them. And here he issues a warning: "If you take it upon yourselves, civilized governments will shame us. . . . Europeans will say to us, 'Look, even the Kurds don't recognize the Caliphate'" (47–49).

The central Ottoman government's fear that eastern Anatolia was under threat of being severed from the empire by greedy foreign governments and disloyal Armenians was real, regardless of the severity

---

7. I thank Fatma Müge Göçek for introducing me to this diary.

(or even the reality) of the threat. But what Sadettin Pasha encountered was the locals' (Kurds' and others') anxiety that this would happen and, moreover, that the central Ottoman government would be complicit in the handing over of eastern Anatolia to the Armenians. Sadettin Pasha counseled Kurds all over the Van province: "Don't believe that the government will give the Armenians a *beylik* [independent or autonomous principality]" ([1896] 2003, 21, 49, my italics). But his advice did little to convince many local Kurds, who instead accused Sadettin Pasha of whitewashing the situation and hiding the realities from them (98), to which he responded dramatically, "[Giving the Armenians a *beylik*] will never happen. Know that if such a thing were to occur, I would be the first to fall before you and die" (99).

In their journals, Kurds also dealt with the fear that Armenians were going to sever the Ottoman East from the empire. At the turn of the twentieth century, Abdurrahman Bedir Khan wrote in the periodical *Kurdistan*,

> What really irritates me in Europe, because of my nationality, of which I am a proud member, are the Europeans' reproachful comments on clashes with Armenians. What are the reasons for this looting and plunder, which make you [Kurds] guilty in the eyes ... of Europe? Believe me, I know all of these reasons. I know everything about how Armenians desire to separate this holy land, Kurdistan, from the Ottoman body, and to make it a land for themselves. ... However, all of these events do not give you the right to clash with the Armenians. It is never right to trust the policies of the government. (1 Oct. 1900, 2)

Some Kurds even published in Armenian journals to the same effect; mostly, this act was less about ambivalence regarding Kurdish–Armenian relations and more about opposition to Sultan Abdülhamid II. In one such article, Abdullah Cevdet, a prominent Kurdish–Ottoman intellectual writing as "Bir Kürd" in 1900, blamed the sultan for paving "the way for an Armenian–Kurdish struggle" through rumor-mongering and inciting Kurds to attack Armenians (quoted in Sasuni 1986, 223–24).[8] Indeed,

---

8. "Bir Kürd" was one of Abdullah Cevdet's pen names. See Klein 2007a, 164n47.

many Kurds also attempted to counter these fears, to expose them as ridiculous, and to explain that Armenians were not, in fact, a threat to either the empire or the Kurds but rather that it was the regime of Sultan Abdülhamid II that was the problem. In *Kurdistan* on 1 October 1900, Abdurrahman Bedir Khan acknowledged that there might have been a handful of Armenian "bandits," but he cautioned his readers to remember that they were very few and that not all Armenians backed the revolutionary program. He urged Kurds to behave well toward the Armenians, to protect them against violence, and to understand that the Kurds' true enemy was not the Armenians but Sultan Abdülhamid II himself.

Many Muslims around the empire blamed their Christian neighbors for foreign intervention, believing that they tried to paint a picture to the world that they were oppressed so that foreigners would intervene on their behalf to grant them autonomy, a view that Sadettin Pasha shared ([1896] 2003, 149).⁹ This perception became more widespread in the Balkans after the Crimean War of 1853–65 (Philliou 2010, 158) and then after events in the eastern Mediterranean in the middle of the nineteenth century (Makdisi 2000). However, it was also evident in eastern Anatolia two decades before Sadettin Pasha toured the region. Indeed, after the reform package put forth following the Treaty of Berlin in 1878, one British agent in Van observed in 1879 that "the Turks in the town as well as the Kurds appear to be deeply irritated at the advent of European consuls. They think the Europeans have been sent here at the instigation of the Christians, to upset the old order of things, to protect and assist the unbelievers whom they detest and to diminish the gains that now flow into their pockets by malversation and open robbery. . . . There is a great danger that they will

---

9. Sadettin Pasha's mission must be viewed with this perception in mind. Others, however, saw it the other way around. In 1876, a British report noted that local Ottoman officials in Erzurum believed that it was the Russians who were trying to incite Christians to draw up petitions to submit to the Great Powers, "setting forth their sufferings in exaggerated terms" and asking for relief from Turkish oppression (Zohrab to Elliot, Erzurum, 18 Sept. 1876, Foreign Office [FO]: Embassy and Consulates, Turkey [formerly the Ottoman Empire]: General Correspondence, FO 195/1100, UK National Archives, London).

wreak their vengeance upon the latter."¹⁰ In fact, the Sheikh Ubeydullah movement of 1880–81 was also significantly inspired by and drew support from these rumors that the sultan, in collusion with foreign powers, would allow the Armenians and even the Assyrians to gain part of Ottoman territory for their own states (Jwaideh 2006, 83).¹¹ It is important to emphasize the impact on locals of the rumor that foreign governments (and perhaps even the sultan himself) were responding to Armenians' desires for autonomy or even independence. This prospect, which was linked to the reform packages from the beginning, was not only alarming but humiliating to local Muslims.¹² Sadettin Pasha exploited this fear, as did his predecessors much earlier, to try to control the Kurds.¹³ After all, the state saw the Kurds as a wild card (in more ways than one); their loyalty was also in question, and they might just collude with Christians or foreign powers,¹⁴ which is why it was important to divide and conquer in the borderlands. And, as noted earlier, some Kurdish writers responded by exposing this "divide-and-conquer" ploy and by calling out to their Kurdish compatriots to see the Hamidian regime, not the Armenians, as the real enemy.

10. Clayton to Trotter, 29 Aug. 1879, Van, FO General Correspondence, FO 195/1237.

11. Wadie Jwaideh (2006) emphasizes the Kurds' fear of Armenian ascendancy in the region as well as the new European consuls in the region (which I have documented in my own review of British archives).

12. Indeed, in 1876, even before the Russo-Ottoman War and the Treaty of Berlin that followed, a British report from Erzurum stated that Muslims saw the "firman of reforms" as humiliating (Zohrab to Elliot, 4 Jan. 1876, Erzurum, FO General Correspondence, FO 195/1100).

13. An agent of the sultan was reported to have traveled to Shemdinan to dissuade Kurds inclined to participate in Sheikh Ubeydullah's movement that rising up would be "just what England wanted in order to carry out her plans of erecting an Armenian State" (Clayton to Goschen, 17 May 1881, Van, FO General Correspondence, FO 195/1376). I should also note that a decade and a half later a Makuri chief in Van told Sadettin Pasha that it was the Van notables and "zaptiyes" who approached Kurdish tribes and stirred them up against the Armenians (Sadettin Pasha [1896] 2003, 149).

14. There are numerous reports on collusion between Kurds and Armenians due to their shared disgust with "Turkish rule." See, for example, Everett to Trotter, 19 Aug. 1882, Erzurum, FO General Correspondence, FO 195/1420.

Making Armenians and Kurds Minorities

An essential element in mass violence is one group's designation of another group as a threat to the "nation" (Moses 2008, 31), and Sadettin Pasha's diary, along with other sources, provide us a glimpse into not just the construction of Armenians (and also of Kurds, albeit on a different level) as a threat to the Ottoman nation but also the construction of Armenians and Kurds as minorities—a process that is, as Pandey (2006) has argued, tortured with violence. Scholars have recently offered nuanced accounts of how Armenians were viewed by their fellow Ottomans as a threat to the Turkish-nation-in-the-making and to the territorial integrity of the Ottoman Empire and of how the Young Turks' demographic policies resulted in genocide (Akçam 2012; Üngör 2011). Taner Akçam highlights in particular the Muslim Ottomans' fear that the reform proposals of 1914 that called for Armenians to participate in the governance of the six provinces on an equal basis would lead to an independent Armenia and how this fear (indeed, panic) was a final contingency that led down the path of genocide (2012, 129–39).

Although these scholars have carefully illustrated how Young Turks constructed Armenians (and later Kurds) as a demographic threat to Turkish hegemony and therefore as a dangerous Other, they (and others) take for granted the concept of "minority" as something that was perhaps sui generis and not in fact constructed through the very dynamics that they detail so well. Drawing on Pandey's work on minorities, I suggest that the anti-Armenian (and later anti-Kurdish) violence was part and parcel of the path toward constructing minorities and what made subsequent treatment of minorities (constructed as such) in the Ottoman Empire and post-Ottoman states so violent. The process of making Armenians, then later Kurds, a minority was, in fact, a core feature in the very development of Turkish nationalism itself. In this process, "Turks" distinguished themselves not just from people across the border but also primarily from Others within, and these Others came to be designated as minorities. Indeed, "Turks" were to identify as "Turks" not simply because they were not Armenians or Kurds—the two most powerful Others—but, indeed, because they were embattled against these two main threats to the "nation" (Armenians in the last half century of the Ottoman Empire's existence and Kurds from at least a decade before the Turkish Republic came into existence).

"Whose country is this anyway?" (Pandey 2006, 84) is the question of the era of nationalism, and it is the question that led to the decimation of the Ottoman Armenian community and the attempted destruction of the Kurdish community as such in Turkey. In the minoritization process, Armenians and Kurds came to have hyphenated identities and became marked citizens, living "under the sign of a question mark." Pandey asks, "[What] are the enabling conditions for such question marks?" He explains that "two tasks confront the advocates of a natural national identity. The first is to establish the oneness of the people claimed as a nation. The second is to find the appropriate political arrangement to make room for those who do not naturally fit into the unified, undifferentiated nation—and we scarcely need to remind ourselves that such groups exist to a greater or lesser extent in all modern political communities" (129). Although it could be predicted that the concept of "majority/minority" would come into play as Ottoman and later Turkish nationalism took shape, because this process is tied to nationalism, Armenians—and later Kurds—did not automatically have to be designated as such but came to be marked citizens as realities of foreign intervention combined with and shaped the concept of the "nation-in-the-making." This process was not inevitable. Armenians in the empire became marked citizens because their loyalty came to be called into question, and with rumors afloat that they were colluding with foreigners to claim a chunk of Ottoman territory for themselves, they needed to demonstrate their loyalty, something that the dominant group never needs to do. After all, "the test of loyalty is in fact required for those who are not real, natural citizens" (i.e., marked citizens) (Pandey 2006, 133). In the late Ottoman period, first Muslims and then Turks became the "we" who needed no articulation.[15] And as the notion of "good" and "bad" community took shape in the Ottoman Empire, the (Turkish) nation became the "good," but the

---

15. Pandey makes this point about Hindus in India (2006, 146).

groups now known as minorities were judged by their ability to conform to "the current state of the national project or, to put it more bluntly, [by] whether [they were] seen as threatening to the nation(al) community or not" (Pandey 2006, 182).

In the Ottoman and then the Turkish Republican context, violence became the way for the dominant group in power to deal with this perceived threat, primarily through the population policies outlined so carefully by Uğur Ümit Üngör (2011), for one. But local Muslims were inserted into and included themselves in this violence as well because of their conviction that the Armenians (and later Kurds) were "real or potential monsters who have done all this and worse to 'us' or will do so if given half a chance" (Pandey 2006, 34). This is the violence associated with minorities and a key element in all genocides. How these perceptions drew people into anti-Armenian violence has been superbly documented, but the story is not complete without recognizing this violence as the result of the process of constructing them (and later Kurds) as minorities.

We can see this process as it took shape in Sadettin Pasha's diary and other sources. Although neither Sadettin Pasha nor the Kurds with whom he spoke explicitly used the terms *majority* and *minority*, it is clear that they nonetheless were thinking along the lines of the various attributes associated with being a majority or a minority as these concepts were being articulated. And yet, despite the fact that the "ingredients" of minorityhood were varied and complex, numbers did matter for some. In a long speech to Armenian clergy and notables, Sadettin Pasha asserted that the Ottoman government had preserved Armenian identity[16] but that Armenians had better remain loyal, or they would be left to the mercy of the Kurds, who outnumbered them. He reminded the Armenians forcefully here that they were numerically inferior—"For every one of you," he said, "there are three of them [Kurds] in this province" ([1896] 2003, 31–36). Elsewhere, he told Armenians gathered before him, "You see, the Kurds here are four times more numerous than you. Not only that, but they also claim that they have been in this land [*memleket*] much longer

---

16. Perhaps as a counterpoint to Russian policy, which was more assimilationist?

than you have. What would become of you if the state withdrew, and you were left alone with the Kurds?" The only way to save yourselves, he said, was through loyalty to the state (66). He emphasized the Kurds' numerical superiority to the Kurds themselves as well, reminding them of the three-to-one (or, elsewhere, four-to-one) population ratio and how, as a result, the reforms would benefit them much more than they would the Armenians (49–50).[17] Sadettin Pasha frequently addressed the Kurds as coreligionists, hence as the "we" that formed the dominant majority, at least at the time. So in our story of the Kurds' minoritization, a first step was being tenuously considered among the majority-in-the-making. But that status was indeed a fragile one and would not last long.

The last point in Sadettin Pasha's diary I would like to highlight here is the one in which he also picked up on the Kurds' claims of unique ties to the land and, indeed, their right to be on and even *in* that soil, which some of them articulated to him ([1896] 2003, 98). At one point, he told his Kurdish audience, "This earth is yours; protect it from the Armenians. . . . Even though they are less populous than you, they are going to steal your land [*memleket*] right from under you. Get your act together!" (156–58). It appears that Sadettin Pasha was manipulating the Kurds' own sense of homeland for the sake of his larger mission, but it is clear from the various ways in which he addressed both Armenian and Kurdish audiences that the elements associated with majorityhood and minorityhood were ever present in his discourse. Population numbers, loyalty, threat, belonging, rights to the land, or lack thereof—they all were there.

Although Kurds were not initially marked as minorities, they, too, would soon see themselves as victims of this process. But Kurds suffered these developments slightly differently than did their Armenian neighbors. The state's approach to Armenians was never to deny Armenian identity but rather to highlight how the Armenians' identity made it such that they would never be "Turks" and, as such, would forever constitute a threat to the Turkish-nation-in-the-making. Seen as imperialist stooges and as a fifth column, Armenians ultimately became the victims

---

17. Clearly, Sadettin Pasha threw out numbers for effect.

of genocidal policies of removal and extermination. Kurds, however, experienced official perceptions of Kurdish identity differently. At first, they were tenuously included in the majority-as-Muslim. Then, this inclusion was soon whittled down to their recognition as Kurds by state officials but now depicted as backward, barbaric, and untrustworthy and in need of adopting "Turkish civilization" and identity to minimize their threat to Turkish unity and territorial integrity. Loyalty here meant maintaining not only the territorial integrity of the empire but also national unity and identity. The only loyal Kurds were those who identified as Turks or who could be considered "potential Turks" (Yeğen 2007, 137).[18]

Kurdish intellectuals attempted to work out what this meant in their publications from the earliest moments of their own minoritization process. Although there is evidence from the first Kurdish journal, *Kurdistan* (published from 1898 to 1902),[19] that Kurds were beginning to feel the pressures of dealing with Kurdish identity on new levels and were working to counter both denialist and what we might call "orientalizing" discourses, these efforts were sharpened in the journals of the Second Constitutional Period, particularly from 1918 on, when the fate of the empire (and, hence, the fate of the Kurds) was in limbo.

Kurdish writers urged their Kurdish compatriots to take an active role in countering early Turkish nationalist discourses that denied the Kurds' unique identity as Kurds. In the Second Constitutional Period, this argument became linked first to an effort to focus on Kurdish history. In this new era in which "the nationalities were being decided and recognized," as Abdullah Cevdet put it in the journal *Rojî Kurd*, the aim of history writing and historical research had changed, and "national" histories had come to dominate the discipline (15 June 1913, 3).

Very aware of the importance of history in the national(ist) project, Abdullah Cevdet urged Kurds to assert their unique history and identity, to

---

18. Mesut Yeğen (2007) rightly argues that in the Republican Era the "gate of assimilation" was largely left open for Kurds as future Turks in a way that was closed to non-Muslim communities, but I would argue that seeing Kurds as future Turks began in the late Ottoman period, as I suggest in this chapter.

19. See Bozarslan 1991 for a collection of *Kurdistan* (1898–1902) issues.

be proactive in this effort. He recognized that the Kurds' future depended on their ability to publicize their own history. He wrote,

> [Just] as an individual who does not possess a certain clearly defined personality, a nation that does not possess a personality cannot be considered anything other than a group of speaking animals who are not called by a name. . . . History plays the role for nations that memory plays for individuals. Human life and even the life of animals can be continued by adding memory. A person who has amnésie complète is nothing more than a plant in our gardens and mountains, [which] blows its leaves from one direction to another. . . . If a nation does not have an excellent history, it is as if that nation has never lived. . . . Do the Kurds have a history? . . . The century we live in, no joke is the twentieth century. A nation that does not possess its history of the past and its future history does not have an identity. Nations and individuals who do not have their own identity will become slaves—the property of others. . . . I said the future history. . . . Many readers might be surprised by this strange phrase; yes, nations must possess their future history in addition to their past histories, and the former is more important. (*Rojî Kurd*, 15 June 1913, 3)

It is important to note that Kurdish intellectuals' assertions of "national" identity were not necessarily separatist or in conflict with remaining in the empire and hoping to keep the empire intact (Klein 2007b). But something else was going on there, too. Although Kurdish writers were asserting their "nationhood," they were also striving to establish that they belonged in the empire and that they were, in fact, an integral part of the Ottoman body. In *Rojî Kurd*, one writer emphasized that the Kurds were "one of the strongest pillars of Ottomanism and humanity" (15 June 1913, 2). Babanzâde İsmail Hakkı suggested in the journal *Kürd Teavün ve Terakki gazetesi* that Kurdishness and Ottomanness were so deeply intertwined that harm to one would result in damage to the other (1 December 1908, 3-4).[20] Still others spoke to their Kurdish readers about finding ways to make their

---

20. See Bozarslan 1998 for a collection of *Kürd Teavün ve Terakki gazetesi* (1908-9) issues.

Kurdishness more valuable to the Ottoman body as a whole. Babanzâde İsmail Hakkı proposed that if their mother tongue were brought to the Kurds, their education would take place more quickly and completely, thus making them "a more valuable member of the Ottoman family" (*Kürd Teavün ve Terakki gazetesi*, 19 December 1908, 2–3).

Whereas these writers worked to counter their minoritization by emphasizing an overarching Ottoman patriotism that consisted of diverse and equal groups (so that all would be citizens, none would be "marked," and there would be no drift toward minority and majority designation for Turks and Kurds), others—although perhaps a smaller number among the writers in the press—considered partial assimilation to Turkishness as the answer. In other terms, writers internalized "orientalizing" discourses that positioned Kurds as backward and in need of civilizing by (majority and dominant) Turks.

By 1918, many Kurdish intellectuals felt that denialist trends were becoming even clearer. Although some wanted to counter the process of minoritization by arguing against suggestions that Kurds were backward and uncivilized or, alternatively, by "fixing" their "backwardness," others worked to expose and reject such assertions. This debate took place in the immediate post–World War I era in a changed political environment, and it was connected to new tensions surrounding the continued existence and sovereignty of the empire as well as the level of sovereignty that would be achieved by non-Turkish groups.

For all enduring Ottoman groups, this urgency was felt even before the war ended, and there is no doubt that they took it upon themselves to explore and extract meaning from the rather vague language of Woodrow Wilson's Fourteen Points, in particular the Twelfth Point, which concerned the sovereignty of what was left of the Ottoman Empire and its diverse peoples.

Some Kurds took this argument in a political direction and made it clear that they were not going to be a minority in a state that denied them equality. Abdurrahim Rahmi wrote in *Jin* on 25 December 1918 that it was true that, "until now, we Kurds have not felt the need to leave the government of the Turkish state, in other words, the Ottoman commonwealth." He continued, though, referring to Wilson's Fourteen Points: "But now we see that Wilson is saying, 'We will not give non-Turks to the Ottomans.' ... They call our place Kurdistan; there, there are no Turks other than two or three who have come and settled as *memur*s [civil servants]. ... As for the Armenians, they do not amount to one-fifth of us. Others amount to only two percent. Therefore, there is no nation other than the Kurds. Therefore, Kurdistan is the right of the Kurds, and is the right of no one else but the Kurds" (14–15).

To demonstrate that Kurds deserved a separate status and were a "majority" in their own region, and to resist becoming minoritized within a larger—and at the time unclear—Turkish or Ottoman entity, they worked to counter claims against their unique identity in several ways. Halil Hayali and Süleymaniyeli Tevfik argued that Kurds needed to stand up to these denialist claims—which asserted that Kurds did not exist as such—through research to demonstrate not only that the Kurds did have a unique identity but also that they were certainly not, according to the latest research methods, Turks. Aware of Orientalist research conducted on the region's peoples by European and Russian scholars, Kurdish writers such as Halil Hayali and Süleymaniyeli Tevfik drew upon the latest in ethnography to demonstrate in the journal *Jîn* that Kurds were not Turks but were the same "race" (*ırk*) as Persians, Nestorians, and even Armenians.[21] In another periodical also titled *Kurdistan*,[22] Barzincizade Abdulvahid criticized the Ottoman official Süleyman Nazif for "the evil policy which evidently aims at Turkifying Kurds, and ... makes the life of an innocent nation a plaything" (29 May 1919).

---

21. Süleymaniyeli Tevfik (1918) continued along these same lines in subsequent issues, highlighting that Kurds were not Turks but were from the Iranic branch of people and that the cities in Kurdistan were and had been historically inhabited by Kurds. Of course, this argument, as I highlight later in this essay, was significant during the postwar negotiations over what would happen to the empire and the peoples within it. See Süleymaniyeli Tevfik's articles in *Jîn* from 25 Dec. 1918, 9 May 1919, 22 May 1919, 4 June 1919, and 18 June 1919. See also "Dehak Efsanesi," *Jîn*, 7 Nov. 1918, 7–11. Some pages of the latter article are illegible; see the transliteration in Bozarslan 1985–88, 189–92.

22. Please note that although the title of this journal is the same as that of the *Kurdistan* gazette published between 1898 and 1902, the two publications are not the same.

Whereas some writers linked themselves "racially" to Armenians to highlight their non-Turkishness, others began to separate themselves from Armenians to justify their claim to Kurdistan. One contributor to *Jîn* denounced those who referred to "Kurdistan" by "such strange names as 'the Eastern provinces,' 'the Eastern regions,' 'Eastern Anatolia,' 'the frontier,' and even 'Armenia'" without calling it by its "real" name (Hizanizade Kemal Fevzi, 10 March 1919, 3). Interestingly, Kurds had to adopt the same language that was being used to minoritize Armenians in order to establish themselves as a majority in eastern Anatolia at the same time as they rejected this language in its use against themselves.

We need to see the efforts of these writers in the context of the aftermath of the Armenian Genocide, during which the vast majority of the Kurds' Armenian neighbors were murdered and displaced as World War I was being fought. The Armenians were seen to have failed the loyalty test; they had become "marked citizens," even though most Armenians had remained loyal to the empire and were certainly not traitors. But decades of thinking about new concepts of citizenship and loyalty had combined with novel global ideas and practices on social engineering, all of which played a role in the Armenian Genocide (Akçam 2012; Üngör 2011). Some Kurds had witnessed the genocide in horror and had tried to shield their Armenian neighbors from the violence. Others, who found it in their interest to profit from Armenian losses or who still believed (as I demonstrated earlier) that Armenians were a threat to their existence, became perpetrators. Whatever their role in the genocide, the tragedy served to further sharpen Kurds' identity as Kurdish and the fear of what would happen to the Kurds (as Kurds) after the conclusion of the war as the fate of the entire empire, in particular the Ottoman East, was uncertain. They also did not want to become a minority in a new, expanded Armenia.

We need, moreover, to situate these writers' new claims against the backdrop of the postwar settlement negotiations and the issuance of Woodrow Wilson's Fourteen Points, the Twelfth Point of which read, "The Turkish portions of the present Ottoman Empire should be assured a secure sovereignty, but other nationalities which are now under Turkish rule should be assured an undoubted security of life and an absolutely unmolested opportunity of autonomous development" (Wilson 2018).

Inspired by the American president's declaration, a number of Kurds began to navigate the possibility of an independent Kurdistan and to distance themselves not just from Armenians but also from Turks. One writer, as mentioned earlier, cited the Fourteen Points to highlight the Kurds' rights to the land they occupied over the rights of Turks and Armenians (Abdurrahim Rahmi, *Jîn*, 25 December 1918, 14–15). In another piece in *Jîn*, Kamuran Ali Bedir Khan called on the "Turkish government" to help the Kurds attain their national rights:

> In Wilson's fourteen principles, it is declared how the principle of each nation's self-determination in the world will now be accepted, and it is made clear that humanity will no longer be a toy for political purposes. . . . In this most important period in our world history, in the beginning of the establishment of a new order, now we want to assert our ideas as openly as possible . . . morally and materially with this living nation's individual appearance. Finally, the previous government that ruled our country and did not depend in any way upon the principles that knowledge has accepted has fallen along with its program. . . . Now, I am calling out to the Turkish government, which is behind the regions of the Crimea, Georgia, and Armenia, whose people are adamant about independence, who are far away from them, and who promise warm and friendly support for those nations whose rights have been seized: in these most crucial moments, remember the cities of the east, some other regions, and Iran as well, in their entirety, and the traditions and national qualities of the Kurds and Kurdistan, who for the sake of religion and virtue, protecting all of their moral and material values, listen to the echoes of the voice of freedom from rough, rocky mountains and who do not hesitate to do anything to uphold their national dignity. . . . Kurdistan, who [once] desired, with a religious ideology and in a national admiration, peaceful unification and obedience to Yavuz Sultan Selim, today also hopes to receive support from the Turkish nation. . . . The Kurdish nation, in order not to meet this [negative] end, [to keep itself] from falling into this dark situation, sees in itself the power and ability to hold itself together. . . . Kurdistan is going to attend, in a way to advance the elevation and progress of all its national strengths, the Peace Conference, whose decisions and negotiations are still unclear. (20 November 1918, 5)

The Kurds attended and had representation at the Peace Conference, but although the Treaty of Sèvres (1920) made provisions for an independent Kurdistan, it was superseded by the Treaty of Lausanne (1923), which recognized Turkish independence based on the new Republic of Turkey and its incorporation of much of geographic Kurdistan into its borders. This new treaty was a coup for the Turkish nationalist leaders who had led the Turkish War of Independence. The British Mandate in Iraq, which was made up of three Ottoman provinces—Mosul, Baghdad, and Basra— was created in 1920 after the British decided that a viable Iraq needed to include the Mosul province for economic, ethnic, and strategic reasons (although that province remained in dispute for a few years). A smaller number of Kurds was incorporated into Syria, and of course Iran, which was not part of the Ottoman Empire, retained the Kurds already in its boundaries. From that point forward, Kurdish identities shifted further in response to the new nation/state-building practices of the new states in which they lived (Klein 2014). From this moment on, the minoritization of the Kurds took on a new life in each of those separate states. Indeed, their actual minority status in the postwar era, when there was now a language to articulate minority protections, may not have been recognized in the states in which they lived (because the recognition of a minority remained connected to religion and not to ethnicity), but their legal status and sociopolitical status did not need to align in order for them to experience an ongoing process of minoritization.

Without seeing minoritization as "primordial, inevitable, or permanent" (Grew 2001, 2), we nonetheless can perceive some common features in this process. This is not just in the Ottoman and post-Ottoman worlds or in the wider Middle East, but, indeed, around the world. Recent comparative studies on the construction of minorities have been fruitful for viewing these developments in a new light. I have worked to highlight part of the experience of minoritization in the Ottoman Empire and have focused on what I'm calling, for now, the late Ottoman "minority extraordinaire"—the Armenians—and their role in the Kurds' own minoritization process. But I have also studied the "minority extraordinaire" in the Turkish Republic and perhaps even in Iraq after the period I am discussing here. Kurds not only became the most prominent "Other" to Turks after the Armenians were gone but also participated in the process through which Armenians were minoritized, and this process played a role in their own later minoritization. The path to the Armenians' and Kurds' minoritization was not inevitable but was the product of certain historical contingencies that I have tried to introduce in this chapter. First, Kurds witnessed the minoritization of Armenians and considered themselves to be part of the "majority" (Muslim) population, although they were quickly disabused of the notion that they might attain equality with Turks in the new "national" setting, whether it was an empire or nation-state that asked the question "Whose country is this, anyway?" They soon began to respond to the devaluation, whether by arguing to be included as full citizens in the new political body or by resisting minoritization in another way—by pushing for separation or by continuing to agitate for those "minority rights" now enshrined (albeit problematically) in international law.

References

Akçam, Taner. 2006. *A Shameful Act: The Armenian Genocide and the Question of Turkish Responsibility*. New York: Holt.
———. 2012. *The Young Turks' Crime against Humanity: The Armenian Genocide and Ethnic Cleansing in the Ottoman Empire*. Princeton, NJ: Princeton Univ. Press.
Bayır, Derya. 2013. *Minorities and Nationalism in Turkish Law*. Surrey, UK: Ashgate.
Bozarslan, M. Emîn, ed. 1985–88. *Jîn (1918–1919)*. 5 vols. Reprints of *Jîn*. Uppsala, Sweden: Weşanxana Deng.
———, ed. 1991. *Kurdistan (1898–1902)*. 2 vols. Reprints of *Kurdistan*. Uppsala, Sweden: Weşanxana Deng.
———, ed. 1998. *Kürd Teavün ve Terakki gazetesi (1908–1909)*. Reprints of *Kürd Teavün ve Terakki gazetesi*. Uppsala, Sweden: Weşanxana Deng.
Bullock, Alan, Stephen Trombley, and Bruce Eadie, eds. *The Harper Dictionary of Modern Thought*. London: HarperCollins, 1988.
Cora, Yaşar Tolga, Dzovinar Derderian, and Ali Sipahi, eds. 2016. *The Ottoman East in the Nineteenth Century*. London: I. B. Tauris.
Der Matossian, Bedross. 2014. *Shattered Dreams of Revolution: From Liberty to Violence in the Late Ottoman Period*. Stanford, CA: Stanford Univ. Press.

Grew, Raymond. 2001. Introduction to *The Construction of Minorities: Cases for Comparison across Time and around the World*, edited by André Burguière and Raymond Grew, 1–14. Ann Arbor: Univ. of Michigan Press.

Jwaideh, Wadie. 2006. *The Kurdish National Movement: Its Origins and Development*. Syracuse, NY: Syracuse Univ. Press.

Klein, Janet. 2007a. "Conflict and Collaboration: Rethinking Kurdish–Armenian Relations in the Hamidian Period (1876–1909)." *International Journal of Turkish Studies*, nos. 1–2 (July): 153–66.

———. 2007b. "Kurdish Nationalists and Non-nationalist Kurdists: Rethinking Minority Nationalism and the End of the Ottoman Empire, 1908–1909." *Nations and Nationalism* 13, no. 1: 135–53.

———. 2011. *The Margins of Empire: Kurdish Militias in the Ottoman Tribal Zone*. Stanford, CA: Stanford Univ. Press.

———. 2014. "The Minority Question: A View from History and the Kurdish Periphery." In *Minority Rights and Multiculturalism in the Arab World*, edited by Eva Pfoestl and Will Kymlicka, 27–52. Oxford: Oxford Univ. Press.

———. 2019a. "Kurdish History: Not a Neutral Pursuit." In *The Future of the Kurds in the Middle East: Representation and Reform after the Arab Spring*, edited by Faleh Jabour and Renad Mansour, 222–43. London: I. B. Tauris.

———. 2019b. "Making Minorities in the Eurasian Borderlands: A Comparative Perspective from the Russian and Ottoman Empires." In *Empire and Belonging in the Eurasian Borderlands*, edited by Krista A. Goff and Lewis H. Siegelbaum, 17–31, 211–16 (notes). Ithaca, NY: Cornell Univ. Press.

———. 2020a. "The Fate of the Kurds." *Origins: Current Events in Historical Perspective* 13, no. 5. At http://origins.osu.edu/article/kurds-stateless-turkey-syria-iraq-iran.

———. 2020b. "The Kurds and the Territorialization of Minorityhood." *Journal of Contemporary Iraq and the Arab World* 14, nos. 1–2: 13–30.

Makdisi, Ussama. 2000. *Culture of Sectarianism: Community, History, and Violence in Nineteenth-Century Ottoman Lebanon*. Berkeley: Univ. of California Press.

Mann, Michael. 2005. *The Dark Side of Democracy: Explaining Ethnic Cleansing*. Cambridge: Cambridge Univ. Press.

Moses, A. Dirk. 2008. "Empire, Colony, Genocide: Keywords and the Philosophy of History." In *Empire, Colony, Genocide: Conquest, Occupation, and Subaltern Resistance in World History*, edited by A. Dirk Moses, 3–53. New York: Berghahn Books.

Pandey, Gyanendra. 2006. *Routine Violence: Nations, Fragments, Histories.* Stanford, CA: Stanford Univ. Press.

Philliou, Christine. 2010. "Communities on the Verge: Unraveling the Phanariot Ascendancy in Ottoman Governance." *Comparative Studies in Society and History* 51, no. 1: 151–81.

Polatel, Mehmet. 2016. "The Complete Ruin of a District: The Sasun Massacre of 1894." In *The Ottoman East in the Nineteenth Century*, edited by Yaşar Tolga Cora, Dzovinar Derderian, and Ali Sipahi, 179–98. London: I. B. Tauris.

Robson, Laura. 2017. *States of Separation: Transfer, Partition, and the Making of the Modern Middle East.* Oakland: Univ. of California Press.

Rodrigue, Aron. 1995. "Difference and Tolerance in the Ottoman Empire." Interviewed by Nancy Reynolds. *Stanford Humanities Review* 5:81–92. At https://www.academia.edu/44088508.

Sadettin Pasha. [1896] 2003. *Sadettin Paşa'nın anıları: Ermeni-Kürt olayları.* Edited by Sami Önal. Istanbul: Rezmi Kitabevi.

Sasuni, Garo. 1986. *Kürt ulusal hareketleri ve Ermeni-Kürt ilişkeler, 15. yy'dan günümüze.* Stockholm: Orfeus.

Üngör, Uğur Ümit. 2011. *The Making of Modern Turkey: Nation and State in Eastern Anatolia, 1913–1950.* Oxford: Oxford Univ. Press.

White, Benjamin. 2007. "The Nation-State Form and the Emergence of 'Minorities' in Syria." *Studies in Ethnicity and Nationalism* 7, no. 1: 64–85.

——— . 2011. *The Emergence of Minorities in the Middle East: The Politics of Community in French Mandate Syria.* Edinburgh: Edinburgh Univ. Press.

Wilson, Woodrow. 2018. "President Woodrow Wilson's Fourteen Points (18 January 1918)." At http://avalon.law.yale.edu/20th_century/wilson14.asp.

Yeğen, Mesut. 2007. "Turkish Nationalism and the Kurdish Question." *Ethnic and Racial Studies* 30, no. 1: 119–51.

Yosmaoğlu, İpek. 2014. *Blood Ties: Religion, Violence, and the Politics of Nationhood in Ottoman Macedonia, 1878–1908.* Ithaca, NY: Cornell Univ. Press.

3

The Turkishness Contract and the Formation of Turkishness

Barış Ünlü

In this chapter, I analyze the historical constitution and everyday practice of Turkishness. In doing so, I draw on the set of concepts generated in another context, whiteness studies in the United States. The rich conceptual framework of whiteness studies, oriented less to the disadvantaged and ostracized groups of race and ethnicity studies than to privileged and ostracizing groups, presents the possibility in different countries and contexts for the sociological and psychological analysis of dominant, privileged racial and ethnic groups. At first glance, whiteness and Turkishness may seem to be incomparable because one is based on race and the other on ethnicity. Yet if we take race and ethnicity not as natural and different categories but rather as historically constructed schemas of thinking and feeling about a particular population (Brubaker, Loveman, and Stamatov 2004; Wimmer 2008), then Turkishness and whiteness are perhaps not beyond comparison.[1]

This chapter is based on my recent book *Türklük sözleşmesi: Oluşumu, işleyişi ve krizi* (Ankara, Turkey: Dipnot, 2018). I also make use of a number of in-depth interviews. I thank my interviewees for helping me to better understand the subject of my work. Perhaps the most important part of my ideas on Turkishness, which I try to summarize here, was developed during my stay as a visiting lecturer at the Centre for Diversity Studies at the University of Witwatersrand in 2015. I am grateful to the center's director, Melissa Steyn, for making this opportunity possible. Finally, I thank my friend John William Day for translating this chapter, including the quotations from sources in Turkish.

1. I specifically conceptualize race and ethnicity as mental and cognitive structures that form our thinking and feeling and provide rules for aggregating, separating, and

Comparing Whiteness and Turkishness

At the core of whiteness studies is the assumption that racism is double-edged; it shapes the material lives, the forms of thinking, feeling, and knowing, the presentations of self, and the techniques of the body of not only Blacks but also whites. Racism, then, becomes analyzable not only as an individual phenomenon but also as a structural phenomenon such that not only individual, overtly racist whites but also those who reject racism also harbor the cognitive structures and forms of thought that underlie and reproduce privilege.[2]

In this sense, there are also important homologies between racism and sexism. It is, for instance, no coincidence that two of the founders of whiteness studies, the social scientists Peggy McIntosh (1988) and Ruth Frankenberg, are white feminists. Frankenberg, in her groundbreaking work, summarizes this overlap:

> Race shapes White women's lives. In the same way that both men's and women's lives are shaped by their gender, and that both heterosexual and lesbian women's experiences in the World are marked by their sexuality, White people and people of color live racially structured lives.

---

classifying a particular population. They specify who belongs and who does not; they define visible and invisible differences. They inform power relations and hierarchies that systematically render certain groups privileged and others underprivileged.

2. Though drawing broadly on what Black intellectuals and activists have long said and written about whiteness (see, e.g., Roediger 1998), whiteness studies really emerged as a distinct literature in the social sciences in the second half of the 1980s. Today, this literature forms an expansive field of research that explores white forms of seeing, hearing, knowing, feeling, and sensing; strategies of ignorance or indifference developed against nonwhites; and the various phenomena of whiteness that whites often unknowingly benefit from and, as in the privileges of whiteness, often unconsciously perpetuate through discourses and acts. Among the particular analytical strengths of whiteness studies are its ability to bring together under the concept of "whiteness" dualities that are so often analyzed separately—the social and individual, the historical and contemporary, the conscious and unconscious, thought and affect—as well as its exploration of the relations between such fields.

> In other words, any system of differentiation shapes those on whom it bestows privilege as well as those it oppresses. White people are "raced," just as men are "gendered." And in a social context where White people have too often viewed themselves as nonracial or racially neutral, it is crucial to look at the "racialness" of White experience. (2005, 1)

Charles W. Mills's well-known and influential work *The Racial Contract* (1997) also touches on the affinities between gender studies and whiteness studies. Mills was inspired by Carol Pateman's (1988) idea that at the heart of the social contract that makes civil society possible lies a patriarchal sexual contract. He therefore posits that behind the privileges and schemas of whiteness, there exists among whites a racial contract that comprises a set of formal and informal agreements that ensure the material and psychological privilege of whites vis-à-vis nonwhites. It should be noted that one of the most important characteristics of the racial contract is that it is not necessary to be a racist white at the individual level to benefit from the contract: "All Whites are beneficiaries of the Contract, though some of them are not signatories to it" (Mills 1997, 11).

Based on the conceptual tools generated around whiteness, I examine the relations among (a) the historical constitution and contemporary functioning of Turkishness, (b) the sociogenesis of the Turkish nation/state and the psychogenesis of the Turkish individual, (c) the thoughts and feelings of Turks, and (d) the structural privileges and unconsciousness strategies of Turkishness. What I mean by "Turkishness" is not an imagined bond of citizenship, a generated cultural identity, or a form of ideological belonging, as in Turkish nationalism. I instead conceptualize Turkishness as a habitus in Pierre Bourdieu's terms—that is, as certain structures of thought, feelings, ways of acting, strategies, and performances that, for all their differences across lines of class, gender, or ideological belonging, also display several important shared characteristics.

However, before I turn to the habitus of Turkishness, it is necessary to identify its origins, the historical process that ensured its emergence. Setting out from Bourdieu's definition of habitus as "history turned into nature" (2010, 78), I discuss the "Turkishness contract" as a medium that transformed history into the habitus of Turkishness. Just as the Turkishness contract constructed the habitus of Turkishness, it also left its imprint on everyday relations between Turks and non-Turks, a phenomenon I analyze here through Erving Goffman's concept of "interaction order." In other words, the Turkishness contract has informed the epistemic, emotive, and behavioral patterns of extracontractual non-Turks who have to interact with Turks in public spaces every single day. Yet non-Turks have to deal not only with Turkish individuals but also with Turkish institutions (schools, universities, mosques, the military, companies, courts, the National Assembly, political parties, and the like) to receive education and compulsory military training, pray, look for a job, bring a lawsuit, do politics, and struggle for their rights. Given its emphasis on shaping the lives of non-Turks, the concept of the "Turkishness contract" will also help us understand the Kurdish issue as the most crucial and bloodiest problem of the Turkish Republic since 1923 on the one side and of the Kurdish liberation struggle on the other.

Historical Framework: From the Muslimness Contract to the Turkishness Contract

In this section, I claim that both the psychogenesis of the Turkish individual and the sociogenesis of the mononational Turkish state, which superseded the multinational Ottoman state, took shape within the historical framework of the Turkishness contract. But to understand the dynamics of the Turkishness contract, one must first examine the preceding Muslimness contract based on a historical process I simplify for heuristic purposes. Between 1912 and 1922, during a near-ceaseless decade of war (the Balkan Wars of 1912–13, World War I of 1914–18, and the Independence War of 1919–22), Muslims already settled in Anatolia as well as émigré Muslims from the Balkans and the Caucasus were able to unite around certain shared feelings and expectations against foreign Christian powers (England, Russia, France, and Greece) and local Christian populations (Armenians, Anatolian Greeks). In the entirety of this consensus and partnership were two basic provisos that, though unwritten, were known to all: (1) to live a secure and privileged life in Anatolia, one had to be a Muslim; and (2) no one is to tell the truth about what was done and will be done to non-Muslims, no one is to sympathize with them or engage in politics on their behalf.

Muslimness Contract

Among the shared sentiments uniting Muslims under such a social contract were four factors based on their personal experiences. First, painful times befell them because of their identity as Muslims; second, they feared to lose their land, their own lives, and the lives of their family members; third, they developed a built-up hatred of all Christians, whom they held responsible for their pains and fears; and fourth, they also had built-up resentment against and envy of local Christians, who they thought were better off than Muslims because the latter had not yet fully adapted to capitalism and modernity. The shared expectations contain aspects that are both negative (the protection of their possessions, property, and life) and positive (the appropriation of the possessions, property, workspaces, and the like of Ottoman non-Muslims). When the risk of losing the Ottoman Empire through the British conquest of the capital Istanbul in the West and the Russian conquest of Anatolia in the East was at its highest in 1915, these emotions and expectations shared by Anatolia's different Muslim peoples grew into a particularly toxic combination,[3] resulting in the Armenian Genocide.[4] As several recent studies of ethnic violence have also emphasized in analyzing such forms of mass violence, it is important to analyze the roles played by elites as well as the impact of popular, collective political emotions such as fear, resentment, and hatred (see, e.g., Petersen 2002).

It is a truism that the Committee of Union and Progress (İttihat ve Terakki Cemiyeti) decided to deport Armenians, which resulted in the genocide. Yet it would have been impossible to get local people to participate in exiling and killing nearly a million Armenians if there were not

---

3. Christian Gerlach (2010) refers to this toxic combination as an "extremely violent society."

4. For more information on the Armenian Genocide, see, for instance, Akçam 2007; Kévorkian 2011; Suny, Göçek, and Naimark 2011.

already strong inclinations and expectations for "ethnic cleansing" (at the time, the Armenians "cleansed" from Anatolia made up nearly 10 percent of Anatolia's population) in the countryside. In other words, Ottoman centers of power and the Ottoman countryside acted on shared emotions and expectations.[5] Recognizing that the Ottoman state and the Union and Progress government did not impose this cooperation from above but that such expectations already existed in the countryside is critical to understanding the horizontal nature of the Muslimness contract. This acknowledgment of course does not mean that all Muslims participated in the crime of genocide but rather that there was sufficiently broad participation to make such destructive events possible. It is also conceivable that Muslims did not see such acts against Armenians as crimes because they considered these acts a form of self-defense out of fear and felt that the Armenians deserved what befell them. Indeed, this emotional perception embedded in the Muslimness contract may explain why for more than a century the Armenian Genocide has been denied not only by the Turkish state but also by Turkish society. Until now, even though most studies on the Armenian Genocide have focused on the Turkish state's mechanisms of denial, this discussion highlights the significance of the everyday, popular forms of denial that exist within Turkish society.

The last round of the decade-long war preceding the official formation of Turkey, from 1919 to 1922, is especially important for understanding the Muslimness contract as a social contract because at this time there was no state left to protect Anatolian Muslims. The Ottoman state had largely collapsed, so the question of who would establish what kind of state in Anatolia moved to center stage. From the perspective of Muslims, the most terrifying of these possibilities was a Greek state in the West and an Armenian state in the East. They believed that in contrast to the incursion of externally induced Western colonialism or mandate rule, the establishment of such states by the Greeks and Armenians on their ancestral lands in Anatolia would amount to a permanent loss for the Muslims, a lasting

---

5. See, for instance, Kaiser 2014 on the extermination of Armenians around Diyarbakir.

separation from their lands, labor, homes, and habitats. In such a context of statelessness, local congresses were held across Anatolia, leading to the penning of many micro Muslimness contracts, as it were.

The basic aim of these congresses, which collected both taxes and soldiers, was to function as a de facto state in the absence of a central authority in Anatolia and to organize Muslim resistance against real and potential Christian occupation of Anatolia (Tanör 1998). One of the great successes of the Ottoman general who then became the founder of the Turkish Republic, Mustafa Kemal (Atatürk), was to unite these local congresses around a set of shared emotions and expectations, first in national congresses and later in the Grand National Assembly located in Ankara, the heartland of Anatolia, as opposed to in the imperial capital, Istanbul. In other words, Mustafa Kemal brought together many micro Muslimness contracts under a macro contract embracing all of Anatolia: the body politic of a Muslim nation had started to take shape. The most important aim of the National Assembly was to establish a state that would transform Anatolia into a Muslim homeland. As a sign of the continuing horizontal nature of the Muslimness contract, the success of this movement rested on a large number of negotiations, concessions, and agreements among Muslim populations. For instance, Mustafa Kemal and his cadre continuously emphasized the religious brotherhood of Kurds and Turks, on the one side, and their common struggle against Christian enemies and Armenians in particular, on the other. Accordingly, the Constitution of 1921, approved by the new assembly in Ankara, foresaw an administrative structure with much power given to local autonomy, specifically to the Kurds on their ancestral lands in southeastern Anatolia.

Turkishness Contract

In delineating the many factors uniting a people into a nation, Ernest Renan emphasizes the emotional impact of suffering as a factor more significant than religion, noting that "suffering in common unifies more than joy does" (1996, 53). Ottoman Muslims believed that the shared suffering and fear of persecution that they experienced were due precisely to their Muslimness. Hence, they shaped their new collective identity around this suffering, defining themselves as a Muslim nation. Also, in the 1910s among Anatolia's Muslim groups, there had yet to emerge a conscious identity of Turkishness. As Turkish nationalist intellectuals of the time so often lamented in their writings, people from Anatolia's various ethnic groups (Bosnians, Circassians, Kurds, Albanians, Turks, Arabs) did not perceive themselves as Turks. Because their shared identity was Muslimness, Turkishness had to be created.

With the end of a decade of war (1922) and the international recognition of a new state through the Lausanne Agreement, resulting in the foundation of the Turkish Republic (1923), a cadre of leaders/founders, now operating in a top-down manner, felt sufficiently empowered to narrow the horizontal Muslimness contract into a vertical imposition—namely, the Turkishness contract. This was accomplished by partially modifying the first clause of the Muslimness contract. Now, to live in this country with security and privileges, it was not enough just to be a Muslim. One also had to be a Turk. That is, one should be both a Muslim and a Turk. Yet, critically, the Turkishness of the Turkishness contract was not necessarily an innate ethnic characteristic. It was rather a world of language, sentiment, and thought that any Muslim could adopt.

What was required from birth was that one be a Muslim, just as it was stipulated in the population exchange between Turkey and Greece in 1923 that the main criterion for the exchange was not ethnicity but religion. It did not matter if someone in Greece spoke Greek and was ethnically Greek; as long as she was a Muslim, she was considered a Turk and was exchanged. Similarly, even if an Orthodox Christian in Turkey spoke Turkish and was ethnically a Turk, she was taken to be Greek and exchanged (Grigoriadis 2013). Hence, the purging of Anatolia's non-Muslims, which began in the 1910s, was largely completed by the founding of the Turkish Republic in 1923. Whereas in 1913 one in five subjects (20 percent) of what is now defined as Turkey was Christian, by 1923 this figure had been decimated to one in forty (2.5 percent) (Keyder 2007, 105). The basic logic behind making Muslimness the fundamental condition of Turkishness was the idea that whereas Muslims could be trusted in the face of "internal and external enemies," non-Muslims could never be trusted. Thus, for the small number of non-Muslims who remained in Turkey, try as they might to pass culturally as a Turk, the gates of the Turkishness contract remained closed to them. They could never be a "real Turk." The second clause of the Muslimness contract, which forbids speaking the truth about what has been done to non-Muslims and extending sympathy to them, was transposed to the Turkishness contract and further strengthened the first clause.

The natural trust felt toward Muslims was based on the presupposition that they could be assimilated to Turkishness without much difficulty. And, indeed, as foreseen, a large part of the Muslim population in Anatolia did abide by the newly narrowed contract. Although cultural factors such as the fact that the majority of Anatolian Muslims already spoke Turkish certainly played a role, I think the main factor had more to do with the logic of the contract itself. Muslims had constructed the contract because they believed that only a state of their own could protect them. Both the Ottoman state under the leadership of the Unionists (carrying out ethnic cleansing) and the Turkish state under the leadership of Kemalists (winning the War of Independence against the Armenians and Greeks and deporting Anatolian Greeks) were able to fulfill this vital mission—that is, to rescue Muslims from a world of insecurity and constant battle on all sides and present them with a secure life. Even though the Kemalists were the ones to establish the new Turkish Republic, they did borrow a great deal from the initial Muslimness contract of the Ottoman Empire.

Rethinking debates on the formation of the Turkish nation and theories of nationalism through the metaphor of contract may offer additional insights. We can approach the Turkish nation, following Ernest Gellner (1983) and Eric Hobsbawm (2012), not as an autochthonous social reality but rather as a modern political/emotional collective invented and produced by Turkish nationalism and the Turkish state. Furthermore, if we think through Benedict Anderson's (2016) famous concept, the Turkish nation may be seen as an imagined community as a consequence of the fact that its members, despite not knowing one another face to face, nevertheless see one another as companions and are prepared to die for one another and for the nation.

Indeed, Turkish nationalism and the Turkish state founded by nationalists undertook an expansive project to invent a collective sense of

Turkish identity and an individual sense of Turkish selfhood, mobilizing a range of institutions and fields (the school, the mosque, the army, the press, the family) for this purpose. Yet they did not produce all the elements of this invention from scratch. I do not mean simply the existence of certain conditions that Anthony D. Smith (1996) sees as necessary for the formation of a nation, such as shared homelands, myths, symbols, memories, and economies. It may be that these conditions existed, but more important, in my opinion, was the existence of a contract. A Muslim community emerged with a Muslimness contract, jointly constructed by Muslims from a range of backgrounds on account of shared interests and emotions as well as shared decades of bloody struggle, massacres, and wars. This Muslim community, formed within a contract and through struggle, established a state that belonged solely to Muslims. It seems to me, then, that one can see the process of the formation of the Turkish nation as a synthesis of the horizontal dynamics of a Muslim community formed largely by its own dynamics and the top-down, imposed nature of the new Turkish state formed from within such horizontality. Simply, the Turkish nation was produced from within the Muslim community, Turkishness from Muslimness, and the Turkishness contract from the Muslimness contract.

Rewards and Punishments

Jean-Jacques Rousseau, who in the mid-eighteenth century developed the idea of a social contract between citizens and their state, wanted to ensure that the terms were equitable for both parties. He specifically noted what needed to be avoided: "I make a covenant between us which is entirely at your expense and entirely for my good, which I will observe as long as I please, and which you will observe as long as I please" (Rousseau 1999, 50, 53). He objected to such a contract, identifying it as "vain and contradictory" (50). Turning to the Turkish case, did the Turkishness contract's narrowed (Turkified) nature make it what Rousseau said must be avoided? I think not. Of course, political oppression and social inequalities have marked the Turkish Republic, just as they did the Ottoman Empire. But beyond such phenomena, there were also expectations of shared interests and privileges that united Turks and the Turkified (or, in other words, those who abided by the Turkishness contract) across different social groups. As long as these rules were followed, the protection of the lives and property of Turks and the Turkified continue. Through a set of material and immaterial privileges, the state would also provide them with political and civil rights. Shared interests included security of life and property (from which all benefited to some degree), a sense of psychological superiority (pride, righteousness, normality) gained from declarations of Turkishness as a legitimate and esteemed culture vis-à-vis that of other ethnic groups (Kurds, Circassians, Bosnians, Arabs), and the possibility or promise of advancing in the sociopolitical hierarchy (class or status advancement). The possibilities for social mobility afforded to Turks and the Turkified by the Turkishness contract and the republic are indeed striking. Countless Turks and Turkified groups hailing from the lowest rungs of society were able to reach the heights of political, economic, bureaucratic, and academic life—to become, for instance, presidents, cabinet ministers, bourgeoisie, generals, professors, and judges. Thus, although those who followed the terms of the contract can be seen to have lost certain cultural or ethnic characteristics, what they gained in return is invaluable.

Yet the Turkishness contract was as much a mechanism of punishment as that of reward. That is to say, those not abiding by the contract had to be punished. Punishment would take many forms, from death to exile, imprisonment to unemployment, or denigration to exclusion; whatever the form of punishment, one thing certain was that they would receive it. Rousseau again provides insight into how to explain this aspect by stating that "in order to ensure . . . that the social pact should not be an empty formula, it contains an implicit obligation which alone can give force to the others, that if anyone refuses to obey the general will, he will be compelled to do so by the whole body" (1999, 58). Specifically, the person who does not abide by the contract and insists on not abiding is a traitor and thus is either exiled or killed "as an enemy rather than as a citizen" (71). Precisely how and by what means those not following the Turkishness contract would be punished was made abundantly clear in the first years of the contract with the Kurdish Sheikh Said Rebellion. It erupted in 1925 when it became clear to the Kurds that the Turks were reneging on their promise of local sovereignty, making the republic not a federated state but solely a Turkish republic instead. Hence, the rebellion displayed Kurdish resistance to the Turkishness contract. After the fierce suppression of the uprising, the Turkish republican elite added the third article to the Turkishness contract: no one is to tell the truth about what has been done to those (Kurds) who have resisted Turkification, and no one is to sympathize with them or engage in politics on their behalf. Those not obeying this new article of the contract have since 1925 been punished in various ways and to different degrees.

I have tried so far to analyze the historical formation of the Turkish state and nation within the framework of the Turkishness contract. Yet this contract is not a relic of the past. The Turkishness contract has been the foundation stone of the Turkish Republic since the 1920s, unwritten yet far more effective than anything in writing. It has defined the functional rules of fields and institutions and formed the schemas of thought, feeling, and action of individuals born, raised, socialized, and working within these fields and institutions, making them all into Turkish subjects.

How to Become Turkish

As the new Turkish state constructed institutions and fields within the framework of the Turkishness contract, what resulted was structural Turkism—an institutional structure and power relation that systematically privileges and extends advantages to Turks and the Turkified but not to non-Turks and/or to those who resist Turkification. Although being a part of such a structure presents a range of real and potential privileges to individuals and families, if one takes a stand against it, certain punishments and disadvantages will follow. Structural Turkism thus explains why people participate in the Turkishness contract ("Why does a person become Turkish?"). But just as important is the question of how ("How does a person become Turkish?"). Exploring the answers to this second question articulates people's individual performances and strategies of

Turkishness, their modes of being and acting in various institutions and fields—in short, what they undertake to become Turkish subjects.

To be Turkish means to learn certain ways of talking, thinking, seeing, knowing, and feeling because certain positive performances are expected of those who belong to and thus wish to benefit from the Turkishness contract—performances in the sense of doing certain things in certain ways. These performances differ according to a person's social class and in relation to the fields or institutions in which she works or the particular political conjuncture in which she is situated. Yet one fundamental performance is expected of everyone, thus transcending class and ideology: to speak Turkish. Hence, if the innate condition of Turkishness is Muslimness, then the most fundamental learned condition is to speak Turkish exclusively. To be sure, to speak or not speak a language is not a simple theatrical act. The actual expected performance is not to speak a particular language but to see, think, and feel and to create meaning in a particular way. If one truly gives up speaking a language not just in public but also in private life, one also gives up thinking and feeling in that language. Such linguistic transition can extinguish one world and re-create a person in another world of thought and feeling.

Like the advantages of whiteness for its holders, then, Turkishness brings significant material and symbolic advantages to a person throughout her life. As such, it can also be conceptualized as a possession (Harris 1993) or a field of investment (Lipsitz 2006) full of resources, opportunities, and power whereby people can accumulate various forms of capital. Turkishness's forms of speaking, seeing, knowing, thinking, and feeling present a person with certain material and symbolic advantages and with a place in—and the possibility for advancement across—various fields of social life. In sum, the resources of Turkishness can be used as capital by people wishing to advance in various fields and institutions.

Yet people do not necessarily invest in Turkishness as a form of rational calculation. Rather, as Bourdieu describes through the notion of strategy, actors follow certain and regular/durable lines of acting, thinking, and feeling thanks largely to naturalized and internalized unconscious predispositions/tendencies. Hence, regardless of the competition with one another in a certain field, not only are actors in agreement regarding the rules of the game, but they all also possess knowledge of and a feel for the game. With such knowledge and sense, a person invests in the field of her interests and expectations, following certain lines within that field. In other words, such concepts as "strategy," "habitus," and "the game" do not point to a constant process of cost-benefit analysis but rather to how one feels like a "fish in water" in the fields (of play) in which one lives and labors. One doesn't feel the weight of the water; one sees the world around one as natural and given (Bourdieu and Wacquant 1992, 127).

Positive and Negative Performances

In the process of becoming Turkish—that is, learning to think, feel, see, and speak like a Turk—playing in accordance with the functions and expected roles of the fields and institutions in which one operates is crucial. Turkishness is of critical importance in every field's specific game, and someone who does not possess the dispositions of Turkishness cannot play the game. To enter a particular institution, a person must possess at least a minimal amount of Turkishness capital, and once she enters an institution, she must know how to meet the expectations of Turkishness specific to that field and institution and to keep developing her Turkishness capital accordingly. Such expectations of Turkishness capital include doing and not doing certain things in certain ways, always doing certain things, and never doing others. For instance, although a judge is expected to be fair and impartial, at the same time she must make her decisions as a Turk. A journalist must be courageous but concurrently report matters as a Turk. An academic must think objectively but also write as a Turk. Most people in these professions do, in fact, act accordingly. Decisions are not taken, the news isn't reported, and books aren't written in favor of those who have been left out of or opted out of the Turkishness contract.

These strategies are acquired through socialization—in the home through the language and gestures of parents and relatives; through education at schools, mosques, and the military; through living in particular neighborhoods and working to meet expectations around roles and performance in different institutions. Everyone thus acquires pertinent knowledge as well as a sense of power relations and hierarchies through this process. These strategies become an internalized part of the habitus, of one's personality, and of Turkishness. If we draw on Carl Jung's description of persona (etymologically meaning "mask") as "a compromise between individual and society as to what a man should appear to be," we can say that Turkish personality emerges through a compromise of sorts formed within the Turkishness contract. Yet to the extent that the mask or role of Turkishness becomes character or persona, it ceases to be a mask and turns into one's individuality or subjectivity. Jung points to this transformation, writing that "it is . . . only a mask of the collective psyche, a mask that feigns individuality, making others and oneself believe that one is individual, whereas one is simply acting a role through which the collective psyche speaks" (1972, 216–17).

One crucial characteristic of both structural racism in the United States and structural Turkism in Turkey is that for a white or a Turk to be a part of this structure, it is not necessary that he be an explicitly racist or Turkist individual. It is possible to participate in the contract and not violate its rules, not so much by doing a particular thing as by *not* doing it. Every interaction, action, thought, and feeling that does not violate the contract indirectly reproduces it. For instance, if an academic or a journalist does not produce a scholarly study or report or take a stance on subjects forbidden by the Turkishness contract, she is in effect participating in and reproducing the contract. We can think of such a process of participation and reproduction through inaction in terms of Thomas Hobbes's remarks on implicit signs: "Signs by inference, are sometimes the consequence of words; sometimes the consequence of silence; sometimes the consequence of actions; sometimes the consequence of forbearing an action: and generally a sign by inference, of any contract, is whatsoever sufficiently argues the will of the contractor" ([1651] 1998, 86).

Personality is therefore not solely formed by positive performances; negative performances, or *not* doing certain things, are just as significant. Specifically, Turkishness is as much a state of not seeing, not hearing, not knowing, and not feeling. A person whose character and ways of acting have been formed by Turkishness is conditioned to see, feel, and be aware of certain things but never others. Yet because inaction is less visible than action, it renders the contract less visible, which in turn makes it more powerful. These negative aspects of Turkishness, of which people are typically unaware in their daily lives, are shaped by apathy and indifference on the one hand and by ignorance on the other, factors that can be identified as the subclauses of the Turkishness contract. According to these subclauses of indifference, one should never sympathize with extracontractual non-Muslims and non-Turkish Muslims or feel any moral obligations (charity, responsibility, or the protection of rights) or moral sentiments (guilt, shame, or compassion) toward them or care about the injustices, lawless acts, oppression, and massacres carried out against them. What this indifference amounts to is the formation of a circle of moral concern, inscribing an affective border between those inside and outside the contract.

Apathy and Indifference

The condition of apathy and indifference or the lack of moral feelings toward those outside the contract is so widespread that, generally, the Turkish state or its institutions do not need to take any measures to ensure the contract's reproduction. Mechanisms of control and warning begin to function the minute such apathy disappears—that is, when someone inside the contract is affected by and feels compassion toward someone outside it. Apathy is not passive. Individuals are, in theory, capable of expanding their sphere of moral concern, of cultivating moral feelings for those beyond received affective borders. Because such a potential exists, and because it poses a danger (for it suggests the possibility of exiting the contract), it may be necessary to resort to a range of emotional strategies to escape from such feelings, to follow certain emotional grooves to prevent the entry of such feelings into one's emotional repertoire. Melissa Steyn, a leader in whiteness studies in South Africa, calls attention to the political and social effects of affects, stating that "we can legitimately ask and must ask, not only what emotions are at play in any context, but what they are doing" (2015, 6). In the context of Turkishness, this question transforms into the question of what the affects of Turkishness as well as of Turkishness's forms of apathy and indifference actually accomplish.

Ignorance

Similar questions can be asked regarding knowledge repertoires and strategies of ignorance. Whites' ignorance both about their own whiteness as well as about the lives of nonwhites is one of the primary areas of interest in whiteness studies, where it is often referred to as the "epistemology of ignorance" (Sullivan and Tauna 2007). According to a growing number of studies, white ignorance is typically not passive. Ignorance persists, in other words, not because of a lack of knowledge. To maintain their self-image, self-respect, and privileges, not to feel complicit, and to feel moral, whites follow a range of familiar strategies and channels to escape from any knowledge that may endanger their position. Put differently, white ignorance is not a harmful absence but a convenient presence. Further, white ignorance stems from privilege, from the power inherent in the luxury of being able to ignore and to lack knowledge without suffering any significant losses. Or, as Steyn notes, the ignorance contract was an important subconstituent of the racial contract in apartheid-era South Africa: "Part of the privilege of being white was that one could choose not to hear, not to know" (2001, 9; see also Steyn 2012).

Because such forms of ignorance stem from the privileged position of racial hierarchies and structural racism, a similar phenomenon can be observed in Turkishness. Even to acquaint oneself with groups outside the contract may bring about different ways of seeing, thinking, and feeling, activities that may bring with them the risk of various forms of punishment because they may involve stepping beyond the boundaries of Turkishness and the Turkishness contract. This is where and why strategies of ignorance come into play. For instance, a Turk may label the knowledge groups that are outside the contract as biased, ideological, self-seeking, nationalist, racist, or imperialist and refuse to take it seriously, thus assuring that he may continue living without upsetting his material and symbolic comforts.

Such ignorance promoted by strategies of dismissing knowledge is not an absence but a privilege. Someone living within the limits of the contract is able not to concern himself with those outside the contract. He is able to disregard their thoughts and not listen to them because he has the power to do so and is thus in no risk of incurring social losses. On the contrary, owing to his power, he has much to gain in the ignorance he reproduces. Yet those outside the contract have no choice but to know what those inside the contract (Turks) think and to listen to what they say because such knowledge is indispensable for their survival. In other words, just as the powerful have a vested interest in remaining ignorant, in not knowing, so too the powerless must invest in knowing. This difference, stemming from whether one is inside or outside the contract, is vital and affects countless interactions on a daily basis.

The Turkishness Contract as an Interaction Order

To the extent that Turks have internalized the forms of Turkishness through socialization and strategies, they experience these forms as if they were natural and neutral. Just as masculinity or heterosexuality or whiteness has its own forms of normativity, there is a normativity proper to Turkishness as well. To speak, think, feel, and act as such is normal; not to do so is abnormal. A Turk and/or Turkified person is not consciously aware of the advantages and privileges he possesses. Just as he is not aware he is in the water, so to speak, he is also not aware that he is swimming with the current, not against it. As social scientists working on privilege note, "Privilege is far less visible to us than its absence; when we are discriminated against, it is much more painfully obvious than when we belong to the groups that benefit from that discrimination" (Kimmel and Ferber 2014, x). Furthermore, those inside the contract also do not want to know because such knowledge not only would make it difficult for them to enjoy the fruits of such privilege but will also throw accessing that privilege into jeopardy.

Yet those outside the contract or out of the water are aware of the water and enter it cognizant of its rules. Entering the water, they also find themselves swimming against the current and as such are constantly reminded that the flow is an obstacle. Another reason why knowledge of Turkishness is quite advanced among those outside the contract is that such knowledge is vital for their survival in spaces where Turkishness predominates; they must know how Turks will think, feel, and act because not to know and thus to act in a wrong, deficient, or inappropriate manner could endanger their lives, security, and/or welfare.

In this chapter, I focus on two social groups outside the contract, non-Muslims and Kurds, who have significant differences in how they lie outside the contract. The most important one predictably is the categorical marginalization of non-Muslims from both the Muslimness contract and the Turkishness contract. Kurds, meanwhile, are among the founders of the Muslimness contract and, hence, like the other Muslim peoples of Anatolia, can be theoretically included in the contract insofar as they wish to be and possess the necessary forms of capital and schemas proper to Turkishness. Indeed, over the past century millions of Kurds have become irreversibly Turkified, thereby joining the Turkishness contract. Yet millions of Kurds conscientiously resist Turkification politically; as such, they differ from almost all the other Turkified Muslim peoples of Anatolia who in large measure have preserved their ethnic identities only through a depoliticized attachment to their "folklore." There are also similarities between Kurds who conscientiously exist outside the Turkishness contract and non-Muslims who are categorically excluded from it.

Non-Muslims

Despite their categorical exclusion, non-Muslims are still expected to follow the rules of the contract—for instance, to speak Turkish and not to produce knowledge about what actions have been executed against those outside the contract or to engage in politics on their behalf. As long as such conditions are met, the Turkish state has allowed apolitical non-Muslims, who comprise less than one percent of the country's population, to reside in Turkey and to work almost exclusively in the private sector, not the public sector. Thus, some doors, if not all, have been left open to them, and they have been able to benefit from certain advantages tied to being a de jure if not a de facto Turk. Those who are able to perform Turkishness well, who generally do not contest Turkish supremacy, or who at least do not publicly live out their own non-Turkish identities are accepted as admissible non-Muslims, whereas those who run counter to the contract are punished.

The fact that, performances of Turkishness aside, non-Muslims are never to be accepted as true Turks has created for many people a number of contradictions and tensions in coping. Regardless of how hard a non-Muslim tries to be a Turk, she can never become a Turk and therefore feels constantly under threat. The most common way of dealing with this tension accompanies Turkey's non-Muslims from birth to death: they execute a particular performance of Turkishness through silence, hiding their true self and identity in the public spaces where Turkishness predominates. For instance, they speak Turkish instead of their own natal language (Syriac, Greek, Armenian, Ladino), use Turkish names instead of their own true names, and demonstrate, when needed, that they think and feel like a Turk. They disguise their languages, their religious symbols and rituals, and any thoughts and feelings outside of or unacceptable to Turkishness. They keep such aspects of their lives inside (both metaphorically and literally, as in concealing one's cross inside of one's clothes) or hide them in the home or in places of worship. Non-Muslims indeed learn at a very young age not to attract attention, to be invisible, through the informal education they receive from their parents and communities (see, e.g., Brink-Danan 2014; Erol 2016). In this sense, a warning by a leading Jewish figure in the 1930s addressed to his community is still valid for all non-Muslims in Turkey: "You shout out in Spanish or French in public places. This has a bad effect. There's a rising trend against us. So speak Turkish, and speak softly. Live a meek life!" (quoted in Bali 2010, 282–83).

Living so is certainly not a mask one can simply put on and take off at a whim. Non-Muslims live in fear because of the traumatic memories they have of being wiped out of Anatolia and live with the anxiety that something similar could again occur at any moment. Because they continue to live outside the contract, they have no protection. Violent history has, in a sense, imprinted meekness and fear onto the bodies and minds of non-Muslims, transforming these contingencies into their natural state. An Anatolian Greek explained this dynamic as follows: "We often carry out such autocontrol upon ourselves. We try not to cause problems. Let's say that we went to a restaurant, for example, and the soup is cold. I'd never say, 'Hey, the soup is cold.' This is a matter of habit for me. And I don't behave differently when I go to Europe. Because this is imprinted on us. We try not to call attention to ourselves, to disturb our surroundings, or create tension. This is my character" (quoted in Koçoğlu 2004, 291). An Anatolian Greek who later migrated to Athens had this to say about character formation, about how being Greek had been worked into his body: "When I was six or seven, I was naturally speaking Greek. 'Hush' became second nature to us, and I'm not sure when I became aware of this. It took me about 5–6 years after coming to Greece for me to speak audibly in public spaces. If you notice, Greeks from Istanbul are always quite genial. They speak gently, don't yell too much, refrain from being seen too often in public, and aren't noisy. Why? Because this is unthinking, second nature to them. This feeling runs that deep" (quoted in Türker 2015, 130).

Kurds

Matters are a bit more complicated for Turkey's non-Turkish Muslim peoples. As noted earlier, over the past century millions of ethnically non-Turkish Muslims have passed into Turkishness, giving up being Kurds, Arabs, Circassians, Pomaks, Georgians, Laz, Albanians, and Bosnians.[6] On this subject, a Kurdish academic I met in Diyarbakir described passing to Turkishness through the metaphor of a centralized exam system. According to him, if one wishes to succeed in the exam (the rules of which are clear to all), "One must enter this road without any internal questioning; one must live according to it, set up a life appropriate to it, and work very hard. If this is the life one chooses, then it determines a person's life, relationships, way of thinking, and emotional life." In addition to Muslims who have become entirely Turkified, there are also millions who have done so while still maintaining aspects of their ethnicity. Such people are aware, to different degrees and forms, of the danger of living outside of Turkishness, so they often feel the need to emphasize their Turkishness and their ties to the Turkishness contract constantly and publicly. For instance, they use a double discourse that legitimizes their ethnic differences strictly

---

6. On the passing of various Europeans and "light-skinned" Blacks to whiteness, see Hobbs 2014 and Roediger 2006, 2007.

through the lens of Turkishness, live their ethnicity in private spaces as a depoliticized cultural identity, and are careful to distance themselves from those Kurds who have resisted the Turkishness contract. As long as they remain within these parameters, they enjoy the support of the Turkish state (see, e.g., Kaya 2011; Serdar 2019).

The position of Kurds vis-à-vis the Turkishness contract differs from that of other ethnically non-Turkish Muslim communities because a significant proportion of Kurds have actively resisted the Turkishness contract since the 1920s. According to the Turkish state, this century-old tradition of resistance has made Kurdish political consciousness and cultural/linguistic continuity the most significant threat to the state and the contract. This threat is significant because it points to the existence of millions of people who do not think, feel, or act like Turks. Because of this resistance and the threat stemming from it, Kurds are frequently punished for being outside the contract, leading them to develop various strategies to survive in spaces where Turkishness predominates.

As for non-Muslims, for Kurds one of the most widespread and useful strategy is to hide themselves, to silence their language, thoughts, and feelings. A Kurdish religious figure I met summarized this strategy: "The personality of every Kurd, every Kurd, is behind the scenes; no Kurd's personality is visible [on stage]." Such a presentation of the self (Goffman 1983) is necessary because the stage is always that of Turkishness, where Turks and the rules of Turkishness predominate, and is not perceived by Turks as a theatrical space but as normal life itself. In passing from behind the scenes to the Turkish stage, Kurds must attend to this stage's rules because not to do so brings a range of problems. A person who is aware that she is outside the contract avoids certain behaviors, such as emphasizing cultural particularities (for instance, ways of dressing) and talking, writing, or commenting on the contract. Forced to live without exposing themselves, they try to conceal their identities as much as possible in the spaces and institutions of their professional and public lives.

In their communication and interactions with people inside the Turkishness contract, Kurds are compelled to be excessively cautious. This caution might show itself in how they try to "act like a Turk." For instance, if they speak proper Turkish and do not touch upon matters forbidden by the Turkishness contract, the person across from them might think they are Turks, and the interaction will proceed smoothly. A researcher and translator I met explained the experience of Kurdishness, or what was termed "hidden lives," through the example of going to the hairdresser:

> I can give many examples about hairdressers. These are spaces full of talk; everyone talks a lot; everyone's out-of-the-blue free and easy. But for me this is frustrating. I immediately put up walls. But everything is open to conversation there. They talk about Kurds, about Turkey's politics related to Kurds. You hear so many negative, foulmouthed, offensive, and degrading statements, yet you sit there and keep silent. You already put up your walls. I'd say you automatically put up those walls with your Kurdish identity. What I mean by walls is, let no one ask me a thing, let the conversation not continue. Because either you will expose your true self and get into an argument, or you will stay silent. And because it would be even worse to act as if you think like them, the best is to make no contact, to try to cut off the interaction, see?

Such cautions in speech, taken because one is not Turkish and is outside the Turkishness contract, also affect bodily practices. A professor who knows several foreign languages in addition to Kurdish and Turkish explained Kurdishness and the bodily effects of being outside the contract: "It's automatic; when you speak Kurdish, you immediately lower your voice. When I switch over to Kurdish, as if by bodily habit I lower my voice. The body's used to this, I mean." In explaining this, he leaned over to a friend sitting next to him and spoke very quietly to illustrate how the body hides Kurdishness from the outside world.

Yet Kurds hesitate in such situations not just from an internalized sense of fear. Shame, too, yields similar results. For instance, because Turkish is the only official language and is further presented by state and society as the language of civilization, speaking Turkish with an accent can produce a sense of shame, a sense of "not being good enough." The source of this shame comes from constantly measuring oneself against the values of a dominant group (here, Turkishness), from seeing oneself through the gaze of others, and from judging one's self-worth accordingly. If we approach this condition within W. E. B. Du Bois's framework, Kurds experience themselves through a "double consciousness" (Du Bois [1903] 1995, 45) marked by the values of a Turkish gaze, and as a consequence they are in a constant state of vigilance regarding how they appear from the outside. Kurds may also not participate in the public sphere because they believe they are unable to fully express themselves. Because Turkishness has been accepted as normal and Kurdishness as abnormal, states of mind such as self-confidence, righteousness, and entitlement that are so internalized by Turks are much less common among Kurds, particularly in spaces where Turkishness predominates. A Kurdish student working on a master's degree in women's studies described this situation in an interview: "To tell you the truth, every place that is under the control of Turks is like a stage of Turkishness to me. It's as if you have to take on the role of a Turk, and to speak you have to be a Turk. Maybe this is something I made up. If you're a Turk, you can speak, you can express yourself. As a Kurd, you can't speak. I feel that my words are worthless."

To summarize, the Turkishness contract has constituted an "interaction order" (Goffman 1983) that shapes countless everyday encounters between individuals inside the contract and individuals outside of it.[7] The Turkishness contract seeps into daily life, giving it shape and color. For instance, a person outside the contract who possesses the knowledge and sense of the basic rules of the contract speaks and acts as if he were inside the contract, thus reducing any potential risks as much as possible. Hence, many of the thoughts, character traits, presentations of self, and body language that are so often taken as personal or individual characteristics are in fact determined by the Turkishness contract. When two people, one within the contract and one without, interact, each interlocutor is not strictly an individual but rather a subject who is socially and historically formed through many power relations. The critical difference marking the encounter of these two imagined individuals is that one possesses a state and a nation, whereas the other does not. The Turk knows that the state and nation that make up one side of the contract will protect him

---

7. As Bourdieu states, the "whole social structure is present in each interaction" (1991, 67).

when needed. This knowledge gives him a sense of trust that is reflected in his actions and his body. In contrast, the non-Turk knows that he will receive no such protection from the state or the nation because he is outside the contact. Thus, the Turkish state and nation have worked in opposing ways on the mentalities and bodies of those inside the contract and those outside it. Because people outside the contract try to conceal their outsider status, it is often not publicly apparent how the contract shapes their everyday interactions. Yet its effects, though unseen, are always there.

Conclusion

The Turkishness contract and the conditions of Turkishness today face a significant challenge that has been growing deeper and more widespread over the past thirty years: I call it "a crisis in Turkishness."[8] The growth of the Kurdish movement in its many forms over time has made it impossible for the Turkish state to continue denying the century-long "Kurdish problem," which is continuously chipping at the power and privilege of Turkish individuals not to see, not to know, and not to care. The ensuing large-scale military and civil challenges also emerge as a crisis of the state, ultimately undermining the state's historical and contemporary legitimacy. In response, the Turkish state has eventually been compelled to accept the existence of Kurds and the Kurdish language and to take steps, however superficial and insincere, toward a political and cultural "opening" vis-à-vis the Kurdish problem.

Meanwhile, when Turks are faced with a new Kurdish historiography that presents Kurds' history as one filled with massacres and oppression by the Turks, they experience crises of identity. It is important to note that a similar development has also occurred in relation to the century-long "Armenian problem" of the Turkish state and society as expressed by the Armenian intellectual Hrant Dink, who was assassinated in 2007, and by his socialist newspaper *Agos*. With the emergence of the Kurdish movement and a new generation of Armenian intellectuals, many Kurds and

---

8. For more information on this "crisis in Turkishness," see Ünlü 2016.

Armenians living outside the contract have gradually been liberated from the forms of meekness and timidity I have described as being typical of outsiders. Instead of continuing to live double lives, they have begun to openly express their "true selves," languages, thoughts, and feelings. The growing courage, audacity, and confidence among Kurds and Armenians, together with the new historiography, have deepened the crisis in Turkishness. Turks, in short, have experienced the growing strength of Kurds and Armenians as a loss of their own power, echoing other confrontations taking place at a global scale, just as whites are faced with the growing strength of Blacks and men are challenged by the growing power of women.

In the face of this crisis, significant numbers of Turks have become more nationalist, more hardened in their stance. Yet equally significant numbers have begun to grow aware of their Turkishness, to comprehend how it has shaped and delimited their personhood, and with this new awareness they have begun to be freed from the burden they unknowingly carried and to see, think, and feel in new ways. My analysis in this chapter can be seen as a product of this ongoing social transformation.

References

Akçam, Taner. 2007. *From Empire to Republic: Turkish Nationalism and the Armenian Genocide.* London: Zed Books.

Anderson, Benedict. 2016. *Imagined Communities: Reflections on the Origins and Spread of Nationalism.* London: Verso.

Bali, Rıfat N. 2010. *Cumhuriyet yıllarında Türkiye Yahudileri: Bir Türkleştirme serüveni (1923–1945).* Istanbul: İletişim.

Bourdieu, Pierre. 1991. *Language and Symbolic Power.* Translated by Gino Raymond and Matthew Adamson. Oxford: Polity.

———. 2010. *Outline of a Theory of Practice.* Translated by Richard Nice. Cambridge: Cambridge Univ. Press.

Bourdieu, Pierre, and Loïc Wacquant. 1992. *An Invitation to Reflexive Sociology.* Cambridge: Polity.

Brink-Danan, Marcy. 2014. *Yirmi birinci yüzyılda Türkiye'de Yahudiler: Hoşgörünün öteki yüzü.* Translated by Barış Cezar. Istanbul: Koç Üniv. Press.

Brubaker, Rogers, Mara Loveman, and Peter Stamatov. 2004. "Ethnicity as Cognition." *Theory and Society* 33 (Feb.): 31–64.

Du Bois, W. E. B. [1903] 1995. *The Souls of Black Folk*. New York: Signet Classics.
Erol, Su. 2016. *Mazlum ve makul: İstanbul Süryanilerinde etno-dinsel kimlik inşası ve kimlik stratejileri*. Istanbul: İletişim.
Frankenberg, Ruth. 2005. *White Women, Race Matters: The Social Construction of Whiteness*. Minneapolis: Univ. of Minnesota Press.
Gellner, Ernest. 1983. *Nations and Nationalism*. Oxford: Basil Blackwell.
Gerlach, Christian. 2010. *Extremely Violent Societies: Mass Violence in the Twentieth-Century World*. Cambridge: Cambridge Univ. Press.
Goffman, Erving. 1983. "The Interaction Order." *American Sociological Review* 48, no. 1 (Feb.): 1–17.
Grigoriadis, Ioannis N. 2013. *Instilling Religion in Greek and Turkish Nationalism: A "Sacred Synthesis."* New York: Palgrave Macmillan.
Harris, Cheryl I. 1993. "Whiteness as Property." *Harvard Law Review* 106, no. 8 (June): 1707–91.
Hobbes, Thomas. [1651] 1998. *Leviathan*. Edited by J. C. A. Gaskin. Oxford: Oxford Univ. Press.
Hobbs, Allyson. 2014. *A Chosen Exile: A History of Racial Passing in American Life*. Cambridge, MA: Harvard Univ. Press.
Hobsbawm, Eric. 2012. *Nations and Nationalism since 1780*. Cambridge: Cambridge Univ. Press.
Jung, Carl Gustav. 1972. *Two Essays in Analytical Psychology*. Translated by R. F. C. Hull. Princeton, NJ: Princeton Univ. Press.
Kaiser, Hilmar. 2014. *The Extermination of Armenians in the Diarbekir Region*. Istanbul: İstanbul Bilgi Üniv. Press.
Kaya, Ayhan. 2011. *Türkiye'de Çerkezler: Diasporada geleneğin yeniden icadı*. Istanbul: İstanbul Bilgi Üniv. Press.
Kévorkian, Reymond. 2011. *The Armenian Genocide: A Complete History*. London: I. B. Tauris.
Keyder, Çağlar. 2007. *Memâlik-i Osmaniye'den Avrupa Birliği'ne*. Istanbul: İletişim.
Kimmel, Michael S., and Abby L. Ferber. 2014. Preface to *Privilege: A Reader*, edited by Michael S. Kimmel and Abby L. Ferber, ix–xiv. Boulder, CO: Westview.
Koçoğlu, Yahya. 2004. *Azınlık gençleri anlatıyor*. Istanbul: Metis.
Lipsitz, George. 2006. *The Possessive Investment in Whiteness: How White People Profit from Identity Politics*. Philadelphia: Temple Univ. Press.
McIntosh, Peggy. 1988. "White Privilege and Male Privilege: A Personal Account of Coming to See Correspondences through Work in Women's Studies."

Working Paper no. 189, presented at the Center for Research on Women, Wellesley College. At https://www.wcwonline.org/images/pdf/White_Privilege _and_Male_Privilege_Personal_Account-Peggy_McIntosh.pdf.

Mills, Charles W. 1997. *The Racial Contract*. Ithaca, NY: Cornell Univ. Press.

Pateman, Carole. 1988. *The Sexual Contract*. Stanford, CA: Stanford Univ. Press.

Petersen, Roger D. 2002. *Understanding Ethnic Violence: Fear, Hatred, and Resentment in Twentieth-Century Eastern Europe*. Cambridge: Cambridge Univ. Press.

Renan, Ernest. 1996. "What Is a Nation?" In *Becoming National: A Reader*, edited by Geoff Eley and Ronald Grigor Suny, 42–56. New York: Oxford Univ. Press.

Roediger, David R., ed. 1998. *Black on White: Black Writers on What It Means to Be White*. New York: Schocken.

———. 2006. *Working toward Whiteness: How America's Immigrants Became White*. New York: Basic.

———. 2007. *The Wages of Whiteness: Race and the Making of the American Working Class*. London: Verso.

Rousseau, Jean-Jacques. 1999. *The Social Contract*. Translated by Christopher Betts. Oxford: Oxford Univ. Press.

Serdar, Ayşe. 2019. "Strategies of Making and Unmaking Ethnic Boundaries: Evidence on the Laz of Turkey." *Ethnicities* 19, no. 2 (Apr.): 335–69.

Smith, Anthony D. 1996. "The Origins of Nations." In *Becoming National: A Reader*, edited by Geoff Eley and Ronald Grigor Suny, 106–30. New York: Oxford Univ. Press.

Steyn, Melissa. 2001. *"Whiteness Just Isn't What It Used to Be": White Identity in a Changing South Africa*. Albany: State Univ. of New York Press.

———. 2012. "The Ignorance Contract: Recollections of Apartheid Childhoods and the Construction of Epistemologies of Ignorance." *Identities: Global Studies in Culture and Power* 19, no. 1: 8–25.

———. 2015. "Feeling White." In *Unveiling Whiteness in the Twenty-First Century: Global Manifestations, Transdisciplinary Interventions*, edited by Veronica Watson, Deirde Howard-Wagner, and Lisa Spanierman, 3–8. Lanham, MD: Lexington.

Sullivan, Shannon, and Nancy Tauna, eds. 2007. *Race and Epistemologies of Ignorance*. Albany: State Univ. of New York Press.

Suny, Ronald Grigor, Fatma Müge Göçek, and Norman M. Naimark, eds. 2011. *A Question of Genocide: Armenians and Turks at the End of the Ottoman Empire*. Oxford: Oxford Univ. Press.

Tanör, Bülent. 1998. *Türkiye'de kongre iktidarları (1918–1920)*. Istanbul: Yapı Kredi.

Türker, Nurdan. 2015. *Vatanım yok memleketim var. İstanbul Rumları: Mekân-bellek-ritüel*. Istanbul: İletişim.

Ünlü, Barış. 2016. "The Kurdish Struggle and the Crisis of the Turkishness Contract." *Philosophy and Social Criticism* 42, nos. 4–5 (Jan.): 397–405.

———. 2018. *Türklük sözleşmesi: Oluşumu, işleyişi ve krizi*. Ankara, Turkey: Dipnot.

Wimmer, Andreas. 2008. "Elementary Strategies of Ethnic Boundary Making." *Ethnic and Racial Studies* 31, no. 6 (Aug.): 1025–55.

4

Kurds in the History of Displacement in Izmir, 1850–Present

Michael Ferguson

As a result of the conflict between the Turkish state and the Kurdistan Workers' Party (Partîya Karkerên Kurdistanê, PKK) in the 1980s and 1990s, an unprecedented wave of displaced Kurdish civilians fled to western Anatolia's large cities, such as Istanbul, Izmir, and Ankara. Many who arrived in Izmir settled around and atop the largest hill overlooking the city, Kadifekale. The location where they settled is not surprising, given that since the 1850s it has been the main site in the city center where displaced people have established themselves.

This chapter examines the history of Kurdish settlement in Izmir within the broader history of displacement to Izmir—specifically to Kadifekale. It argues that successive waves of displaced peoples, including those from the Balkans, Crete, the Crimea, Africa, and Syria as well as Kurds from within Turkey, have formed "layers" that make up the urban fabric of this part of the city. In so doing, this chapter sheds light on the complex processes of settlement, emphasizing the importance of the long-term historical context in examinations of one or another specific ethnic or religious group within a particular cityscape. It also counters much of the existing historiography on Kurds in Turkey, which largely mutes the discussions of lived realities in favor of political and ideological analysis and presents the Kurds' history in isolation from the histories of other ethnic and religious groups. Thus, examining Kurdish displacement alongside other historical displacements enables new questions to be asked about how and why Kurds' experiences in some ways differ and in other ways overlap.

Historiographical and Theoretical Overview

This chapter's line of argument challenges the received narrative of the city's historical transformation, which portrays Ottoman Izmir as a wealthy port city with a significant European and Europeanized community that was destroyed following the chaos of the Greek occupation and resulting fire in 1922 (Milton 2008). As a result, the narrative continues, Izmir was thrown off its course of both economic prosperity and cosmopolitan modernity and was rebuilt as a model city of Turkish secularism following the establishment of the republic, creating a supposed homogenized ethnic-majority population. Works of this type often limit their focus both spatially to the port and commerce and socially to the business owners and merchants. This chapter examines a space not featured in this historiography: Kadifekale (also known as Mount Pagus)—a settlement site of marginal peoples in Izmir since the 1850s.

Taking a holistic approach to the influx of people to Kadifekale, this chapter situates itself in the emergent subfield of displacement studies in the Middle East (Chatty 2017). As the anthropologist Dawn Chatty notes, "The topic of dispossession and resulting involuntary migration has not been rigorously examined" in Middle Eastern history (2010, 17). As she points out, academics, with some exceptions, have poorly conceived of the different kinds of reasons for "involuntary" migration and its causes (17). To this, one can also add that although historians of the Ottoman Empire have produced a robust literature on migration, they have organized their analysis primarily around the particular trajectory of one or another ethnic group or of a limited time period, *which often aligns with the end of the Ottoman Empire and the advent of the nation-state.*[1] For Izmir, most notably, there currently exist no studies that examine displacement, forced

---

1. One exception is Ryan Gingeras's (2009) work on conflict in the Sea of Marmara littoral region following World War I; yet the chronological scope of his study is relatively small and thus leaves long-term transformational trends unnoticed. For southeastern Anatolia prior to the end of the Ottoman Empire, see Kasaba 2009.

migration, or refugees in the long term.[2] The goal of this chapter is to provide such a framework that situates the history of Kurdish displacement within the long history of migration to the city and to demonstrate the usefulness of this approach for further research on the lived experiences of different ethnic groups.

The history of Kadifekale is not well understood, and the existing studies do not take into account the long history of settlement in the district. Most of the recent research on this large hill in Izmir's city center is on the current situation of Kurds and has been done by the sociologists Cenk Saraçoğlu and Neslihan Demirtaş-Milz. Saraçoğlu's publication *Kurds of Modern Turkey: Migration, Neoliberalism, and Exclusion in Turkish Society* (2011) is perhaps the only book-length study on the topic of the Kurds of Kadifekale. His work demonstrates the xenophobia and racism of the middle classes of Izmir through their everyday interactions with Kurds in the city, in particular those from Kadifekale.[3] It is particularly notable for being among the few studies on racism in Turkey published in English.[4]

However, methodological choices undermine the significance of Saraçoğlu's findings. First, he interviewed only local middle-class people who harbor anti-Kurdish sentiments, which makes it difficult to draw broad conclusions about middle-class people of Izmir as a whole. Second and more importantly, Saraçoğlu does not interview any Kurds in Izmir and thus neglects the very people discriminated against. Doing so without explanation has the unintentional effect of implying that the lives of long-settled, middle-class, non-Kurdish residents are worthy of examination, whereas the concerns, experiences, and lives of Kurds are not. Third, the

---

2. A recent contribution is Mümtaz Peker's (2015) work, although it focuses on migration more broadly and only incidentally discusses forced migration. Some recent scholarship has also posed a challenge to the narrative centered on Izmir's elite and state actors; see, for example, the essays in Yıldırım and Haspolat 2010.

3. Saraçoğlu argues that local "Izmirlis'" negative views of Kurds constitute what he calls "exclusive recognition" (2011, 4, 29, 79).

4. The most notable studies in English are Ergin 2016 and Maksudyan 2005.

focus on Kurds assumes that negative perceptions of Kurds in Izmir are unique; he does not compare those perceptions to the locals' perceptions of newcomers at other points in history (Saraçoğlu 2011, 4). He brushes aside discrimination of "ethnically" non-Turkish Muslim communities living in Turkish cities, such as Bosnians, Lazs, Georgians, and Circassians, without citing any evidence to back up his dismissal (Saraçoğlu 2011, 4). Nor does he address the scholarship on negative stereotypes of long-standing "minority" communities in the city, Roma and Jews (Bali 2005; Kolukırık 2009), or the experiences of Greek-speaking Muslim refugees from Greece in the 1930s, a period of heightened discourse against "others." The most notable event from this period was the "Citizen Speak Turkish!" campaign, wherein the new Turkish Republic portrayed non-Turkish speakers as working against the state and so encouraged citizens to report on neighbors who failed to abide by strict language laws (Aslan 2007). Likewise, Saraçoğlu's reasoning behind his emphasis on the differences instead of on commonalities between forms of discrimination is not clear. Indeed, a study on shared traits might yield entirely different results and be arguably more effective for understanding the broader history of settlement in the city. Last, his brief mention of the long history of Kadifekale before the arrival of Kurds is also problematic, going back only to 1950. He states that "the first squatter settlements were built in this area in as early as 1950 and then spread rapidly across other vacant state lands in the city" and suggests that many of its residents before then were from central Anatolia (Saraçoğlu 2011, 120). As this chapter shows, however, "squatter settlements" indeed existed on Kadifekale one hundred years earlier.

In contrast, Neslihan Demirtaş-Milz and Saraçoğlu's (2015) coauthored chapter in the volume *The Kurdish Issue in Turkey* represents a much more refined approach to the lives of residents atop Kadifekale. It draws our attention to the complex dynamics of the reshaping of urban space by a neoliberal regime, using fieldwork that shows perspectives of the space held by both insiders (Kurdish residents) and outsiders (middle-class Izmirlis). They convincingly demonstrate that the perception of Kadifekale as a site of disorder, urban decay, immorality, and PKK activity has contributed to the justification for the "urban-renewal" process now underway. However, Demirtaş-Milz and Saraçoğlu do not examine the history of Kadifekale or, indeed, find any reason to. Their assertion that the problems of Kurds atop Kadifekale today are not "related to local conditions in Izmir" as well as their choice to limit their discussion of the history of this space to only as far back as the 1960s (Demirtaş-Milz and Saraçoğlu 2015, 180n4) are highly problematic. Although the Kurdish experience atop Kadifekale no doubt has unique features, there is a fair amount of commonality across Kadifekale's 165-year history of settlement that should be taken into account in any analysis of that space, as I show here.

These scholars' neglect of Kadifekale's history before the arrival of Kurds is somewhat understandable—they are sociologists interested in studying present-day problems, not the past. From a historian's perspective, however, the notion that the problems in Izmir began as a result of the arrival of Kurds, particularly since the emergence of the PKK, without a look at a deeper history of marginalization and discrimination in the city and indeed elsewhere in Turkey, implies that these places were fine before the arrival of Kurds. Thus, it reinforces the notion that Turkey's "troublemakers" are the Kurds and only the Kurds.[5] This chapter offers a corrective to approaches that convey this belief.

A Brief History of Displacement around Kadifekale

The First Settlers: Enslaved and Emancipated Africans in Izmir

Perhaps the least-acknowledged group of displaced people in the historical record of Izmir is African slaves and their descendants. Approximately sixteen thousand to eighteen thousand men and women were transported into the Ottoman Empire per annum during the peak years of the slave trade in the nineteenth century between the 1840s and the 1860s.[6] In total, roughly 1.3 million Africans were brought to the empire as slaves in the nineteenth century. I have estimated elsewhere that three thousand

---

5. My thanks to Azat Zana Gündoğan for suggesting this argument to me as well as for his other critical comments.

6. The most reliable work estimating the volume of the African slave trade to the Ottoman Empire is Austen 1988.

slaves per year were settling in or passing through Izmir in this period (Ferguson 2015, 47). Following the prohibition of the slave trade in 1857, the Ottoman state attempted to manage the lives of manumitted Africans after their "liberation." Beginning in the 1870s, it planned to move all emancipated Africans to Izmir in an attempt to redirect their labor toward the empire's bourgeoning agricultural hinterland and port. As a result, Izmir had the highest proportion of emancipated slaves of any city in the empire, second only to Istanbul (Ferguson 2015, 80). Many of the emancipated Africans who settled in the city established themselves in the space nearest to employment opportunities, where they could also find inexpensive (or free) land: Kadifekale. There they formed distinct neighborhoods and even held their annual African festival, the Calf Festival. Indeed, many of their descendants, known as Afro-Turks, still live on and around Kadifekale. It was reported that for years this festival was attended by outsiders, including the famed novelist and Izmir resident Halit Ziya Uşaklıgil. By the late nineteenth century, however, local newspapers took a decidedly negative view of the annual African festivities. Believing the festival to be a site of immorality, public disorder, and un-Islamic practices incompatible with modernity, they called for its prohibition. In 1895, it was allegedly banned by the governor, Hasan Fehmi Paşa. However, it is unclear if the ban was ever actually enforced. Regardless, by this period Kadifekale had been branded in local newspapers and public discourse as a dangerous place that needed to be brought into order (Ferguson 2015, 120–39). These notions of Kadifekale as a site of disorder echoed similar ideas that emerged around Kurdish settlement more than a hundred years later in the same space, suggesting a form of continuity.

Wars of Russian Expansion

The number of people fleeing from the contracting northern borders of the Ottoman Empire due to conflict with the Russian Empire beginning in the mid-nineteenth century is staggering. In essence, the Crimean War (1853–55) displaced approximately one to two million people (Ağanoğlu 2001, 30; Kiper 2006, 41). But migration waves that had the most significant impact on Izmir were those following the Russo-Turkish War of 1877–78, in which a similar number were uprooted (Ağanoğlu 2001, 33–40; Kiper 2006, 56–59). The Ottoman state established a Refugee Commission to manage and control the flow of displaced people into major ports such as Izmir and to expedite their resettlement with varying levels of success.[7] According to British officials in Izmir in 1878, within the span of a few weeks roughly twenty-seven thousand refugees had poured into the city, overwhelming its resources as well as those of local and foreign aid groups. The condition of the refugees was "one of extreme destitution and starvation."[8] An order from the Ottoman government in 1878 indicates that state-owned and abandoned properties as well as those possessed by religious endowments were to be used to help settle the displaced (Kiper 2006, 173).[9] In the eyes of the state, the unprecedented number of newcomers represented a threat to the existing urban order, so it attempted to guide and monitor their settlement. "Planned immigrant districts" were established to enable active surveillance. For the most part, however, the state left it up to the refugees themselves to construct new homes wherever and however they could. The informal housing from these waves of migration still shapes the urban layout of certain parts of the city, especially on the slopes of Kadifekale and neighboring Değirmendağı. Numerous other conflicts and territorial losses, such as Crete, contributed to the growing number of refugees in Izmir. In 1899 alone, some twenty thousand displaced peoples arrived in Izmir from Crete, many of whom established themselves on and around Kadifekale (Ağanoğlu 2001, 40).[10]

---

7. For a full discussion of this topic, see Kiper 2006, chap. 5.

8. Reade to Layard, Smyrna, 4 Feb. 1878, copy of no. 5, pp. 36–38, 78/2850, Foreign Office, London.

9. Whereas indigenous forms of urban settlement had used cul-de-sacs to create semiprivate spaces in neighborhoods, these new state-planned districts were to have a grid system, dramatically increasing the ability of local authorities to pass into these neighborhoods. See Bilsel 1999, 227, and Temizsoy 2006, 744, 750.

10. One such building project in 1900 was designed to help some of the recently arrived refugees from Crete labeled "homeless and helpless" by a Cretan charity. They were able to construct thirty-seven small dwellings in different parts of the city (Kiper 2006, 176).

World War I to Turkish Independence

The largest and perhaps most well-known displacement to and from Izmir began during World War I and ended in 1923. Greece, allied with the victorious powers, occupied Izmir and a large portion of western Anatolia in 1919. By 1922, though, the Greek military occupation had overextended itself and was being pushed back to the Aegean by the newly formed Turkish nationalist forces in central Anatolia. Following the retreat of the Greek army to Izmir and out of Anatolia by sea, Turkish forces arrived in the city by land. In the chaos of mid-September 1922, a fire broke out that destroyed the city center and its extensive port infrastructure and businesses.[11] Christians (mainly Greeks and some Armenians), fearing reprisals from the victorious Turkish army, gathered at the shore safe from the flames and awaited help from European and American vessels, which refused to intervene. Some opted to throw themselves into the sea in the hope of being saved rather than face death by fire or the Turkish army. Although estimates vary dramatically, approximately 30,000 were killed, and 100,000–150,000 were displaced to Greece.[12]

Because the new Turkish state was founded on ethnic-religious nationalism (just like its neighbor Greece), Christians who survived the fire were legally displaced by an agreement between Greece and Turkey the following year. The Greek–Turkish Population Exchange of 1923 required the forced "transfer" of all Greek Orthodox Christians from Turkey to Greece and obliged Muslims living in Greece to depart for Turkey (with some exceptions).[13] In total, 1.2 million Greeks left Anatolia (Turkey), and 350,000 Muslims left Greece. Owing to the lack of records, it is unclear exactly how many Greeks left Izmir at this time and how many Muslims

---

11. For further discussion, see Neyzi 2008.

12. The most authoritative monograph in English on this topic, devoid of nationalist distortions, remains O. Yıldırım 2006.

13. There were some exceptions, including the Orthodox of Istanbul and neighboring islands and the Muslims of Thrace. For the text of the treaty, see appendix 1 in Hirschon 2003, 281–87. For a more general discussion of the social history of these events, see Clark 2006.

settled in their place. Many Greeks had lived on the lower, northern slopes of Kadifekale, and those slopes became empty when they were forced to leave. Muslims arriving in Izmir came mainly from Salonica or Kavala, and many settled in that same space, which had been mostly unaffected by the fire. The Greek–Turkish Population Exchange ended one of the most traumatic chapters in the history of Izmir. Because Turkey was not involved in World War II, the global mass migrations following that war did not have a major effect on the city that they had elsewhere in the region. The movement of displaced people into, out of, and through Izmir was reduced largely to a trickle by the middle of the twentieth century. Thus, the third quarter of the twentieth century in Izmir is one where no new major waves of displacement occurred, making it the first "stable" period since the 1850s.

Displacement of Kurds to Izmir since 1980

Kurdish speakers have certainly lived in Izmir since the early Ottoman period. Many were long-distance traders, some soldiers, and a few were forcefully settled in and around the city by the Ottoman government's tribal-settlement programs in the late nineteenth century. From the mid-twentieth century on, industrialization brought people from all over Turkey, including Kurds, to Izmir in search of employment opportunities (Saraçoğlu 2011, 76–77). However, beginning in the early 1980s, displaced Kurds from Turkey's Kurdish-majority southeastern region, known as Northern Kurdistan (Bakurê Kurdistanê), arrived in Izmir and dramatically reshaped its urban landscape. The conflict between the Turkish military and the PKK was the cause of most of this displacement. This struggle, whose initial phase lasted from 1984 to 1999, continues intermittently (the latest phase having started in 2015). The process of displacement of civilians from their hometowns and villages has been extensively documented. According to a Human Rights Watch report in 1996,

> Some 2,685 villages and hamlets in Turkey's southeastern provinces have been completely or partially depopulated since fighting broke out in the region in August 1984 between government forces and the [PKK].... [M]ost of the depopulation has been the result of a government

counterinsurgency campaign intended to deprive the PKK of logistical support. The PKK has also targeted state-sponsored village civil militia settlements, forcing some inhabitants to flee. . . . Most of this forced migration has occurred since 1992 and estimates of the number of individuals displaced range from 275,000 to two million. (Human Rights Watch 1996)[14]

Further research has established that since the early 1980s the majority who fled Kurdistan were forced to do so because "their security and livelihood were threatened" and not simply because they had employment opportunities or a network of contacts such as relatives in western Anatolian cities (Saraçoğlu 2011, 96). As Saraçoğlu notes, "The 25 years of political conflict in eastern Anatolia had a significant effect on everyday urban life in the western cities in general and Izmir in particular" (2011, 94). Indeed, state and society writ large were transformed by this conflict. According to Saraçoğlu's calculations, in 2008 the population of Izmir was 3.8 million, which included 291,000 displaced Kurds, 7.6 percent of the total population (2011, 102). This number of Kurds does not include those who had already been living in Izmir for a longer period. Just like previous waves of displaced people arriving in Izmir, many of the displaced Kurds settled atop Kadifekale. Most of them were largely from one particular southeastern province, Mardin (Mêrdîn), likely a result of chain migration. Many moved from villages en masse, and a great many social welfare and solidarity organizations specific to individual villages were established atop and around Kadifekale (see figure 4.1).

According to state census data from 2015, in a population of 4.2 million, 139,313 people living in Izmir registered Mardin as their home province, the second largest of any group of non-Izmir origin after those from the neighboring city Manisa. Indeed, many more Kurds claim origin in Mardin even if they were born in Izmir (*Ege'de SonSöz* 2016; *Yeni asır* 2015). This connection between Izmir and Mardin is well known throughout the city. Izmir's central bus station features a disproportionate number of travel companies catering to those heading to and from Mardin. Atop

---

14. For further discussion on this topic, see Jongerden 2010.

4.1. Building that housed the Mardin–Midyat Üçağıl (Kozê) Village Cooperation and Solidarity Association, Kadifekale, Izmir, 2013. Photograph by Michael Ferguson.

Kadifekale, several businesses feature the name "Mardin."[15] The selling of mussels (*midye*) in the city center is known to be a trade controlled and operated by Kurds from Mardin (Saraçoğlu 2011, 108).

The interaction between Kurdish newcomers from Mardin and locals in Izmir has, according to Saraçoğlu, resulted in the latter holding negative perceptions of the former. The extreme form of anti-Kurdishness in Izmir is typified by the parliamentary campaign of the independent ultranationalist candidate of the now-defunct National Party (Ulusal Parti), Tuncer Sümer, in the Turkish general election of 2011. His election poster projected him as a strong man, stating: "Turkey is for the Turks, Izmir for the Izmirlis. Protect Izmir from the PKK."

15. Observed during my fieldwork atop Kadifekale, Izmir, during visits in 2009–13 and 2016.

The local press denounced this message that very bluntly linked all Kurdish inhabitants of Izmir to "terrorism." Likewise, local human rights associations organized to file a hate-speech crime against him (*soL haber* 2011; *Ege'de SonSöz* 2011). Even though Sümer was unsuccessful in his parliamentary campaign, the fact that he made such public declarations about Kurds in Izmir is significant. It points to one of the many challenges for displaced peoples from Mardin in Izmir: a lack of understanding of their lives in the homelands they were forced to leave behind.

The Effects of Displacement: The Case of Rahşan Demirel's Self-Immolation

Although studies on the lasting social, economic, and psychological impact of displacement and marginalization of Kurds in Izmir are not yet available, one way to glimpse this reality is through the life and death of Rahşan Demirel. Rahşan was born on 15 August 1975 in the border town of Nusaybin (Nisêbîn) in the southern part of Mardin province.[16] In 1977, before the major wave of displacements resulting from the state–PKK conflict, Rahşan's family moved to Izmir, likely in search of new employment opportunities.

On the night of 22 March 1992, news reports emerged of around one hundred lives lost during a state crackdown on Kurdish New Year (Newroz) celebrations in Rahşan's hometown, Nusaybin, as well as in nearby Cizre (Cizîra Botan) and other Kurdish-majority cities and villages in southeastern Turkey. In her bedroom at home in Izmir, Rahşan recorded a message on a cassette, declaring that she would provide a response to these events and make her own Newroz (*Yoldaş Pançuni* 2011). Reportedly leaving her house without her mother noticing, she joined other Kurds atop Kadifekale celebrating Newroz. There, in front of numerous witnesses, she lit herself on fire (*Milliyet* 1993; *Yeni asır* 1992b). Rahşan killed herself

---

16. Conflicting information suggests that in fact Rahşan was from the village of Doğanlı (Talatê) outside of Nusaybin's city center (Aledîn Sinayic, personal communication to the author, 18 July 2018).

in the same dramatic fashion as numerous Kurdish political activists in the Diyarbakir (Amed) Prison had years earlier and as another young Kurdish woman, Zekiye Alkan, had in Diyarbakir two years earlier (Açık 2014, 121).

The circumstances of Rahşan's self-immolation reflect the links she maintained with her homeland. Her inability to return home to the town of her youth, given its geographic location in the Turkish state–PKK conflict, and a sense of helplessness for her kin there no doubt played an important role in her choice to end her life. In death, however, Rahşan was able to return to her hometown because her mother found a way to have her buried there (*Yeni asır* 1992b). Thus, her actions could be read as rescripting her and her family's history of displacement by emplacing and re-placing herself at home, where she would have never been able to return to otherwise.

Rahşan's death has had a lasting impact on the Kurdish movement in many ways and continues to do so to this day. Even Abdullah Öcalan himself, most prominent among the founders and leaders of the PKK, discusses Rahşan's self-immolation in his writings (Öcalan 1966, 288). A song dedicated to her simply titled "Rehşan" appears on Agirê Jiyan's politically charged recording *Adarê*, one of the most important Kurdish-language music albums of the mid-1990s (and, indeed, of all time).[17] The women's military wing of the PKK, the Free Women's Units (Yekîneyên Jinên Azad ên Star, or YJA-Star), indicates on its website that its members draw their inspiration from Rahşan's death and from the deaths of other young women who killed themselves in the early 1990s in the name of freedom for Kurdish peoples (YJA Star n.d.).

Rahşan's life is often memorialized at Newroz celebrations. In Izmir in 2015, Newroz events were formally dedicated to her memory (*ANF News* 2015). At Newroz in Nusaybin in 2017, speeches were made recognizing her as among the important natives of the city who have fought for Kurdish rights (*Evrensel* 2017). In Izmir in March 2018, with Newroz events

---

17. Agirê Jiyan, "Rehşan," on *Adarê* (KOM Müzik, 1996). See also Kuruoglu and Hamelink 2017, 112.

approaching, witnesses of her self-immolation in 1992 suggested that her spirit lives on in the Kurdish resistance to the Turkish invasion of northwestern Syria, also known as Afrin (Efrîn) (Mezopotamya Ajansı 2018).

Like many mothers who lost children, relatives, husbands in the conflict between the Turkish state and Kurdish opposition and activism, Rahşan's mother, Emine, continues to speak openly about Rahşan's death. She has given speeches at Newroz events in Nusaybin and been interviewed by many journalists (*Rojeva Kurdistan* n.d.). Rahşan's life and death, although seemingly one small part of the broader forced migration and related trauma, have become a prominent symbol of the experiences of Kurds in Izmir.

Urban Renewal in Kadifekale and Further Displacement of Kurds

Kadifekale is in the midst of a major "urban-renewal project," which is effectively displacing many of its residents anew. The foundations of this process were established in 2005 when the Izmir Chamber of Commerce published a report on life atop Kadifekale, detailing both the current conditions of the people who live there and the plans for the neighborhood. The report emphasized the squalid housing conditions, lack of access to medical clinics, high crime rates, limited transportation, and even the low levels of literacy among Kurds (one neighborhood, Alireis, having a shocking rate of 52 percent) (Karayiğit 2005, 14–15, 19–25).[18] Thus, the Turkish state began to build a biopolitical argument to justify the destruction and reconstitution of Kadifekale and the displacement of its residents.

In the first stage of this project in 2007, the neighborhoods at the summit of Kadifekale were partially demolished. In their place, new roads and parks were created. The municipality planted hundreds of small trees, emphasizing the importance of the "greenification" of Kadifekale and its

---

18. It should be noted that it's unclear whether "literacy" in this study includes only Turkish or Kurdish as well.

benefits in terms of health, aesthetics, and sense of regeneration (*Milliyet* 2011). The city is also in the process of moving many of the residents of these demolished neighborhoods to a new development specifically built for them, called Uzundere. This large apartment complex is in the sprawling southern limits of Izmir, near the city's airport (Saraçoğlu 2011, 121).

For the residents, this move to Uzundere represents another forced removal from their homes. Although it is true that the city and the project have promised to raise the standard of their living conditions, the psychological trauma brought about by being the target of government projects that force them to leave their homes once again is not insignificant. For residents, the demolition is also a breaking up of their common public, Kurdish space. The courtyards that had allowed friends and families to congregate are gone. The Kurds of Kadifekale have been forced to move into small, nuclear-family-size apartments, where a sense of community is likely eroded. Demirtaş-Milz and Saraçoğlu (2015) show how these actions were fueled by the interrelated goals of reducing a perceived PKK threat to Izmir and reordering Izmir's urban space shaped by neoliberal economics.

In addition, it should be noted that as Izmir/Kadifekale undergoes this transformation, it continues to receive displaced Kurds from Turkey's Southeast. Although the demographic impact of Turkish security forces' recent sieges on Kurdish cities since the autumn of 2015 is not entirely clear, a United Nations High Commissioner for Refugees report indicates that "government security operations affected more than 30 towns and neighborhoods and displaced between 335,000 and half a million people"(*UN News* 2017). Many of these people fled to cities in western Turkey, although the exact number that came to Izmir is unknown. Circumstantial evidence and my observations on the ground, however, do point to another significant wave of Kurdish migration to Kadifekale. In June 2016, one of my interlocutors who had just arrived from Nusaybin confirmed many more displaced Kurds from Mardin province were arriving daily.[19]

---

19. Anonymous Kadifekale resident, personal communication to the author, 14 June 2016.

The Newcomers: Syrian Refugees

Since 2011, new groups of displaced people have arrived in Izmir: Syrians, Iraqis, Afghans, and others from sub-Saharan African countries. At the height of the so-called refugee crisis in 2015 resulting from the Syrian Civil War, Izmir municipal officials estimated that roughly one hundred thousand people, most of them Syrians, were living in or transiting through the city in their attempt to enter the European Union (EU) via sea crossings mainly to the nearby Greek islands of Samos, Chios, and Lesvos.[20] The large number of people seen sleeping in city parks, desperate and destitute, in some ways recalls the situation in Izmir in 1878, noted earlier. Following the enforcement of the EU–Turkey migrant agreement (signed 18 March 2016), the movement of these people has dramatically slowed (Council of the EU 2016). Many have become effectively trapped in and around Izmir without a clear way to enter the EU. A great number of Syrians have settled in the Basmane area, at the base of Kadifekale, and on its slopes as well. Although no demographic data are available, during my fieldwork in 2016 I encountered both Arabic- and Kurdish-speaking Syrian refugees, indicating that some are of Kurdish origin, likely from Afrin.

Conclusion: Toward Identifying a Shared Experience of Displacement and Solidarity

The various displaced peoples living in Izmir discussed in this chapter are connected through their shared experience of forced removal from their homelands and settlement in the city. Many residents of Kadifekale are keenly aware of this continuity. One example is Yalçın Yanık, an Afro-Turk, resident of Basmane, leftist activist, and community organizer for the pro-Kurdish rights umbrella political party, the People's Democratic Party (Halkların Demokratik Partisi, HDP). Yanık, a tailor by trade, has both worked with the Africans' Culture and Solidarity Association

---

20. Sema Pekdaş, mayor of Konak (Izmir), personal communication to the author, 10 June 2016.

(Afrikalılar Dayanışma, Kültür ve Yardımlaşma Derneği, operating since 2006) and organized his own social welfare association, Kapılar (Doors), which promotes itself as an "open social space in Izmir for the communities of Basmane." The association organizes regular events, including daycare, literacy, and cooking classes for Kurds from southeastern Turkey as well as for Syrians and other displaced peoples living in the area.

Yanık's work of connecting people with a shared experience was made even more evident during his campaign for the Izmir first-district seat in the Turkish Parliament. Because of his identity as an Afro-Turk and perhaps his unusual commitment to inclusive and progressive politics, he caught a flurry of media attention (*Evrensel* 2018). In one interview, Yanık clearly outlined his thinking about the bonds of solidarity that form around displacement and settlement atop and around Kadifekale: "Even if my ancestors actually came to this country as slaves, they too were refugees. Whatever my identity is in Turkey, I have created a connection with the refugees to my ancestors' refugeeness" (*BBC News* 2018).

Yanık moves beyond ethnic/religious/linguistic/national divides to cultivate a form of political solidarity among the displaced. Although he was unsuccessful in his bid for Parliament, his ideas will likely play an important part in how the peoples of Kadifekale will organize themselves in the future and in many ways reflect the broader point of this chapter: that Kadifekale's long history as a site for the settlement of displaced people is worth studying as a whole.

The history of settlement in Kadifekale is the history of displacement to Izmir. Examining this history thus tells us about the global processes occurring not just in the region but across a large portion of eastern Europe, the Middle East, and even Africa. Each successive group has established itself as a constituent part of Izmir's urban fabric. Thus, any understanding of Kadifekale should acknowledge the importance of its long history as a site of displacement.

This chapter has shown how political violence, centered on the conflict between the Turkish state and the PKK in the rural, southeastern part of the country, has contributed to another layer of the history of displacement in Izmir's Kadifekale neighborhood. As such, it has connected Kurdish experiences with other displaced groups in Izmir's history and revealed the complexities of life in displacement. Given this complexity, the displaced Kurds' experiences in Kadifekale need to be interpreted within the historical context of displacement in Izmir. Those who acknowledge this complexity, such as the Afro-Turk tailor Yanık, welcome new Kurds as members of another wave of displacement in the history of Izmir. However, those who deny it by constructing an imagined (but not realized) Turkishness, such as the ultranationalist politician Tuncer Sümer, foster marginalization, exclusion, and violence against the Kurds. Settlement in Kadifekale is, however, just one example of how local, urban dynamics have been shaped by this conflict. Applying a similar approach in other locales will therefore prove fruitful to broadening our understanding of the various impacts that political violence continues to have on life in Anatolia and Mesopotamia.

References

Açık, Necla. 2014. "Re-defining the Role of Women within the Kurdish National Movement in Turkey in the 1990s." In *The Kurdish Question in Turkey: New Perspectives on Violence, Representation, and Reconciliation*, edited by Cengiz Gunes and Welat Zeydanlıoğlu, 114–36. London: Routledge.

Ağanoğlu, H. Yıldırım. 2001. *Osmanlı'dan cumhuriyet'e Balkanlar'ın makûs talihi: Göç*. Istanbul: Kum Saati.

ANF News. 2015. "Newroz Celebrated All over Turkey." 22 Mar. At https://anfenglish.com/news/newroz-celebrated-all-over-turkey-10732.

Aslan, Senem. 2007. "'Citizen, Speak Turkish!': A Nation in the Making." *Nationalism and Ethnic Politics* 13, no. 2: 245–72.

Austen, Ralph. 1988. "The 19th Century Islamic Slave Trade from East Africa Swahili and Red Sea Coasts: A Tentative Census." *Slavery and Abolition* 9, no. 3: 21–44.

Bali, Rıfat N. 2005. *Cumhuriyet yıllarında Türkiye Yahudileri: Bir Türkleştirme serüveni, 1923–1945*. Istanbul: İletişim.

BBC News. 2018. "Yalçın Yanık: HDP'nin Afrika kökenli İzmir milletvekili adayı." 4 June. At https://www.bbc.com/turkce/haberler-turkiye-44331693.

Bilsel, Cânâ. 1999. "The Ottoman Port City of Izmir in the 19th Century: Cultures, Modes of Space Production, and the Transformation of Urban Space." In *7 Centuries of Ottoman Architecture: "A Supra-national Heritage,"* edited by Afife Batur, 222–33. Istanbul: YEM Yayınları.

Chatty, Dawn. 2010. *Displacement and Dispossession in the Modern Middle East.* New York: Cambridge Univ. Press.
———, ed. 2017. "Forced Displacement and Refugees." Special issue of *International Journal of Middle East Studies* 49, no. 4 (Nov.).
Clark, Bruce. 2006. *Twice a Stranger: How Mass Expulsion Forged Modern Greece and Turkey.* London: Granata Books.
Council of the EU. 2016. "EU–Turkey Statement, 18 March 2016." Press release, 18 Mar. At http://www.consilium.europa.eu/en/press/press-releases/2016/03/18/eu-turkey-statement/pdf.
Demirtaş-Milz, Neslihan, and Cenk Saraçoğlu. 2015. "Space, Capitalism, and Kurdish Migrants in Izmir." In *The Kurdish Issue in Turkey: A Spatial Perspective,* edited by Zeynep Gambetti and Joost Jongerden, 185–212. New York: Routledge.
Ege'de sonSöz. 2011. "İzmirli adaydan tepki çeken söylem." 26 May. At http://www.egedesonsoz.com/haber/izmirli-adaydan-tepki-ceken-soylem/794094.
———. 2016. "İzmir nüfusunun 'memleket' dağılımı: En çok nereli var?" 3 Feb. At http://www.egedesonsoz.com/haber/izmir-nufusunun-memleket-dagilimi-en-cok-nereli-var/919129.
Ergin, Murat. 2016. *Is the Turk a White Man? Race and Modernity in the Making of Turkish Identity.* Leiden, Netherlands: Brill.
Evrensel. 2017. "Newroz'un ilk kutlaması Nusaybin'de yapıldı." 17 Mar. At https://www.evrensel.net/haber/312584/newrozun-ilk-kutlamasi-nusaybinde-yapildi.
———. 2018. "HDP'nin Afrikalı adayı: Mültecilerin sesi parlamentoda olmalı." 24 May. At https://www.evrensel.net/haber/353304/hdpnin-afrikali-adayi-multecilerin-sesi-parlamentoda-olmali.
Ferguson, Michael. 2015. "The African Presence in Late Ottoman Izmir and Beyond." PhD diss., McGill Univ.
Gingeras, Ryan. 2009. *Sorrowful Shores: Violence, Ethnicity, and the End of the Ottoman Empire, 1912–1923.* Oxford: Oxford Univ. Press.
Hirschon, Renée, ed. 2003. *Crossing the Aegean: An Appraisal of the 1923 Compulsory Population Exchange between Greece and Turkey.* New York: Berghahn Books.
Human Rights Watch. 1996. *Turkey's Failed Policy to Aid the Forcibly Displaced in the Southeast.* Vol. 8, no. 9 (D). New York: Human Rights Watch, June. At https://www.hrw.org/reports/1996/Turkey2.htm.
Jongerden, Joost. 2010. "Village Evacuation and Reconstruction in Kurdistan (1993–2002)." *Études rurales* 186:77–100.

Karayiğit, Ahmet. 2005. *Kadifekale'nin sosyo-ekonomik profili ve sorunları*. Izmir, Turkey: Izmir Ticaret Odası.

Kasaba, Reşat. 2009. *A Moveable Empire: Ottoman Nomads, Migrants, and Refugees*. Seattle: Univ. of Washington Press.

Kiper, Nilgün. 2006. "Resettlement of Immigrants and Planning in Izmir during the Hamidian Period." PhD diss., Izmir Institute of Technology.

Kolukırık, Suat. 2009. *Dünden bugüne Çingeneler: Kültür, kimlik, dil, tarih*. Istanbul: Ozan Yayıncılık.

Kuruoglu, Alev, and Wendelmoet Hamelink. 2017. "Sounds of Resistance: Performing the Political in the Kurdish Music Scene." In *The Politics of Culture in Turkey, Greece, and Cyprus: Performing the Left since the Sixties*, edited by Leonidas Karakatsanis and Nikolaos Papadogiannis, 103–21. New York: Routledge.

Maksudyan, Nazan. 2005. "The *Turkish Review of Anthropology* and the Racist Face of Turkish Nationalism." *Cultural Dynamics* 17, no. 3: 291–322.

Mezopotamya Ajansı. 2018. "'Rahşan'ın yaktığı ateş bugün Efrin'de gürleşiyor." 14 Mar. At https://mezopotamyaajansi.com/components/88122611/content/view/17766.

Milliyet. 1993. "Nevruz ateşiyle intihar etti." 23 Mar.

———. 2011. "Kadifekale'de yeşil kuşak genişletiliyor." 29 Nov. At http://www.milliyet.com.tr/kadifekale-de-yesil-kusak-genisletiliyor/ege/haberdetay/29.11.2011/1468712/default.htm.

Milton, Giles. 2008. *Paradise Lost: Smyrna 1922—the Destruction of Islam's City of Tolerance*. London: Sceptre.

Neyzi, Leyla. 2008. "Remembering Smyrna/Izmir: Shared History, Shared Trauma." *History & Memory* 20, no. 2: 106–27.

Öcalan, Abdullah. 1996. *Devrimin dili ve eylemi*. Cologne, Germany: Weşanên Serxwebûn.

Peker, Mümtaz. 2015. *Sahil kasabasından büyükşehire evrimleşme sürecinde İzmir'e göç*. Izmir, Turkey: İzmir Büyükşehir Belediyesi.

Rojeva Kurdistan. N.d. "Newroz ateşini Rahşan Demirel'in annesi yaktı." At http://rojevakurdistan.org/guendem/13310-newroz-ateini-rahan-demirelin-annesi-yakt.

Saraçoğlu, Cenk. 2011. *Kurds of Modern Turkey: Migration, Neoliberalism, and Exclusion in Turkish Society*. London: I. B. Tauris.

soL haber. 2011. "İzmir'de ırkçı aday tepki çekiyor." 29 May. At http://haber.sol.org.tr/kent-gundemleri/izmirde-irkci-aday-tepki-cekiyor-haberi-42989.

Temizsoy, Arzu. 2006. "Cultural and Architectural Significance of Planned Refugee Houses in Izmir (Turkey) from the Point of Conservation." In *1st International CIB Endorsed METU Postgraduate Conference: Built Environment & Information Technologies*, 741–56. Ankara, Turkey: Middle East Technical Univ.

UN News. 2017. "Turkey: UN Report Details Allegations of Serious Rights Violations in Country's Southeast." 10 Mar. At http://www.un.org/apps/news/story.asp?NewsID=56330#.WPEQuWelvAU.

Yeni asır. 1992a. "Kadifekale diken üstünde." 24 Mar.

———. 1992b. "Nevruz için kendini yaktı." 23 Mar.

———. 2015. "İzmir'de yaşayanların sadece yüzde 41'i İzmirli." 16 Feb. At http://www.yeniasir.com.tr/ekonomi/2015/02/16/izmirde-yasayanlarin-sadece-yuzde-41i-izmirli.

Yıldırım, Deniz, and Evren Haspolat, eds. 2010. *Değişen Izmir'ı anlamak.* Ankara, Turkey: Phoenix Yayınları.

Yıldırım, Onur. 2006. *Diplomacy and Displacement: Reconsidering the Turco-Greek Exchange of Populations, 1922–1934.* New York: Routledge.

YJA Star. n.d. "Tarihteki ilk kadın ordusu 5." At http://www.yja-star.com/tr/bolumler/savasan-kadn/314-tarihteki-ilk-kadn-ordusu-5.

Yoldaş Pançuni. 2011. "Rahşan Demirel." 29 Mar. At http://yoldaspancuni.blogspot.com/2011/03/rahsan-demirel.html.

Part Two

Racialization and Violence

5

The Making of Coloniality in Turkey

Racialization of Kurds in a Working-Class District in Istanbul between 1950 and 1980

Güllistan Yarkın

This chapter focuses on the "racialization of Kurds" in the working-class district Zeytinburnu in Istanbul between 1950 and 1980. It examines the subordination and racialization of Kurdish migrant workers as an effect of the colonial relationship that the Turkish state formed with Northern Kurdistan[1] despite the lack of such official status (Beşikci 1990; Duruiz 2020; Yarkın 2019). Workers' experiences of the unequal division of labor informed by racialized ideologies and practices help us trace the effects in Zeytinburnu of Turkish colonial domination in Northern Kurdistan. Based on workers' testimonies, the chapter analyzes how racism and coloniality are reproduced outside Kurdistan—in particular how the Turkish colonial imaginary negates, oversimplifies, essentializes, insults, subordinates, and dehumanizes Kurdish workers.

My analysis draws on the literature that explains racism in connection with the historical processes of colonization—conquest, enslavement, peonage, indentured servitude, and colonial or neocolonial labor immigration

---

1. I use "Northern Kurdistan" (Bakurê Kurdistanê) in reference to the contemporary Kurdish regions. These regions were historically also the land of Armenian and Assyrian people, who were erased from the region by the Turkish state forces. Many Turkish, Kurdish, Circassian, and other non-Turkish Muslim civilians also participated in the genocide.

(Bonilla-Silva 1997, 471; Cox 2000, 72; Fanon 1963; Jordan 2000; Omi and Winant 1994, 55–56; Quijano and Wallerstein 1992; Wallerstein 1991). Racism emerged to legitimize the conquest and exploitation of colonized people and to serve the needs of capitalist modes of production and different forms of labor domination (Bonacich 1972; Cox 2000; Hall 2019; Quijano and Wallerstein 1992; Rex 1986; Wallerstein 1991; Wolpe 1986). Colonial subjects are dehumanized and portrayed as biologically and culturally inferior (Bonilla-Silva 1997; Grosfoguel 1999; Miles and Brown 2003; Solomos 2003). Colonization oversimplified the culture of the conquered people and negated their national existence by expropriation, enslavement, and abolishment of natives' customs (Fanon 1959, 1963). Although the term *colonialism* generally refers to the oppressive relationship in history, the term *coloniality* indicates its continuing forms today. As the Peruvian sociologist Anibal Quijano (2000) argues, social discrimination as well as racial, political, and economic hierarchical relations persist in contemporary societies as living legacies of colonialism. This chapter traces how persisting Turkish colonialism in Northern Kurdistan emerges as coloniality in an Istanbul district and informs the racialization of Kurdish workers.

Given that the Turkish state constitutionally denies the existence of non-Turks living within the borders of Turkey, there are no official statistics about the housing, education, or employment conditions of Kurds, nor do periodic population surveys collect information on ethnicity. Notwithstanding the challenges of conducting research in the context of a lack of comprehensive data, the analysis here is built on a mixed-methods approach, including archival records, oral histories, in-depth interviews, focus-group discussions, and ethnographic observations.

During fieldwork from June 2014 to March 2017, I conducted open-ended, in-depth interviews with ninety Kurds, eighty Turks, and ten Albanians—workers, retired workers, housewives, wholesalers, retailers, and students in Zeytinburnu. Only half of the interviewees have direct experience of the period from 1950 to 1980 that this chapter focuses on, but the narratives of even the younger interviewees provided valuable insight into the memory of the district's past.

This chapter contains five sections. The first lays out the colonial background of Kurds and Kurdistan, connecting Ottoman rule and then the modern Turkish Republic's rule in colonial domination of Northern Kurdistan. The second section focuses on Zeytinburnu to examine the urban development and ethnic formation of the district. The third reflects on the biological and cultural aspects of the racialization of Kurds in Zeytinburnu. The fourth focuses specifically on Alevi Kurds and examines how their religious difference from the dominant Sunni Muslim majority intensifies stigmatization and exclusion. The fifth section displays how the subordinate position of Alevi and Sunni Kurdish workers is produced and reproduced in the labor market in Zeytinburnu.

The Colonial Background of Kurds and Kurdistan in Turkey

Since the fifteenth-century conquest of the capital city of the Roman Empire by the Ottoman Turks, Istanbul (Constantinople) has become one of the most important Muslim Turkish–dominated cities of the world. Under the Ottomans, Muslim, non-Muslim, Turkish, and non-Turkish communities lived together in the religiously and ethnically hierarchical social millet system. Sunni Muslim Kurdish settlement in Istanbul started in the fifteenth century along with the Turkish Muslim occupations of Christian lands (Çelik 2005, 142), and the Sunni Muslims' movement to Istanbul later increased in the nineteenth century in conjunction with the Ottoman state's modern colonial policies in the Kurdish regions that led to out-migration.

Until the nineteenth century, the Kurdish region had a semiautonomous status in the empire and was governed by local Kurdish tribal leaders. Sometime in the nineteenth century, the Ottoman elites adopted the European colonial approach toward the empire's periphery (Deringil 2003, 311–28; Klein 2011, 15–16; Powell 2003). In what Selim Deringil calls "borrowed colonialism," the Ottoman elites began to view the nomads and tribes as "savage." They recommended that these "savage" people needed to be civilized through political and economic intervention, which would be facilitated by means of local tribal leaders' loyalty to and cooperation with the state. For this intervention, it was crucial to build state buildings, courts of law, military outposts, and roads in these regions (2003, 311–28). According to Edhem Eldem, the Ottoman state consolidated the homogeneity of the "core regions of the empire"—namely, the Anatolian Peninsula and the eastern regions of Thrace—within a proto-nationalist vision, pushing the Arab provinces to become the "peripheral regions" of the empire (2000, 223). Experiencing the impact of the change in the Ottoman state, Kurdish provinces were also transformed into colonial regions of the empire. Hence, the historically semiautonomous status of Kurds was eliminated entirely, and their right to self-determination was eradicated through Ottoman policies (Alakom 2011, 25–26; Özoğlu 2004)

Kurds were predominantly an agrarian population and thus adversely affected by the political, economic, and cultural destruction visited upon their regions through colonialism. Many were forced to become colonial migrants in Istanbul. In the nineteenth and early twentieth centuries, these migrants became part of Istanbul's labor force, doing low-skill, low-wage, and less desired jobs. They worked mostly as porters, living in poverty and working in harsh conditions (Alakom 2011, 70–174; Serfiraz 2016). At the time, the Ottoman state recognized Kurds as part of the millet system and constructed Kurdish migrants as a colonial-racialized minority in the dominant Turkish imaginary. Many idioms and proverbs pertaining to Kurds in the Turkish language and in Turkish literature testify to this colonial-racialized image of them: for instance, "You cannot make a fur from a bear, a friend from a Kurd" (Ayıdan post Kürtten dost olmaz); "the God of a Kurd and a dog is the same" (Kürt ile itin Allahı birdir); and "a donkey called Kurdish did not eat food for forty years" (Eşeğe Kürt demişler eşek kırk yıl yem yememiş) (Alakom 2010).

After the foundation of the Republic of Turkey, the colonial imaginary about Kurdistan and its people continued, this time to assimilate them into the Turkish nation in the making. Official top-secret reports recommended that the name "Kurdistan" and "Kurds" be replaced with the geographical markers "the East" and "easterners." Through boarding schools, forced-settlement policies, and national disciplining in the military service, the state sought to eliminate Kurdish nationalism and Kurdish nationalists and to assimilate Kurds into Turkish society (Bayrak 1994; Yayman 2011).

In 1925, for instance, Prime Minister İsmet İnönü's Eastern Reform Plan proposed that a public inspector should rule Kurdistan in a "colonial way," and the plan went into effect that year (Bozarslan 2004, 64). Similarly, another state official, the Turkish general inspector Avni Doğan, suggested in a report in 1943 that "the settlement of the republic in the East" was akin to "the settlement of civilized nations in Africa." He urged his fellow statesmen to consider: "Who dares to argue that we lack something in us that [is possessed by] the civilized nations settling in Africa[,] where the weather conditions are worse than Diyarbakir?" (quoted in Yayman 2011, 155).

In contemporary Turkey, the Kurds are equal citizens on paper. However, in reality they are denied their most basic human and citizenship rights, such as access to public education in their mother tongue, equality before the law, and equal political participation. One of the freedoms they possess has been labor mobility within Turkey. This mobility is important to the state not only because it provides a reserve army of labor for Turkish agriculture and industries but also because migration has been beneficial for the Turkish state's assimilationist policies. Since the 1980s, the Turkish state has forcefully displaced around 3 million Kurds (Barut 2002), with many of them migrating to Turkish cities in the West or South, mostly Istanbul. Such migration has significantly increased since the 1990s due to forced Kurdish village evacuations by the military with the auspicious intent to eliminate the Kurdish guerrilla movement known as the Kurdistan Workers' Party (Partîya Karkerên Kurdistanê, PKK).

Urban Development and Ethnic Formation of Zeytinburnu

As one of the oldest working-class districts of Istanbul, Zeytinburnu—its name meaning "Cape of Olive"—is located in the European part of the city, at the seaside on the northern Marmara coast. Throughout Ottoman history, it served as the site of tanneries, an industry often located on the urban margins owing to the foul smell it produces, and was populated by the poorest sections of the immigrant population to the city. In the late nineteenth century, in addition to tanneries, other industrial sites producing iron, gunpowder, and weaponry were also constructed in Zeytinburnu (Özvar 2006, 70–72). Zeytinburnu continued to be the most crucial leather-production site in republican Turkey. At the same time, it also became more industrialized, especially with the expansion of manufacturing between the 1950s and the 1980s, when 325 new factories producing textiles, food, metal, paper, rubber, plastic, chemicals, electrical motors, and medicine were constructed (Akbulut 2006, 383–84; Akçay 1974, 304–27).

Despite the development of industrial areas, until the 1950s Zeytinburnu by and large remained an agricultural site in which nearly all the land belonged to the state (Kaya 2004, 90). Starting from the 1950s, Istanbul received massive rural-to-urban migration from different parts of the Balkans, Anatolia, and Northern Kurdistan. Because the state did not regulate the urban infrastructure processes and did not meet the housing needs of the rural migrants, the housing shortage became one of the most severe urban problems in Istanbul and other major cities (Işık and Pınarcıoğlu 2013, 111). Under these conditions, most of the rural migrants illegally occupied the unused public lands by building makeshift single-story houses called *gecekondu* (literally "built at night") near the factories (Keleş 1972). Zeytinburnu experienced the same transformation. The first *gecekondus* were made of wood, package box, tin, mud brick, and linoleum (Kaya 2004, 93), and they had no water, no electricity, no roads, no sewers (Zürcher 2012, 327–30). Later, stone, brick, glass, cement, and building tile were used (Kaya 2004, 93). By 1963, more than 40 percent of the district's population were factory workers, 17 percent were self-employed, and 13 percent were state officials (Hart 1969, 67).

From 1945 to 1965, the population of the district rose from 8,970 to 102,874, and in 1980 its population reached 124,543 (İstanbul Büyükşehir Belediyesi 2005; Kaya 2004). The district's new residents were from diverse ethnic backgrounds, including Turks, Albanians, Kurds, Bosniaks, and Pomaks (Kaya 2004, 90), but, according to a survey in 1963, more than 50 percent of the population were Turkish migrants from the Balkans, and a small group was from Central Asia (Çakırer 2012, 90–122). The rest of the population originated from within the borders of modern Turkey.[2]

2. Accordingly, the percentages of migrants' place of origin were the following: Black Sea region (23.7 percent), eastern Anatolia region (6.2 percent), central Anatolia region (5.6 percent), Thrace (4.5 percent), Marmara region (3 percent), Aegean region (1.7

Kurdish migrants from Northern Kurdistan—whom the state officially referred to euphemistically as "migrants from eastern and southeastern Anatolia"[3]—composed a small minority (7.4 percent). In the district's Sunni Muslim Turkish-majority population, the Kurds and the Albanians constituted the two significant non-Turkish Sunni and Alevi minority groups. Although a small number of Greeks and Armenians also lived in the district, most of them left it following the Istanbul pogrom in 1955.

Turkish and Albanian migrants from the Balkans were identified as *muhajirs* (Tanc 2001, 49). The term *muhajir*, meaning "refugee," has Islamic connotations deriving from Arabic roots and can be translated as "those who leave their homes in the cause of Allah after suffering oppression."[4] With the emergence of the national independence wars in

---

percent), southeastern Anatolia region (1.2 percent), and Mediterranean Sea region (0.9 percent) (Hart 1969, 133–40; Kaya 2004, 98).

3. Until the founding of the Republic of Turkey, Kurdistan was not called "Anatolia." During the Ottoman Empire, Armenia and Kurdistan were referred to as geographical entities. For instance, in the nineteenth century the region between Arapkir, Musul, and Van used to be called "Kurdistan," and the region at the northern border of Kurdistan, Erzincan, Van, and Kars used to be called "Armenia." However, many Armenians and other Christians lived in Kurdistan, and numerous Kurds also lived in Armenia (Kiesser 2005, 63). These regions were the common lands of Armenians and Kurds as well as of other Christian and non-Muslim communities, such as the Yezidis.

4. A *muhajir* is not just a refugee but specifically a Muslim refugee (Tanc 2001, 10). During the Ottoman Empire, before becoming *muhajirs*, not all but most of these people were the Muslim settlers or their grandchildren who were previously used by the Ottoman state for its imperial expansionist purposes into Christian territories. In its classical era, the empire produced settlement policies to direct the inflow of Muslims to newly acquired territories (Karpat 2015, xxvii). It used various methods to encourage the Muslim Turkish subjects to settle in designated places. The Ottoman state provided Anatolian Turkish-speaking Muslims with incitements such as free land, exemption from tax, and military service to encourage their settlement in the region. When these incitements did not work to make them settle in designated areas, the state applied deportation methods (Dündar 2008, 41–42). In the fifteenth and sixteenth centuries, the number of Turkish Muslims who settled in the Balkans (especially in Bulgaria, Macedonia, and Dobruja) was estimated at around 400,000 to 500,000. Later, following the conversion of Albanians and Bosnians to Islam, the number of Muslims in the Balkans significantly increased (Karpat 2015, xxvii).

the Balkans against the Ottoman Empire, thousands of Muslims settlers and autochthonous Muslim groups were forced to migrate to the mainland, and this migration continued after the foundation of the Turkish Republic (Tanc 2001, 49). According to my respondents, *muhajir* inhabitants of Zeytinburnu, who constituted the majority of the district's population during the *gecekondu* period, either came to Turkey before the 1950s, settling in other places before moving to Istanbul, or came to Zeytinburnu directly from Yugoslavia in the 1950s.

Although colonial oppression was the primary motivation for Kurdish migration, Kurdish migrants to Istanbul were never referred to as *muhajirs*. In my fieldwork, I found that before the 1980s the Kurdish migrants came mainly from Malatya (Meletî in Kurdish), Erzincan (Erzingan), Bingöl (Çewlîg), and Tunceli (Dêrsim).[5] Although most of the migrants from the historical Dêrsim region, including parts of Erzincan, Bingöl, and Tunceli, were Alevi (Qizilbash) Kurds, some from Malatya and other Kurdish regions were Sunni Kurds. Some of these Alevi Kurds spoke the Kurmanckî (Zazakî) dialect of Kurdish, but others spoke the Kurmancî dialect.[6] According to the 1965 census data analyzed by Faik Akçay (1974), 2,052 Zeytinburnu residents were born in Erzincan, 1,419 in Malatya, 464 in Tunceli, and 254 in Bingöl.[7] Although not all migrants from these

---

5. In 1935 parts of Dêrsim were named "Tunceli," a Turkish word that means "hand of bronze."

6. The population censuses of 1960 and 1965 contained a question on the language spoken at home among family members. According to the census of 1965, the total population of Zeytinburnu was 102,874, and 100,004 (97.2 percent) of them reported to the state officials that the language spoken in their home was Turkish. The following languages were reported as languages spoken at home: Albanian (1,056), Greek (631), Armenian (513), Serbian (200), Kurdish (125), Bulgarian (68), Arabic (31), Bosnian (26), Circassian (20), Lazish (3), Pomak (32), Hebrew (7), German (7), English (3), French (1), Italian (18), Romanian (4), Russian (7) (Akçay 1974, 243–44). However, Akçay, a teacher from Zeytinburnu, notes that even though many people from the eastern regions spoke Kurdish, the Kurds, unlike other groups, did not report their language to state officials (1974, 244).

7. According to the same data, the number of those born in Kurdish regions were recorded as follows : Adıyaman, 31; Ağrı, 51; Bitlis, 47; Diyarbakir, 127; Elazığ, 302; Hakkari, 6; Mardin, 217; Muş, 57; Siirt, 72; Urfa, 200; Van, 53 (Akçay 1974, 231–33).

regions were ethnically Kurdish, one can claim that until the 1990s the Kurds living in Zeytinburnu came predominantly from these regions. Yet it is also likely that these figures underestimate the actual number of Kurdish inhabitants owing to the illegal nature of *gecekondu* dwellings and the fact that many Kurds at the time lived in workers' lodges.

Racialization of Kurds

Turkish *muhajir*s from the Balkans came to Zeytinburnu with the decolonization of the Balkans, whereas the Kurds arrived there as a result of the Turkish state's colonial policies. Although *gecekondu* studies in Turkey have chosen not to account for non-Turkish ethnic identities of people (e.g., Erman 2001), during my fieldwork I found that the inhabitants not only recognized these ethnic identities but also commonly used them. For instance, referring to someone by the nickname "Kurd" or "Laz" or "Albanian" was a common practice in the district.

Today, the Turkish respondents I interviewed tend to romanticize their relations with their Kurdish neighbors when they all were living in *gecekondu* neighborhoods. They indicate a feeling of loss of "traditional" Zeytinburnu to urban renewal and the advent of "apartmentalization." This sense of nostalgia is also connected to the emergence of the national Kurdish armed movement since the 1980s and the political transformation of the district's Kurds. They identify Kurds living in the district during the *gecekondu* period as "old Kurds" and those moving to Zeytinburnu after the 1990s as "new Kurds." Whereas they idealize "old Kurds" as "loyal" and "obedient" citizens who do not create problems for the state, the Turkish nation, or the Turkish inhabitants of the district, they see the "new Kurds" as "bigoted," "violent," "quarrelsome," and "suspect" "traitors" and as natural supporters of the "terrorist PKK." The following remarks by a Turkish man in his late forties who runs a convenience store evince how some Turks categorize the Kurds:

> M: There are big differences between the Kurds of the 1970s and those coming here since 2000, 1995.
> G: Could you explain it more?

M: Old Kurds are more temperate. They have adapted better here. Because, I think, there was not a sentiment of Turkishness–Kurdishness in the past. This is a significant factor; look, now even a ten-year-old kid is inclined toward violence. Kurds see us as an enemy. . . . However, this did not exist in the past because we could sit on the same side and could become neighbors.

G: Why?

M: Because [they say], "We are oppressed people." By saying "we have been oppressed like that," "our rights have been taken away like that," by saying stuff like that, they [Kurdish youth] are imitating things they see from their parents. They are multiplying like that at the moment. (ellipses indicate omission)

When colonial migrants arrive in metropols, they enter spaces that are already "polluted" by racial power relations informed by a long colonial history, colonial imaginary, colonial knowledge, and racial/ethnic hierarchies (Grosfoguel, Oso, and Christou 2015). The particular encounter between the Turks and the Kurds took place in Zeytinburnu within a space that was already "polluted" by racial-national-ethnic power relations with a long colonial history. Establishing "loyalty" to the Turkish state and nation, to the flag, to the culture has been one of the main goals of Turkish nationalism (Beşikci 1991; Ülker 2007), which informed the construction of Kurds. For instance, in the 1930s when the Alevi Kurdish Genocide in Dêrsim and the other massacres against Kurds occurred, the Turkish state and especially the Turkish military referred to all the Kurdish rebels and Kurdish victims as "feudal," "savage," "backward," and "ignorant" "bandits" and "brigands" (Genelkurmay Belgelerinde Kürt İsyanları 2011). The official stigmatization pattern of the 1930s was reproduced after the 1980s when the state and the Turkish media portrayed the Kurdish national movement and its supporters as "terrorists" and "traitors" (Erdem 2014). Hence, the local distinction between "old Kurds" as "good Kurds" and the "new Kurds" as "bad Kurds" emerges as an important form of the articulation of coloniality in Zeytinburnu. The "old Kurds" are good, unlike the "new" ones, because they did not establish Kurdish political organizations challenging the principles of Turkish nationalism, the state, and Turkish supremacy. When Kurds came to the city before the 1980s, the PKK had not yet emerged. The construction of "old Kurds" as "desirable" and of "new Kurds" as "undesirable" in the Turkish imaginary reveals how Turkish nationalism has affected the racialization of Kurds differently at different historical junctures.

Yet even though the Turks romanticized the "old Kurds" as desirable citizens, they also stigmatized them as unskillful, uncivilized, illiterate, and dirty. My Turkish and Kurdish respondents stated that the dehumanizing stereotypes such as "Kurd with a tail" still existed in Zeytinburnu, persisting from the Ottoman Empire (Serfiraz 2016, 27). For instance, a sixty-seven-year-old Kurdish man whose father was a porter from Malatya and who lived among Turks stated:

G: Has anybody called you a Kurd with a tail?
A: Yes, they used to when I was a kid. At school, my friends used to tell me jokingly that Kurds had tails. Once, I showed to my male friends that I do not have a tail.

As Frantz Fanon notes how "a normal negro child, having grown up within a normal family, will become abnormal on the slightest contact with the white world" (1986, 111). Similarly, a normal Kurdish child will lose his sense of normality when he has to prove that he has no tail, that he is not an animal, that he is a human. The dehumanization of Kurds has a long colonial history that can be traced back to the Turkish soldiers in Northern Kurdistan. For instance, after the Dêrsim Genocide of 1938, many female children of the remaining Alevi Kurdish families in Dêrsim were kidnapped by Turkish soldiers and taken to the Elazığ Girls' Institute. When these Kurdish youth arrived there, they were humiliated by soldiers calling them "mountain bears" and "Kurds with tails." This dehumanization presumably legitimated their subsequent treatment as war captives in which their hair was scraped off and their traditional clothes burned (Türkyılmaz 2015). Likewise, Kurdish memoirs of the 1920s and the 1930s frequently refer to "the tail issue" as part of Turks' portrayal of Kurds (Diken 2010). This racist remark reproduced across time and space indicates how the colonial domination established in Kurdistan was rearticulated in a Turkish-dominated district in Istanbul.

The Turkish military plays a crucial role in feeding the racist Turkish imaginary about the Kurds. Many of my respondents mentioned that it was during their military service that they encountered for the first time the Kurds who could not speak Turkish. They also became accustomed to the rank-and-file soldiers' racist attitudes and behavior toward Kurdish soldiers and Kurdish civilians. The number of Kurds living in the *gecekondu* settlements between the 1950s and the 1980s was quite low, and the Kurds in Zeytinburnu were mostly single men who were living in workers' lodgings. Many Zeytinburnu Turkish inhabitants' perceptions of Kurds were formed during their military service.

In accounting for his time in the military, one of my Turkish respondents said that the Kurdish men carried out the worst jobs in the military. A well-known Turkish idiom, "Dirty tricks make Kurdish Memet go to sentry duty" (Alavere dalavere Kürt Memet nöbete), testifies that the understanding that Kurds are suited to the most onerous and unwanted tasks is ingrained in the general culture. Furthermore, historical archives indicate that this understanding indeed informed a long-term Turkish state policy. For instance, in 1924 the Azadî Kurdish national organization submitted a letter to the British forces in Iraq, noting that "Kurds in the army were pressured, badly treated, [and] generally assigned the most difficult and unwanted tasks" (quoted in van Bruinessen 2005, 153–54).

Racialization of Alevi Kurds

Although all Kurds are subjected to racialization, Alevi Kurdish residents in Zeytinburnu carried a double burden of diverging from the dominant Sunni Muslim Turkish identity not only by ethnicity but also by religion. In contrast to Sunni Kurds, who built *gecekondus* near Sunni Turk neighborhoods—thanks to the Sunni brotherhood—the Alevi Kurdish workers predominantly resided in workers' lodgings or in crowded and smelly dwellings in the tanneries, which were very cold in the winter and humid in the summer. It was only in the late 1970s and early 1980s that they were able to move into *gecekondu* neighborhoods because of changing housing laws.

Even though the Alevi Kurds composed the majority of the Kurdish population in the district, their numbers did not help them express their identity freely in public amid the historically established religious and ethnic hierarchies in Turkey. The Ottoman millet system defined Alevis as "heretics," while explicitly identifying Muslims as the dominant community (*millet-i hakime*) and non-Muslims as the subordinate community (*millet-i mahkume*) (Türköne 1991, 63). Among the dominated groups, Christians and Jews were communally protected as "people of the Book" but nevertheless lived as secondary subjects and were required to pay a special poll tax called the *jizya* to the state (Zürcher 2012, 26–28). The remaining dominated groups were categorized as "heretics," such as the Alevis, and did not have the same legal rights as the "people of the Book" (Ateş 2011; Makdisi 2002, 774). Hence, the "uncivilized" Alevi "heretics" of the Kurdish Dêrsim region suffered from severe state discrimination and were constantly subjected to massacres and forced displacements (Bayrak 1997, 169).

In comparison to Alevi Turks, Alevi Kurds experienced oppression in the Ottoman Empire and then in the republic. The official Ottoman documents of the nineteenth century classified the people of the historical Dêrsim region, which also included the Alevi populations in Bingöl and Erzincan, as "disobedient people" who needed to be "civilized," whose "wildness" should be eliminated, and whose religious beliefs should be "corrected." In 1912 an Ottoman bureaucrat confessed that since the Tanzimat period of 1839–76, the state had targeted the Alevi Kurds many times, massacring them, seizing their properties, and burning their homes, yet it had still failed to "eliminate the savagery and ignorance of the people of this place" (quoted in Gündoğdu and Genç 2013, 13–43).

The modern Turkish Republic, which spurned the Ottoman past as "backward," had no qualms in employing the same violent measures in Dêrsim. In 1931, Fevzi Çakmak, the first chief of the General Staff, stated: "People of Dêrsim cannot be acquired through caresses. An armed intervention would have more impact. Dêrsim's governance should be perceived as the administration of a colony, and a colonial government should be established here" (quoted in Yayman 2011, 106). It was no accident that in 1938 the Turkish state responded to the Dêrsim rebellion by brutally killing thousands of Alevi Kurds (Akyürekli 2011, 78–130; Beşikci 1990). These colonizing and racializing policies have continued in different forms throughout the history of modern Turkey up to the present.

Alevi Kurds who migrated to Zeytinburnu were not expressive about their identity, nor did they openly practice their religion. For instance, they only secretly fasted during the month of Muharrem. And although they did not fast during Ramadan, they pretended to do so. They prayed secretly and organized their funerals in mosques according to Sunni traditions. Even today, older people avoid talking about their Alevi identity in public. The first public appearance of the Alevi identity and claim to the public space in Zeytinburnu was the opening of a place of worship, Erikli Baba Cemevi, in 1993.

Sunni and Alevi Kurdish Workers in the Turkish Labor Market

When rural migrants arrive in cities, the help provided by previous migrants from their home villages and towns has vital importance. Various problems, such as finding a job, finding accommodation, and building a home, are solved within these solidarity groups (Kaya 2004, 98). The labor market is structured in connection with people's geographic and ethnic origins. For instance, my interviews indicate that before the 1980s most of the textile workers in Zeytinburnu were Turks, and they came either from the Balkan regions as *muhajir*s or from the Black Sea region. Turkish workers also worked in all manufacturing industries in the district.

Most Kurdish workers occupied subordinate positions in the labor market, as they had done during the Ottoman period. They were incorporated into the Zeytinburnu labor market as porters, leather-tanning workers, and hippodrome workers. Whereas the Alevi Kurdish workers toiled at the tanneries in the Kazlıçeşme neighborhood, Sunni Kurdish workers were by and large porters; a minority of Sunni Kurds also worked at the hippodrome as horse groomers. Both the working conditions and wages for the latter jobs were worse than those for manufacturing jobs.

Among the three sectors, the tanning industry located in the Kazlıçeşme neighborhood, which involves converting animal skins and hides into leather, was one of the most hazardous industries because of the use of various toxic chemicals.[8] According to the accounts by retired Alevi Kurdish leather workers, they were surrounded by worms while working. They often fainted from the effect of the arsenic and lime used to remove the hair from the animal skins. Workers used very primitive machines for emerying and liming and powerful chemicals for painting. Owing to the primitiveness of the machines, some leather workers lost their arms. The streets surrounding the tanneries were full of animal pelts. Some residents mentioned that the smell was so strong that they would almost faint when they walked by the area. One Alevi Kurdish respondent who worked as a leather worker said that no matter how frequently they washed, they could not remove the bad smell from their bodies and their clothes. This probably affected their interactions with others in the district, further contributing to their stigmatization.[9]

In many parts of the world, racialized groups work in the tanning industry—for instance, Chamars (a group of "untouchables," or Dalits, located at the bottom of the caste system) in India (Rawat 2011, 93) and Blacks and immigrants in the United States (Schereuder 1990, 406–10). Different modes of labor domination occurred in the modern colonial-capitalist world system, and racism was a central mechanism for the maintenance of different forms of labor control (Quijano and Wallerstein 1992, 549–51; Wallerstein 2011, 94–127). In sum, the bottom layer of the labor

---

8. In 1976 the National Institute of Occupational Safety and Health in the United States reported that the accident and illness rate in tanneries was five times higher than the average for all other industries (Nihila 1999, WS-24).

9. In 1987 the movie *Çark* (The Cog) by Muzaffer Hiçdurmaz portrayed the bad working conditions in tanneries. In the movie, Turkish glass workers living and working in Zeytinburnu have to start working in a tannery after losing their jobs due to the neoliberal policies applied to the glass factories in the 1980s. Depicting all leather workers as Turkish, this movie was blind to the real ethnic composition of tannery workers, although it illustrated well the working conditions by showing how the workers would vomit as soon as they arrived at work or faint due to the horrible smell or die in work accidents.

and housing markets that Kurdish workers were obliged to inhabit indicate to us how racial and ethnic hierarchies and coloniality informed their experiences in Zeytinburnu.

Conclusion

This chapter has analyzed how coloniality and racism were articulated and reproduced in the Turkish-dominated working-class district of Zeytinburnu in Istanbul. It has demonstrated that racism functioned to keep the Kurdish workers at the bottom layer of the labor market and that the origins of this racism were deeply connected to the Turkish colonial domination in Northern Kurdistan. In comparison to Sunni Kurdish workers, Alevi Kurdish workers experienced further subordination due to their doubly subordinate position according to the two hierarchies of religion and ethnicity in colonial Northern Kurdistan. Nevertheless, even though Sunni Kurds were in a relatively advantageous position within the hegemonic Sunni structure, they, too, were subject to racism along with the Alevi Kurds, although to different degrees, and Kurdish ethnicity was racialized regardless of the Sunni–Alevi divide. The origins of this racialization can be traced back to the Ottoman period, when Kurds as a whole were stigmatized as uncivilized, illiterate, unskillful, and dirty people who had tails. The Turkish state and society mobilized existing racialized biological and cultural discourses and stereotypes concomitantly. They distinguished between "old Kurds" and "new Kurds" as another form of coloniality and racism. Turkish male workers in particular drew upon their experiences during military service, where the military displayed the most racist attitudes and practices against the Kurds. In all, then, the formation and evolution of the racist imaginary across time and place affected Turkish–Kurdish relations in the working-class district of Zeytinburnu as well.

References

Akbulut, M. Rıfat. 2006. "Spatial Transformation in Zeytinburnu." In *Surların öte yanı / The Other Side of City Walls Zeytinburnu*, edited by Burçak Evren, 376–413. Istanbul: Zeytinburnu Belediyesi Kültür Yayınları.

Akçay, Faik. 1974. *Zeytinburnu gerçek yönleriyle bir gecekondu kenti.* Istanbul: Çelikcilt Matbaası.
Akyürekli, Mahmut. 2011. *Dersim Kürt tedibi 1937–1938.* Istanbul: Kitap Yayınevi.
Alakom, Rohat. 2010. *Türk edebiyatında Kürtler.* Istanbul: Avesta Yayınları.
———. 2011. *Eski İstanbul Kürtleri.* Istanbul: Avesta Yayınları.
Ateş, Kâzım. 2011. *Yurttaşlığın kıyısında Aleviler "öz Türkler" ve "heretik ötekiler."* Ankara, Turkey: Phoenix Yayınları.
Barut, Mehmet. 2002. *Zorunlu göçe maruz kalan Kürt kökenli T.C. vatandaşlarının göç öncesi ve göç sonrası sosyo ekonomik, sosyo kültürel durumları, askeri çatışma ve gerginlik politikaları sonucu meydana gelen göçün ortaya çıkardığı sorunlar ve göç mağduru ailelerin geriye dönüş eğilimlerinin araştırılması ve çözüm önerileri (1999–2001).* Istanbul: Göç-Der.
Bayrak, Mehmet. 1994. *Açık-gizli/resmi-gayrıresmi Kürdoloji belgeleri.* Istanbul: Özge Yayınları.
———. 1997. *Alevilik ve Kürtler.* Istanbul: Özge Yayınları.
Beşikci, İsmail. 1990. *Devletler arası sömürge Kürdistan.* Istanbul: Alan Yayıncılık.
———. 1991. *Kürtlerin mecburi iskânı.* Ankara, Turkey: Yurt Kitap Yayın.
Bonacich, Edna. 1972. "A Theory of Ethnic Antagonism: The Split Labor Market." *American Sociological Review* 37, no. 5: 547–59.
Bonilla-Silva, Eduardo. 1997. "Rethinking Racism toward a Structural Interpretation." *American Sociological Review* 62, no. 3: 465–80.
Bozarslan, Hamit. 2004. *Türkiye'nin modern tarihi.* Istanbul: Avesta Yayınları.
Çakırer, Yasemin. 2012. "İstanbul—Zeytinburnu'nda ulusötesi kentleşme aktörleri olarak Türk kökenli göçmenler." PhD diss., Istanbul Technical Univ.
Çelik, Ayşe Betül. 2005. "'I Miss My Village': Forced Kurdish Migrants in Istanbul and Their Representation in Associations." *New Perspectives on Turkey* 32:137–63.
Cox, Oliver C. 2000. "Race Relations: Its Meaning, Beginning, and Progress." In *The Theories of Race and Racism,* edited by Les Back and John Solomos, 71–78. London: Routledge.
Deringil, Selim. 2003. "'They Live in a State of Nomadism and Savagery': The Late Ottoman Empire and the Post-colonial Debate." *Society for Comparative Study of Society and History* 45, no. 2: 311–42.
Diken, Şeyhmus. 2010. *İsyan sürgünleri.* Istanbul: İletişim Yayınları.
Dündar, Fuat. 2008. *Modern Türkiye'nin şifresi İttihat ve Terakki'nin etnisite mühendisliği (1913–1918).* Istanbul: İletişim Yayınları.

Duruiz, Deniz. 2020. "Tracing the Conceptual Genealogy of Kurdistan as International Colony." *Middle East Report*, no. 295 (Summer). At https://merip.org/2020/08/tracing-the-conceptual-genealogy-of-kurdistan-as-international-colony/.

Eldem, Edhem. 2000. "Istanbul: İmparatorluk payitahtından periferileşmiş bir başkente." In *Doğu ile batı arasında Osmanlı kenti Halep, İzmir, İstanbul*, edited by Ethem Eldem, Daniel Goffman, and Bruce Masters, 152–230. Istanbul: Tarih Vakfı Yurt Yayınları.

Erdem, Derya. 2014. "The Representation of the Democratic Society Party (DTP) in the Mainstream Turkish Media." In *The Kurdish Question in Turkey: New Perspectives on Violence, Representation, and Reconciliation*, edited by Cengiz Gunes and Welat Zeydanlıoğlu, 47–67. London: Routledge.

Erman, Tahire. 2001. "The Politics of Squatter (*Gecekondu*) Studies in Turkey: The Changing Representation of Rural Migrants in the Academic Discourse." *Urban Studies* 38, no. 7: 983–1002.

Fanon, Fanon. 1959. "Reciprocal Bases of National Culture and the Fight for Freedom." At http://www.marxists.org/subject/africa/fanon/national-culture.htm.

———. 1963. *The Wretched of the Earth*. Translated by Richard Philcox. New York: Grove Weidenfeld.

———. 1986. *Black Skin White Masks*. Translated by Charles Lam Markmann. London: Pluto Press.

Genelkurmay Belgelerinde Kürt İsyanları. 2011. *Genelkurmay belgelerinde Kürt isyanları 1*. Istanbul: Kaynak Yayınları.

Grosfoguel, Ramon. 1999. "Introduction: 'Cultural Racism' and Colonial Caribbean Migrants in Core Zones of the Capitalist World-Economy." *Review* (Fernand Braudel Center) 22, no. 4: 409–34.

Grosfoguel, Ramon, Laura Oso, and Anastasia Christou. 2015. "'Racism,' Intersectionality, and Migration Studies: Framing Some Theoretical Reflections." *Identities* 22, no. 6: 635–52.

Gündoğdu, Cihangir, and Vural Genç. 2013. *Dersim'de Osmanlı siyaseti izâle-i vahşet, tashîh-i itikâd ve tasfiye-i ezhân 1880–1890*. Istanbul: Kitap Yayınevi.

Hall, Stuart. 2019. *Essential Essays*. Vol. 1. Edited by David Morley. Durham, NC: Duke Univ. Press.

Hart, Charles W. M. 1969. *Zeytinburnu gecekondu bölgesi*. Istanbul: İstanbul Ticaret Odası Yayınları.

Işık, Oğuz, and Melih Pınarcıoğlu. 2013. *Nöbetleşe yoksulluk gecekondulaşma ve kent yoksulları: Sultanbeyli örneği*. Istanbul: İletişim Yayınları.

İstanbul Büyükşehir Belediyesi (Istanbul Metropolitan Municipality). 2005. *Zeytinburnu stratejik eylem planı raporu.* Istanbul: İstanbul Büyükşehir Belediye Başkanlığı Kentsel Dönüşüm Müdürlüğü.

Jordan, Winthrop D. 2000. "First Impressions." In *The Theories of Race and Racism*, edited by Les Back and John Solomos, 33–50. London: Routledge.

Karpat, Kemal. 2015. "Önsöz." In *Türkiye'nin göç tarihi 14. yüzyıldan 21. yüzyıla Türkiye'ye göçler*, edited by M. Murat Erdoğan and Ayhan Kaya, xxi–xi. Istanbul: İstanbul Bilgi Üniv. Yayınları.

Kaya, Muzaffer. 2004. "Siyasal katılım: Zeytinburnu örneği." Master's thesis, Yıldız Teknik Üniv.

Keleş, Ruşen. 1972. *100 soruda Türkiye'de şehirleşme, konut ve gecekondu.* Istanbul: Gerçek Yayınevi.

Kiesser, Hans-Lukas. 2005. *Iskanlanmış barış doğu vilayetlerinde misyonerlik etnik kimlik ve devlet 1839–1938.* Istanbul: İletişim Yayınları.

Klein, Janet. 2011. *The Margins of Empire Kurdish Militias in the Ottoman Tribal Zone.* Stanford, CA: Stanford Univ. Press.

Makdisi, Usama. 2002. "Ottoman Orientalism." *American Historical Review* 107, no. 3: 768–96.

Miles, Robert, and Malcolm Brown. 2003. *Racism.* London: Routledge.

Nihila, Millie. 1999. "Marginalization of Women Workers: Leather Tanning Industry in Tamil Nadu." *Economic and Political Weekly*, 34, nos. 16–17 (Apr. 17–30): WS21–WS27.

Omi, Michael, and Howard Winant. 1994. *Racial Formation in the United States from the 1960s to the 1990s.* New York: Routledge.

Özoğlu, Hakan. 2004. *Kurdish Notables and the Ottoman State: Evolving Identities, Competing Loyalties, and Shifting Boundaries.* Albany: State Univ. of New York Press.

Özvar, Erol. 2006. "Zeytinburnu at the Time of Ottomans." In *Surların öte yanı / The Other Side of City Walls Zeytinburnu*, edited by Burçak Evren, 70–97. Istanbul: Zeytinburnu Belediyesi Kültür Yayınları.

Powell, Eve M. Troutt. 2003. *A Different Shade of Colonialism: Egypt, Great Britain, and the Mastery of Sudan.* Berkeley: Univ. of California Press.

Quijano, Anibal. 2000. "Coloniality of Power, Eurocentrism, and Latin America." *Nepantla: Views from South* 1, no. 3: 533–80.

Quijano, Anibal, and Immanuel Wallerstein. 1992. "Americanity as a Concept, or the Americas in the Modern World-System." *International Social Science Journal* 134:549–59.

Rawat, Ramnarayan S. 2011. *Reconsidering Untouchability: Chamars and Dalit History*. Bloomington: Indiana Univ. Press.

Rex, John. 1986. "The Role of Class Analysis in the Study of Race Relations—Weberian Perspective." In *Theories of Race and Ethnic Relations*, edited by John Rex and David Mason, 42–64. Cambridge: Cambridge Univ. Press.

Schereuder, Yda. 1990. "The Impact of Labor Segmentation on the Ethnic Division of Labor and the Immigrant Residential Community: Polish Leather Workers in Wilmington, Delaware, in the Early Twentieth Century." *Journal of Historical Geography* 16, no. 4: 402–24.

Serfiraz, Mesud. 2016. "Osmanlı dönemi kürt basınında Kürt işçi sınıfına dair haberler." *Kürt tarihi*, no. 22: 22–27.

Solomos, John. 2003. *Theorizing Race and Racism in Britain*. New York: Palgrave Macmillan.

Tanc, Barbaros. 2001. "Where Local Trumps National: Christian Orthodox and Muslim Refugees since Lausanne." *Balkanologie* 1–2. At https://journals.openedition.org/balkanologie/732.

Türköne, Mümtaz'er. 1991. *Siyasi ideoloji olarak İslamcılığın doğuşu*. Istanbul: İletişim Yayınları.

Türkyılmaz, Zeynep. 2015. "Dersim'den Tunceli'ye bir kolonizasyon projesi Sıdıka Avar ve dağ çiçeklerim." *Kürt tarihi*, no. 21: 32–41.

Ülker, Erol. 2007. "Assimilation of the Muslim Communities in the First Decade of the Turkish Republic (1923–1934)." *European Journal of Turkish Studies*, Jan. At https://journals.openedition.org/ejts/822.

Van Bruinessen, Martin. 2005. *Kürdistan üzerine yazılar*. Istanbul: İletişim Yayınları.

Wallerstein, Immanuel. 1991. "The Ideological Tensions of Capitalism: Universalism versus Racism and Sexism." In *Race, Nation, Class: Ambiguous Identities*, by Étienne Balibar and Immanuel Wallerstein, 29–36. New York: Verso.

———. 2011. *The Modern World-System I: Capitalist Agriculture and Origins of the European World-Economy in the Sixteenth Century*. Berkeley: Univ. of California Press.

Wolpe, Harold. 1986. "Class Concepts, Class Struggle, and Racism." In *Theories of Race and Ethnic Relations*, edited by John Rex and David Mason, 110–30. Cambridge: Cambridge Univ. Press.

Yarkın, Güllistan. 2019. "İnkâr edilen hakikat sömürge kuzey kürdistan." *Kürd araştırmaları* 1. At https://www.kurdarastirmalari.com/yazi-detay-nk-r-edilen-hakikat-s-m-rge-kuzey-k-rdistan-26.

Yayman, Hüseyin. 2011. *Türkiye'nin Kürt sorunu hafızası*. Istanbul: SETA Yayınları.

Zürcher, Erik J. 2012. Modernleşen Türkiye'nin tarihi. Istanbul: İletişim Yayınları.

6

"I Would Have Recognized You from Your Smell"

Racialization of Kurdish Migrant Farmworkers in Western Turkey

Deniz Duruiz

Batuhan,[1] a Turkish agricultural engineer working at a seed-production company in Bursa, was both amused by and in awe of finally having discovered the identity of the mysterious woman working among the Kurdish laborer group in the cornfield under his supervision: a Turkish anthropologist doing her PhD in the United States. He called his friend Tuğba on her cellphone and invited her to the fancy restaurant that he insisted on taking me to and said: "I'm having a beer with one of Zubeyr's laborers, come, join us!" He told me that I would get along well with Tuğba; she was a tough girl, just like me. When she arrived, Batuhan introduced us with a mischievous grin, watching the puzzled look on Tuğba's face as I proceeded to answer her questions, "But you're not actually one of those laborers, are you? How do you know them? So, you really worked in the field all day? Did you stay in their tents? Have you seen the toilets? Oh, my God!"

I had gone to that farm because two worker families I had spent the previous six months with in Kurdistan[2] were working there. Their labor

---

1. I used pseudonyms in this chapter to protect the anonymity of my interlocutors.

2. In this chapter, I use the name "Kurdistan" to refer to the Kurdish provinces that remain within the borders of Turkey. There are many names used for the land currently

intermediary, Zubeyr, had heard of me from those workers, who were also his neighbors, and he wanted to meet me. We were staying at a tent camp of about four thousand workers from Kurdistan with a few Syrian families among them, all of whom were working mostly for the large seed-production company. On the days that the company needed fewer workers than usual, they went to work for smaller farmers in the area. Zubeyr was in charge of organizing the worker groups and assigning tasks to 106 workers that he had recruited, and among that many workers I could go unnoticed for a while.

I had been working among that group of laborers for eight days when the engineers finally noticed me. On my second day in the cornfield, I had asked Zubeyr if I could introduce myself to the engineers. He said it would be better if I did not since they could suspect I was there to document the company's illegal labor practices, such as employing Syrian workers. So I spoke in Kurdish in the presence of the Turkish engineers, avoided eye contact, and thought that I had managed to go under the radar for the following few days. Batuhan said he thought I was Zilan's friend from the university. He thought maybe my folks were in need, so I had come here to work for the summer. He said, "It wasn't until Şervan [the labor intermediary's son] called you Deniz *Hanım* [Miss Deniz] that I realized that there was something else." Tuğba jumped in: "I would have immediately recognized you from your smell! The cornfield has a smell, and then when one hundred workers go into the field, it changes. Every group of workers has a smell." Batuhan said that he and other agricultural engineers used to wear sunscreen, deodorant, perfume, collared shirts, and sunglasses, but then they realized that the laborers "find that odd," so they gave it all up. If you wear them, he said, the workers call you a "gentleman" (*kibar*

---

predominantly inhabited by the Kurds that remains within the borders of Turkey. Each of the names used to replace or nuance "Kurdistan"—such as "the Eastern and Southeastern Anatolian Regions," "the East," "the Southeast," "the Kurdish Provinces," "Turkish Kurdistan," "Northern Kurdistan," "Bakur" (which simply means "North" in Kurdish), "Western Armenia," and "the Region"—are loaded with historical and political baggage. I prefer to use "Kurdistan," the name that the vast majority of the people of this land as well as of my interlocutors use when they do not think it would be dangerous for them to do so.

adam) and don't take you seriously. A gentleman cannot do our job, they say. "You need to be stern with workers, if need be," he said, "although I feel bad when I do so; they already work for twelve hours under the sun." But one cannot always have a firm hand on the workers, either; sometimes one needs to joke around. How can one tell a worker not to talk to anyone for twelve hours straight?

Tuğba said that I was lucky: "Zubeyr's workers are a good group; their cultural levels are high, and they know the job." After asking me if I always work with Kurdish workers, "the ones from the East," she said, "I no longer say I hate Kurds as I used to. We make them do all our work. And one works with them; one gets to know them. . . . But it is very hard [to work with them]."[3] Batuhan turned to Tuğba and laughed. He said that Tuğba is a really tough girl; she is the only woman working in the production department, but sometimes things happen that she can't take, either. "Once I saw her coming from the field; her face looked like a disaster," he said. "I asked what happened; she said she caught two workers having sex in the field. You can't imagine the things we see. They ask for permission to go to the toilet and go sit in the shade, so many things."

What gave me away in my unsuccessful attempt to pass as a Kurdish worker, even before Şervan called me out as "Miss Deniz," was first and foremost the fact that I did not belong to a particular family. I had lunch with one family, spent my tea break with another, sat among men, smoked, talked about politics (as I later learned, Batuhan was informed that I support the pro-Kurdish movement), and spoke in an overconfident tone for a single young woman. Also, I had arrived late in the summer, as many university students do; I was too inexperienced for my age, which was why Şervan was following me around to make sure I was assigned to the correct row of corn; and again, despite my age, I was single. Batuhan probably also read other clues—such as a slight difference in my accent in Turkish, my bodily comportment, the patterns on some of my headscarves

---

3. In quotations from my interlocutors, the ellipses indicate omissions of statements rather than pauses in speech.

showing that they are from western Turkey—and assumed that I was a friend of Zilan's from the university.

However, none of these clues came to Tuğba's mind as possible indicators of my difference. For her, I could have worked for twelve hours with Kurdish workers under the sun; I could have stayed in a tent; I could have had the same limited access to water; yet, regardless of my living conditions, I could never have smelled like "them." Unlike the remaining ninety-nine of Tuğba's one hundred imaginary workers that smell up the cornfields, I would, of course, smell like roses, so much so that she would be able to single me out by my smell. Batuhan's emphasis on the workers' finding deodorant and perfume "odd" did not seem to be limited to the context of a cornfield, either. To him, it pointed to a radical difference between the embodiment of a "gentleman" and those who find the ways of a gentleman odd.

Following this conversation, both engineers said that they envied the workers because no matter how hard their work was, it would end at six o'clock, and they no longer had any responsibilities until the next morning, whereas the work of the engineer would not end until everything was in order. Then they went on to tell me how they hacked the GPS of the clocking-in system installed on the company iPads to control their working hours so that they can chill out at a fancy restaurant while their boss thinks they are still in the cornfield. Yet it did not occur to either of them that what they were doing was essentially the same thing as the workers when they slack after a toilet break. When Tuğba said, "*We* make them do *our* work," she was identifying with the owner of the company and papering over the class antagonism that she was quite aware of in the instance of hacking the company iPad. What allowed her statement to make sense to her was the racialized figure of the Kurdish worker, whose uncultured, lazy, smelly, dirty, overly sexualized body meant that neither her nor I could ever be put in the same category.

The vast majority of agricultural work in western Turkey is done by Kurdish families from Kurdistan, known in the mainstream media as "seasonal agricultural workers." Depending on the monetary needs of the family, "the season" of their stay in rural western Turkey ranges from forty days to nine months. The racialization of Kurds is prevalent in everyday life, not only in the cities of western Turkey (Gönen 2011; Saraçoğlu 2009; Yonucu 2008) but also in rural contexts, where labor relations and hierarchies between Turks and Kurds create significant social tensions. Focusing on the everyday struggles of migrant workers in navigating these power relations allows us to understand how anti-Kurdish politics and the Kurdish political movement are experienced beyond the level of national politics and permeate the capillaries of social life.

Here, I focus on race and racialization as they are experienced by Kurds and examine how racialization draws on the emotional, affective, and embodied social registers. In Turkey, it is generally considered extremely rude to observe let alone talk to a stranger about other people's bodily processes or the details of their intimacy. Yet when it comes to Kurds, especially working-class Kurds, all this talk becomes acceptable. The aversion with which two Turkish engineers described the Kurdish workers' smell, the disgust with which Tuğba commented on the toilets, the horror the workers incited through their "improper sexuality," and the resentment the engineers felt toward the workers' disobedience are essentially emotional and affective components of the racial anxieties about Kurds in Turkey. These affects are heightened by contact or proximity to working-class Kurds and are crucial to the operation of the racialization of Kurdish migrant workers as well as to the self-making of the Turkish engineers in distinction to the workers.

The racialization of Kurdish migrant workers is a collective embodied and affective experience of paramount importance to the formation of their subjectivities. As William Mazzarella argues, affect provides "a way of apprehending social life that does not start with the bounded, intentional subject while at the same time foregrounding embodiment and sensuous life" (2009, 291). The emphasis on subjectivation as a continuous process grounded in embodiment and affect allows us to go beyond an a priori subject endowed with a stable body and an interiority to experience the social world around her. Affect is not only constitutive of the subject's recurrent embodiment but also equally integral to the making of its social worlds. Approaching racialization from the point of affect allows us to look beyond ethnoracial groups as given collectives that share linguistic, cultural, or biological characteristics. It instead helps us see race and racialization as social processes that form individual and collective subjects by signifying, experiencing, and resignifying difference. More concretely, in this perspective, being Kurdish or Turkish is not a singular identity shared by a predetermined group of people. Rather, subjects become Kurdish or Turkish as an affective and embodied experience that forms the self through imaginary and real encounters with the other, while at the same time signifying that experience through a symbolic universe, which itself is always under construction.

The focus on affect here aims to emphasize two significant aspects of the process of racialization. First, affects arise "in the midst of in-betweenness" (Gregg and Seigworth 2010, 1) and saturate spaces, relations, and encounters. "The relational and spatial character of affect transcends the sphere of the personal as affect defines the impact of feelings on bodies, objects and spaces" (Gutierrez-Rodriguez 2014, 47). Thus, the affective aspect of racialization shows us that racialization does not necessarily act on already-formed human subjects but might work through spaces, relations, encounters, bodies, objects, sensory information (sights, smells, sounds), habits, individual and collective feelings, moods, and environments.

Second, affects disseminate through "a kind of involuntary and powerful learning and participation" (Stewart 2007, 40). Ana Yolanda Ramos-Zayas argues that racial learning in each specific context occurs through mostly unpleasant feelings, transgressions in practice, and emotional dissonance. In line with this pattern of learning, "an embodied racialized affect centers on how the poor and marginal examine their affective and sentimental experiences, enter social consciousness through affect, and might explain conditions of social subordination accordingly" (2011, 27). Moreover, this learning informs not only the subordinated but also the unmarked (dominant) raced subjects, whose subjectivities are formed through this involuntary expression and through participation in the recurrent formation of the self and the other.

As Neferti X. M. Tadiar observes about Filipino domestic workers, the historical conditions that turned them into a global migrant domestic labor force through imperial heteronormative gender norms were also the conditions that allowed them to invent caring and life-making qualities for their communities through the same gendered and raced norms that were brought about by those conditions in the first place. She asks: "What, then, might it mean to reconsider 'race' as a theoretical question and political intervention rather than a category of social exemption or exclusion or a descriptive category of 'difference' (as a sign of marginalized social being)?" She answers, "It means attending to these subaltern pathways of social and self-formation that remain beneath the threshold of visibility of raced subjects (both dominant and subordinate), the proper borders of their own self-presencing" (2015, 156).

Inspired by Tadiar's question, I examine the racialization of Kurdish migrant workers not only as instances of marginalization and subordination but also as instances of self-making as raced and classed subjects. I pay particular attention to the embodied and affective responses the workers give to their racialization and how they in turn participate in racializing logics with reference to the imaginary racial figures of "the Gypsy" and "the Syrian." Although this experience of racialization is also inextricably tied with the experience of social class, the idioms of marginalization and self-making come from racialized terms and racial references. In other words, Kurdish migrant workers experience discrimination, subordination, and marginalization as Kurds, which they respond to by resignifying their Kurdishness and distinguishing themselves from other racialized groups while at the same time contributing to those groups' racialization.

The Racialization of Kurds in Turkey

It is no easy task to define racialization and race and to distinguish them from ethnicization and ethnicity. The problem of definition is not only about the intellectual genealogies of these terms but also about the sociopolitical contexts out of which they were born and the histories of their usage and circulation. Hence, many scholars have used the terms *race* and *ethnicity* interchangeably (Bourgois 1989), resorted to the composite term *ethnoracial* (McLaughlin 2005), written one or both in quotation marks (De Genova 2005), or argued that the terms *ethnicity, race* (Miles 1989), and *racialization* (Goldberg 2009) should be abandoned for their lack of specificity and because they occlude the analysis of more complicated and singular social, political, and economic processes.

Whether one chooses to employ the terms *race, ethnicity, ethnicization*, and *racialization*, one common emphasis is that they do not signify empirical realities in the world but rather social processes of boundary making. Nevertheless, in both the academic and the lay uses of the terms, *ethnicity* and *race* signal culture and biology, respectively (Munasinghe 1997). However, this distinction is an uneasy one, too, because whatever is defined as biology or the body is already determined socioculturally: "Although the concept of race appeals to biologically based human characteristics (so-called phenotypes), the selection of these particular human features for purposes of racial signification is always necessarily a social and historical process" (Omi and Winant 1994, 59). To highlight the embodied aspect of racialization, in my work I draw on Robert Miles and Malcolm Brown's definition of *racialization*: "Where biological and/or somatic features (real or imagined) are signified we speak of racialization as a specific modality of ethnicisation" (2003, 99). Affect situates this real or imagined somatization of difference within the broader political and economic context by working through classed and gendered forms of subjectivation. As Berg and Ramos-Zayas argue, "The consequences of both affective manifestations (self-fashioning) and affective being (self-reflection) carry significantly different political-economic consequences for racialized populations" (2015, 656).

Among the scholars of the Ottoman Empire and modern Turkey, there is considerable resistance to employing "race" as an analytical category based on a narrow definition. According to these scholars, it is not racism or racialization unless there is an explicit reference to race (*ırk*). On the one hand, this distinction is a necessary precaution: race is the central logic and the most dominant element of marking the social difference in the European colonial and postcolonial experience, and it is important to read the history of the Ottoman Empire and modern Turkey on its own terms rather than through the lens of European history (Göçek 2013). In addition, "race" has a dangerous history of reiteration in the social sciences, which was criticized for contributing to the racialization of social difference (Banton 1977; Webster 1992). However, relegating race and racism solely to European colonial experience and denying the profound influence of European racism on Turkish nationalism run the risk of overlooking how racial grammars operate through different vocabularies in various social settings by acquiring gendered, sexualized, and classed meanings (Wekker 2016). Moreover, racialization operates not only through explicit references to racial hierarchies articulated as biological differences but also through silences, omissions, gestures, imaginaries, and affects. Refusing to read those signs as racialization has rendered the racial and colonial imaginaries[4] at work in Turkish society invisible and has contributed to the erroneous conceptualization of Turkish nationalism as "civic" and "inclusive" rather than ethnoracial and discriminatory as well as to the fervent denial of racism in Turkish society (Gökay and Whitman 2017).

Throughout the histories of the Ottoman Empire and the Turkish Republic, racial and colonial imaginaries, discourses, and moral/affective tropes have been mobilized in many instances to define Kurds (Klein 2011; Makdisi 2002a; Maksudyan 2005), enabling the Turkish state to implement policies ranging from assimilation to massacres.[5] The Orientalist and

---

4. What I refer to here as "colonial imaginaries" and "colonial tropes" are the discursive elements that link the real or imagined features of Kurdistan to the people living there. These features are derived from or show a significant resemblance to Western colonial imaginaries. An example comes from Ayşe Öncü's analysis of the contemporary Turkish TV series that takes place in Kurdistan, in which "the East," a euphemism used to represent Kurdistan, is denoted as a harsh and unyielding landscape, causing the moral codes of the "eastern people" to be merciless and ruthless. Öncü draws parallels between the description of the East as empty and barren lands and the Zionist narrative of Palestine as "empty land" and argues that the colonial trope of emptiness situates the colony outside of time and history and resignifies it as in need of Western intervention and cultivation (2011, 57).

5. Although tracing the genealogy of the racialization of Kurds in Turkey is a long-neglected and important intellectual task, it exceeds the limits and aims of this chapter. However, influenced by postcolonial studies, historians and sociologists of the Ottoman Empire and the Turkish Republic in particular have been attending to the construction of social difference (Göçek 2013; Tezcan 2012), the intellectual roots and practices of modernization, centralization, and nation-state formation in the management of social difference (Deringil 1999; Yosmaoğlu 2006). Scholars have read the concurrent transformation

colonial discourses on Kurds have always drawn on metaphors of animality, savagery, primitiveness, and monstrosity (Deringil 2003; Türkyılmaz 2016; Yonucu 2008) and have included details such as skin color, body hair, and even a widespread belief that Kurds have tails. Three decades of war between the Kurdistan Workers' Party (Partîya Karkerên Kurdistanê, PKK) and the Turkish state has also added the term *terrorists* to this racializing vocabulary. However, neither was Turkish nationalism, which constructed Turkishness as the identity of the dominant/ruling people, a singular narrative, nor did the racialization of Kurds follow a linear path or a coherent ideology.

Building on the concept of the racial contract in critical whiteness studies, Barış Ünlü argues that the construction of Turkishness was based on "two unspoken and unwritten agreements among Muslims of Anatolia between 1915 and 1925, what I call the Muslimness Contract and the Turkishness Contract, respectively" (2016, 399).[6] Ünlü argues that after the non-Muslim population of the empire in Anatolia was largely eliminated by a series of population exchanges, massacres, and genocides, it was stipulated that Muslims of different ethnic origins (Circassian, Bosnian, Bulgarian,

---

of the peripheries of the Ottoman Empire in conjunction with the rise of colonial modes of thinking toward the periphery (Deringil 2003; Makdisi 2002a, 2002b), regimes of movement and mobility (Kasaba 2009), and the transformation of the eastern Kurdish peripheries and borderlands (Ateş 2013; Klein 2011; Özok-Gündoğan 2014). The rise of Turkish nationalism and histories of racial thinking and race science (Alemdaroğlu 2005; Eissenstat 2005; Üngör 2008) are crucial for understanding not only the foundational violence of the Turkish Republic (Üngör 2011) but also the interconnected histories of inclusion/exclusion of non-Muslim minorities and Kurds (Cora 2015; Ekmekçioğlu 2014), the relation of Turkish nationalism and the nation-state with Kurds (Aslan 2011; Yeğen 2007, 2011), and the Orientalism and colonial modes of governing inherent to the Turkish nation-state (Türkyılmaz 2016; Zeydanlıoğlu 2012). In addition, there is a sizable literature on Kurdish nationalism and other ideological, historical, and political modes of self-making of Kurds (Bozarslan 2003; Gündoğan 2015; Vali 2003; van Bruinessen 2003; Watts 2010). All this literature prepares the groundwork for a genealogy of the racialization of Kurds in Turkey to reveal not only discrimination and marginalization of Kurds but also the processes of the self-formation of Kurdish people as a collective subject through the political acts of ethnoracial boundary making.

6. *Volume editors' note*: See also chapter 3 by Ünlü in this volume.

Kurdish, Arab, and so on) should be assimilated into the dominant Turkish identity. They could enjoy the privileges of being Turkish as long as they did not resist assimilation and did not pronounce the atrocities that happened to non-Muslims and Kurds. This actively sought ignorance was the guarantee not only of privilege but also of a clear conscience.

Among the Muslim groups targeted, Kurds made up the largest and were the only ones with a history of self-government in their homelands that was far from the Turkish state's reach due to those homelands' geographic and demographic qualities. Therefore, the state took much more violent measures against the Kurds, such as massacres, deportations, social engineering, and memory politics (Üngör 2011). Kurds have also been the only Muslim ethnic group to resist assimilation and to actively struggle throughout the past century for various forms of self-determination. Since the beginning of the 1980s, the PKK's armed struggle and Kurdish politics have made it impossible to ignore the Kurdish people, leading to a crisis of Turkishness. As Ünlü (2016) notes, within the relatively liberal climate of the 2000s, "the Kurdish question" began to be more freely discussed, further leading to the disruption to the official state narrative, while also evoking intense feelings of loss and resentment in those who have thus far harvested the benefits of Turkishness.

From the long history of ideologies, discourses, and practices of inclusion/exclusion of the Kurds in Turkey, what has survived to the present in Turkey's contemporary social imaginary are fragments of discourses, racial grammars, and affective, imaginary, symbolic elements of discrimination. As Dicle Koğacıoğlu notes, the racialization of Kurds in Turkey is not an incitement to discourse in which race is pronounced explicitly; instead, "it work[s] by silencing even the name of what it bans" (2011, 204). In other words, the racialization of Kurds generally does not include explicit references to a "Kurdish race" as different from a "Turkish race." However, the absence of the term *race* has not made "racial" perception and racist measures disappear. The latter are instead expressed with a different term, *culture* (Koğacıoğlu 2011, 204).

Étienne Balibar, building on Pierre-André Tagiuieff's definition of *differentialist racism*, argues that the new racism of the era of decolonization in France "fits into a framework of 'racism without races.' ... It is a racism whose dominant theme is not biological heredity but the insurmountability of cultural differences," and in this way "culture can also function like a nature [sic]" (1991, 21). However, as Ann Laura Stoler argues, cultural criteria have always been formative of categories of political exclusion and racial membership: "'Cultural racism' was not a recent, postmodern variation on an old theme but itself a colonial phenomenon" (2002, 17). Hence, the absence of the term *race* concerning the Kurds indicates neither newer nor milder forms of racism compared to a biological racism that builds on explicitly pronounced biological differences.

In recent years, some scholars have turned to the terms *ethnicization*, *racialization*, *racism*, and *coloniality* to analyze the attribution of negative qualities to Kurdish identity in contemporary Turkish and Kurdish publics (Dirik 2018; Ergin 2014; Gönen 2011; Saraçoğlu 2008, 2009; Yarkın 2020, Yıldırım 2019). Cenk Saraçoğlu defines the subject of his study as "ethnicization": "The processes through which middle-class people in Izmir, a metropolis in Turkey, construct the migrants from Eastern Anatolia as 'Kurdish' and as 'ethnic others'" (2008, 44). His research reveals the contemporary language of racialization in western Turkey, in which the stereotypes of Kurds as "ignorant and cultureless," "benefit scroungers," "invaders," "separatists," "disrupters of urban life" prevail, with quite typical racist explanations such as Kurds having many children being offered as proof of "invasion." Similarly, Murat Ergin (2014) identifies the social process of assigning negative qualities to Kurds after the 1990s as racialization and pays particular attention to embodied racial stereotypes. Saraçoğlu and Ergin argue that racialization is a recent phenomenon that became prevalent only after being Kurdish was recognized as a distinct identity. This argument, however, is built on the assumption that the previous modality of racialization—namely, the erasure of Kurdishness from public discourses—allowed Kurds to remain a racially unmarked group. It neglects the continuities between the previous forms of racialization of Kurds and the contemporary ones. It also undermines the role of Turkish state racism in the ethnoracial distribution of privilege in Turkey.

Zeynep Gönen, in her research in Izmir, the third-largest city of Turkey, focuses on the restructuring of the police force and its "deliberate strategy of profiling and criminalization of ethno-racially differentiated and gendered urban poor populations, especially Kurdish migrants and Roma people" (2011, 2–3). Her work recognizes earlier forms of racialization of Kurds as part of the political history of the construction of Kurdish people and sees both the continuities and the breaks in these processes (248). Gönen, like Ergin, underlines the systematic and institutional nature of racialization. She argues that racialization draws on certain bodily features (dark skin, hairy body) as well as on negative cultural markers attributed to Kurds (crude manners, unruliness, propensity for violence, moral depravity, the production of many children, backwardness, laziness, incivility) and operates through other social categories of social difference, such as gender, class, place of origin, language, and accent.

Finally, Güllistan Yarkın (2020) examines Kurdish homeownership as an antiracist practice among Kurdish migrants who fled from the war in Kurdistan in 1990s and settled in a slum neighborhood of Istanbul. She demonstrates that racist tropes such as "dirty Kurds," "they breed quickly," and "they are terrorists" have very real material consequences in the everyday lives of Kurdish migrants because homeowners and contractors, the majority of whom are Turkish, do not rent to Kurds, which forces them to live in their workplaces and to endure hunger to save money to buy a home. Yarkın's study also shows how racism against Kurds should be analyzed in relation to the colonial violence of the Turkish state as well as to the coloniality of a Turkish identity that is based on an imagined superiority over Kurds. Without the analysis of Turkish coloniality and its racialized hierarchies, studies of anti-Kurdish racism are doomed to remain descriptive and to fall short of explaining how it constitutes the backbone of Turkey's political economy (from homeownership to labor regimes) and social life (e.g., who marries whom, who neighbors whom).

The two modalities of racism—namely, the erasure of Kurdishness from public life and its reformulation as "culture"—allow the reproduction of racism by reinforcing the Turkish nationalist claim that there is no racism against Kurds and that the symbolic and sometimes physical violence toward them is a reaction only to those Kurds who are involved in the Kurdish political movement. The next section examines how the stigma of potential support for the movement, which implicates all Kurds (supporters and nonsupporters alike), is only one link in a long chain of racialized signification of more clearly colonial and racial elements such as dark skin color, affects such as pity and disgust, and bans on speaking one's native tongue.

The Hallmark of Racialization: The Materiality and Affectivity of Dark Skin

The preoccupation with skin color is a distinct feature of racialization in Turkey. Even though Kurds and Turks are phenotypically indistinguishable from each other, attributing darker skin and darker hair to Kurds is a discourse firmly rooted in their public representations. For instance, as Murat Ergin notes, "In popular culture, Kurdishness is associated with a prototype combining culture and physical features: the *kıro*. *Kıro* is a distorted version of the Kurdish word *kuro*, which means boy or son, a stereotype in Turkish meaning uncouth, vulgar, and lowbrow. In Turkish humour magazines, the uncivilized characters with dark skin and hairy bodies always turn out to be Kurds, sometimes euphemistically called Easterner[s]" (2014, 330). This public representation is deeply tied to class and gender. *Kıro* is a Kurdish working-class young man who has recently migrated from Kurdistan to the metropolitan cities of western Turkey, who works in informal and temporary jobs such as construction, shipping and handling, and selling fresh produce in open-air markets and who speaks Turkish with a Kurdish accent.[7]

Dark skin is a marker of race and class in the context of farm labor as well. It also has a gender aspect to it because most Kurdish women on the farm are at pains to protect their skin from the sun to meet with the normative standards of beauty. They wear several layers of clothing, covering as much of their skin as possible, and use socks, gloves, and rags to cover

---

7. The representation of the Kurds as having a darker complexion has also been taken up subversively by Kurds themselves, as in the naming of the Kurdish popular-culture magazine *Esmer*. Etymologically rooted in the Arabic word meaning "dark-colored," especially "brown," the Turkish word *esmer* is used exclusively to describe a darker complexion. However, the proud ownership of the dark skin does not resonate with the broader Kurdish public or get resignified in a cultural movement such as "Black is beautiful."

the areas in between clothes. They wear caps, cover their faces and necks with several headscarves and find different methods of creating as much shade as possible around their eyes. Men, in contrast, wear only T-shirts, pants, and sometimes hats and thus perform the meticulously calculated masculine indifference to normative beauty.

The day before Zilan and I were supposed to go downtown to shop at the marketplace, Zilan came up to me:

ZILAN: We all get sunburnt here together, so we don't realize [how much we have burned], [and when] we go to the town to shop, we become blue!
DENIZ: What do you mean?
ZILAN: I mean our skin gets so dark that "black" is not enough to describe us. Once we went to the town, and we got off the truck, a woman turned to us and said: "Gypsies invaded the town."
DENIZ: No way! Also, what's wrong with being a Gypsy?
ZILAN: Yeah, they are also human.

I would experience the uncomfortable gaze of the women of the town as we were getting off the truck the next day. Zilan approached me and said: "You see how they look at us? They must have never seen a human before!" I nodded silently. Among the dozens of times that I had been to a marketplace in Turkey, with other women and alone, I had never been pushed around as much as I was that day. We were always in the wrong: accused of blocking a customer's view and another's access to the counter, of sitting on benches for too long—in short, of taking up too much space in their world. In Zilan's words, we had become "blue," a color that no human skin is tinted.

Blackness is always entangled with dehumanization through metaphors used to describe racialized populations, such as "primitive," "animal," "savage," and "monster," as well as through its implicit or explicit historical references to racial slavery, colonial genocides, and everyday forms of political violence. Alexander Weheliye defines blackness[8] as "a

---

8. I choose not to capitalize the *b* in *blackness* because the proper name "Black" is used primarily to refer to the people of African descent in the Euro-American context.

changing system of unequal power structures that apportion and delimit which humans can lay claim to full human status and which humans cannot" (2014, 3). Race, Weheliye argues, disciplines humanity into full humans, not-quite humans, and nonhumans. The constantly changing designation of the degree of humanness of a racialized group involves not only a socially cultivated practice of seeing their skin color but also the affects and sensory information that an encounter with the other generates.

Zilan's response to her racialization by the townspeople was not an appeal to universal humanity. She instead morally condemned the owner of the gaze and reversed their discourse to deny them humanity: if they have never seen a human before, they cannot be human. Furthermore, she adopted the gaze she morally condemned and took it to its extreme through a discursive transgression of color, from black to blue. Underlying the sarcastic statement that Kurdish workers turn blue, there is the reinforcement of a community of those whose skins get darker under the sun together gradually and to whom one another's blackness is not visible. Nevertheless, the moral objection to the experience of being racialized by Turks does not take the edge off the Kurds' reluctant acceptance of the third, the "Gypsy," as being "also human."

The reproduction of the racial gaze does not take place only between the seer and the seen. As Michel Serres (1982) argues, history is based not on the slave's recognition of the master and the master's appropriation of the slave's world-transforming action but on the inclusion of a third element in the parasitic relation through which they make sense of each other. Sometimes the third is the color blue, which makes sense of black and white; other times, it is an anthropologist from America who talks to both Turkish engineers and Kurdish workers; at other times, it is the imaginary "Gypsy," who for both Kurds and Turks is undeniably black.

Not surprisingly, during my fieldwork in 2014 and 2015 "the Syrian" also became the third of racialization in Turkey. Since the beginning of

---

As I argue later, I believe the grid of blackness is more global than it is imagined in the Western academy.

the Syrian War in 2011, millions of Syrians have fled from war to Turkey. Turkey does not recognize them as refugees but has granted them the vague and precarious status of "persons under temporary protection." Being deprived of refugee rights such as residency and work permits as well as material support from international organizations, Syrian refugees quickly got integrated into the informal labor force of Turkey, including migrant farm labor. In Turkish public discourses, "the Syrian" came to be defined through a plethora of embodied and affective racializing tropes previously used for working-class Kurds, such as "poor and needy" but also "greedy scroungers," "overly sexualized," "ill-mannered," "dirty," and "dangerous." Their skin color was also assumed to be undeniably black. The racialization of Syrians, just like that of Kurds and Gypsies, was not a unidirectional discourse used by the dominant against the subordinate but was more often than not triangulated through other groups' racialization and processes of social and self-formation.

No wonder the story of the Turkish woman who mistook Baran, a young Kurdish worker, for a Syrian refugee became the hit story of the summer. Baran was the dream child of all Kurdish migrant workers. His grandfather, who was previously a migrant farmworker, had moved to western Turkey permanently in the 1990s. After twenty years of doing agricultural work, the family bought a few small fields and moved from being farmworkers to being small farmers. Now they were paying four additional farmworkers from their extended family in Kurdistan, who came to work for them for a couple of months. Baran and his unmarried siblings kept working in the fields along with the additional farmworkers they hired, but they also attended much better schools in western Turkey than they would have if the family had stayed in Kurdistan. Eventually that spring, Baran took the national university exam and scored high enough to get into medical school.

On four different occasions, I heard Baran tell the story of his being mistaken for a Syrian refugee by this woman. First, I overheard him while he was whispering it to his brother with a grim face, after making him promise not to tell anyone. Then, realizing I was working close by, he told it to me as a story of discrimination with much resentment. The next day, I heard him giggling with his sister about what had happened. After dinner that day, as the family was sitting in the courtyard of their house, his sister Evîn poked him and said, "Come on, tell it, it's hilarious!" This time, he recounted it as stand-up comedy in the presence of all family members.

Baran was walking on the street when an old woman came out of her house and told him, "Come here." When he went up to her, she asked if he was from Syria. He said, "No, I'm from Mardin." She said that there was baklava left over from the Eid: Would Baran like to eat it? It had been eight or nine days since Eid had passed. Baran told this part of the story with a spectacular mix of mimics and gestures: "I looked at the baklava; it had gone soooo black [pekleve bû rrrrrrreş]! I said, 'You eat it; we don't eat this.'" Then she looked at him, she looked at the baklava, and she walked over to the garbage bin in the street and threw it out. Upon hearing this story, the entire family burst into laughter, and Evîn said: "The woman is right; he has become just like the Syrians: he's the same height, he's black, so the woman said, 'He's from Syria, let him eat this' [Ma newe? Ew eyn Sûrî bû. Boy eyn ye, e reş e. Jinik got qey ew Sûrî ne. Bila bixwe]!" Another burst of laughter. . . .

The first question that the old woman asked Baran was "Are you from Syria?" By simply looking at him, the old woman knew that he was not Turkish. She might have come to that conclusion from his darkened skin, his height, or other bodily features, as his sister remarked. The old clothes he wore on the farm and the dust on his shoes might also have been clues implicating his class. The majority of the Turkish children in the area where Baran works do not work in the fields; Kurdish and Syrian children work in their stead. When the woman asked Baran if he was from Syria, she was actually asking about a class difference mapped onto the racialized body of the Syrian.

Place of origin is an important identity marker across Turkey; each place-name gives clues about the ethnoracial and religious background of the persons from there. However, in the case of Kurdish-majority provinces, the name of the province immediately becomes a marker of an ethnoracial difference, just like the larger geographic referents "the East" and "the Easterner" are used as euphemisms for "Kurdistan" and "Kurds," respectively. When Baran told the women that he was from Mardin, that information did not change anything for the Turkish woman; in her mind, both Kurds and Syrians would yearn for the old baklava that she would otherwise throw away.

For Baran, the difference between him and the old woman was no less essential: although he was born in Bursa, the western city where both he and the woman lived, he told her that he was from Mardin, the Kurdish city where his parents had been born. The strong ties of Kurdish identity to the Kurdish homeland make the latter a source of pride in the self-making of Kurdish people, as it was in Baran's case. Yet when we look at how the story was shared, how it acquired different affective features as he told it, and how it ended up in the genre of farce as he recounted it in front of the whole family, it is not hard to see that pride is not the only affective relation Baran and his family have to their Kurdishness. What was it that made the doubling of the blackness of the baklava with that of Baran's skin laughable? And what was it that got released in the communal laughter?

It could be argued that they laughed at the woman's ridiculousness. However, no one showed any objection to the woman's image of "the Syrian." On the contrary, they shared the same image of the Syrian as a dark-skinned, short, and pitiful figure, as Evîn pointed out. Furthermore, it is highly doubtful that the story would have been equally laughable if Evîn—Baran's sister, who is very resentful of not having been sent to school and who is as careful as any other woman Kurdish migrant worker to protect her skin from getting darker—had been mistaken for a Syrian refugee. Could it be that the story was laughable because Baran was so undeniably different from a Syrian refugee that the old woman's racialization of him did not matter? But if that were the case, he would not have been offended so much in the first place. In addition, as more and more Syrian refugees started working as migrant farmworkers alongside workers from Kurdistan since 2011, Kurdish farmworkers developed a collective resentment toward being equated with Syrians. As several Kurdish migrant workers said to me, "You know Syrians; we are the Syrians of here."

Let us remember that what changed the tone of the story was the family's laughter, starting with Baran's sister's giggling. Later, it was the family's collective laughter that changed this instance of racialization into farce, while reproducing the racialization of "the Syrian" and reaffirming Baran's difference from him. It was an instance of racialization similar to when the women of the town said, "Gypsies invaded the town," and Zilan's reluctant acceptance that Gypsies were "also human" even after I insisted on asking, "What's wrong with being a Gypsy?" Zilan's distortion of the discourse that denied her humanity by redirecting it at the Gypsies, Baran's family's laughter at his supposed similarity to a Syrian, and the resentful comment "You know Syrians, we are the Syrians of here" shatter both the binary distinction of the dominant versus subordinate ethnic groups mapped over the binary of the oppressor and the oppressed as well as the progressive fantasies of the solidarity of the oppressed. Tadiar argues: "Beneath the level of given social identities, whose genealogies we participate in making and revising so they become the proper protagonists of our critique, remaindered forms of life point to subaltern human pathways of transmission and influence through which life-making affective properties and sensibilities are invisibly passed across distinct communities" (2015, 155).

None of the migrant workers' reactions depicted earlier allows us to make the workers into "the proper protagonists of our critique." Nevertheless, these reactions are the life-making pathways formed through embodied and racialized affects that Kurdish migrants adopt and, as Ramos-Zayas notes, "enter social consciousness affectively" (2011, 27), allowing them to cope with racialization through life-making and self-affirming discursive and affective interventions.

The racialization of Kurdish workers may operate through overtly racist mechanisms, such as employers' bans on speaking Kurdish on the farms of western Turkey, which many workers have experienced. In such cases, Kurdish workers have sometimes stood up against their employers but at other times have bit their tongues and kept working for fear of losing their jobs. Therefore, although in other contexts the refusal to see a difference between two groups of people could mean resisting racialization, in the case of Kurds the reduction of their self-identified difference as a people distinct from Turks—with their own language, homeland, and "ways of doing" (Stewart 1996)—to a difference of geographic origins redefined as "the East" should also be seen as a modality of racialization.

However, racialization also relies on covert symbols that do not have a racist meaning outside specific contexts and work through absences and silences that invite inferences (Hill 2009, 41). Zilan and Baran's self-observation of their bodies as black, short, and not properly human through the colonizer Turks' eyes is a major aspect of being a colonial subject, as are their desire to be white and not to be seen as less than human. Yet there is no neat division between the colonizer and the colonized, the white and the black, but rather continuous negotiations over the definitions of who is less black, less monstrous, more cultured, and so on. Homi Bhabha draws on Frantz Fanon's brilliant analysis of the always-incomplete identification of the black man with the colonizer or with himself and argues: "It is not the colonialist Self or the colonized Other, but the disturbing difference in-between that constitutes the figure of colonial otherness—the white man's artifice inscribed on the black man's body" (1994, 45). In the instances described earlier, it is through "the Gypsy" and "the Syrian" that this distance is measured, and it is through their affective and embodied negation that the colonized Kurdish working-class body aims at whiteness. It is a whiteness that, by the very nature of the relationship of coloniality, can neither be achieved nor be abandoned.

In the case of Kurdish migrant workers in Turkey, these silently invited inferences, racialized images, and affects are sometimes used to justify the disproportional economic exploitation of Kurds compared to Turks; at other times, they are mapped on to discourses of "terrorism" and "separatism" to justify the militarization of the workplace, which replaces the formal mechanisms of labor control and labor discipline. Since the end of the latest cease-fire between the Turkish state and the PKK in 2015, these images and affects not only have increasingly been used to racialize Kurds as "terrorists" but also have added to the Turks' identification with the Turkish state, reinforcing the colonial nature of the Turkish farm as an economically deregulated and politically securitized workplace.

Conclusion

Racialization shapes the Kurdish migrant laborers' experience in rural western Turkey not only in terms of their marginalization and subordination but also in terms of their self-formation and boundary making through embodied and affective ways of making sense of that subordination. Between the metaphors of animality and the racialized affects of aversion to Kurds' "improper sexuality," a Turkish engineer can erase his feelings of pity for Kurds working twelve hours under the sun. Another Turkish engineer, who had overcome her hatred for Kurds to a certain degree by getting to know them in person, can instantaneously reverse her discourse by extending her disgust for the toilets in the camps to the bodies of the Kurdish workers through their smell. Her racialized self-making as a Turk who is undeniably different from and superior to the Kurd depends on making the camp's toilets "their toilets" and the labor for the firm "our work." As she remarked, "*We* make *them* do all *our* work," although she knew very well on which side of the labor–capital divide she stood. Thus, racialization not only displaces class antagonism onto racial and colonial difference but also replaces the formal structures of labor control and labor discipline with racialized affective mechanisms. Thus, the workplace hierarchies, which demand that Kurdish workers be reprimanded like children, if need be, are justified through the translation of the worker's class position into the racialized other's moral failure and "lack of culture."

Neither race and racialization nor whiteness and blackness are metaphors in this study. My choice to analyze the ethnoracial marginalization and self-making of Kurds in this framework does not come from these factors' *similarity* to "Blackness" in the Euro-American colonial contexts. Histories, vocabularies, collections of images, and affects entangled with race, blackness, and whiteness travel and get translated in all kinds of unexpected ways. In Stoler's words, they become "gut feelings" and prepare the conditions for "the instantiation of inequalities" in different colonial and postcolonial contexts (2018, 220). In the ethnographic instances I have described in this chapter, anxieties about those who present as black-skinned display so many elements of the racialization of colonized subjects (smell, dehumanization, oversexualization, cultural appropriateness, and so on) that those references alone show us how intertwined Turkish coloniality is with its Euro-American counterparts. Therefore, instead of repeating the obsolete questions "But is the oppression of Kurdish people really about race or class?" and "Are Kurds treated as an ethnic or racial group in Turkey?," focusing on how Kurds continuously *become black* in particular ways opens up a new field of inquiry on the specificities of Turkish coloniality and its relationship to the racialization of Kurds. More concretely, doing so allows us to ask: What constitutes Kurdish blackness? What is its affective baseline? What are its material support mechanisms? How does it operate differentially for working-class versus upper-class Kurds? How does it relate to spectacular and mundane forms of political violence? And how are the ways of seeing, feeling, and sensing blackness formed, negotiated, and resisted in everyday encounters with others?

However, Kurds are not just victims in these processes; they also participate in these racializing logics and react in ways that do not necessarily challenge the racial hierarchies pervasive in society. Then, as Tadiar asks, can race as a theoretical question and political intervention reveal the colonial relations embedded not only in this labor practice but also in society at large? Can we, for example, analyze the self-making of a migrant Kurdish family through laughter as an affective racial strategy that aims to keep distance both from the whiteness of the Turkish woman that they deem immoral and from the absolute blackness of the Syrian refugee, which they think they have surpassed by having moved up the social ladder? What does it tell us about the relationship between the legacies of the contested blackness of the Kurd, the continuously reaffirmed blackness of the "Gypsy," the newly forming blackness of the Syrian as the poster child of human tragedy, and the effects of the Kurds' anxious attempts to differentiate themselves from the Syrians in their self-making?

As Tadiar notes, "Colonialism was itself the invention of racism as we know it," and decolonization today must build on understanding the contemporary racial logics of the contemporary workings of empire (2015, 137). In looking at the everyday struggles of Kurdish migrant workers in rural western Turkey, my work examines a broader base of colonial relations in Turkey than a simple confrontation between state violence and anticolonial Kurdish resistance. Racialization embedded in this migrant labor regime operates by reorganizing relations of production at a national level and thus turns Kurdistan into a repository of labor for western Turkey. It shows how the embodied and affective economy of racialization, which operates through the formation of Kurds, Turks, and others as gendered, raced, and classed subjects, is not simply a social by-product of power relations in Turkish society but constitutes the affective backbone of Turkey's political economy.

References

Alemdaroğlu, Ayça. 2005. "Politics of the Body and Eugenic Discourse in Early Republican Turkey." *Body & Society* 11, no. 3: 61–76.
Aslan, Senem. 2007. "'Citizen, Speak Turkish!': A Nation in the Making." *Nationalism and Ethnic Politics* 13, no. 2: 245–72.
Ateş, Sabri. 2013. *Ottoman-Iranian Borderlands: Making a Boundary, 1843–1914*. New York: Cambridge Univ. Press.
Balibar, Étienne. 1991. "Is there a 'Neo-Racism?'" In *Race, Nation, Class: Ambiguous Identities*, by Étienne Balibar and Immanuel Wallerstein, 17–28. London: Verso.
Banton, Michael. 1977. *The Idea of Race*. London: Tavistock.
Berg, Ulla D., and Ana Y. Ramos-Zayas. 2015. "Racializing Affect: A Theoretical Proposition." *Current Anthropology* 56, no. 5: 654–77.
Bhabha, Homi. 1994. *The Location of Culture*. London: Routledge.
Bourgois, Philippe. 1989. *Ethnicity at Work: Divided Labor on a Central American Banana Plantation*. Baltimore: Johns Hopkins Univ. Press.
Bozarslan, Hamit. 2003. "Kurdish Nationalism in Turkey: From Tacit Contract to Rebellion (1919–1925)." In *Essays on the Origins of Kurdish Nationalism*, edited by Abbas Vali, 163–90. Costa Mesa, CA: Mazda.
Cora, Yaşar Tolga. 2015. "Doğu'da Kürt-Ermeni çatışmasının sosyoekonomik arkaplanı." In *1915: Öncesi ve sonrasıyla Ermeni siyaseti, tehcir ve soykırım*, edited by Fikret Adanır and Oktay Özel, 126–39. Istanbul: Tarih Vakfı Yurt Yayınları.
De Genova, Nicholas. 2005. *Working the Boundaries: Race, Space, and "Illegality" in Mexican Chicago*. Durham, NC: Duke Univ. Press.
Deringil, Selim. 1999. *The Well-Protected Domains: Ideology and the Legitimation of Power in the Ottoman Empire*. London: I. B. Tauris.
———. 2003. "'They Live in a State of Nomadism and Savagery': The Late Ottoman Empire and the Post-colonial Debate." *Comparative Studies in Society and History* 45, no. 2: 311–42.
Dirik, Dilar. 2018. "The Revolution of Smiling Women: Stateless Democracy and Power in Rojava." In *Routledge Handbook of Postcolonial Politics*, edited by Olivia Rutazibwa and Robbie Shilliam, 222–38. London: Routledge.

Eissenstat, Howard. 2005. "Metaphors of Race and Discourse of Nation." In *Race and Nation: Ethnic Systems in the Modern World*, edited by Paul Spickard, 239–57. Abingdon, UK: Routledge.

Ekmekçioğlu, Lerna. 2014. "Republic of Paradox: The League of Nations, Minority Protection Regime, and the New Turkey's Step-Citizens." *International Journal of Middle East Studies* 46, no. 4: 657–79.

Ergin, Murat. 2014. "The Racialization of Kurdish Identity in Turkey." *Ethnic and Racial Studies* 37, no. 2: 322–41.

Göçek, Fatma Müge. 2013. "Parameters of a Postcolonial Sociology of the Ottoman Empire." In *Decentering Social Theory*, edited by Julian Go, 73–104. Wagon Lane, UK: Emerald Group.

Gökay, Bülent, and Darrell Whitman. 2017. "'No Racism Here': Modern Turkey and the Question of Race and National Identity." *Links International Journal of Socialist Renewal*, June 12. At http://links.org.au/no-racism-here-modern-turkey-race-national-identity.

Goldberg, David Theo. 2009. *The Threat of Race: Reflections on Racial Neoliberalism*. Malden, MA: Blackwell.

Gönen, Zeynep. 2011. "Neoliberal Politics of Crime: The Izmir Public Order Police and Criminalization of the Urban Poor in Turkey since the Late 1990s." PhD diss., State Univ. of New York at Binghamton.

Gregg, Melissa, and Gregory J. Seigworth. 2010. "An Inventory of Shimmers." In *The Affect Theory Reader*, edited by Melissa Gregg and Gregory J. Seigworth, 1–25. Durham, NC: Duke Univ. Press.

Gündoğan, Azad Zana. 2015. "Space, State-Making, and Contentious Kurdish Politics in the East of Turkey." In *The Kurdish Issue in Turkey: A Spatial Perspective*, edited by Zeynep Gambetti and Joost Jongerden, 27–62. New York: Routledge.

Gutiérrez-Rodríguez, Encarnación. 2014. "Domestic Work–Affective Labor: On Feminization and the Coloniality of Labor." *Women's Studies International Forum* 46:45–53.

Hill, Jane H. 2009. *The Everyday Language of White Racism*. Chichester, UK: Wiley.

Kasaba, Reşat. 2009. *A Moveable Empire: Ottoman Nomads, Migrants, and Refugees*. Seattle: Univ. of Washington Press.

Klein, Janet. 2011. *The Margins of Empire: Kurdish Militias in the Ottoman Tribal Zone*. Stanford, CA: Stanford Univ. Press.

Koğacıoğlu, Dicle. 2011. "Knowledge, Practice, and Political Community: The Making of the 'Custom' in Turkey." *differences* 22, no. 1: 172–228.

Makdisi, Usama. 2002a. "Ottoman Orientalism." *American Historical Review* 107, no. 3: 768–96.

———. 2002b. "Rethinking Ottoman Imperialism: Modernity, Violence, and the Cultural Logic of Ottoman Reform." In *The Empire in the City: Arab Provincial Cities in the Ottoman Empire*, edited by Jens Hanssen, Thomas Philipp, and Stefan Weber, 29–48. Würzburg, Germany: Ergon Verlag.

Maksudyan, Nazan. 2005. "The *Turkish Review of Anthropology* and the Racist Face of Turkish Nationalism." *Cultural Dynamics* 17, no. 3: 291–322.

Mazzarella, William. 2009. "Affect: What Is It Good For?" In *Enchantments of Modernity: Empire, Nation, Globalization*, edited by Saurabh Dube, 291–309. New Delhi: Routledge.

McLaughlin, Eugene. 2005. "Recovering Blackness—Repudiating Whiteness: The *Daily Mail*'s Construction of the Five White Suspects Accused of the Racist Murder of Stephen Lawrence." In *Racialization: Studies in Theory and Practice*, edited by Karim Murji and John Solomos, 163–84. New York: Oxford Univ. Press.

Miles, Robert. 1989. *Racism*. London: Routledge.

Miles, Robert, and Malcolm Brown. 2003. *Racism*. London: Routledge.

Munasinghe, Viranjini. 1997. "Culture Creators and Culture Bearers: The Interface between Race and Ethnicity in Trinidad." *Transforming Anthropology* 6, nos. 1–2: 72–86.

Omi, Michael, and Howard Winant. 1994. *Racial Formation in the US: From the 1960s to the 1990s*. New York: Routledge.

Öncü, Ayşe. 2011. "Representing and Consuming 'the East' in Cultural Markets." *New Perspectives on Turkey* 45:49–73.

Özok-Gündoğan, Nilay. 2014. "Ruling the Periphery, Governing the Land: The Making of the Modern Ottoman State in Kurdistan, 1840–70." *Comparative Studies of South Asia, Africa, and the Middle East* 34, no. 1: 160–75.

Ramos-Zayas, Ana Yolanda. 2011. "Learning Affect/Embodying Race." In *A Companion to the Anthropology of the Body and Embodiment*, edited by Frances E. Mascia-Lees, 24–45. Malden, MA: Wiley-Blackwell.

Saraçoğlu, Cenk. 2008. "Migration, Neoliberalism, and Ethnicization: The Middle-Class Construction of Kurdish Migrants in Izmir, Turkey." PhD diss., Univ. of Western Ontario.

———. 2009. "'Exclusive Recognition': The New Dimensions of the Question of Ethnicity and Nationalism in Turkey." *Ethnic and Racial Studies* 32, no. 4: 640–58.

Serres, Michael. 1982. *The Parasite*. Translated by Lawrence R. Schehr. Baltimore: Johns Hopkins Univ. Press.
Stewart, Kathleen. 1996. *A Space on the Side of the Road: Cultural Poetics in an "Other" America*. Princeton, NJ: Princeton Univ. Press.
———. 2007. *Ordinary Affects*. Durham, NC: Duke Univ. Press.
Stoler, Ann Laura. 2002. *Carnal Knowledge and Imperial Power: Race and the Intimate in Colonial Rule*. Berkeley: Univ. of California Press.
———. 2018. "The Politics of 'Gut Feelings': On Sentiment in Governance and the Law." *KNOW: A Journal on the Formation of Knowledge* 2, no. 2: 207–28.
Tadiar, Neferti X. M. 2015. "Decolonization, 'Race,' and Remaindered Life under Empire." *Qui Parle: Critical Humanities and Social Sciences* 23, no. 2: 135–60.
Tezcan, Baki. 2012. "Ethnicity, Race, Religion, and Social Class: Ottoman Markers of Difference." In *The Ottoman World*, edited by Christine Woodhead, 159–70. London: Routledge.
Türkyılmaz, Zeynep. 2016. "Maternal Colonialism and Turkish Woman's Burden in Dersim: Educating the 'Mountain Flowers' of Dersim." *Journal of Women's History* 28, no. 3: 162–86.
Üngör, Uğur Ümit. 2008. "Geographies of Nationalism and Violence: Rethinking Young Turk 'Social Engineering.'" *European Journal of Turkish Studies* 7. At http://ejts.revues.org/2583.
———. 2011. *The Making of Modern Turkey: Nation and State in Eastern Anatolia 1913–1950*. New York: Oxford Univ. Press.
Ünlü, Barış. 2016. "The Kurdish Struggle and the Crisis of the Turkishness Contract." *Philosophy and Social Criticism* 42, nos. 4–5: 397–405.
Vali, Abbas. 2003. "Genealogies of the Kurds: Constructions of Nation and National Identity in Kurdish Historical Writing." In *Essays on the Origins of Kurdish Nationalism*, edited by Abbas Vali, 58–107. Costa Mesa, CA: Mazda.
Van Bruinessen, Martin. 2003. "Ehmedi Xani's Mem û Zin and Its Role in the Emergence of Kurdish National Awareness." In *Essays on the Origins of Kurdish Nationalism*, edited by Abbas Vali, 40–57. Costa Mesa, CA: Mazda.
Watts, Nicole F. 2010. *Activists in Office: Kurdish Politics and Protest in Turkey*. Seattle: Univ. of Washington Press.
Webster, Yehudi O. 1992. *Racialization of America*. New York: St. Martin's Press.
Weheliye, Alexander G. 2014. *Habeas Viscus: Racializing Assemblages, Biopolitics, and Black Feminist Theories of the Human*. Durham, NC: Duke Univ. Press.

Wekker, Gloria. 2016. *White Innocence: Paradoxes of Colonialism and Race*. Durham, NC: Duke Univ. Press.

Yarkın, Güllistan. 2020. "Fighting Racism in Turkey: Kurdish Homeownership as an Anti-racist Practice." *Ethnic and Racial Studies* 43, no. 15: 2705–23.

Yeğen, Mesut. 2007. "Turkish Nationalism and the Kurdish Question." *Ethnic and Racial Studies* 30, no. 1: 119–51.

———. 2011. "The Kurdish Question in Turkey: Denial to Recognition." In *Nationalisms and Politics in Turkey: Political Islam, Kemalism, and the Kurdish Issue*, edited by Marlies Casier and Joost Jongerden, 67–84. London: Routledge.

Yıldırım, Umut. 2019. "Space, Loss, and Resistance: A Haunted Pool-Map in South-Eastern Turkey." *Anthropological Theory* 19, no. 4: 440–69.

Yonucu, Deniz. 2008. "A Story of a Squatter Neighborhood: From the Place of the 'Dangerous Classes' to the 'Place of Danger.'" *Berkeley Journal of Sociology* 52:50–72.

Yosmaoğlu, İpek. 2006. "Counting Bodies, Shaping Souls: The 1903 Census and National Identity in Ottoman Macedonia." *International Journal of Middle East Studies* 38, no. 1: 55–77.

Zeydanlıoğlu, Welat. 2012. "Turkey's Kurdish Language Policy." *International Journal of the Sociology of Language* 217:99–125.

7

Anti-Kurdish Communal Violence in the Twenty-First Century

Origins, Patterns, Directions

Şefika Kumral

Kurdish civilians in the western towns and cities of Turkey have increasingly become targets of lynch mobs and riots in the twenty-first century. Since 2004, the instances of mob violence against Kurdish civilians have increased fourfold. The "trigger" or the "exogenous shock" of violence was different in each case. In certain cases, a personal fight sparked mass violence against Kurds; in other cases, workers speaking in Kurdish became targets of lynch mobs. Most importantly, whereas initial cases of anti-Kurdish mob violence in the early 2000s were met with shock and fear by the commentators and society in general, by 2020 they were by and large accepted as *business as usual*. This form of violence has become so regular and frequent that, in the words of a Kurdish resident, Kurdish civilians are "no longer safe" in the twenty-first-century cities and towns of Turkey.

This is a new form of ethnic violence, which is fundamentally different from the secessionist armed conflict between the Kurdistan Workers' Party (Partîya Karkerên Kurdistanê, PKK) and the Turkish armed forces that took place in the Kurdish region (corresponding to southeastern and some eastern parts of Turkey) throughout the 1980s and 1990s (Ergin 2014). The primary novelty of the post-2000 wave of ethnic violence resides in its *civic/popular nature*, whereby groups of civilians are the perpetrators of lynching attempts and collective raids against the Kurdish population. In other words, this violence can be categorized as *violence from below* because civic populations rather than the state are the main perpetrators of ethnic violence. Moreover, it can be characterized as *popular violence* because it goes beyond the confines of violence associated with nonstate political actors (such as skinhead violence against immigrants in Europe). This form of ethnic violence corresponds to what James Fearon and David Laitin call *communal or societal ethnic violence*, which is "violence between members of different ethnic groups that do[es] not directly involve arms of the state on either side" (1999, 9) and takes on various forms, such as ethnic riots, pogroms, feuding, and hate crimes.

In this chapter, I analyze the origins of anti-Kurdish communal violence in Turkey in the early twenty-first century and discuss it in light of competing explanations for the recent rise of ethnic violence in the world. In focusing on everyday and communal aspects of politics and violence targeting the Kurds of Turkey, the chapter goes beyond the study of state-perpetrated violence and large-scale armed conflict that dominates the literature on anti-Kurdish violence. Overall, the chapter brings a ground-up perspective by looking closely at why and how ordinary people are involved in and experience violence as both perpetrators and victims within the broader theoretical approaches/discussions of ethnic violence, including (1) economic deprivation/competition, (2) state capacity/weakness, and (3) authoritarianism/democratization. To assess the explanatory power of competing explanations in the context of anti-Kurdish communal violence in Turkey, the chapter relies on original quantitative and qualitative data I have compiled.

This chapter first and foremost shows that anti-Kurdish communal violence in western cities and towns of Turkey has been on the rise since the 2000s, when Turkey witnessed high growth rates and a relative decline in the intensity of armed conflict (see figure 7.1). Most importantly, the communal violence emerged in a period of *contested democratization*, whereby Kurdish masses actively pushed the government for inclusion, political recognition, and peace through social movement and electoral mobilization. Instead of economic grievances, resource-based competition, state incapacity, or fear associated with a security dilemma, the key process that produced the anti-Kurdish communal violence targeting Kurdish civilians in western parts of Turkey in the early 2000s was the political empowerment, collective action, and visibility of the Kurdish civilian population in this period. The overall

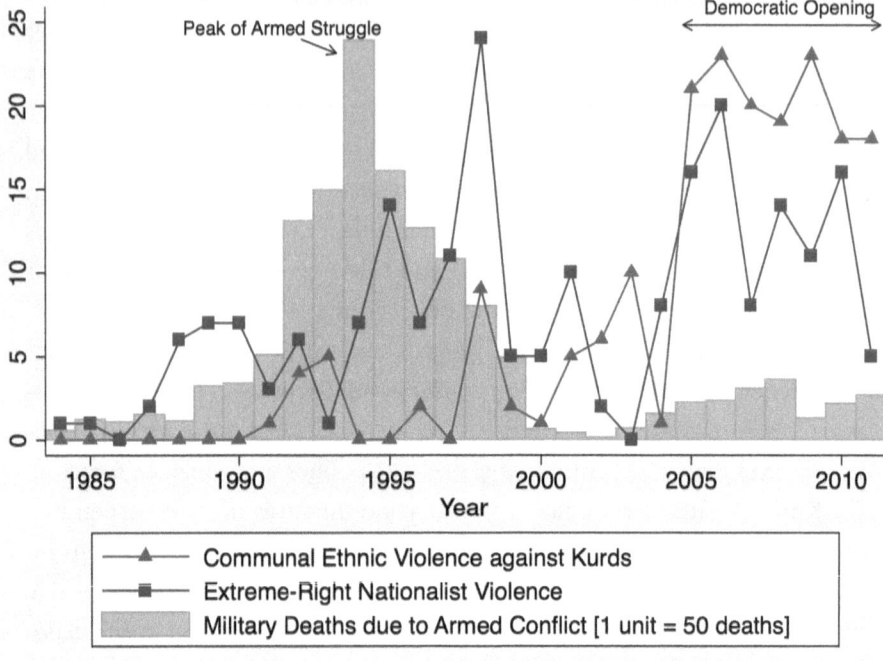

7.1. Trends in communal versus extreme-right nationalist violence and military deaths, 1984–2011. *Source*: The data on frequency of communal ethnic violence and extreme-right nationalist violence were calculated from the ENViT) database; the data on military deaths due to armed conflict are from Şener 2010.

analysis demonstrates the centrality of "democratic mobilization" of Kurds, but the in-depth qualitative analysis also shows that (1) economic factors were only partially relevant in relation to political factors, and (2) although *security fear* in relation to the armed conflict was not a major indicator to explain the upsurge of violence in the 2000s, it is nevertheless important in understanding how violence was framed by perpetrators.

A New Geography and Target of Violence

Incidents of anti-Kurdish communal violence take place in various cities and towns of western, northern, southern, and central Turkey, which are geographically detached from the primary locations of the armed conflict

(Bora 2008; Ergin 2014; Gambetti 2007; Patterson 2007). These new centers of societal ethnic violence also happened to be destination points for hundreds of thousands of internally displaced Kurds, who had migrated to metropolitan and industrial cities of western Anatolia in the late 1980s and 1990s, when the armed conflict between the Turkish armed forces and the PKK had come to a peak (Ayata and Yükseker 2005). These "new" Kurdish residents of historically "Turkish" cities and towns make up the primary targets of this new wave of nationalist collective violence in Turkey.

The targets of this violence are also new. Although there have been many incidents of deadly communal violence in the history of modern Turkey, their targets were often religious/sectarian minorities, who were openly perceived as "the other" in both official and societal conceptions of the Turkish nation. The riots targeting non-Muslims in Istanbul in September 1955, the anti-Alevi pogroms in Maraş and Çorum in 1978, and the massacre of Alevi intellectuals in Sivas in 1993 in the name of the "Turkish nation" and "Sunni Islam"—all belong to the darkest pages of the history of modern Turkey. The twenty-first-century violence is the first time that Kurds—who have historically been considered by official Turkish ideology as an integral part of the Turkish nation and regarded as *eastern Turks* by both official state ideology and the general public—have become targets of communal violence in the name of the Turkish nation.[1]

The instances of communal violence in Istanbul, Maraş and Çorum, and Sivas were very deadly incidents, but they did not produce a rising wave of communal violence. Anti-Kurdish communal violence in western Turkey, however, has been increasing throughout the 2000s and has gradually built up to a significant wave. Hence, it bears a historical resemblance to the wave of anti-Armenian violence in the Ottoman Empire in the late nineteenth and early twentieth centuries.

---

1. State-led violence targeting Kurdish civilians has been prevalent since the foundation of the Turkish Republic. Examples include the brutal repression of the Sheikh Said Rebellion in 1925 (approximately fifteen thousand deaths); the mass deportations following the Ararat rebellions; the Dêrsim massacre in 1937–38 (see van Bruinessen 1994); state violence in the Kurdish region after the military coup of 1980; as well as state repression, village evacuations, and forced migration of two to four million Kurdish civilians during the Kurdish rebellion in the 1980s and 1990s.

Methods and Data

To understand the mechanisms and dynamics behind this new wave of communal violence against the Kurdish population in Turkey, this chapter utilizes mixed methods and data-triangulation strategies. Mixed-method analysis, which combines different forms of quantitative and qualitative evidence, is frequently utilized in studies of communal violence because such studies necessitate different analytical and methodological approaches to examine the various aspects of a problem (Wilkinson 2004).

For the quantitative analysis, I rely on the Ethnic and Nationalist Violence in Turkey (ENViT) database, which I compiled using historical archives of the newspaper *Milliyet* and a wide range of reports by human rights associations and institutions. The ENViT database is the first comprehensive data set of ethnic and nationalist collective violence in Turkey. I included in the database every reported incident of ethnic and nationalist collective violence in Turkey from 1980 to 2011, recording information on the type of collective violence, the actors and victims of incidents, the locations of these events, the number of people who participated in the incidents, the number of people who were killed or injured in the incidents, reported causes of events, attitudes of the state and government institutions, and the roles played by other political organizations (extreme-right groups, left-wing organizations, etc.). The quantitative analysis also includes various secondary data on electoral statistics, macroeconomic and political indicators (including indices of democratization), employment statistics, reports about the level of social mobilization of the Kurdish population, census data, and various opinion polls.

To evaluate the explanatory power of these competing accounts in the context of anti-Kurdish violence in Turkey, first I used negative binomial time-series regression analysis to test the viability of competing explanations in the literature, including socioeconomic, political, demographic, and fear–retribution explanations as well as different approaches to the democracy–ethnic violence relation. Tables 7.1 and 7.2 present the Pearson correlation coefficients and negative binomial regression analysis. In this analysis, the dependent variable is the number of anti-Kurdish communal violence incidents aggregated by year. These data are filtered from the

Table 7.1
Pearson Correlation Coefficients for Selected Variables

	[1]	[2]	[3]	[4]	[5]	[6]	[7]	[8]	[9]	[10]	[11]	[12]
[1] Communal Violence against Kurds	1.0											
[2] Existence of Military Junta	-0.4	1.0										
[3] Annual GDP per Capita Growth	0.03	0.1	1.0									
[4] Annual Change in Unemployment	0.1	0.02	-0.52	1.0								
[5] Wages in Manufacturing Sector	0.27	-0.77	0.01	-0.16	1.0							
[6] Urban Population Growth Rate	-0.5	0.89	0.02	-0.06	-0.68	1.0						
[7] Percentage of Kurdish Forced Migrants	-0.5	-0.11	0.0	-0.15	0.39	0.11	1.0					
[8] Military Deaths in the State—PKK Armed Struggle	-0.18	-0.37	-0.1	-0.25	0.47	-0.34	0.54	1.0				
[9] Political Instability Index (CNTS)	-0.15	-0.22	0.09	-0.26	0.26	-0.17	0.3	0.5	1.0			
[10] Votes for Kurdish Parties in General Elections	0.69	-0.73	0.05	0.11	0.43	-0.87	-0.5	-0.05	-0.02	1.0		
[11] Democratization Index (Unified Democracy Score)	0.32	-0.63	0.09	0.05	0.61	-0.7	0.22	0.17	0.07	0.57	1.0	
[12] Election Year	0.04	-0.24	-0.21	0.13	0.24	-0.27	0.1	0.15	0.19	0.23	0.32	1.0

Table 7.2
Coefficients of Negative Binomial Regression Analysis of Annual Frequency of Communal Violence against the Kurdish Population

	Model 1	Model 2	Model 3	Model 4	Model 5	Model 6	Model 7	Model 8
Number of Communal Violence Incidents (t-1)	0.103*** (0.03)	0.061** (0.02)	0.103** (0.03)	0.090*** (0.03)	0.109** (0.03)	0.056* (0.03)	0.059* (0.03)	0.056* (0.02)
Annual GDP per Capita Growth (t-1)	17.759* (7.00)							5.218 (6.30)
Annual Change in Unemployment (t-1)	5.240* (2.63)							0.83 (2.39)
Wages in Manufacturing Sector 1997 = 100 (t-1)	0.033 (0.02)							0.025 (0.02)
Urban Population Growth Rate (t-1)	-1.651**	(0.59)						
Percentage of Kurdish Forced Migrants (t-1)	-0.037	(0.09)						
Military Deaths in the Armed Struggle with the PKK (t-1)	-0.34e^{-3}		(0.001)		0.001	0.001		
Political Instability Index (CNTS) (t-1)			-0.29e^{-4} (0.075e^{-3})				-0.01e^{-3} 0.05e^{-e}	-0.02e^{-3} 0.05e^{-3}

Table 7.2 (Con't.)

Coefficients of Negative Binomial Regression Analysis of Annual Frequency of Communal Violence against the Kurdish Population

	Model 1	Model 2	Model 3	Model 4	Model 5	Model 6	Model 7	Model 8
Democracy Indicator from Unified Democracy Scores Data Set (t-1)	5.903*	5.116*	2.464	2.415 (2.30)	-0.211 (2.28)			
Is this an election year? 1 = yes; 0 = no (t-1)			-0.617	-0.615	-0.623 (0.57)	-0.608 (0.44)		
Votes of Kurds in General Elections (t-1)			0.956*** (0.44)	1.069***	1.180***			
Constant	-2.824 (1.64)	5.406*** (1.25)	0.942* (0.44)	-1.298 (0.87)	-0.916 (0.89)	-4.225*** (1.25)	-4.983** (1.60)	-6.885** (2.35)
Ln(alpha)	0.191 (0.40)	-0.683 (0.49)	0.56 (0.38)	0.12 (0.42)	0.079 (0.42)	-0.721 (0.50)	-0.773 (0.51)	-0.826 (0.51)
McFadden's adjusted R-Square	0.042	0.163	0.003	0.072	0.067	0.146	0.128	0.106
N	30	30	30	30	30	30	30	30

* $p < 0.05$, ** $p < 0.01$, *** $p < 0.001$.

ENViT database, which categorizes different forms of ethnic and nationalist violence incidents. As noted earlier, following Fearon and Laitin, I defined communal violence as "violence between members of different ethnic groups that does not directly involve arms of the state on either side" (1999, 9). Incidents of anti-Kurdish communal violence in the ENViT database correspond to civilian forms of physical violence directed toward Kurds in the form of lynchings, beatings, riots, fights, and clashes. It also includes violent attacks targeting homes, shops, and institutions belonging to or associated with Kurds (civil society organizations, political parties, etc.). I aggregated the data per year because other variables used in the analysis are available at the year level.

The quantitative analysis presented in this chapter does not aim to establish causality but to illustrate the historical patterning of the anti-Kurdish violence in Turkey and its relationship with various macro indicators. Hence, the analysis will complement these quantitative findings with evidence and insights from qualitative evidence based on interviews conducted between 2010 and 2013 in districts with high levels of anti-Kurdish violence.

Table 7.3
Geography and Demographics of Interview Locations

City	Northwestern Turkey (Marmara / Catalca-Kocaeli Region)		Northwestern Turkey (Southern Marmara Region)		Mediterranean Region		Aegean Region
Districts (pseudonyms)	Isler	Durusu	Karatepe	Kirazli	Senkoy	Bayramli	Tepe
Percentage of Kurds (estimated)	24.71	26.54	6.57	2.02	37.64	29.98	8.68
Total Population	167,717	270,951	238,502	82,980	279,142	33,401	63,312
Unemployment Rate (%)	14.3	14.3	11.4	11.4	14.1	14.1	8.0
Urban/Rural Status	Urban District	Urban District	Urban District	Rural Town	Urban District	Rural Town	Rural Town

Source: Data collected from Turkish Institute of Statistics 2010, "Household Workforce Statistics 2010."

The qualitative data are drawn from seventy-seven in-depth interviews conducted from 2010 to June 2013 in seven districts of four cities of Turkey (see table 7.3). All selected locations are home to Kurdish forced migrant populations and have high levels of communal violence against Kurdish civilians. The locations I chose for interviews are situated in three different regions of Turkey—the western (Aegean), northwestern (Marmara), and Mediterranean (Akdeniz) regions—and include both urban districts and rural towns. The specific location names used in this chapter are pseudonyms.

Findings and Discussion

Socioeconomic Deprivation, Competition, and Anti-Kurdish Communal Violence

Materialist theories of economic deprivation, competition, and underdevelopment have been the most popular explanations of ethnic and racial conflict in the literature (Hechter 1975; Kim and Conceicao 2010; Nairn 1977; Olzak 1989, 1990). Ethnic antagonism and violence are expected to rise owing to competition between ethnic groups for jobs and scarce resources, especially in times of heightened migration/immigration and economic crisis/contraction (Bonacich 1972; Myers 1997; Olzak 1990), as well as to scapegoating of minorities in times of socioeconomic deprivation (Krell, Nicklas, and Ostermann 1996). With the rise of immigration and economic crises in the period of globalization, socioeconomic competition and deprivation theories are used to account for a variety of cases, including extreme-right violence in Europe; anti-Chinese riots in Xinjiang, where international and internal migration has altered existing labor relations; communal violence in post-Sukharto Indonesia; and Hindu–Muslim riots in India (Betz 1994). These perspectives also echo the recent Polanyian explanations that show ethno/religious conflict as part of the "worldwide wave of dismantling the developmental regimes" (Derluguian 2013, 177; see also Polanyi [1944] 2001). A particular appeal of these explanations is the emphasis they put on the grievances of ordinary people. Yet although major economic transformations in world history coincide with ethnic and racial violence, economic factors such as crisis, unemployment, and contraction are shown to be neither necessary nor sufficient conditions for ethnic violence to erupt (Gurr 1993).[2]

Model 1 and Model 2 in table 7.2 aim to evaluate the power of *socioeconomic deprivation and ethnic competition* theories in the case of anti-Kurdish communal violence in Turkey. Model 1 uses one-year lagged values of annual gross domestic product (GDP) per capita levels, yearly changes in the unemployment level, and average wages in the manufacturing sector.[3] In the literature, although all three measures are widely used to assess the level of socioeconomic deprivation, the unemployment level and annual wages of industrial laborers are commonly used to measure the effects of ethnic competition.

As table 7.2 shows, the effects of economic indicators on communal violence are decidedly mixed. In contrast to the expectations, the results suggest that economic growth—rather than decline—increases the levels of communal violence. Likewise, in contrast to the expectations outlined in economic-competition theories, wages in manufacturing do not have a significant impact on communal violence. Among economic indicators, only unemployment seems to have a meaningful and significant impact. In accordance with economic-competition and deprivation theories as well as with Polanyian approaches, communal violence seems to increase with levels of unemployment. The impact of unemployment, however, disappears once controlled with other political variables (see Model 8). Likewise, table 7.2 also shows that the impact of demographic indicators, including urban population growth and Kurdish migration to western

---

2. Steven Wilkinson (2004) also rightly points out in the case of India that sometimes socioeconomic theories mistake outcomes of violence for its causes.

3. In the preliminary analysis, I also considered rate of unemployment, number of forced Kurdish immigrants to cities in western Turkey, and the percentage of the Kurdish population in internal migration in Turkey as possible alternative measures. The findings were not robust, however, and did not alter the existing results, so I did not use these variables.

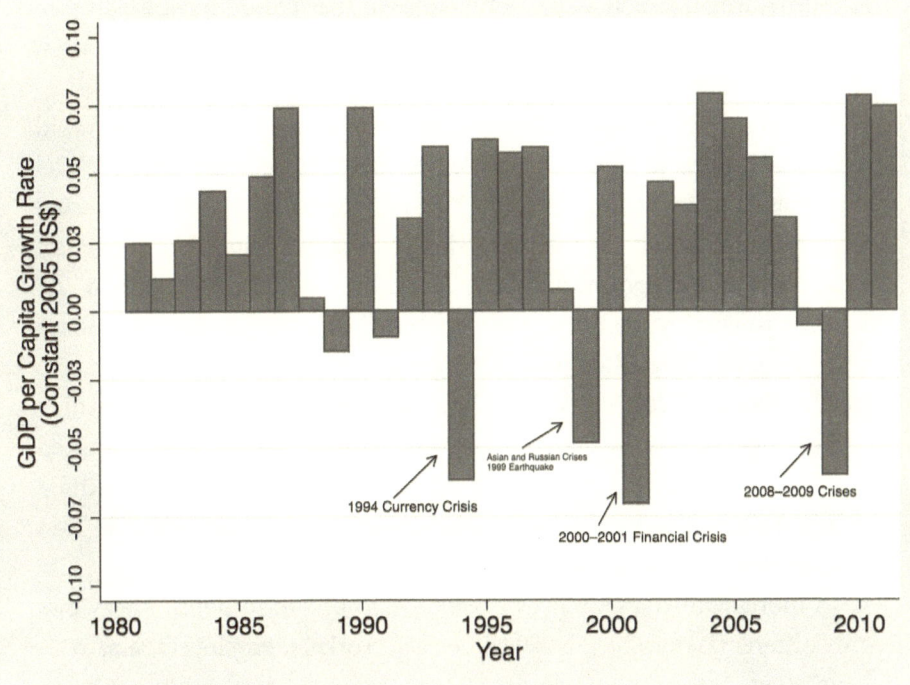

7.2. Annual GDP per capita growth rate, Turkey, 1981–2011. *Source*: World Bank n.d.

cities, did not have an immediate impact on communal violence in the 1990s (see Model 2).

These findings also resonate with the secondary literature on economic transformations in Turkey from 1980 to 2010. The intensity of anti-Kurdish communal violence rose particularly in the 2000s, even though it was a period characterized by "good growth coupled with single-digit inflation for the first time in several decades" (Öniş 2010, 55). Compared to previous decades, the economic performance of Turkey significantly improved in the first decade of the twenty-first century. The economic crises were less frequent, and despite the effects of the 2008–9 global financial meltdown, the growth rate in Turkey temporarily remained around 7 percent (figure 7.2). These observations suggest that the 1990s were more fertile for the emergence of violence linked to economic grievances.

Yet anti-Kurdish violence did not emerge in that period but instead in a decade characterized by "good growth coupled with single digit inflation for the first time in several decades" (Öniş 2010, 55).

The major economic problem throughout the 2000s was that rapid growth and the rise in exports were not matched with the desired level of increase in the number of jobs (Yeldan 2013, 123), which is in accordance with the results of the regression analysis showing the correlation between the rise of communal violence and the rate of unemployment. Yet the high unemployment rate was counterbalanced by increasing welfare provisions, which resulted in declining levels of income inequality in this decade (Karatasli 2015). Likewise, because Turkish workers and Kurdish workers operated in a dual labor-market system, where Kurds worked mostly in the undesired, low-paid, precarious jobs that required unskilled or low-skilled labor, resource-based competition between Kurdish and Turkish workers was not very common.

A more detailed analysis of violent events and of in-depth interviews with different actors in the field (victims, workers, employers, and residents) suggests the partial relevance of economic explanations for violence. The ENViT database on anti-Kurdish communal violence suggests that 3.31 percent of instances of violence were triggered by economic disputes. For instance, in 2009 when Kurdish seasonal farmworkers in a village in Ordu picking hazelnuts demanded their unpaid wages, their demand resulted in a violent attack against them by the villagers. In a similar incident in southern Turkey, 150 Kurdish workers who came to Tepekoy village in Mersin to pick peaches were attacked by villagers shouting, "Damn the PKK!" A lynching attempt was triggered by a dispute over the workers' daily wages. Likewise, in 2011 a dispute over picking cherries turned into an attack against Kurdish seasonal farmworkers in central Anatolia (Eskisehir, Omerkoy). Three hundred villagers attacked the workers, singing the national anthem, unfurling a large Turkish flag, and injuring six workers (Özer 2012). In 2005, a similar economic dispute ended up with an ethnic clash between Kurdish and Turkish residents in the town.

According to the ENViT database, although only 3.1 percent of the anti-Kurdish violence events were triggered by economic disputes, around 17 percent of targets of this violence were reported as "workers." Of importance here is that most of the contentions involving "Kurdish workers" were not economically driven disputes but rather primarily political in nature. Qualitative data give additional insights into understanding the relationship between economic factors and anti-Kurdish violence. An incident in one of my fieldwork locations, Kirazli, which is a small conservative town in northwestern Turkey and home to some well-known members of the ultranationalist Nationalist Movement Party (Milliyetçi Hareket Partisi, MHP) in Turkey, was a typical example indicating the political nature of violence against Kurdish workers. The town hosts Kurdish migrant workers during the hazelnut-harvesting season. Besides there being only some minor contentions, the town witnessed a large-scale attempt to lynch Kurdish workers in 2006. The event started with an exchange of words between workers who were speaking in Kurdish in a grocery store and a local resident who told them to stop speaking Kurdish. When the Kurds did not stop speaking Kurdish, the resident spread a rumor that the Kurdish workers had hung a PKK flag in the town, which led to the gathering of a lynch mob in the thousands.

Although the event was triggered by political reasons, could there have been a hidden economic rationale behind it? After all, every year a large number of Kurdish workers were brought to the villages by the orchard owners from the Kurdish provinces, especially from Diyarbakir. According to the orchard owners, the local residents' demand for hazelnut-picking jobs in the summer was very low. Furthermore, to "protect the local workers," the township decided to pay different rates for local and migrant workers. Hence, there was no indication of open resentment that "Kurds were stealing the jobs" of the locals. In the words of the head of the association of mukhtars, "Kurds are doing a job that no one wants to do it here." There was much less evidence of potential resentment that "Kurds are stealing jobs" in neighborhoods with Kurdish migrant residents—mainly because Turkish and Kurdish workers in western cities operate mostly in a dual labor-market system where Kurdish migrant workers participate mostly in the most precarious sectors with the lowest pay, longest work hours, and no security (e.g., construction work, dock work, seasonal work, etc.), which local residents ("Turkish" workers) do not compete for. In Durusu, most Kurds became the precarious workforce in the "basement textile workshops," which are the sweatshops owned by local residents to produce garments for small and big firms.

When I asked my interlocutors about potential economic hostility as a source of violence, two themes emerged that suggest how economic hostility as a source of violence is conditional on other political factors. First, in comparison to the case for other racial and ethnic groups as well as for migrants, the existence of economic hostility alone cannot account for the emergence of violence against Kurds in these neighborhoods. For instance, the residents were comparing Kurds with Bulgarian Turks, who came to the neighborhood in 1989–90 due to the mass emigration of the Turkish minority from Bulgaria to Turkey, which had resulted from the increasing ethnic tensions between Bulgarian Turks, the dominant population, and the Bulgarian state, which escalated in the second half of the 1980s. Unlike Kurdish migrants, who did not have any possessions because they were forced migrants, and most of their possessions were left behind or burned with the villages, the Bulgarian Turkish immigrants were supported by the state upon their arrival in Turkey and were relatively well off. A local resident who participated in large-scale anti-Kurdish riots noted: "The main focus of economic hostility was Bulgarian Turks when they first arrived. They were given taxi plate numbers[4] and everything. But they were not against the Turkish flag."

This conditionality, "but they were not against the Turkish flag," also revealed itself in relation to state and welfare support that Kurds receive in these neighborhoods. In Turkey, the neoliberal economic growth in the Justice and Development Party (Adalet ve Kalkınma Partisi, AKP) era, which conversely increased precarious work conditions as well as unemployment, was also paralleled by the rise of informal forms of welfare provisions for the poorest segments of the society. Resembling similar informal welfare regimes that incorporate "aids" in various countries in the Global South (Harris and Scully 2015), the Turkish government engaged in material aids (cash transfers, food, coal, etc.), and, not

---

4. Taxi plate numbers are very expensive and hard to get in Turkey due to high demand—particularly in big cities.

surprisingly, Kurds have been one of the major recipients of these aids. A mukhtar in Durusu noted: "This state gives them everything. Green card [basic health-care insurance targeting poor segments of society that do not have formal employment and are without any official and private coverage], aids, etc. . . . However, they are still not grateful. They still protest against Turkey."

As a whole, the interview data showed that socioeconomic-competition theories have limited explanatory power. However, both interviews and the broader fieldwork suggest that the economic hostilities that do exist are triggered mainly through *political contentions*, which manifest in a peculiar form of welfare chauvinism. To understand these links, I focus on the political contentions in the next section.

State Collapse, Security Fear, and Violence

Aside from economic explanations that focus on mass grievances, various scholars in the literature also draw attention to how weak state institutions, declining state capacities, and heightened political instability give way to ethnic and communal violence. Theories of state weakness and failure—both Hobbesian and Weberian variants—are particularly dominant in the post–Cold War period, which is marked by "disorder and the lack of governmental control" (Desjarlais and Kleinman 1994, 10). In their review of the vast literature on ethnic violence, Roger Brubaker and David Laitin emphasize that "weakly Weberian states or quasi-states" of the Third World—with their decreasing repressive capacities—are more prone to ethnic violence (1998, 424). Various scholars also argue that fear regarding group security and physical safety in times of armed conflict (Lake and Rothchild 1996; Posen 1993) has had a role in promoting genocidal violence in various cases, including the Rwandan genocide (Prunier 1995).[5] Despite these theories' strength, too much emphasis on state

---

5. Likewise, a history of armed conflict is also seen as a factor in the escalation and/or transformation of violence into communal clashes and deadly forms of ethnic cleansing. One strand in the literature draws attention to the cycle of "retributive violence," which is driven by revenge and retaliation in times of inter- and intrastate armed conflict.

weakness and armed conflict may lead to faulty generalizations. Some studies found that political instability does not have a significant effect on the outbreak of ethnic wars (Fearon and Laitin 2003). Furthermore, various studies actually document the *roles that states play* in the emergence and institutionalization of ethnic violence (Brass 2003b; Das and Kleinman 2000; Wilkinson 2004). In these formulations, *state inaction* rather than incapacity emerges as a key reason why ethnic riots develop.

Theories of state weakness and security fear are particularly relevant for the Turkish case; most commentators on anti-Kurdish communal violence in Turkey generally refer to feelings of retribution and fear among the Turkish population in the face of Kurdish armed rebellion. Put differently, the dominant discourse tends to understand the current rise of communal violence in Turkey as a nationalist backlash motivated by feelings of group insecurity and by the perception of a threat to territorial integrity. The most widely held argument about the rise of popular violence against Kurds or the electoral support for extreme-right parties is the "rising national reflex" in Turkish society as a result of the Kurdish question in Turkey. Although the armed conflict is an important factor without which current anti-Kurdish communal violence cannot be understood, explaining anti-Kurdish communal violence only within the framework of civilian response to armed conflict perpetuates the state-centric and ultranationalist justification of civilian violence.

It is true that since the 1990s, the decade when the state–PKK armed conflict reached its peak, the ultranationalist MHP presented itself as the only party to take a tough and uncompromising position vis-à-vis the Kurdish movement in Turkey, and the capture of the PKK leader Abdullah Öcalan in 1999 directly resulted in the rise of votes for the MHP (Arıkan 2008; Başkan 2006). Yet the tempo of the armed conflict between the state and the PKK and the tempo of the rise of communal violence are out of synchrony: communal violence increased when the armed conflict decreased.

For instance, Paul Brass (2003a) shows how the violence that preceded the partition of India is critical to understanding the retributive genocide in Punjab.

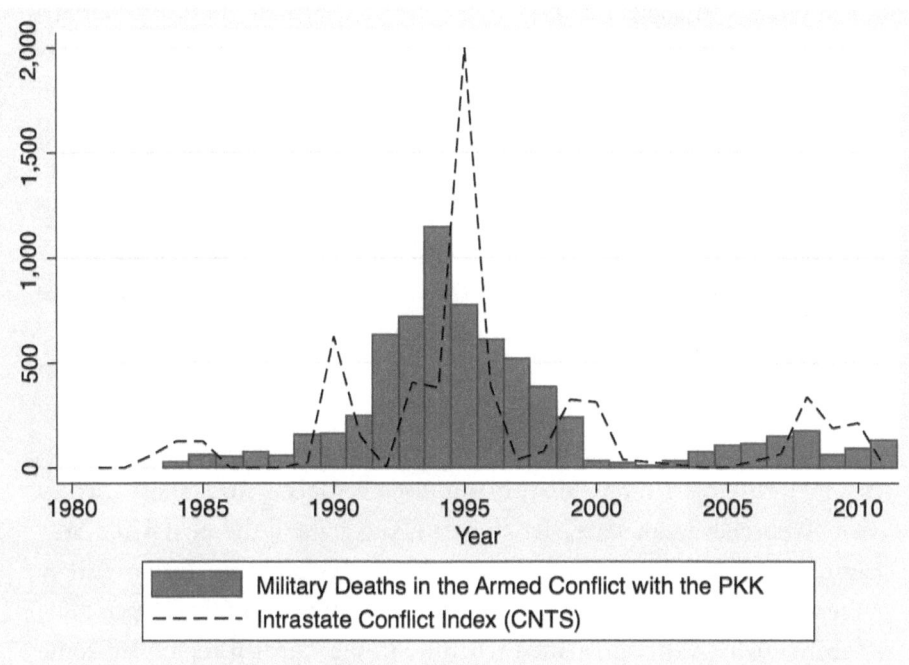

7.3. Political Instability Index and military deaths in the Turkish state's armed conflict with the PKK, 1981–2011. *Source*: CNTS data are from Banks and Wilson 2021.

The quantitative analysis does not provide support for political-instability/state-weakness arguments either. In Model 3 of table 7.2, I used two indicators to assess the validity of *state-weakness* arguments. The first one is the political-instability variable from the Cross-National Time-Series data set (Banks and Wilson 2021), which is a weighted conflict index that includes assassinations, general strikes, guerrilla warfare, government crises, purges, and antigovernment demonstrations. The second indicator aims to capture the intensity of armed conflict between the Turkish state and the PKK because armed conflict tends to increase state fragility and to decrease state repressive capacity. As an indicator of the intensity of armed conflict, I used the number of battle deaths from armed conflict between the PKK and the Turkish armed forces (figure 7.3).

Model 3 in table 7.2 tests these explanations in the case of anti-Kurdish violence in Turkey. This model addresses theories of state weakness as well as theories that underscore the role of fear and retribution in the face of actual or potential threats to physical security.[6] This model tests the impact of political instability and the intensity of armed conflict on communal violence. Contrary to expectations raised by theories drawing attention to retributive violence and security fear, my findings show that the intensity of ethnic armed conflict with the PKK does not have any statistically significant impact on communal violence. Furthermore, levels of political instability do not have a statistically significant impact on communal violence, either.

These findings are not accidental, and they resonate with the secondary literature on Turkey. First, it would be erroneous to classify Turkey as a "Weberian weak state," let alone a failed state in the post–Cold War period. Various scholars of Turkish politics have underlined that Turkey inherited a "strong state" tradition from the Ottoman Empire (Heper 2005; Mardin 1973). Although armed rebellion in the Kurdish region led some analysts to categorize Turkey among the "states to watch" (Rice and Patrick 2008), characterized by "moderate state fragility" (Marshall and Cole 2011), the communal violence in Turkey erupted in the 2000s when the armed conflict started to wane. Despite the high level of armed conflict with large numbers of casualties in the 1990s, communal violence targeting Kurds didn't erupt until the 2000s, when the scale of armed conflict, casualties, and hence actual threats to security and state integrity *declined*. Thus, although the Kurdish demand for separate statehood, the armed conflict, and the high number of casualties aggravated Turkish nationalist sentiments to an unprecedented level after 1984, they cannot explain the

---

6. These two indicators of state weakness also help us test theories of retribution and security fear, for two reasons. First, state weakness and collapse constitute an important intermediate variable that increases a particular group's fear regarding physical security (Posen 1993). The intensity of armed conflict is utilized as an actual proxy for the existence of group security. The number of battle deaths due to armed conflict between the PKK and the Turkish army is also used as an intermediate variable, increasing the likelihood of retributive violence.

huge difference in levels of communal violence targeting Kurdish civilians between the 1990s and the 2000s.

The quantitative analysis does not point to the significant role of state weakness and armed conflict, but a closer look at the events recorded in the ENViT database reveals that around 14.51 percent of the anti-Kurdish communal-violence events took place in the aftermath of an armed conflict between the Turkish state and the PKK. This is a much higher percentage compared to the percentage of violence due to economic grievances, and it resonates with approaches that highlight "retributive violence" and "fear and security." Likewise, my interviews showed that armed conflict and news about "martyrs" played a critical role in shaping the emotions of the broader masses, pushing them into the streets to protest and thus providing opportunities for ultranationalist "violence specialists" to turn nonviolent nationalist demonstrations into violent ethnic riots.

In approximately half of my interviews, the themes of "death of our soldiers" and "martyrs" came up in discussions of violence. Many respondents said that in their neighborhoods the violent events often took place in the aftermath of "soldier deaths." It is interesting that although the number of "soldier deaths" and armed conflict were quantitatively far less common in the 2000s compared to the 1990s, which is reflected in Model 3 of the regression analysis, the perception was that they were much more common during negotiations between the government and the PKK:

> What concerns people is damage to property, life, and our soldiers. People especially react when they receive the news about martyrs. After the "opening" [the "Kurdish Opening," or peace negotiations between the PKK and the Turkish state], there was more news [about the martyrs]. . . . Here, there is a specific reaction against the BDP [the pro-Kurdish Peace and Democracy Party (Barış ve Demokrasi Partisi)]. The way they talk, the way they rally against our soldiers bother [us] the most. They show how much they love this country by calling those [who die] in the mountains [the PKK guerilla fighters] as their martyrs. (anti-Kurdish riot participant, Durusu)

This account suggests that "perceived threats to group security and fear," as emphasized by David Lake and Donald Rothchild (1996) as well as by Barry Posen (1993), might have played a greater role than implied by the quantitative analysis. In the same neighborhood, a representative of the Republican People's Party (Cumhuriyet Halk Partisi, CHP) explained that this perception was created by the framing of the news about martyrs by mainstream media: "To me, the greatest role is played by the media. The constant news about martyrs triggers such [violent] events. They often do this right before the elections. In the violent riot that took place here, the way the media framed the news triggered the events."

A Turkish human rights organization in Karatepe shared a similar view: "When there are soldier deaths, you hear some people saying, 'We should hang a couple of these Kurds so that they will behave,' or 'The best Kurd is a dead Kurd.' The serious problem is the funerals of the martyrs. . . . Media always show soldier deaths. They show this news in such a way that people feel as if Kurds will come and shoot them in their neighborhoods."

In addition to the media framing of the Turkish soldiers' funerals, local-level rumors that spread after news of soldier deaths also escalate such perceived threats to security and fear. Most of these rumors have been produced by ultranationalist youth groups such as *ülkücü* groups,[7] which also play a key role in the production of violent ethnic riots (Kumral 2017). For instance, a Kurdish resident whose coffeehouse was destroyed during an ethnic riot in Durusu stated: "After the coffeehouse was destroyed, we learned that [before the riots] some [*ülkücü* groups] spread some rumors saying that we were aiding the PKK. They spread the rumor that we were happy with the soldier deaths. Now, people are no longer coming to the coffeehouse. They are not even using this street to walk."

Members of ultranationalist youth organizations that I talked to in interview locations also explained to me how important soldier deaths were for their anti-Kurdish attitude. Many young members of the *ülkücü* movement informed me that they and many of the ultranationalist youth were politicized due to martyr deaths in their families. They also

---

7. "*Ülkücü* youth" are members of the organization Hearth of Idealists (Ülkü Ocakları), an unofficial youth branch of the ultranationalist MHP.

explained that they can mobilize many more people in the aftermath of soldier deaths and during martyr funerals. During an interview, a young *ülkücü* in Isler stated: "There is a neighborhood here that all supports the [pro-Kurdish] BDP. No other party can mobilize there except for the Kurds and the communists. We always organize car convoys there after our soldiers die. . . . [The other day] we organized a rally for our martyrs. Five thousand people gathered, and after a while they suddenly started throwing stones [at Kurds' houses and BDP buildings]."

The overall analysis demonstrates that although communal violence actually increased at a time when the intensity of armed conflict had declined, ultranationalist organizations (i.e., the ultranationalist *ülkücü* movement) still utilized the armed conflict as a primary tool to spread rumors, instigate masses, and frame communal violence that targets Kurdish civilians.

Democratization, Authoritarianism, and Anti-Kurdish Communal Violence

Democracy has long been associated with internal and international peace. Particularly in the post–Cold War period, democratization was adopted as *the* key solution to various ethnic wars. Because democratic regimes provide nonviolent means of claim making, competition, and protest, they are expected to provide peaceful resolution of conflicts (Tilly and Tarrow 2015). Owing to the sudden escalation of ethnic violence in parallel with the global spread of democracy (Diamond and Plattner 1994; Olzak 2011; Saideman et al. 2002; Snyder 2000), however, many scholars have started to contest the view that democracy is a magical solution to ethnic conflicts (Mann 2004; Mousseau 2001; Reilly 2001; Roeder and Rothchild 2005; Snyder 2000; Wimmer 2013). Various studies have shown that although democracy brings about stability in the long run, the *transition to democracy* is actually a violent process (Mann 2004; Reilly 2001). Another group of scholars in the literature point out the conflict-bearing potential of electoral competition/challenge in democratic regimes (Brass 2003b; Dhattiwala and Biggs 2012; Olzak 1990; Wilkinson 2004). Another strand of political-competition theories draws attention to the political and electoral challenge posed by minority populations as a source of racial and ethnic violence by dominant populations (Olzak 1990). Despite their important insights, these approaches do not focus on how democratic contention unfolds on the ground in the arena of *social movement mobilization.*

To assess the validity of competing positions in the relationship between democracy and ethnic violence in the Turkish case, Models 4–8 in table 7.2 incorporate the impact of qualitatively different democracy measures on anti-Kurdish communal violence. It must be noted that these models do not include transition theories—how early democratic transition from nondemocratic regimes to parliamentary democracies produces violence—because in Turkey the transition to parliamentary democracy took place after the Young Turk Revolution of 1908. Although the newly established Republic of Turkey had a single-party rule from 1924 to 1946, after 1946 the transition to a multiparty parliamentary regime was complete. Hence, there is no need and no way to assess the validity of transition theories in the case of Turkey. If "transition" in these theories can also be extended to incorporate the transition from temporary interruptions of this multiparty parliamentary regimes due to military coups, it will be captured by Model 4.

Model 4 shows that increasing levels of democracy in Turkey do not prevent communal violence. On the contrary, the intensity of communal violence increases with democratization. This finding resonates with the secondary literature on Turkey. After all, various liberal scholars welcomed the initial decade of the AKP as a period of liberalization owing to the introduction of a variety of political reforms. Overall, the reforms entailed the introduction of laws and measures against torture, "adoption of [European Union] standards for the death penalty," and "retrial of all the cases in Turkey decided in State Security Courts" (Muftuler Bac 2005, 25–26) as well as the democratization of civil–military relations (Altunisik 2005; Muftuler Bac 2005; Narli 2011). In this period, the AKP government also promised and partially engaged in various "political opening" initiatives pertaining to ethnic and religious minorities, commonly known as the "Kurdish Opening" and the "Alevi Opening." As shown in figure 7.4, however, this engagement resulted in an only partial and limited extension of rights to Kurds and other minorities in the cultural sphere, such as

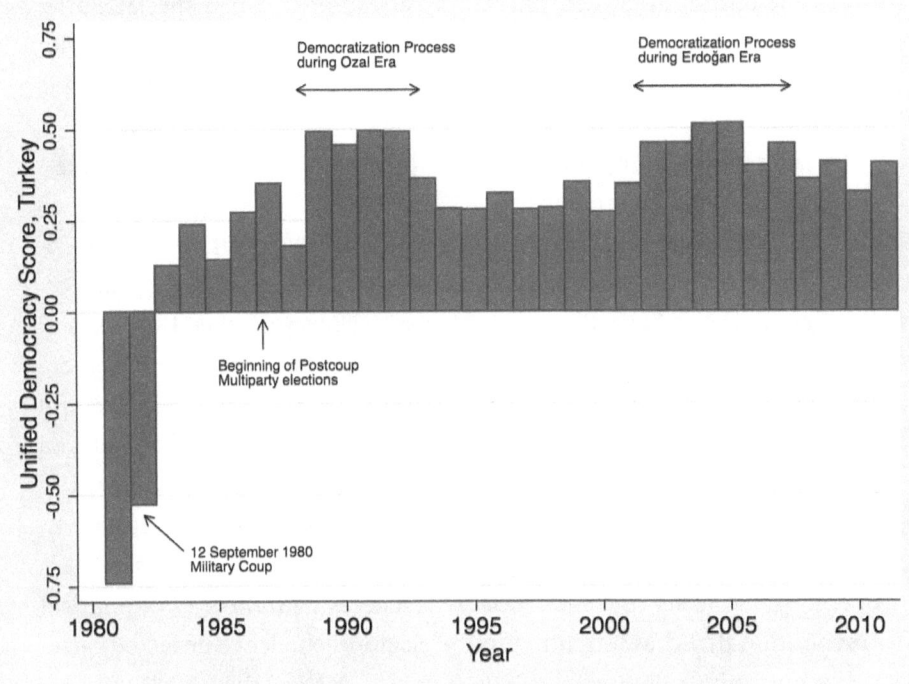

7.4. Unified Democracy Score in Turkey, 1981–2011. *Source*: Pemstein et al. 2010. Data available at http://www.unified-democracy-scores.net/index.html.

the lifting of the legal ban on broadcasting in other languages (Altunisik 2005; T. Smith 2005).

Can the significant effect of democratization on violence be interpreted as partial support for the modified version of the "democratic transition" theory, suggesting that anti-Kurdish communal violence is a temporary outcome of a partial opening? There are several problems with such an interpretation. First, it must be noted that despite the limited extension of rights in the cultural sphere, the extension of political rights to Kurds was never actualized. On the contrary, the AKP government responded to the popular political challenge by the pro-Kurdish political parties with repression through party bans and the arrest of pro-Kurdish political activists (Kumral 2017). Second, in contrast to the predictions made by democratic transition theories, it was not ethnic violence that disappeared over time but the AKP's partial-democratization efforts. Especially after 2013, the AKP took a sharp authoritarian turn that further intensified violence. Hence, to understand why there is a positive relationship between democracy and violence, we need to focus on alternative accounts.

The inclusion of "election year" in Models 5–8 of table 7.2 aims to test the effects of electoral-competition and electoral-challenge theories on anti-Kurdish violence. Model 5 does not change the positive and significant impact of democracy levels on communal violence; it shows that election year does not have a significant impact. However, when the electoral power of pro-Kurdish parties is added in Model 6, the impact of democracy levels on communal violence disappears. In this model, the electoral power of pro-Kurdish parties is the only variable with a significant and positive impact on communal violence. Among all other measures of democracy, this impact is the only significant indicator. Put differently, electoral challenge and empowerment of Kurdish parties increase levels of communal violence, which broadly resonates with theories of political competition that draw attention to the electoral challenge posed by racial and ethnic minorities (Olzak 1990). Models 7–8 show that this is the only robust finding in the analysis.

The results are also in accordance with the sociopolitical context of Turkey in which communal violence erupted. Communal-violence events erupted mainly in the 2000s, the period in which the PKK gave up arms and the Kurdish movement started to embrace electoral politics and social movement mobilization on the ground. Pro-Kurdish political parties in the 2000s (the BDP; the People's Democratic Party [Halkların Demokratik Partisi, HDP]; and the Democratic Society Party [Demokratik Toplum Partisi, DTP]) became central actors in Turkish politics and gradually increased their electoral power and presence in Parliament. What is not evident from the regression analysis is that the electoral challenge posed by the Kurdish political parties in this period had a strong social movement component. In this period, various cities in western Turkey had become important centers of social and electoral mobilization, thanks to the sizeable Kurdish forced-migrant population in these cities. Figure 7.5 shows the rapid increase in social movement mobilization of Kurds—including

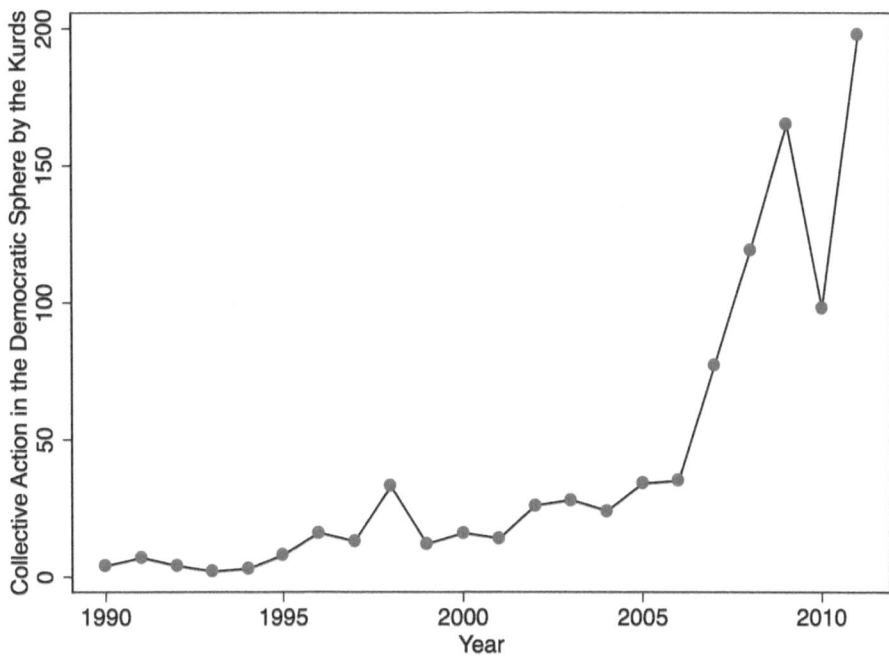

7.5. Social movement mobilization of the Kurds, 1981–2011. *Source*: Authors' calculations using *Milliyet* news archives.

protests, electoral rallies, demonstrations, and other forms of collective action in the public sphere—in the twenty-first century.

The social movement aspect of this sociopolitical challenge is best captured by a more detailed analysis of targets and contexts of violence, as presented in table 7.4. According to the ENViT database, almost half of these violent events (49.67 percent) take place in the context of a collective action led by Kurds, such as protests, rallies, demonstrations, and public celebrations. The action is followed by episodes of military clashes between the Turkish armed forces and the PKK (14.57 percent). As mentioned earlier, only 3 percent of these episodes take place for economic reasons. Targets of the violence also show that around 44.53 percent of anti-Kurdish communal-violence incidents target Kurdish protesters or activists. These findings highlight the central role of social movement mobilization of Kurds as a major political challenge.

Table 7.4
Context and Targets of Collective-Violence Events

Context of Violence	Percentage	Targets of Violence	Percentage
Political Contention (e.g., protests, demonstrations, rallies)	49.67	Kurdish Protestors/Activists	44.53
Military Clash with the PKK	14.57	Kurdish Workers	16.79
Unidentified	11.26	Kurdish Individuals	11.68
Criminal Events	10.6	Institutions (e.g., political party buildings)	9.49
Speaking Kurdish in Public	6.62	Generalized Violence against Kurds	9.49
Nationalist Hatred/Identity Related	3.97	Other	5.11
Nationalist Hatred/Economic Reasons	3.31	Kurdish Students	2.92

Source: ENViT data set.

The impact of this political challenge is also evident on the ground. In interviews, the increasing political impact of pro-Kurdish parties on Kurdish masses in western cities and towns was often commented on by Kurdish politicians as well as by local politicians of different parties. "Kurds started to be politicized in the 2000s. This created a problem for the [political] system. We have been in this district since 1990, when HEP [the People's Labor Party [Halkın Emek Partisi], one of the first pro-Kurdish parties] was founded. The party members in the district have increased throughout the 2000s. While we received six hundred votes in the district in 1991 local elections, we received more than four thousand in 2011" (representative of the pro-Kurdish BDP, Isler).

The local population and politicians did not welcome this increasing Kurdish political activism, which also translates into votes and thus electoral empowerment of pro-Kurdish parties. A BDP representative in the Durusu neighborhood, where electoral support for the pro-Kurdish parties is substantially high, recounted the responses to those parties after the local elections in 2011: "We are very well organized in this district.... We succeeded to become the third-largest party in local elections [in 2009]. [After the elections], the district mayor said on CNN Turk that 'there is a grave threat in our district. For the first time, an ethnic party came third in elections, which made me anxious.'"

This political mobilization, which both incorporated and resulted in electoral mobilization and empowerment, made pro-Kurdish political parties and ordinary Kurdish civilians central actors in the Turkish political scene. A major outcome of this process was that the "Kurdish issue" became a major point of contestation between ordinary civilians in western cities and towns rather than solely between the state and the Kurdish "rebels" in distant Kurdish provinces.

Conclusion

In this chapter, I have examined the increasing anti-Kurdish communal violence in Turkey's recent history and have argued, in contrast to dominant theories about ethnic violence, that this violence owes less to (1) the *economic competition* between Turks and Kurds and (2) *security fear* in relation to declining state capacity and armed conflict with the PKK than to electoral empowerment and the increasing collective action and visibility of the Kurdish population in a period of *contested democratization*. Put differently, the social origin of anti-Kurdish communal violence in Turkey is the emergence of Kurdish masses as a major, strong, and active political force for democratization in Turkey in the first decade of the 2000s.

This conclusion might seem unusual considering Turkey's explicit authoritarian turn, which has led to the escalation of various forms of political violence. Since 2013, we have been living in a categorically different phase of violence directed against the Kurdish population. This is not surprising. As mentioned at the beginning of this chapter, the anti-Kurdish communal violence of the 2000s was categorically distinct from the military conflict between the Turkish armed forces and the PKK in the 1990s. Likewise, the current moment is neither a direct continuation of the 2000s nor a return to the 1990s, but rather a new radical phase of the struggle wherein the dynamics of both eras—that is, state-led and communal forms of violence—are in play.

It is already apparent that the dynamics of ethnic violence in the post-2015 era are different from the dynamics of the 2000s. Turkey no longer enjoys the relatively better economic-growth environment of the 2000s but is on the eve of one of the most serious economic crises of its history. Peace negotiations between the Turkish state and the PKK have collapsed, so armed conflict has once again escalated, creating a much more unstable and fragile political environment compared to the 2000s. Hence, economic grievances interlinked with aggravated political contention might play a more decisive role in this new era. Likewise, as signaled by both the deadly bombing attacks on the eve of the snap elections in November 2015 (e.g., the Suruc bombing on 20 July 2015) and Recep Tayyip Erdoğan's electoral campaigns since the snap elections—based on the platform "Without my rule, there will be chaos"—today there is a closer relationship between electoral politics and violence. Hence, the post-2015 phase of anti-Kurdish violence has also started to resemble the case of anti-Muslim violence in Narendra Modi's India. Most importantly, however, in this new era there appears to be a clearer relationship between de-democratization and violence.

Most commentators today seem to be puzzled by how Erdoğan and his party, the AKP, who were once supported by the United States and its Western allies as champions of democracy, have suddenly taken such an authoritarian turn. Many scholars wonder what changed to bring about this turn. The analysis presented in this chapter provides important insights to answer this question as well. For one thing, it shows that Turkey's recent authoritarian turn and escalation of violence directed against Kurds are not as recent as they seem. On the contrary, seeds of authoritarianism and intensified violence had already been planted during the contentious democratization process in the first decade of the AKP government in the 2000s, when the AKP was seen as a "champion of democracy" in the West. Likewise, this analysis suggests that there is a rather thin line between contentious democratization and authoritarianism, whose coordinates are determined by a power struggle.

This dynamic is very similar to the relationship between working-class mobilization and democracy in modern world history. As Dietrich Rueschemeyer, Evelyne Huber Stephens, and John Stephens (1992) show, although working-class mobilization has always been the primary motor of democratization processes, a mobilization that is too strong challenges dominant power blocs and thus brings about repression and authoritarianism. In Turkey's case, the strength and success of democratic mobilization by the Kurds—especially the HDP's electoral victory in the elections of June 2015 and the political success of Kurds in the Rojava region of Syria—have proven to be critical in the pendulum swing. In hopes to gain and maintain hegemony over politically active Kurdish masses that challenge the AKP's power in Turkey and Turkey's efforts to become a regional hegemon in the Middle East, Erdoğan's AKP has been using brute force without consent, hence relying on coercion without hegemony. The most alarming nature of this new period is that anti-Kurdish violence in today's Turkey incorporates state violence and repression, societal violence, and paramilitary violence all at the same time.

References

Altunisik, Meliha Benli. 2005. "The Turkish Model and Democratization in the Middle East." *Arab Studies Quarterly* 27, nos. 1–2 (Winter–Spring): 45–63.

Arıkan, E. Burak. 2008. *Milliyetçi Hareket Partisi—MHP: Türk sağının Türk sorunu*. Istanbul: Agora Kitaplığı.

Ayata, Bilgin, and Deniz Yükseker. 2005. "A Belated Awakening: National and International Responses to the Internal Displacement of Kurds in Turkey." *New Perspectives on Turkey* 32, no. 1: 5–42.

Banks, Arthur S., and Kenneth A. Wilson. 2021. "Cross-National Time-Series Data Archive." Databanks International, Jerusalem. At https://www.cntsdata.com/.

Başkan, Filiz. 2006. "Globalization and Nationalism: The Nationalist Action Party of Turkey." *Nationalism and Ethnic Politics* 12, no. 1: 83–105.

Betz, Hans-Georg. 1994. *Radical Right Wing Populism in Western Europe*. New York: St. Martin's Press.

Bonacich, Edna. 1972. "A Theory of Ethnic Antagonism: The Split Labor Market." *American Sociological Review* 37, no. 5 (Oct.): 547–59.

Bora, Tanıl. 2008. *Türkiye'nin linç rejimi*. Istanbul: İletişim Yayınları.

Brass, Paul R. 2003a. "The Partition of India and Retributive Genocide in the Punjab, 1946–47: Means, Methods, Purposes." *Journal of Genocide Research* 5, no. 1: 71–101.

———. 2003b. *The Production of Hindu–Muslim Violence in Contemporary India*. Seattle: Univ. of Washington Press.

Brubaker, Roger, and David D. Laitin. 1998. "Ethnic and Nationalist Violence." *Annual Review of Sociology* 24:423–52.

Das, Veena, and Arthur Kleinman. 2000. Introduction to *Violence and Subjectivity*, edited by Veena Das, Arthur Kleinman, Mamphela Ramphele, and Pamela Reynolds, 1–19. Berkeley: Univ. of California Press.

Derluguian, Georgi M. 2013. "Does Globalization Breed Ethnic Violence?" In *Rhetorics of Insecurity: Belonging and Violence in the Neoliberal Era*, edited by Zeynep Gambetti and Marcial Godoy-Anativia, 175–96. New York: New York Univ. Press.

Desjarlais, Reynolds, and Arthur Kleinman. 1994. "Violence and Demoralization in the New World Disorder." *Anthropology Today* 10, no. 5 (Oct.): 9–12.

Dhattiwala, Raheel, and Michael Biggs. 2012. "The Political Logic of Ethnic Violence: The Anti-Muslim Pogrom in Gujarat, 2002." *Politics & Society* 40, no. 4: 483–516.

Diamond, Larry, and Marc F. Plattner. 1994. Introduction to *Nationalism, Ethnic Conflict, and Democracy*, edited by Larry Diamond and Marc F. Plattner, ix–xxx. Baltimore: Johns Hopkins Univ. Press.

Ergin, Murat. 2014. "The Racialization of Kurdish Identity in Turkey." *Ethnic and Racial Studies* 37, no. 2: 322–41.

Fearon, James D., and David D. Laitin. 1999. "Weak States, Rough Terrain, and Large-Scale Ethnic Violence since 1945." Paper presented at the Annual Meetings of the American Political Science Association, Sept., Atlanta, GA. At https://www.researchgate.net/publication/251847236_Weak_States_Rough_Terrain_and_Large-Scale_Ethnic_Violence_Since_1945.

———. 2003. "Ethnicity, Insurgency, and Civil War." *American Political Science Review* 97, no. 1: 75–90.

Gambetti, Zeynep. 2007. "Linç girişimleri, neoliberalizm ve güvenlik devleti." *Toplum ve bilim*, no. 109: 7–34.

Gurr, Ted R. 1993. "Why Minorities Rebel: A Global Analysis of Communal Mobilization and Conflict since 1945." *International Political Science Review / Revue internationale de science politique* 14, no. 2: 161–201.

Harris, Kevan, and Ben Scully. 2015. "A Hidden Counter-Movement? Precarity, Politics, and Social Protection before and beyond the Neoliberal Era." *Theory and Society* 44, no. 5: 415–44.

Hechter, Michael. 1975. *Internal Colonialism: The Celtic Fringe in British National Development 1536–1966*. Berkeley: Univ. of California Press.

Heper, Metin. 2005. "The European Union, the Turkish Military, and Democracy." *South European Society & Politics* 10, no. 1: 33–44.

Karatasli, Sahan S. 2015. "The Origins of Turkey's Heterodox Transition to Neoliberalism: The Ozal Decade and Beyond." *Journal of World-Systems Research* 21, no. 2: 387–416.

Kim, Namsuk, and Pedro Conceicao. 2010. "Economic Crisis, Violent Conflict, and Human Development." *International Journal of Peace Studies* 15, no. 1: 29–36.

Krell, Gert, Hans Nicklas, and Anne Ostermann. 1996. "Immigration, Asylum, and Anti-foreigner Violence in Germany." *Journal of Peace Research* 33:153–70.

Kumral, Şefika. 2017. "Ballots with Bullets: Elections, Violence, and the Rise of the Extreme Right in Turkey." *Journal of Labor and Society* 20, no. 2: 231–61.

Lake, David A., and Donald Rothchild. 1996. "Containing Fear: The Origins and Management of Ethnic Conflict." *International Security* 21, no. 2: 41–75.

Mann, Michael. 2004. *The Dark Side of Democracy: Explaining Ethnic Cleansing.* Cambridge: Cambridge Univ. Press.

Mardin, Serif. 1973. "Center–Periphery Relations: A Key to Turkish Politics." *Daedalus* 102, no. 1: 169–90.

Marshall, Monty G., and Benjamin R. Cole. 2011. "Global Report 2011: Conflict, Governance, and State Fragility." Center for Systemic Peace. At http://www.systemicpeace.org/vlibrary/GlobalReport2011.pdf.

Mousseau, Demet Yalcin. 2001. "Democratizing with Ethnic Divisions: A Source of Conflict?" *Journal of Peace Research* 38, no. 5: 547–67.

Muftuler Bac, Meltem. 2005. "Turkey's Political Reforms and the Impact of the European Union." *South European Society and Politics* 10, no. 1: 17–31.

Myers, Daniel J. 1997. "Racial Rioting in the 1960s: An Event History Analysis of Local Conditions." *American Sociological Review* 62:94–112.

Nairn, Tom. 1977. *The Break-Up of Britain: Crisis and Neo-nationalism.* London: NLB.

Olzak, Susan. 1989. "Labor Unrest, Immigration, and Ethnic Conflict in Urban America, 1880–1914." *American Journal of Sociology* 94, no. 6: 1303–33.

———. 1990. "The Political Context of Competition: Lynching and Urban Racial Violence, 1882–1914." *Social Forces* 69, no. 2: 395–421.

———. 2011. "Does Globalization Breed Ethnic Discontent?" *Journal of Conflict Resolution* 55, no. 33: 3–32.

Öniş, Ziya. 2010. "Crises and Transformations in Turkish Political Economy." *Turkish Policy Quarterly* 9, no. 3: 45–61.
Özer, Evren. 2012. *Türkiye İnsan Hakları Raporu 2011*. Report no. 77. Ankara: Türkiye İnsan Hakları Vakfı Yayınları.
Patterson, Ruairi. 2007. "Rising Nationalism and the EU Accession Process." *Turkish Policy Quarterly* 7, no. 1: 131–38.
Pemstein, Daniel, Stephen A. Meserve, and James Melton. 2010. "Democratic Compromise: A Latent Variable Analysis of Ten Measures of Regime Type." *Political Analysis* 18, no. 4: 426–49.
Polanyi, Karl. [1944] 2001. *The Great Transformation: The Political and Economic Origins of Our Times*. 2nd ed. Boston: Beacon Press.
Posen, Barry R. 1993. "The Security Dilemma and Ethnic Conflict." *Survival* 35, no. 1: 27–47.
Prunier, Gérard. 1995. *The Rwanda Crisis: History of a Genocide*. New York: Columbia Univ. Press.
Reilly, Benjamin. 2001. *Democracy in Divided Societies: Electoral Engineering for Conflict Management*. Cambridge: Cambridge Univ. Press.
Rice, Susan E., and Stewart Patrick. 2008. *Index of State Weakness in the Developing World*. Washington, DC: Brookings Institution.
Roeder, Philip G., and Donald S. Rothchild. 2005. "Dilemmas of State-Building in Divided Societies." In *Sustainable Peace: Power and Democracy after Civil Wars*, edited by Philip G. Roeder and Donald S. Rothchild, 1–25. Ithaca, NY: Cornell Univ. Press.
Rueschemeyer, Dietrich, Evelyne Huber Stephens, and John D. Stephens. 1992. *Capitalist Development and Democracy*. Chicago: Univ. of Chicago Press.
Saideman, Stephen M., David J. Lanoue, Michael Campenni, and Samuel Stanton. 2002. "Democratization, Political Institutions, and Ethnic Conflict: A Pooled Time-Series Analysis, 1985–1998." *Comparative Political Studies* 35:103–29.
Şener, Nedim. 2010. "26 Yılın kanlı bilançosu." *Milliyet*, 26 Apr. At https://www.milliyet.com.tr/gundem/26-yilin-kanli-bilancosu-1254711.
Smith, Thomas W. 2005. "Civic Nationalism and Ethnocultural Justice in Turkey." *Human Rights Quarterly* 27, no. 2: 436–70.
Snyder, Jack L. 2000. *From Voting to Violence: Democratization and Nationalist Conflict*. New York: Norton.
Tilly, Charles, and Sidney Tarrow. 2015. *Contentious Politics*. New York: Oxford Univ. Press.

Turkish Institute of Statistics. 2010. "Adrese Dayalı Nüfus Kayıt Sistemi (ADNKS) verileri." At https://data.tuik.gov.tr/.

Van Bruinessen, Martin. 1994. "Genocide in Kurdistan? The Suppression of the Dersim Rebellion in Turkey (1937–38) and the Chemical War against the Iraqi Kurds (1988)." In *Conceptual and Historical Dimensions of Genocide*, edited by George J. Andreopoulos, 141–70. Philadelphia: Univ. of Pennsylvania Press.

Wilkinson, Steven I. 2004. *Votes and Violence: Electoral Competition and Ethnic Riots in India*. Cambridge: Cambridge Univ. Press.

Wimmer, Andreas. 2013. *Ethnic Boundary Making: Institutions, Power, Networks*. New York: Oxford Univ. Press.

World Bank. N.d. "GDP per Capita Growth (Annual %)—Turkey [1961–2021]." World Development Indicators, World Bank Group. At https://data.worldbank.org/indicator/NY.GDP.PCAP.KD.ZG?locations=TR.

Yeldan, Erinç. 2013. "The Turkish Experience with Work-Sharing Policy during the Global Economic Crisis, 2008–2010." In *Work Sharing during the Great Recession: New Developments and Beyond*, edited by John C. Messenger and Naj Ghosheh, 119–50. Geneva: International Labour Office; Cheltenham, UK: Edward Elgar.

8

Homo Sacer at the Border

Turkish Narrative Violence in the Representation of the Roboskî Massacre

Ali Eşref Keleş

This chapter aims to critically examine the Turkish media representation of the Roboskî massacre against the Kurds. This massacre took place on the Turkey–Iraq border on 28 December 2011. Based on drone intelligence provided by the United States, the Turkish military bombed a group of thirty-eight Kurdish villagers, mostly teenagers who were citizens of Turkey engaged in routine cross-border smuggling of basic goods such as sugar and cigarettes. Thirty-four of the thirty-eight Kurds died in the attack. For the Turkish media coverage of the event, I focused on three highly circulated Turkish newspapers with different ideologies: the pro-Kemalist and central-right *Hürriyet*, the pro-government *Sabah*, and the left-wing *Birgün*. I analyzed the period between 2009 and 2015, employing critical discourse analysis. The analysis temporally commences in 2009, when the Turkish state was officially negotiating with the Kurdish Workers' Party (Partîya Karkerên Kurdistanê, PKK), which provides leadership to the Kurds, with the intent to end the civil strife between the Turkish state–society and the Kurds in Turkey. It ends in 2015, when the negotiation collapses and is replaced by systemic state and societal violence against the Kurds.

The analysis enabled me to socially construct the Turkish media's "narrative violence" against the Kurds. I define *narrative violence* as unjust storytelling whereby in constructing their narration, certain social actors highlight particular elements of an event that benefit their own interests while silencing others that reflect the interests of humanity. I then present a theoretical framework in which narrative violence has three levels: the first level commences with the denial of the event; the second level moves to blaming the victims—in this case, the Kurdish smugglers—for the event; and the third level proceeds to expand the category further by not only specifically blaming the victims but also reducing *all* Kurds to bare life (the life of the *homo sacer*). In all, then, events involving Kurds are subverted through denial, blaming first the victim and then all the Kurds and thereby silencing the agency of all Kurds in Turkey. In doing so, the narrative violence helps reproduce the existing power relations at the expense of the Kurds.

I reached two significant findings. First, in the case of this mass killing, the Turkish media discourse almost directly reflects the official Turkish state discourse. As such, the hegemonic state narrative is reproduced almost untouched in the media narrative, which is supposed to be based on the experiences and knowledge emanating from civil society, not from the Turkish state. Second, this synergy between the Turkish media discourse and Turkish official discourse not only shapes the general public opinion but also reproduces narrative violence that ultimately others, excludes, and silences the Kurds within the Turkish body politic. In summary, the sovereign power that shapes the Turkish media ends up eventually turning Kurds into *homos sacer* so that they can then be destroyed with impunity.

Method and Operationalization of the Data

Selected Newspapers

To fully portray the Turkish media's discourse of the Roboskî massacre, the data I use consist of more than one thousand articles I collected from *Hürriyet*, *Sabah*, and *Birgün* during my fieldwork in 2017. Table 8.1 conveys the ideological alignment, political affiliation, and ownership of these newspapers during the period covered, between 28 December 2011 and 31 December 2014.

Table 8.1

Ideological Affiliation and Ownership of Turkish Newspapers, 2009–2015

Newspaper	Ownership	Ideological Orientation/Bent	Relation with the Government (AKP)	Number of Relevant Articles
Hürriyet	Doğan Holding	Kemalist/Mainstream/Central Right/Relatively Secular	Moderate conflict/partially pro-government	632
Birgün	Independent cooperation	Leftist/Liberal Democrat/Secular	In conflict	114
Sabah	Çalık Holding (2008–13), Kalyon Holding (2013–present)	Mainstream/Central Right/Conservative/Political Islam	Pro-government/cooperating with government	294

I chose these three Turkish newspapers because they had the highest public-circulation rates and different ideological stances spanning the political spectrum right to left. Here is a brief account of the political economy of these three newspapers.

Hürriyet (Liberty) is well known for its nationalism, with its cover-page motto declaring, "Turkey belongs to the Turks," next to a small Turkish flag and the picture of Mustafa Kemal Atatürk, the official founder of the Turkish Republic. The paper was owned during the 2011–14 period by the Doğan Holding[1] business conglomerate, which operated largely in energy, trade, tourism, industry, and media and turned into one of the largest conglomerates in Turkey. *Hürriyet* was Turkey's first commercial newspaper, had the highest circulation number in the period discussed, greater than 300,000, and politically represents Kemalist and other political elites of the mostly center-right political persuasion.

Sabah (Morning), another newspaper with a conservative and pro-JDP (Justice and Development Party [Adalet ve Kalkınma Partisi], which has been in government since 2002) stand, had the second-highest circulation rank, also higher than 300,000. As part of the Turkuvaz Media Group, *Sabah* was owned by Çalık Holding for a short period, 2008–13. It

---

1. In April 2018 Doğan Holding sold *Hürriyet* to Demirören Holding, which is pro-government because of the state's subsidization of business.

is worth noting that the CEO of Çalık Holding was Berat Albayrak, Turkish president Recep Tayyip Erdoğan's son-in-law, who is now the minister of treasury and finance in Turkey. Then in 2013 *Sabah* was bought by Cemal Kalyoncu (Kalyon Holding), which was commissioned by the JDP government to undertake many extremely lucrative state-subsidized megaprojects, such as the Third International Airport and Metrobus system in Istanbul. Media ownership of *Sabah* in this case and ownership of a media outlet in general have emerged as a precondition that the JDP seems to stipulate in return for receiving lucrative contracts for state-subsidized megaprojects from the JDP government. *Sabah* has naturally now turned into the flagship newspaper of JDP's conservative and nonliberal politics in Turkey. Although the Kemalist *Hürriyet* and the Erdoğanist *Sabah* have different political aspirations, they are nevertheless instrumentalized by the government as its mouthpiece due to their owners' business interests in government subcontracts—Kalyon Holding in large-scale construction, Doğan Holding in energy, tourism, and industry (Hacisabanoglu 2015; Tunç 2015; Yılmaz 2016).

Birgün (Someday) is the only left-leaning independent newspaper in Turkey, with a much lower circulation, in the ten thousands, although it once had a higher circulation of thirty thousand between 2005 and 2009. Unlike the other two newspapers, *Birgün* was much more recently established, in 2004, and is supported largely by labor unions and various left-wing organizations through the advertisements these groups give to the newspaper. Because it is not owned by a conglomerate, it is more independent and therefore able to assume a more critical stance toward the state and the JDP government, but it is also limited to leftist politics at the expense of Kurdish identity politics. Thus, deep down, it also maintains if not a pro-government stand, then certainly a pro-state stand.

Method

For data analysis, I primarily employed the critical discourse analysis (CDA) approach to interpret the data and especially to scrutinize the ideological production of reality and meaning beyond the text by focusing on the context. Norman Fairclough efficiently sheds light on analyzing language, discourse, text, and context in his renowned works *Media Discourse* (1995) and *Language and Power* (2001). When investigating news reports, it is necessary to consider language and discourse as social practices and to focus on the analysis of "the relationship between text, processes and their social conditions" as well as the circumstances generated by social structure and institutions (Fairclough 2001, 21). Rather than taking it as given that media texts such as news articles fully mirror reality, CDA argues that what is narrated are texts that reflect partial accounts of social reality constructed according to the political, economic, and social interests of those in positions of power (Fairclough 1995, 2003; Fairclough and Fairclough 2012).

CDA is thus concerned largely with the production and reproduction of social inequalities because it focuses on the manufacturing of consent and domination in discursive practices through prejudice, discrimination, and disempowerment. CDA investigates the naturalization and opacity of language, exposes power relations embedded within the text, and reveals concealed meaning in the text by focusing on wording, context, source attribution, naming, rhetoric, presence of different voices, and nonverbal components such as images (Fairclough 1995; Reisigl and Wodak 2001; Richardson 2007). For instance, Fairclough's method of analyzing the representational process in newspaper texts dwells on "what choices are made—what is included and what is excluded, what is implicit and what is explicit, what is foregrounded and what is backgrounded, what is thematized and what is unthematized, what process types and categories are drawn upon to represent events, and so on" (1995, 104). Hence, by applying CDA to the Turkish media coverage of the Roboskî massacre, I was able to move beyond the rhetoric in the media texts to chart how the Turkish state intervenes in and penetrates all these newspaper articles to further its own interests. I describe this process as *narrative violence* against the Kurds.

Empirical Background:
Roboskî Village, Borders, and Borderlands

On 28 December 2011, while flying over the mountains along the Turkey-Iraq border, a Turkish Predator drone exported from the United States detected a group of people crossing the border into Turkey with about fifty mules. Subsequently, between 21:39 and 22:44, more than an hour, Turkish artillery aided by F-16 jets bombarded the group. The airstrike continued for an additional forty-five minutes close to Roboskî (in Kurdish; in Turkish: Ortasu) and Bêcih (in Kurdish; in Turkish: Gülyazı) villages in the Uludere (Qaliban in Kurdish) district of the Şırnak province, which is a part of the Kurdish region of southeastern Turkey. Because Roboskî is the village closest to the place where this mass killing took place, I prefer to refer to this violent event as the "Roboskî massacre," as many other critical researchers do, rather than as the "Uludere event," which "official" or Turkish state researchers prefer to use. I want to emphasize here the politics of naming in Turkey: the state and military banned, changed, and replaced the Kurdish names of cities, villages, and regions with Turkish names during the systematic assimilation politics employed by the Turkish Republic against all non-Turkish elements, ethnic or religious (Al 2015; Aslan 2015; Beşikçi 1991; Gunes 2013; Romano 2006). Hence, I use Kurdish names to counter the challenge of Turkish state discursive practices that constantly redraw boundaries, remap the Kurdish-populated geography, and Turkify the land by eliminating Kurdish place-names as well as property and land ownership.

Soon it became evident through local sources that the thirty-eight villagers were on a routine round trip, traveling to Iraqi Kurdistan with cash and returning with their mules burdened by packs full of sugar, cigarettes, and gasoline. The bombardment killed thirty-four of them. Nineteen were children younger than eighteen, who were "smuggling," as the Turkish state discourse refers to the activity, to support their education and the economic well-being of their families in the village. Around fifty mules carrying the burden were also killed on the spot. The Turkish army refused to be held accountable, claiming that the group had been mistakenly interpreted as PKK armed militia clandestinely crossing the Turkish border. Yet this explanation did not make sense because such border crossing for trade was routine, carried out at the same time and on the same day of the week for many months. Hence, the Turkish army was fully aware of this kind of trade and the border-crossing activities it entailed. According to the accounts of the victims' families and experts, the Turkish army already knew that the group consisted of villagers and not PKK militias because some state officials turned a blind eye to these activities in return for receiving their cut from this "smuggling" in the form of a bribe (Eralp 2015; Geerdink 2015; Oral 2015). Illegal trade with neighboring countries is not a rare practice for citizens of Turkey, and the state from time to time had attacked the Kurds for cross-boarding trade, but until this violent incident there had not been a similar case with such a high death toll.

In 2013 the Roboskî case was sent from the Turkish civilian court to the military court, and the Turkish military court dropped the charges against the army in 2014. Justice for the victims and their families has thus remained elusive. Since then, the Turkish legal system's guarantee of the rights of all citizens, including Kurds, has also vanished. As local residents of the broader region, Kurds had historically lived, traded, traveled, and become neighbors with each other regardless of borders. Yet with the formation of the new nation-states of Turkey, Iran, Iraq, and Syria to replace the Ottoman and Iranian Empires, Kurdistan was literally divided into four pieces that were soon strewn with violence (Beşikçi 1991). The Kurdish question was not merely a question of identity but now the consequence of the region's interstate colonization (Beşikçi 1990; Dirlik 2002; Gambetti and Jongerden 2015). These new artificially drawn borders turned the trading done by Kurds into "smuggling" and traders such as the villagers of Roboskî into illegal "smugglers." These unfairly drawn political territorial borderlines produced countless stories of smuggling, banditry, death, loss, and separation in the lives of all Kurds (Aras 2014a). So far, the people of Roboskî have experienced the most disastrous violence. All four nationalist governments of Turkey, Iran, Iraq, and Syria have favored their own ethnic majority in the allocation of local resources, forcing the Kurds in each of these nation-states into poverty, underdevelopment, and deprivation. Aside from centuries of cross-border trade, it was these conditions that impelled the Roboskî villagers across the border in search of inexpensive goods and trading, despite the nation-states' definition of these activities as illegal.

Nation-states formulate severe policies against their inhabitants to create a piece of homogenized land that excludes the existence of the other within them. Establishing the margins of the nation-state enables the nation to reinstate itself in those spaces, exercising power there to decide "what/who is going to be inside and what/who is going to be left out" (Akyüz 2013, 20). Local Greeks and Armenians (non-Muslims) were violently excluded during the drawing of the boundaries of the modern Muslim Turkish nation-state, but the Kurds were initially invited to fight alongside the Turks against western European powers as useful allies during the War of Independence, which lasted from 1919 to 1922. The Turkish leaders of the new republican state promised the Kurds, in return for their participation, equal rights and local sovereignty. Yet after the Lausanne Treaty of 1923 secured the borders of the new Turkey internationally, the Turkish leadership reneged on their promise, resorting instead to violence and oppression. Although Kurds were given citizenship, they were treated as second-class citizens. They could become equal citizens symbolically if and when they erased their Kurdish identity, thereby becoming "Turkified."

Reflecting on the connection between borders and national identities, John Agnew suggests that "national identities have been crafted after borders are more or less in place by ethnic cleansing or expulsions, forced assimilation, and other planned or spontaneous, but usually violent efforts at cultural homogenization by central authorities and their local agents" (2007, 400). Likewise, during the process of national border making, to construct the "appropriate" citizen the Turkish state has executed massacres, oppression, and forced assimilation against the Kurds during the past century. Many Kurdish revolts, such as the Sheikh Said (1925), Mount Ararat (1930), and Dêrsim (1937–38) Uprisings, were started with the intent to get Turkey to fulfill its initial promise of full equality to the Kurds, but they failed (Aras 2014b; Beşikçi 1991; Bozarslan 2008; Çiçek 2016; Gunes 2013; Orhan 2016; Ünver 2015). Within this larger historical and analytical framework, the violence experienced by the Roboskî villagers can be interpreted as yet another attack by the Turkish state, randomly enacted to suppress the Kurds and to reiterate that any violence carried out against them will never be tried in the Turkish justice system to hold the Turkish state and the military accountable for this grave massacre.

Representation of the Kurdish Question in the Turkish Media

Turkish media have always played a strong ideological role in the production of Turkish national identity, an identity that systematically discriminates against the non-Turk and the non-Muslim, excluding these social groups as the "Other" (Akan 2011). Also, Turkish media have always had to rely on the state and its governments because of the lack of democratic institutions, an independent bourgeoisie, and an autonomous civil society in Turkey. As a consequence, from the start of the republic in 1923 to the present, the Turkish state media as well as mainstream private media have always backed the interests of the official elites and media owners, promoting the state official discourse (Heper and Demirel 1996; Kaya 2009; Kaya and Çakmur 2010). This official discourse has constantly marginalized and delegitimized Kurds as backward reactionaries who choose to exist as tribes, who are economically underdeveloped by their own choice, and who are potential traitors backed by Western imperialist powers against the Turkish nation (Aras 2014b; Ünver 2015; Yadirgi 2017; Yegen 1999; Zeydanlıoğlu 2006). Such a depiction places the blame squarely on the Kurdish victims rather than holding the Turkish official perpetrators accountable for reneging on the promise they made to Kurds for local sovereignty.

The Turkish media have fully embraced this derogatory official discourse, thereby representing the Kurds within frameworks filled with prejudice, xenophobia, and discrimination. Despite the pressure to acknowledge the civil rights of the Kurds during the European Union accession process, the Turkish media have continually reinforced banal nationalism by employing the narrative of othering that constantly associates the Kurds with terrorism and depicts them as a domestic threat to the Turkish nation. With this reinforcement from the Fourth Estate, the Turkish state has continued to sustain its hegemony and control over the Kurds through various forms of violence (Sezgin and Wall 2005; Yumul and Ozkirimli 2000). For instance, the media frequently targeted the Kurdish Democratic Society Party (Demokratik Toplum Partisi, DTP), which was banned in 2009 by the Turkish Constitutional Court, continuously portraying it and the Kurds as terrorists posing a national threat (Köker and Doğanay 2010).

Theoretical Argument: Social Construction of Narrative Violence in the Turkish Media

The empirical and methodological analysis I undertook enabled me to develop a more complete picture of the violence enacted against the Kurds by the Turkish state, society, and media. Moving beyond the physical violence that has been amply demonstrated in scholarship and media, I analyze the discourse in Turkish media regarding the Roboskî incident to flesh out another kind of violence that I refer to as narrative violence. I present the framework of this argument in figure 8.1. The figure presents the social construction of Turkish narrative violence through the interaction of Turkish national ideology with Turkish state discourse at three levels: denial, blaming the victim, and erasing Kurds as a social group. Although the state somewhat moderated this stance at the beginning of peace talks with the PKK in 2009, it soon abandoned that moderation, and the physical violence that ensued was supported with narrative violence. As the figure indicates, Turkish national ideology interacts with the media discourse regularly and quickly at the three levels of denial, blaming the victims, and erasing the agency of all Kurds. Based on this theoretical model, I have analyzed the Turkish media coverage of the Roboskî massacre in detail.

Initially, during the first twelve hours after the attack, the Turkish mainstream media remained silent, thereby violating media reporting ethics by depriving the public of the knowledge of the incident. Turkish

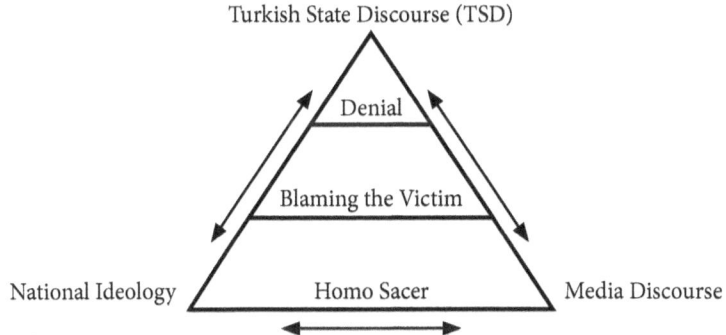

8.1. Social construction of Turkish narrative violence against the Kurds.

TV channels and in particular news channels such as NTV, CNN Turk, and TRT did not announce the air-strike attack for half a day. Apart from the Kurdish press agencies, neither Turkish TV stations nor newspapers provided any information on the air strike. They self-censored, starting their coverage of the incident only after Turkish officials and officers started to give briefings on it. Because of social media, however, news of the incident and photographs of the victims had already started to circulate widely by this point. The Dutch journalist Fréderike Geerdink,[2] who was carefully following the case, states that a colleague of hers who was working for one of the major TV channels told her that the station was unable to broadcast the massacre instantaneously because Prime Minister Recep Tayyip Erdoğan did not give the Turkish media permission to do so (2015, 13). Many hours after the bombardment, the Turkish TV channels started their broadcast of the incident not by covering the massacre but by unanimously repeating the following short statement from the Turkish army: "An abnormal activity has been detected on our border, which terrorists frequently use as a gateway. The decision was taken to hit the target, which had been bombarded between 9:37 p.m. and 10:24 p.m." Turkish media have adopted and widely circulated such official statements with similar formal, indirect discursive practices since the foundation of the republic; in all these cases, ideological obedience replaces the critical questioning of the credibility of the news source, on the one side, and independent explanation of what happened on the ground, on the other.

Finally, on 30 December 2011, two full days after the massacre, Turkish newspapers started to report it by employing somewhat different narrations. The headline of the pro-government newspaper *Zaman* (Time), which was a mouthpiece of the religious Gülen movement, a staunch ally of the JDP back then, read "Fatal Intelligence," with the subheading "35 of Our Citizens at the Border of North Iraq Lost Their Lives." The newspaper carefully chose to state that "the mistake" had happened in northern

---

2. Fréderike Geerdink is a journalist and Turkey expert who has done research on the conflict resolution and Kurdish question in Turkey. Her book on the Roboskî massacre, *The Boys Are Dead: The Roboski Massacre and the Kurdish Question in Turkey* (2015), provides extensive information.

Iraq, not within Turkish borders, refraining to refer to the region by its official name, "Iraqi Kurdistan." It has been a political taboo in Turkey to refer to the region as anything other than "the Southeast," thereby silencing the facts that the region is called "Kurdistan" in general and that the land of the Kurds residing in Turkey is called "Northern Kurdistan," or "Bakur" (Bakurê Kurdistanê) in Kurdish. A similar heading was employed by another pro-JDP Islamist newspaper, *Yeni şafak* (New Dawn): "Fatal Mistake," accompanied by the subtitle "35 People Lost Their Lives" (30 December 2011).

When covering this massacre, the secular Kemalist and religious Islamist newspapers put aside their inherent conflicts and hostility against each other, uniting along the nationalist anti-Kurdish stand. The conspicuous headline of the pro-Kemalist and nationalist newspaper *Sözcü* (Spokesperson) on 30 December read "They Were Carrying Weapons." Hence, unlike the Islamist papers *Zaman* and *Yeni şafak*, the secularist *Sözcü* vilified the victims by alluding that they deserved the violence directed at them because they were allegedly carrying not basic goods but rather weapons for the PKK. Indeed, the Turkish media have often adopted the transportation of illegal weapons as the dominant official excuse to legitimate the Turkish state and society's use of disproportionate violence and destruction against the Kurds and thereby not to hold the state–society accountable. Time and again, the Turkish media have not engaged in investigative journalism but instead cheered on the state violence executed against the Kurds. A case in point is the Dêrsim massacre in 1937–38, where about forty thousand Kurds were murdered, and many thousands more were forced to leave their ancestral homes, with no accountability asked of the Turkish state or society (Bulut 2005).

Contrary to the pro-JDP and Kemalist newspapers, the liberal newspaper *Taraf*'s (Side) headline condemning the airstrike read "The State Bombed Its Citizens: 35 Dead" (30 December 2011). Likewise, the left-leaning *Evrensel*'s (Universal) headline referred to the military strike as the "Uludere Massacre." Hence, these liberal and left-leaning papers challenged the discourse of the dominant mainstream newspapers. However, the most radical headline, "Genocide" (30 December 2011), belonged to the pro-Kurdish newspaper *Özgür gündem* (Free Agenda). This newspaper went on to state that the JDP's policies toward the Kurds had turned genocidal. Its subheading stated that the Turkish army had deliberately massacred thirty-five villagers, most of whom were children. That these victims were children, that they had crossed the border as part of their traditional trading activities practiced for centuries, and that they had done so with the knowledge of Turkish officials and officers were never discussed in the mainstream newspapers. The negligence of and silence toward the whole story behind the air strike produced a half-truth, committing narrative violence that only helped solidify the prejudicial press coverage of the Kurd as a violent traitor instead of an innocent victim.

Layers of narrative violence eventually emerged, starting with the official denial at level I, moving on to blaming the victims at level II, and finally ending with erasing the agency of all Kurds at level III.

Level I. The Official Denial:
"The State Does Not Bomb Its Citizens"

Hürriyet juxtaposed the image of a funeral convoy with Prime Minister Erdoğan's statement overtly denying the collective violence executed by the Turkish state against its Kurdish citizens. Erdoğan stated that no such action could have been taken under the current government and that his administration would examine the tapes and "do whatever needs to be done." Indeed, Prime Minister Erdoğan not only asked rhetorically, "Does the state bomb its people?" (figure 8.2), and answered, "The state does not bomb its citizens," but also conveyed the following: "Our sorrow is enormous. No state bombs its people. In the past, these kinds of things might have happened, but under our government, such a thing cannot happen" (*Hürriyet*, 31 December 2011). Erdoğan's narrative perfectly demonstrates the triple advantage of denial: by "ignoring the presentness of the present" (Bakić-Hayden 2016, 922), one distorts the reality and at the same time refuses to take on the responsibility for the violence. Indeed, in the coverage of the massacre after this date, the Turkish state's denial of this crime against its villagers became one of the dominant discourses in *Hürriyet* and *Sabah*. In addition to embracing the official narration that the state could never commit such a crime against its own citizens, *Hürriyet* then

8.2. A *Hürriyet* headline quotes Erdoğan: "Does the state bomb its own people?" (31 December 2011).

bolstered and legitimized this stand by giving voice to the leading republican official, Prime Minister Erdoğan. These first two moves enabled the newspaper to totally dismiss and forever silence the accounts of bombardment by the victims' families and the survivors.

Hürriyet and *Sabah* ultimately privileged the sources of information provided by the state, emphasizing that the air strike was an "operational accident" rather than routine for the Turkish state to conduct such an operation against "our" citizens. This "interpretive denial" (Cohen 2001, 105) constructed the Kurds as citizens encountering an accident rather than being intentionally and systemically executed by the state. The papers also did not acknowledge the inherent prejudice and discrimination in the definition and practice of citizenship in Turkey: although everyone living in Turkey appears to have equal rights, the Turkish Constitution and political codes define and privilege the citizenship of those with Turkish ethnicity (Aslan 2015; Bayır 2013). Likewise, the conservative pro-JDP newspaper *Sabah* proclaimed that the air strike was an "unwanted accident" that occurred when the army misrecognized the target. Rather than contextualizing what the innocent victims were doing, the paper instead associated—and thereby legitimized—the army's violent actions by arguing that it was merely trying to prevent PKK assaults. PKK assaults were apparently so frequent that the newspaper referred to the "Gediktepe syndrome," whereby the Turkish military was conditioned to react violently without first checking what was going on.

Under the headline "Gediktepe Syndrome Hits the Smuggler" (30 December 2011), *Sabah* aimed to exonerate the Turkish army based on the official accounts: "The previous night, a group with mules infiltrated the border. The army, knowing that previous attacks on Gediktepe and Dağlıca had been carried out by weapon-loaded mules, went on alert and then bombed the group with F16s." *Sabah* deliberately mentioned Gediktepe and Dağlıca (thus silencing Roboskî and Uludere) because these two places housed the headquarters of the Turkish army and had once been once attacked by the PKK years earlier. It thus falsely associated Roboskî with the PKK so that the public could be convinced that the Roboskî "attack" was a military precaution taken to prevent a possible incursion by the PKK. *Sabah* also further attempted to justify the air strike by explicitly stating that the bombed civilians "looked like PKK members." Indeed, the subsequent news article read, "They were shot being mistaken for terrorists": "It was commented that the [earlier] Gediktepe experience [of the military] was effective in the bombarding that killed 35 people," and "the dead people were smugglers."

Sabah and *Hürriyet* constantly referred to the Roboskî massacre as the "Uludere incident" or "Uludere accident," thereby criticizing and delegitimizing alternative narrative versions of the bombardment as a massacre. It should be noted here that media representation is *not* the re-representation and mirroring of objective reality (Hall 2013; B. Poole 2010). Rather, it is a practice by which an event is processed; in this case, the massacre is filtered and reconstructed through reference to the Turkish state ideology. For instance, Taha Akyol, a senior columnist at *Hürriyet*, uncritically accepted the dominant narrative that the killing of the Kurds at Roboskî was an accident rather than mass murder. In his column, he was more concerned with counternarratives and with the perception of the massacre by other actors: "[But] it is another thing to agitate for Kurdish nationalism. *Özgür gündem* newspaper cited this situation as a 'physical genocide' executed by the state over the Kurds. . . . Murat Karayılan said, 'It is an attack on the Kurdish people. . . . The massacre that was carried out with a plan!' . . . Karayılan's real 'strategic' statement, which is described as '*serxildan*' [revolt], is as follows: 'If our people do not react, massacres like this will continue!' No need to comment on what he called for" (*Hürriyet*, 2 January 2012). Akyol warned that the nonmainstream discourse on the violence of the massacre was agitating the Kurds so much that it could eventually lead to another Kurdish rebellion. Elizabeth Poole states that the biased media representation that Akyol exemplifies here "appears to tell us more about the representers than the represented" (2009, 47). In this regard, the denialist and distorted image of Roboskî in *Sabah* and *Hürriyet* reveals not what actually happened but rather the extent to which both newspapers were willing to internalize the false accounts generated by the Turkish state.

Unlike this discourse of denial and accident advocated by *Sabah* and *Hürriyet*, the left-wing paper *Birgün* condemned the bombardment in the headline "Uludere Massacre" (30 December 2011), using the same photograph as *Sabah*. The article further articulated the paper's critical stand: "The Turkish Army bombed 36 villagers, many of whom were between the ages of 15–20, massacring [them] close to Ortasu [Roboskî] [located] in Uludere, a district of Şırnak, [and did so] while they tried to cross the border." *Birgün* thus provided an alternative voice, mentioning the child victims, elaborating on their reasons for crossing the border, and, in doing so, challenging the dominant Turkish state narrative. The provision of the larger context regarding the age of the victims and their poverty made it possible for the audience to access a fuller picture of the case and thus to move beyond the dominant state propaganda. Yet *Birgün* did some of its own silencing, too: it highlighted only the massacre's material conditions, not mentioning its *ethnic* dimension. It did not stress that the victims were not only poor villagers but also Kurds so that it could be seen that in this event poverty intersected with ethnicity. This form of silencing also contributed to the denial. Indeed, in this mode of ethnic silencing, *Birgün* followed the lead of *Sabah* and *Hürriyet*, which almost never mentioned the victims' Kurdish ethnic background. In summary, such silencing indirectly legitimated the violence continually committed against the Kurds by the Turkish state since the establishment of the Turkish Republic.

Level II. The Politics of Blaming the Victim: A "Deserved" Death

Despite their different political ideologies, both *Sabah* and *Hürriyet* accommodated another discursive practice of the state: its veiled xenophobia. They implied that the victims were "dishonest smugglers" who had been involved in criminal activities. Indeed, Yılmaz Özdil, a passionate Kemalist and a popular columnist at *Hürriyet*, perfectly illustrated this stand in his column:

> Dear smuggler
>
> The donkey bangs the horse. The mule is born ... smuggling is the mule, the fruit of forbidden love. It does not matter whoever or whichever bangs one another, the end result is the mating of the state and smuggler ... [e]ach time it [the mule] is able to carry 140 cans of diesel or 400 packs of cigarettes. According to TÜİK [the Turkish Statistical Institute], there are 50,000 mules, [and] 30,000 of them are there [in the Kurdish lands]; count that! The romantic crew of pups say, "The innocent villager ... has to put his life in danger for 50 liras," but that innocent makes [up to] 15,000 lira when he goes [smuggling] twice a week! (6 January 2012)

The naturally attuned elements of racism and sexism diffuse into the author's rhetoric to legitimize the killing of the victims, the majority of whom were younger than eighteen. In addition, the author ridicules those who sympathize with these young victims, stating that the poor victims were not risking their lives for a few dollars but instead making money hand over fist. The author also defines the trade between the Kurds across borders as smuggling, presenting the victims not as innocents but rather as criminals. It is significant to note that smuggling was not categorized and defined as "illegal" until after the partition of Kurdistan by the four nation-states in the region (Kentel 2015). In the Foucauldian sense (Foucault 1972), one could argue that smuggling is not just an already-said utterance but a discursive strategy that establishes a connection between an illegal activity and the Kurdish "other." This strategy helps legitimate and reestablish Turkish state hegemony in Kurdistan.

Sabah's discourse between 2011 and 2014 shifted in accordance with the shifting Turkish state discourse toward the Kurds. In 2012, the hegemonic discourse continued both to regularly blame the victims and their families as well as to associate the Roboskî villagers with the PKK. However, *Sabah* then started to moderate its discourse in 2013 and 2014 by referring to the massacre as a "conspiracy" that had been plotted against the JDP government for starting official peace talks with the Kurds.

Through the first year after the massacre, to legitimize it and silence potential public outcry, the newspaper linked the villagers to the PKK as collaborators. For instance, a few days after the air strike, *Sabah* announced in its headline, "Four Members of the Family [of the Victims] Are in Prison Because of Espionage" (3 January 2012). It then provided the following details: "While grieving the death of 35 villagers and smugglers in the air-strike operation, the new details about the relatives of the villagers resurfaced. . . . Four people [relatives of the family] have been detained for three years and are awaiting trial since they sold [Turkish] state secrets to the intelligence service of the Democratic Party of Iraqi Kurdistan." The article contents actually refuted the headline because the people had *not* been tried and imprisoned but were merely awaiting trial. Yet the headline summarily convicted the detainees, in the process associating them with the massacre victims. Many similar articles in *Sabah* and *Hürriyet* linked the murdered villagers to crime, enemies of the state, illegal activities, and material greed; they all did so with the intent to condemn the victims rather than the perpetrators. Judith Herman elucidates how the vicious discourse of the perpetrator comes about:

> To escape accountability for his crimes, the perpetrator does everything in his power to promote forgetting. Secrecy and silence are the perpetrator's first line of defense. If secrecy fails, the perpetrator attacks the

credibility of his victim. If he cannot silence her absolutely, he tries to make sure that no one listens. To this end, he marshals an impressive array of arguments, from the most blatant denial to the most sophisticated and elegant rationalization. After every atrocity one can expect to hear the same predictable apologies: it never happened; the victim lies; the victim exaggerates; the victim brought it upon herself; and in any case it is time to forget the past and move on. The more powerful the perpetrator, the greater is his prerogative to name and define reality, and the more completely his arguments prevail. (1997, 8)

The Turkish state's denialist strategy continued in mainstream newspapers despite contradictory accounts by the survivors and local villagers. *Sabah* discredited the victims by quoting the deputy prime minister, who stated, for instance, that "the group was warned with signal rockets. . . . [S]ince the group did not stop, the bombardment started" (3 January 2012); it thereby persisted in presenting the official account as truth.

Both *Hürriyet* and *Sabah* likewise joined in blaming other Kurdish actors who were criticizing the government and advocating for the victims' rights. *Sabah* routinely quoted in its headlines Prime Minister Erdoğan's accusations against the Kurdish Peace and Democracy Party (Barış ve Demokrasi Partisi, BDP). For instance, on 4 January 2012 *Sabah*'s headline quoted Erdoğan as stating, "They [the BDP] are walking on the path of Satan." Through this association, the news report delegitimated Kurdish actors' criticisms of the state's and media's reports related to the massacre by alleging that actually the Kurds were the ones "abusing" the Roboskî massacre. Nationalist antagonism against the Kurds then united the Islamist paper *Sabah* and the Kemalist paper *Hürriyet*. Because of the BDP's solidarity with the Roboskî villagers during the mourning process, senior columnist İsmet Berkan of *Hürriyet* explicitly argued that the PKK and BDP were "carrying out a political and public-relations campaign against Turkey" (3 January 2012). *Birgün*, however, continued to blame the Turkish state and the JDP government as perpetrators of the massacre. It also continued to give voice to the families of the victims, allowing them to speak for themselves, not as criminal subjects that the state made them out to be but rather as victims of state persecution.

Level III: The Death and Bare Life of Homo Sacer

The reaction of Turkish state institutions, especially the judiciary and the government, toward the perpetrator of the massacre, the Turkish army, remained uncritical and even supportive. This was the case because Prime Minister Erdoğan implied that the air strike had been an "indispensable" measure. One day after the air strike, on 29 December 2011, Erdoğan explicitly stated, "We have seen similar border activities, where they [the PKK] were smuggling arms prior to massive terrorist raids. The public had demanded to know then as to why we hadn't stopped them. This is what we did now [as a consequence]." A day later he explicitly congratulated the army for its "sensitive" performance (Bianet English 2012). Both *Sabah* and *Hürriyet* reported Erdoğan's biased state-centric interpretation uncritically as if it were the truth. They circulated these official statements even though it was a well-known "secret" that the "smugglers" had not crossed the border without first informing local military officers (Oral 2015).

The congratulations offered to the Turkish army and its exemption from being held accountable for such a horrendous crime can be interpreted through Giorgio Agamben's concept of the *homo sacer* and his bare life. Roman law defined the *homo sacer* as a person who cannot be sacrificed. Yet if another person kills the *homo sacer*, the act is not considered a homicide, and therefore the perpetrator is not punished by death (Agamben 1998). Legally defined as a bad and impure man, *homo sacer* cannot be considered a citizen; he has been bestowed merely with bare life (*la nuda vita*), which is excluded from the juridical law of the sovereign power. *Homo sacer* can then be killed, and the killer will have impunity because human and divine law leave out the execution and death of *homo sacer*. By the same token, in the case of the Roboskî massacre, the Kurdish victims' diminished legal status means they gradually come to resemble *homo sacer*; they possessed bare lives that were exposed to violence in a vulnerable moment, during which the sovereign power of the Turkish state froze and discarded their human rights as a state of exception.

In addition, both newspapers carefully avoided bringing the perpetrator into the story by employing a sentimental tone and passive language to contend that no one should be punished for this crime. A day after the strike, *Hürriyet*'s second headline on the front page read: "35 Dead, We Are Very Sorry" (30 December 2011). As such, the sentimental sorrow was supposed to blanket the rational issue of public responsibility and accountability for the committed violence. Along the same lines, four days after the air strike, *Sabah* quoted one of the JDP ministers: "The state is the one that is damaged the most by this [massacre]." He then elaborated: "Even though the terrorist organization [the PKK] is trying to take advantage of this [massacre], we [are the ones that] suffered from this [massacre]. . . . Who is the one that suffered the most morally and economically? The state, the government, and JDP." The article barely mentioned the suffering of the villagers who died and of their families. It instead emphasized the state's "great loss" without at all explaining what that loss may have been. In line with the government's discourse of strategic silence and misrepresentation, *Hürriyet* normalized and presented the massacre as a political tool abused by the Kurds to criticize the Turkish state. The columnist Rauf Tamer declared that "they [the Kurds] have seized [the] pretext [of the massacre]; of course, they will use it. The villagers who lost their lives in Uludere will always be brought into the discussion as a massacre, even genocide" (*Hürriyet*, 24 May 2012). The author claimed that even though the PKK had killed thousands of Kurds, "they" (referring to Tamer's imagined Kurds) do not hold the PKK accountable and claim such killing "is warfare." Then Tamer implied that the Turkish army should not be held accountable for this "incident" because they (the Turks this time) can also say it is "warfare."

In her book *The Cultural Politics of Emotion* (2014), Sara Ahmed claims that only empathy will "allow us to transform [someone else's] pain into our sadness" (31). However, in Tamer's column, the pain of the victims' families is willfully ignored and politicized, and the dire consequences of the massacre are rationalized; there is not a single trace of sadness or mourning for the victims. Such a punitive stand can only constantly keep reproducing the victims as the enemy and the perpetrators as free of responsibility and accountability.

Taking an opposite stand, *Birgün* acknowledged that the Turkish state and government had committed a crime against the villagers. Yet *Birgün* constructed the crime solely as yet another case of the lack of social justice in Turkey, thus totally omitting the ethnic dimension of the incident. In this context, however, as Ahmed (2017) asserts, the violence was directed more toward some bodies than toward others. Not all citizens of Turkey were equal in terms of the violence directed at them. As Sarita Malik (2002) articulates with respect to Blacks and Asians in Great Britain, the newspaper acted morally in accordance with the notion of solidarity and communality on behalf of victims, yet it was too afraid to take a step further into the origins of the violence to see and acknowledge the underlying issues of the claim that the Kurdish race and ethnicity are much more subject to violence than are the hegemonic Turkish race and ethnicity.

The official Turkish discourse mimicked by the mainstream media started to change over time. In 2013, the second year after the Roboskî massacre, the JDP government started to officially negotiate with the PKK for peace. At the same time, it started parting ways with the Gülen movement, excluding it from the Turkish body politic so much that the Turkish state eventually got the movement reclassified as a terror organization. This peace period with the Kurds moderated and changed the discourse of *Sabah* and *Hürriyet* on Roboskî. First, the newspapers, in particular *Sabah*, started to associate the Gülen movement with the massacre, claiming that it had bombed Roboskî with the intent of derailing the peace negotiations. As more time passed, Roboskî appeared in the newspapers less and less, except for in *Birgün*, which tried to follow the court process that was presumably going to identify and hold accountable those who gave the orders for the artillery bombing and air raid.

Despite the peace process and the positive shift in the Turkish state discourse, none of the perpetrators had yet been convicted as of 2018, seven years after the massacre.[3] The military court started to investigate the case in 2013 when the civil court transferred it to military jurisdiction. In 2014, after gathering information and preparing reports, Turkish military prosecutors decided to go for nolle prosequi (Söylemez 2014)—that is, a formal notice of abandonment of all or part of a suit or action. When

---

3. BBC Turkish 2017 summarizes what happened in Roboskî and after it until the end of 2017.

the Turkish military court dropped the charges, the families of the victims took the legal decision to the European Court of Human Rights (ECHR). However, not only the Turkish state and media but apparently also the pro-Kurdish HDP and the lawyers of the Roboskî families neglected to follow through in the quest for social justice: in May 2018, the ECHR rejected the case on the grounds that the lawyers did not submit missing documents (Bianet English 2018).

Conclusion

In this chapter, I have examined three newspapers—the center-right Kemalist *Hürriyet*, the pro-JDP and political Islamist *Sabah*, and the left-wing *Birgün*—for their representations of the Roboskî massacre. I observed that *Hürriyet* and *Sabah* fully adopted the Turkish government's narration of the massacre. *Sabah* in particular mirrored the JDP's discourse throughout the four years of coverage I examined. Regardless of their ideological differences, both newspapers presented the case in line with the Turkish official narrative, which denied the state crime, blamed the victims, and tried to delegitimize them and the pro-Kurdish actor HDP, which was advocating for their rights, by associating them with the PKK. These two newspapers also ended up supporting the exemption and immunity of the perpetrators. I have defined this process as *narrative violence*. Both of these central-right newspapers failed to challenge the Turkish state's denialist and discriminatory discourse regarding the massacre and instead presented the violence as an accident that could be blamed on the victims, while systematically privileging official voices and silencing the voices of the Kurdish victims.

The rather independent left-wing *Birgün* did provide an alternate account of the massacre, including some historical background to the victims' cross-border actions. Unlike other newspapers, it did not label the victims as greedy smugglers and did not associate them with crime and treason against the Turkish state. Yet although *Birgün* did indeed blame the Turkish state and government, it failed to mention the ethnic origins of the violence—that is, that the ethnicity of the Kurds made them more susceptible to such violence. In the end, no perpetrator was found guilty and punished either during the peace talks or afterward, even to this day. Let me conclude by stating that eventually making the perpetrators accountable for the Roboskî massacre would be one significant step toward achieving peace and democracy in Turkey. At the moment, however, the existing Turkish official narrative of the massacre and the mainstream Turkish media continue to commit narrative violence.

References

Agamben, Giorgio. 1998. *Homo Sacer: Sovereign Power and Bare Life*. Stanford, CA: Stanford Univ. Press.

Agnew, John. 2007. "No Borders, No Nations: Making Greece in Macedonia." *Annals of the Association of American Geographers* 97, no. 2: 398–422.

Ahmed, Sara. 2017. *Living a Feminist Life*. Durham, NC: Duke Univ. Press.

Akan, Aysun. 2011. "A Critical Analysis of the Turkish Press Discourse against Non-Muslims: A Case Analysis of the Newspaper Coverage of the 1942 Wealth Tax." *Middle Eastern Studies* 47, no. 4: 605–21.

Akyüz, Latife. 2013. "Ethnicity and Gender Dynamics of Living in Borderlands: The Case of Hopa-Turkey." PhD diss., Middle East Technical Univ.

Al, Serhun. 2015. "Elite Discourses, Nationalism, and Moderation: A Dialectical Analysis of Turkish and Kurdish Nationalisms." *Ethnopolitics* 14, no. 1: 94–112.

Aras, Ramazan. 2014a. "Border and Borderland Studies in Turkey: A Critical Evaluation." *Journal of Mukaddime* 5, no. 2: 15–38.

———. 2014b. *The Formation of Kurdishness in Turkey: Political Violence, Fear, and Pain*. Oxford: Routledge.

Aslan, Senem. 2015. *Nation-Building in Turkey and Morocco: Governing Kurdish and Berber Dissent*. New York: Cambridge Univ. Press.

Bakić-Hayden, Milica. 2016. "Nesting Orientalisms: The Case of Former Yugoslavia." *Association for Slavic, East European, and Eurasian Studies* 54, no. 4: 917–31.

Bayır, Derya. 2013. "Representation of the Kurds by the Turkish Judiciary." *Human Rights Quarterly* 35, no. 1: 116–42.

BBC Turkish. 2017. "28 Aralık 2011'de Roboski'de neler yaşandı?" 28 Dec. At http://www.bbc.com/turkce/haberler-turkiye-42501681.

Beşikçi, İsmail. 1990. *Tunceli Kanunu 1935 ve Dersim Jenosidi*. Istanbul: Belge Yayınları.

———. 1991. *Devletlerarası sömürge Kürdistan*. Ankara, Turkey: Yurt-Kitap.

Bianet English. 2012. "Timeline: What Happened in Roboski?" 31 Dec. At https://bianet.org/english/human-rights/143200-timeline-what-happened-in-roboski.

———. 2018. "ECtHR Rejects Application about Roboski Massacre." 17 May. At https://bianet.org/english/human-rights/197265-ecthr-rejects-application-about-roboski-massacre.

Bozarslan, Hamit. 2008. "Kurds and the Turkish State." In *The Cambridge History of Turkey*, edited by Resat Kasaba, 333–56. Cambridge: Cambridge Univ. Press.

Bulut, Faik. 2005. *Türk basınında Kürtler: Inceleme*. 2nd ed. Istanbul: Evrensel Basım Yayın.

Çiçek, Cuma. 2016. "Kurdish Identity and Political Islam under AKP Rule." *Research and Policy on Turkey* 1, no. 2: 147–63.

Cohen, Stanley. 2001. *States of Denial: Knowing about Atrocities and Suffering*. Cambridge: Polity.

Dirlik, Arif. 2002. "Rethinking Colonialism: Globalization, Postcolonialism, and the Nation." *Interventions* 4, no. 3: 428–48.

Eralp, Doga Ulas. 2015. "The Role of U.S. Drones in the Roboski Massacre." *Peace Review* 27, no. 4: 448–55.

Fairclough, Isabela, and Norman Fairclough. 2012. *Political Discourse Analysis: A Method for Advanced Students*. Oxford: Routledge.

Fairclough, Norman. 1995. *Media Discourse*. London: E. Arnold.

———. 2001. *Language and Power*. 2nd ed. Harlow, UK: Pearson Education.

———. 2003. *Analyzing Discourse: Textual Analysis for Social Research*. London: Routledge.

Foucault, Michel. 1972. *The Archaeology of Knowledge*. Translated by A. M. Sheridan Smith. New York: Tavistock.

Gambetti, Zeynep, and Joost Jongerden. 2015. "Introduction: The Kurdish Issue in Turkey from a Spatial Perspective." In *The Kurdish Issue in Turkey*, edited by Zeynep Gambetti and Joost Jongerden, 1–21. Oxon: Routledge.

Geerdink, Fréderike. 2015. *The Boys Are Dead: The Roboski Massacre and the Kurdish Question in Turkey*. London: Gomidas Institute.

Gunes, Cengiz. 2013. *The Kurdish National Movement in Turkey: From Protest to Resistance*. Oxford: Routledge.

Hacisabanoglu, Mehmet Sagnak. 2015. "Media Ethics and CSR." *British Journal of Arts and Social Sciences* 19, no. 1: 13–23.

Hall, Stuart. 2013. "The Work of Representation." In *Representation*, edited by Stuart Hall, Jessica Evans, and Nixon Sean, 1–13. London: Sage.

Heper, Metin, and Tanel Demirel. 1996. "The Press and the Consolidation of Democracy in Turkey." *Middle Eastern Studies* 32, no. 2: 109–23.

Herman, Judith Lewis. 1997. *Trauma and Recovery: The Aftermath of Violence— from Domestic Abuse to Political Terror.* New York: Basic.

Kaya, A. Raşit. 2009. *İktidar yumağı: Medya–sermaye–devlet.* Ankara, Turkey: İmge Kitabevi.

Kaya, Raşit, and Barış Çakmur. 2010. "Politics and the Mass Media in Turkey." *Turkish Studies* 11, no. 4: 521–37.

Kentel, Ferhat. 2015. "Savaş kültüründe barış yapmak." In *Barış açısını savunmak çözüm sürecinde ne oldu?*, edited by Necmiye Alpay and Hakan Tahmaz, 138–53. Istanbul: Metis.

Köker, Eser, and Ülkü Doğanay. 2010. *Irkçı değilim ama: Yazılı basında ırkçı ayrımcı söylemler.* Ankara, Turkey: İnsan Hakları Ortak Platformu Yayini.

Malik, Sarita. 2002. *Representing Black Britain: A History of Black and Asian Images on British Television.* London: Sage.

Oral, Sibel. 2015. *Toprağın öptüğü çocuklar: Adaleti beklerken Roboski.* Istanbul: Can Yayınları.

Orhan, Mehmet. 2016. *Political Violence and Kurds in Turkey: Fragmentations, Mobilizations, Participation, and Repertoires.* Oxford: Routledge.

Poole, Brian. 2010. "Commitment and Criticality: Fairclough's Critical Discourse Analysis Evaluated." *International Journal of Applied Linguistics* 20, no. 2: 137–55.

Poole, Elizabeth. 2009. *Reporting Islam: Media Representations of British Muslims.* London: I. B. Tauris.

Reisigl, Martin, and Ruth Wodak. 2001. *Discourse and Discrimination: Rhetorics of Racism and Antisemitism.* London: Routledge.

Richardson, John E. 2007. *Analysing Newspapers: An Approach from Critical Discourse Analysis.* New York: Palgrave Macmillan.

Romano, David. 2006. *The Kurdish Nationalist Movement: Opportunity, Mobilization, and Identity.* Cambridge: Cambridge Univ. Press.

Sezgin, Dilara, and Melissa A. Wall. 2005. "Constructing the Kurds in the Turkish Press: A Case Study of *Hürriyet* Newspaper." *Media, Culture, & Society* 27, no. 5: 787–98.

Söylemez, Ayça. 2014. "Nolle Prosequi in Roboski Massacre Case." Bianet English, 7 Jan. At http://bianet.org/english/human-rights/152644-nolle-prosequi-in-roboski-massacre-case%20takipsilik%20karari%202014.

Tunç, Asli. 2015. *Media Ownership and Finances in Turkey: Increasing Concentration and Clientelism*. Report, South East European Media Observatory, Nov.

Ünver, H. Akin. 2015. *Turkey's Kurdish Question: Discourse and Politics since 1990*. Oxford: Routledge.

Yadirgi, Veli. 2017. *The Political Economy of the Kurds of Turkey: From the Ottoman Empire to the Turkish Republic*. Cambridge: Cambridge Univ. Press.

Yegen, Mesut. 1999. "The Kurdish Question in Turkish State Discourse." *Journal of Contemporary History* 34, no. 4: 555–68.

Yılmaz, Gözde. 2016. "Europeanisation or De-Europeanisation? Media Freedom in Turkey (1999–2015)." *South European Society and Politics* 21, no. 1: 147–61.

Yumul, Arus, and Umut Ozkirimli. 2000. "Reproducing the Nation: 'Banal Nationalism' in the Turkish Press." *Media, Culture, & Society* 22:787–804.

Zeydanlıoğlu, Welat. 2006. "'The White Turkish Man's Burden': Orientalism, Kemalism, and the Kurds in Turkey." In *Neo-colonial Mentalities in Contemporary Europe? Language and Discourse in the Construction of Identities*, edited by Guido Rings and Ann Ife, 155–74. Newcastle, UK: Cambridge Scholars.

Part Three
Micropolitics of Resistance

9

Youth and Politics in Diyarbakır

Delal Aydın

Look here, here, underneath this black marble
A child is buried; if he had lived for one more recess
He would have risen from nature to the blackboard.
He was killed in a lesson of the state.

The wrong question of nature and the state was
—Where does the Mavarannahr flow?
The only correct response from a raised hand in the last row
—Into the heart of the insurrection of a pale people's children.
—Ece Ayhan, "Monument of the Unknown Student" /
"Meçhul öğrenci anıtı" (Ayhan 2014)

This chapter examines political mobilization among the Kurdish youth in the 1990s when clashes between the Kurdistan Workers' Party (Partîya Karkerên Kurdistanê, PKK) and the Turkish military heightened, and it empirically focuses on the formation of the Yurtsever (Patriotic) Youth Movement. The 1990s were marked by the intersection of extensive Turkish state violence against the Kurds and a condensed revolutionary movement of Kurdish subjects. It was a period of turmoil, when the Kurdish masses demanded recognition of their existence, while the Turkish state attempted to violently repress their resistance. When faced with such escalated violence, the Kurdish youth became receptive to the PKK's call for struggle; they mobilized around the public identity of the *yurtsever* (patriot) to display their allegiance to the PKK and to stand united with it against the state.

My argument here has two parts. First, I challenge the claim that the Kurdish *yurtsever* as a political subject emerged solely from the clash of two fixed and bounded imaginaries—namely, the Turkish state on the one side and the Kurdish resistance on the other. Second, I argue that the emergence of the *yurtsever* was the end result of a process, "a reconfiguration of the political" (Rancière, Panagia, and Bowlby 2001, 9) by various actors; this reconfiguration not only shattered and reconstituted previous meanings, significations, and definitions but, more importantly, also led to the emergence of *new* relations. Specifically, the formation of the *yurtsever* subject marked a fundamental change in the political relationship between Kurdish society and the Turkish state, a change that placed the "Kurdish question" (*Kürt sorunu*) at the heart of Turkish politics. Here I empirically analyze this reconfiguration of the political in the formation of revolutionary subjects in a high school setting in southeastern Turkey, or Bakur Kurdistan. I specifically focus on how the Turkish state elites invited Kurdish youth to participate in the republican project of building and reproducing the Turkish nation and how the students responded. I interpret the mobilization of Kurdish *yurtsever* students as a historical process of the revolutionary subject formation when Kurdish students rejected assimilation into Turkishness and chose instead to be a part of a struggle for recognition even at the cost of their own lives. I argue that the *yurtsever* Kurdish political identity emerged through two processes: (1) the creation of a *new* social space for the excluded and the marginalized and (2) the mobilization of those systematically excluded from the Turkish state space.

Empirical Context

The analysis is based on the field research I conducted at Ziya Gökalp High School (Ziya Gökalp Lisesi) in Diyarbakir between January 2015 and January 2016. To study the formation of *yurtsever* subjecthood, I combined in-depth and semistructured interviews, archival research, and autoethnography. In all, I interviewed twenty-one former students of Ziya Gökalp High School, concentrating mainly on those actively involved in the *yurtsever* movement in the early 1990s. In addition, I talked to six teachers who worked at the school during the same decade to grasp the extent of identity contestation at the school. Also, I carried out semistructured interviews with graduates from other high schools to better understand the extent of Kurdish youth mobilization in Diyarbakir in the 1990s. To get access to the PKK's viewpoint, I conducted archival research at the Parliamentary Library in Ankara, which houses the entire collection of newspapers and journals published by the PKK; I specifically explored PKK statements regarding its strategy to mobilize Kurdish youth.

Because I am a Kurdish woman who has lived in this political environment, I also employed autoethnographic methods to better understand what Begoña Aretxaga calls "the deep plays of subjectivity" (1995, 125). In the 1990s, I experienced the process of *yurtsever* subjectification, although I was living in western Turkey at the time. My own experience as a *yurtsever* guided me in choosing a state school to examine the subject formation of Kurdish youth; after all, Kurdish youths' encounter/experience with the Turkish state occurs daily through schooling. While conducting interviews and examining PKK publications, I also documented the feelings and reactions that these interactions evoked in me. By doing so, I could analyze how power operated at a deeper level (Ellis and Borchner 2006), thereby constructing another venue to better understand Kurdish youth mobilization in the struggle for recognition. I need to point out, however, that there was a large difference between my experience of being a *yurtsever* in western Turkey and the experiences of my respondents, who lived in Diyarbakir: western Turkey is populated largely by Turks, so the Kurds there experienced state violence in different forms than the Kurds in eastern Turkey, including Diyarbakir, who lived in constant political violence. I therefore decided to prioritize my respondents' narratives over mine.

ZGL: A Site of Youth Mobilization

Diyarbakir, where Ziya Gökalp Lisesi (ZGL) is located, is the largest city of the Kurdish region in southeastern Turkey, with about a million inhabitants; it is considered the political and symbolic center of the Kurdish (autonomy) movement and, hence, the unofficial capital of the Kurdish homeland for the Kurds of Turkey. Yet the city is also central for the Turkish state as it attempts to build a Turkish society in the middle of a majority-Kurdish population. ZGL, established in 1893, was initially known as

Diyarbakir High School (Diyarbakir İdadisi). It was one of the first secular high schools established by the state that smoothly transitioned from the Ottoman Empire to the Turkish Republic.

In 1953 the school was renamed after the famous sociologist, writer, and poet Ziya Gökalp, who also taught at the school. Gökalp's ideas had a very strong ideological influence on the Young Turk Revolution in general and on the Committee of Union and Progress (İttihat ve Terakki Cemiyeti) in particular. It was ultimately Gökalp's writings that fundamentally informed the construction of Turkish nationalism and especially its "moral ethos";[1] he is ironically therefore known in official Turkish discourse as "the founder of Turkism," even though he was ethnically Kurdish. In his theory of corporatist nationalist ideology, influenced by Émile Durkheim, Gökalp argued that it was the political elite's corporate responsibility to alter the composition of society with the intent to enhance cultural unity and solidarism (Üngör 2011, 31, 35). This stand legitimated the social engineering practiced by the Committee of Union and Progress, especially as it forcefully deported and massacred the non-Muslim imperial subjects—the Armenians, the Pontus, the Greeks, the Syriac, and the Assyrians. Gökalp's famous poem "Red Apple" ("Kızılelma") articulates his social vision well:

> He said it was important to get to know the East
> said the people are a garden and we are gardeners
> trees are not rejuvenated by grafting alone
> first it is necessary to trim the tree. (Gökalp 2011, 35)

Among the imperial subjects, Kurds were like Greeks and Armenians in that they all belonged to social groups that challenged Turkist state ideology. Yet Gökalp also believed that Kurds, unlike Greeks and Armenians,

---

1. I borrow the emphasis on moral ethos in the formation of states from Philip Corrigan and Derek Sayer; they define state forms as "animated and legitimated by a particular moral ethos" in history (1985, 4). The militarized and ethnicized form of the Turkish state has been "animated and legitimated" by the moral ethos of a limited and totalizing imaginary of the nation.

would be more easily assimilated given their cultural (religious) affinity to Turks (Üngör 2011, 38). It is this legacy that led Ziya Gökalp to be honored by the Turkish state, which named a school after him right in the middle of Kurdistan. It is as if Gökalp were personally inviting Kurdish youth to the school to participate in the project of building the Turkish nation that he started. After all, Ziya Gökalp, "the founder of Turkism," was once one of them, born in Diyarbakir and working as a teacher in their school. Indeed, many prominent statesmen, academics, and artists were among ZGL alumni who integrated into the larger Turkish society.

For almost a century, ZGL was the Kurdish region's preeminent school due to its intellectual legacy in republican history, its deep-rooted school culture, its experienced teachers, and its students from the upper echelons of society at large. The school's legacy was important in educating its students to become "good" subservient citizens of the Turkish Republic. Like all other schools in the country, ZGL was administered under the oversight of the Turkish Ministry of Education, which appointed its administrators and teachers and determined its curriculum and budget. At ZGL, the Kurdish youth, whose parents were defined and dismissed by the Turkish state as "backward" and "ignorant," were invited to instead become a part of "civilization" and the Turkish nation. ZGL was thus one of the narrow channels that the Kurdish youth followed if they wanted to be integrated into Turkish society at large. Also, because ZGL was located at the heart of the most populous Kurdish city, it was accessed very easily by all urban inhabitants.

During the 1990s, however, the school transformed from being a narrow mobilization channel to Turkish society to becoming a center of the opposition for pro-PKK youth mobilization. Before the transformation, students from other Diyarbakir high schools had referred to ZGL as the "High School of Punk Youth" (Zibidi Gençler Lisesi). The young urban poor had a much less pleasant way of referring to the school as the "High School of Rich Assholes" (Zengin Götverenler Lisesi). Indeed, the students of ZGL were from the most affluent neighborhoods in Diyarbakir. Thanks to its central location and good reputation, the school also included a considerable number of students from the families of Turkish officers and civil servants. Students from lower-economic classes also attended the school, but their numbers were much more limited there than at other public high schools in the city.

Turkishness at School and the Symbol of the Officer's Kid (*Subay Çocuğu*)

At ZGL, as at any other public high school in Turkey, incessant representations and rituals of Turkish nationalism were indispensable components of the educational system. Students had to collectively sing the Turkish national anthem every Monday and Friday as well as on national days. Every classroom had a picture of Mustafa Kemal Atatürk, a Turkish flag, and a copy of the student oath. Students had to recite this oath at the start of every school day, pledging their allegiance to Turkishness. Here is the oath in English:

> I am a Turk, honest and hardworking. My principle is to protect the younger, to respect the elder, to love my homeland and my nation more than myself. My ideal is to rise, to progress. O Great Atatürk! On the path that you have paved, I swear to walk incessantly toward the aims that you have set. My existence shall be dedicated to Turkish existence. How happy is the one who says, I am a Turk!

It is no accident that the schools in Turkey dispersed more than simple practical knowledge; the state funded all the schools and tasked them with the mission of instilling Turkish national consciousness in all students. How (Turkish) nationalism would be instilled through education is perhaps best articulated by Ismet İnönü, the second president of the republic, in a speech directed to teachers in 1925. For İnönü, as the excerpt from him here also suggests, the goal of Turkish national education was to create a "monolithic" nation where political, cultural, and ethnic differences would be fully eliminated:

> We can consider two parts in national education as regards the political and patriotic character of national education. There is a Turk that gives the Turkish character to all these territories. However, this nation

has not yet become the monolithic nation we desire. If this generation works seriously and consciously under the guidance of science and life by devoting its entire lifetime, then may the political Turkish nation become a full and mature Turkish nation culturally, ideationally, and socially. Within this monolithic nationality foreign cultures must completely dissolve. . . . If we shall live at all, we shall live as a mass of a monolithic nation. This is the general purpose of the system we call national education. (quoted in Kaplan 2002, 143)

Indeed, due to its location at the heart of the Kurdish region, ZGL had an important role to play in transforming Kurds into Turkish citizens. Turkishness in ZGL was taught and learned through the teachers, curriculum, and everyday educational rituals of nationalism. At the same time, there was a model to aspire toward: the *subay çocuğu* (officer's kid). My respondents used the term *subay çocuğu* to refer to the daughters and sons of the Turkish military personnel in Diyarbakir. It is sometimes also used as an umbrella name for all students from the families of Turkish public officials. The officers' daughters and sons occupied a significant place in my respondents' accounts because they were the primary carriers of the symbolic violence of Turkishness that my respondents had to encounter daily in high school. In such accounts, the figure of the *subay çocuğu*, which interlocks ethnicity and class, emerges as one of the most representative symbols of Turkishness to the students.

The *subay çocuğu*s were the beloved pupils of the teachers, the "apples" of their eyes. Being the children of the "proper" citizens of the state, these kids knew how to act in the classroom, how to dress, how to style their hair, and how to speak proper Turkish. They were the exemplars for teachers to demonstrate to Kurdish children what it looks like to be a civilized member of the Turkish society. When Helin,[2] one of my respondents, started ZGL's middle-school classes, she immediately felt the difference between the *subay çocuğu*s and the Kurdish kids:

---

2. The names of all individuals except public figures referred to in this work are pseudonyms.

There was something different from primary school. It was something like, you start becoming urban or westernized or civilized there.... The teachers were mostly from the outside, not local people. Maybe only a few teachers were local. The teachers came from the outside, and we [Kurds] were like animals to manage.... They [the teachers] were acting like that. I remember we were insulted many times.... If one of us said something [wrong], all of us were scolded. But, for example, the [Turkish] kids of officials were always exempted. I never forget that.... They [the teachers] would say things like "We have hardworking girls here; there are ones who are not like you; you should take them as an example."[3]

Knowing that Helin had graduated from one of the best universities in Turkey, I asked her about her academic standing at ZGL. Although she had very good grades there, she never felt that she was celebrated by the teachers as a role model. She said: "I couldn't be an example. My hair was always messy [*laughing*]. Everything about me—I mean, I had nothing to do with them [the *subay çocuğu* exemplars]."

Because Kurds and Turks share a geography that has been inundated with large migration waves throughout history, they display a variety of hair and skin-color types. Hence, there are no clear-cut phenotypical differences between them.[4] However, Helin's "messy hair" operates in her account almost as if it were a racial category,[5] sharply dividing her from the teachers' "blue-eyed" *subay çocuğu* girl. For young girls, having "messy

---

3. Ellipses in quotations from my interlocutors indicate omissions of parts of what they said rather than pauses.

4. In a most general way, we can say that whereas the peoples of the eastern part of Turkey (e.g., Kurds, Armenians, Azeris) are more like their neighbor Iranians, who have darker hair and larger eyes, the peoples of the western part of Turkey (Turks, Greeks, Bosniacs, etc.) are more like their neighbor Balkan peoples. But these differences are not exact enough to identify someone's ethnic origin if they are not accompanied by accent, birthplace, and a name representing a distinct ethnic origin. Kurds in Turkey are especially recognizable by their distinct language and their accent when they speak Turkish.

5. For an analysis of the stigmatization of Black women's hair in the United States, see King 2017.

hair" has been one of the stereotypical signs of Kurdishness in Turkey, signifying the unruliness of Kurdish subjects. The *subay çocuğu* girl's tidy hair, in contrast, displays her parents' attention to their daughter's appearance. This attention, first of all, is a feature of the modern understanding of the distinction between public and private spheres. Also, the entire country has been structured in relation to the norms, values, and principles of the Turkish educated classes, and the school system was from the beginning rigged in favor of their imagination of proper Turkish citizens. While the teachers at ZGL, most of whom were Turkish, aimed to teach their students to be mindful about their appearance in public settings so that they could become part of the "civilized" world, they further favored the ones—the Turkish students from educated families—who already practiced this mindfulness and who mimicked them. Helin's "messy hair" prevented her from being acknowledged by her teachers as a "good student" despite her good grades precisely because "messy hair" with all its connotations worked as a category pertaining to Kurdishness, the "backward" one, the one who lacks civilization.

The autobiography of Sıdıka Avar, *My Mountain Flowers* (*Dağ çiçeklerim*, 1999), offers a striking example of Turkish teachers' efforts to change the appearance of their Kurdish students in order to turn them into "civilized" members of Turkish society. Avar was the model of all idealist teachers during the early republican period, aiming to fulfill by means of education the civilizing ideals of the republic at the "furthest places" (i.e., the Kurdish region); the contemporaneous national press represented teachers like her as "Turkish raiders" or "Turkish missionaries." Avar's book includes photographs of her students, first one before they entered the girls' institute that she directed and then another one later on, displaying their transformation into "civilized" girls. In these photos in contemporaneous newspapers, one can visually follow how the "messy hair" of Kurdish girls was eventually carefully tidied into buns.

I would argue that the teachers' mission as carriers of the Turkish nation-building process into the Kurdish regions was as important as İnönü's speech. The Turkish elite developed their definition of the Turkish nation and Turkish citizens in conversation with the western European colonial experience. A colonial definition of the ideal Turkish citizen emerged from this process. For this citizen, who was considered to be a representative of the state, his or her public appearance signaled belonging both to the state and to civilization. Within this system of symbols, the Turkish state was interpreted as the "giver" of civilization, providing the "civilized" form of tidy hair, white collar, student dress, shoes, and the like; the same state also generated, controlled, and reproduced the Turkish forms of being in the world, centered on the Turkish language and Turkish ways of self-perception and self-expression.

Having tidy or messy hair related to one's social class as well.[6] Helin's mother, who was in serious financial stress, Helin confided to me, probably did not have enough time and energy to tend to her daughter's hair. The *subay çocuğu*, however, was a very effective representative of the Turkish state's bourgeois self-image. Önder, who was from one of the poorest neighborhoods of Diyarbakir, succinctly portrayed the difference between the *subay çocuğu*s and Diyarbakir kids in terms of social class:

> Their clothes, their allowance, their everything was different from [those of] the Diyarbakir people. For example, I always worked after school. I worked for subsistence; I tried to do things for my livelihood. With the little money that I reserved from my earnings, I could, for example, eat a meatball at school, and I could do so only once or twice a week. But for them, there was no such problem. They could eat meatballs at every break and even treat friends to meatballs. Their clothes were totally different from ours. They wore more quality, fashion-brand clothes. Even our sports activities were different. They generally played basketball; they were basketball players. . . . We played soccer. We were different and separated from each other in everything about us.

---

6. In fact, "messy hair" has also been one of the most striking signs of class in relation to the Kurdish issue. In one approach, "messy hair" has represented the impoverishment of Kurdish subjects due to their colonial relation with the Turkish state. For example, the photographs taken in poor neighborhoods of Diyarbakir and surrounding towns display young girls with messy hair and large eyes and thus have been an important part of the Kurdish popular self-imaginary, especially since the 1960s and 1970s, when the Kurdish movement started to define itself in anticolonialist and leftist terms.

I asked Önder additional questions to better understand what had hurt him the most about the figure of the *subay çocuğu*. He gave an example from his physical-education classes to demonstrate how the curriculum as well as the teachers favored the dispositions and skills of *subay çocuğu*s as well as the feelings that this favoritism instigated among others.

> There was a sports hall at ZGL. It was like, this sports hall was dedicated to them. You know, we didn't even know how to play basketball. . . . Teachers favored them. For example, in gym classes. . . . Today the world's most favorite sports activity is soccer, right? . . . But there were no soccer classes at school even for a day, not even one single day. But who knows why one of two gym classes was always on basketball? How to make a basket, how to run in a basketball game, which moves are foul play, and so on. Even this makes you distinct from each other. As the core course, you [teachers] are showing me a sports activity in which I have no interest or skill. In one class, maybe at most three people would play this basketball thing. And these three were among them [the *subay çocuğu*s]. The rest is all soccer players. But you [teachers] suggest no training or support or an agenda for the present or future [for the Kurdish students]. But you do provide that for the others. Unavoidably, it created a feeling of hatred inside me. I couldn't succeed in this basketball thing, but he [the *subay çocuğu*] did.

One also needs to add that basketball courts were inaccessible to local kids because most were located inside large military housing complexes. Therefore, playing basketball spatially divided the *subay çocuğu*s from the local Diyarbakir kids, for whom only soccer was available in the city's dusty alleys. In addition, what makes playing basketball or soccer an issue of class distinction is, as Önder explains, the way this difference is "encouraged" or "discouraged" at school. While the *subay çocuğu* dressed in his fancy gym clothes was admired by the teacher, Önder and others resented the lack of opportunity for success. Within this context, playing basketball operated like the "tidy hair" of *subay çocuğu* girls in that both signified how students experienced Turkish nationalism at school through the intersection of class and ethnicity. Furthermore, some activities and types of knowledge did not have any value in the educational system: the ability to play soccer did not count as a skill, just as the ability to speak Kurdish did not count as a language skill.

The figure of the *subay çocuğu* also displayed the class system of the Turkish state within the nation-building process in Diyarbakir. Philip Corrigan and Derek Sayer understand state formation as the "cultural revolution" of the bourgeoisie, where state institutions actively produce the "bourgeois self-image" to be the norm for society. The "bourgeois self-image" is produced by constructing new integrative social identities (such as nation and citizenship) to displace the experiences of differences in people's lives. The modern state then actively produces its citizens through moral regulation by encouraging some practices and constraining and dismissing others. As Corrigan and Sayer note, "Out of the vast range of human social capacities—possible ways in which social life could be lived—state activities more or less forcibly 'encourage' some whilst suppressing, marginalizing, eroding, undermining others. . . . Certain forms of activity are given the official seal of approval, others are situated beyond the pale" (1985, 4). The continuous forced chain of the "encouragement" and "discouragement" of certain modes of being and acting produces and reproduces the entire societal organization in line with bourgeois state norms. As such, the figure of the *subay çocuğu* at ZGL worked to showcase the bourgeois self-image of Turkishness as a form of citizenship that was actively (re)produced by the Turkish state through schooling. Kurdish children and youth differed from this bourgeois image, which excluded both their class position and ethnicity; both the teachers and the national curriculum they followed dismissed, marginalized, and humiliated Kurdish children and youth.

The figure of the *subay çocuğu* not only displayed the ethnic and class character of the Turkish state but at times was also literally the "child of the state." As Osman put it,

> There was always a difference between us and them. I used to play basketball, too, so I was good with them. But in the end, when the final bell rang—I mean, when the school day ended—there was a green bus waiting for them to take them away. So we would stay behind with each other as Diyarbakir kids. We would hang out together, go and eat meatballs,

go and play billiards or Okey and the like. So as a consequence we were closer to each other among ourselves. Because they were in a different world. They would come to our lives, then they would leave. They wouldn't stay. In the end, they would always go. They had their school services, and these services had guards, soldiers waiting with guns. There I would feel like "here is the state, and they are the children of the state." I would feel they were not one of us when I saw the soldiers waiting for them in front of their vehicles. I mean, I knew that.

The military buses that transported *subay çocuğu* students were mentioned in almost all interviews as a source of resentment and discontent. Indeed, soldiers waiting in front of the school building with guns must have generated a strong image of the "compartmentalization" of the city, especially because these buses traveled to the military housing areas that occupied almost a third of the entire city center. Such compartmentalization, as Frantz Fanon remarked about colonial settings ([2004] 2007, 5), produced sharp divisions that cut across not only territories but also human psyches, making a real connection between the two worlds impossible, even for teenagers. Given that their age group is inclined to romance, the kids of the two different worlds might have fallen in love with each other, but even their love could not pass through those borders. My respondents told me that all they could experience was platonic love.

This spatial and social compartmentalization in Diyarbakir—such as the military buses and soldiers waiting for officers' kids at the school gate—was in stark conflict with the republican ideals of bringing up youth with a national consciousness to entrench unity. Every school day, Kurdish students entered and left the school in the presence of the military buses, feeling increasingly alienated from the state that these buses represented. In the classroom, they were excluded based on the ideals of the republic that the officer's kid embodied but that they somehow lacked. The Turkish state invited all its citizens to be a part of the nation and sought their integration via schools. However, the figure of the officer's kid at ZGL was the only emblem of an ideal that was too far from Kurdish students' reach. The Turkishness promoted at school was, if anything, experienced by Kurdish students as a source of division, separation, and exclusion.

A New Encounter with the Turkish State

By 1990, PKK mobilization had gained momentum in towns and cities. That PKK militants had extended their activities from the countryside to cities became most evident in collective rituals. Kurds increasingly started to participate en masse in guerrilla funerals and Newroz (Kurdish New Year) celebrations in Southeast Turkey/Bakur Kurdistan, especially in Nusaybin, Cizre, Idil, and Silopi. This was not how the PKK mobilized in Diyarbakir, however. My respondents and interlocutors went back to the summer of 1991 and selected to narrate the "Vedat Aydın event," as they called it. Vedat Aydın was a human rights activist and chair of the Diyarbakir branch of the People's Labor Party (Halkın Emek Partisi, HEP). The police raided his apartment and took him away on 5 July 1991, and his tortured dead body was found a few days later (see Türkiye İnsan Hakları Vakfı 1991).

The murder of Vedat Aydın marked the start of thousands of extrajudicial murders of Kurds during the 1990s. Tens of thousands of mourners from Diyarbakir and the surrounding towns peacefully participated in Aydın's funeral. Turkish security forces opened fire on the crowd, leaving seven people dead and hundreds injured (Göral, Işık, and Kaya 2013). According to the people of Diyarbakir, the number of dead was much higher, around fifty to one hundred. Vedat Aydın's son, Felat Aydın, stated that at least twenty people died at his father's funeral (Türkiye Büyük Millet Meclisi 2013, 141). One reason for this discrepancy between the official count and local counts is that some of the casualties were not reported. Also, as I understand the situation from the way my interlocutors in Diyarbakir described the funeral, it could be that, given the extensiveness of the shootings and violence, the local people surmised there were more casualties. According to oral accounts, it was indeed an apocalyptic day when the famed Hevsel gardens by the Tigris River were filled with injured people who had to jump over the city walls to escape the gunshots.

Because the murder of Vedat Aydın created fractures within existing state–society relations, it can be referred to as what Veena Das calls a "critical event." Das specifically underlines that after critical events "new modes of action come into being to redefine traditional categories" (1995,

6). As a critical event, the murder and funeral of Vedat Aydın in Diyarbakir at the start of the 1990s framed a new configuration of relations between the Turkish state and the Diyarbakir people and generated a new politics of mass uprising. As soon as I asked my respondent Necmi how Kurdish students first started to mobilize at ZGL in Diyarbakir, he immediately referred to Vedat Aydın's funeral, explaining its immense impact on Diyarbakir:

> Diyarbakir saw that atrocity; everyone was heavily influenced by that atrocity. And this was, at the same time, the beginning of politicization in Diyarbakir. I mean, there already was resistant organizing [among the people], but with the Vedat Aydın event it turned into a massive force. . . . OK, everyone in Diyarbakir was Kurdish, but Diyarbakir was not a PKK supporter, or Diyarbakir didn't embrace an identity or politics associated with or approved by the PKK. But that event . . . of Vedat Aydın, his murder, was a trauma in itself. He was merely a political man with no gun or anything, yet he was brutally murdered. This resulted in trauma in Diyarbakir. As if this were not enough, the people who took the responsibility of their trauma [by attending the funeral] were also brutally murdered. They killed everyone, targeted everyone without separating women, children, or men. . . . It meant that the state didn't want us anymore. It was no longer our state. . . . And the PKK was right all [along regarding] what they had said about the state. . . . By doing this, the state messaged, "I am the occupier; I do not belong to you. If you don't accept my presence, I am going to slaughter you."

Thus, for Necmi, the Vedat Aydın incident was a constitutive event in terms of building a new type of relationship between the state and people of Diyarbakir. First, by murdering Vedat Aydın and opening fire on those who attended his funeral, the Turkish state performatively disclosed its colonial characteristic ("I am the occupier, I am not yours"). And second, this state framing positioned the Diyarbakir people as if they were colonial subjects, just as the PKK had argued all these years. The Turkish state, in other words, appeared to them as a form of state power defined by colonial violence rather than providing a common political ground to present demands for recognition.

State violence during the ensuing years of the 1990s continued to mobilize ZGL students irrespective of their class positions. My respondent Cemal, who is a 1994 graduate, was from a very wealthy Kurdish family, but he participated in *yurtsever* mobilization as a leading member. Cemal frequently transferred his father's generous allowance to his political activities and his needy friends, causing his father to object by complaining, "Your brother is hanging out with aghas and beys [traditional Kurdish elites], but you are always with the punks [*zibidi*]!" Cemal explained his involvement with the *yurtsever* mobilization:

> It was forbidden to speak in Kurdish, for example. The policemen would curse the Kurds during the [singing of] the national anthem [at school].... Once they made us lie down on the ground because we didn't sing the anthem properly. We were on the ground lying face downward. Hundreds of students. In the schoolyard. It was the antiterror police ... and Yeşil,[7] as he was called. One day something had a great impact on

---

7. Yeşil (Mahmut Yıldırım) was one of the hit men of what was called the "deep state" (*derin devlet*) in the 1990s, who was known for his cruelty and high number of killings. The *Susurluk Report* (Savaş 1998), which was prepared after the Susurluk scandal to investigate the close relations among the Turkish government, the military, security forces, and the mafia to suppress the Kurdish insurgency, dedicated twelve pages specifically to Yeşil. In a press conference, Kutlu Savaş, the head of the board investigating the scandal, stated that the board gave special attention to Yeşil because he was "an important part of an organization" and was thus "to be an example" of people who were involved in this organization (see Özgönül 1998). According to the *Susurluk Report*, Yeşil worked as a contract killer for the Turkish National Intelligence Organization (Milli İstihbarat Teşkilatı) and the Gendarmerie Intelligence and Counterterrorism Unit (Jandarma İstihbarat ve Terörle Mücadele Grup Komutanlığı). He organized and/or carried out many extrajudicial killings, including the assassinations of Kurdish leaders Vedat Aydın, Musa Anter, and Mehmet Sincar (a member of Parliament for the Democracy Party [Demokrasi Partisi]). In the report, Yeşil was also pointed out as responsible for the attacks on some high state officials in 1993, primarily the assassination of Ahmet Cem Ersever, a high-ranking military officer and one of the founders of the Gendarmerie Intelligence and Counterterrorism Unit. He was also responsible for an incident in Budapest in 1996 when an unknown assailant punched Mesut Yılmaz, the former premier and the chair of the Motherland Party (Anavatan Partisi).

me. They killed someone, and while that person's body was still bleeding... they left it on the car, on [the hood] of one of those white Renault Tauruses. The blood flew over the car. A white car covered with blood at the front. They drove the car around Diyarbakir without cleaning [it] for days. They didn't wash the car; they didn't wipe the blood. I was impacted a lot by that.

Cemal's account reveals how the state violence on the streets in the 1990s was layered upon the symbolic violence of enforced Turkishness at school. The police were at the school to contribute to the sacred national duty of disciplining students into obedient citizens; they were there because the usual disciplining tools of the school were no longer sufficient to contain the rebellious students of ZGL. On one occasion, for example, as Kurdish students were forced by policemen to lie face down in the schoolyard when they refused to sing the Turkish national anthem, police violence represented the state for them, further underlining the constant forms of everyday symbolic violence that they were exposed to throughout their school years. From this standpoint, it makes sense for Cemal's explanation to move from the school to the blood-covered car that was driven around to intimidate the Diyarbakir Kurds. Cemal's account is an example of a mode of knowing referred to as situational knowledge, stemming from a "situational relation to the state" (Gupta 1995, 390; Navaro-Yashin 2002, 165), where the Kurds understood the Turkish state as a unified and concrete entity that they constantly confronted in every sphere of life. For Cemal, the Turkish methods of forced assimilation, discipline, management, and regulation that he was exposed to at school were different facets of the same state; when deemed necessary, the state did not hesitate to kill the people of his city with impunity. The *yurtsever* identity offered Cemal a channel by which to resist the humiliation he felt daily when he witnessed state violence. In doing so, the difference between his class position and that of his Kurdish peers at ZGL did not matter at all.

As my respondents often pointed out, state violence made *yurtsever* mobilization as much a moral duty as a political one. Many of my respondents explained their participation in *yurtsever* mobilization in terms of morality. Helin, for example, recounted her initial feelings about getting involved in *yurtsever* mobilization by referring to the concept of (social) responsibility; she noted, "On the one hand, it was a state of juvenile behavior, but on the other hand [there was] an incredible sense of responsibility. A country is on fire, and you must take responsibility." Bülent pointed to moral conscience in justifying his political participation: "I am not talking about an ideological or theoretical decision. . . . If someone had a conscience, I mean a person with a conscience, what was happening was very clear—they had to act accordingly."

The *yurtsever* was thus a product of the 1990s when the Kurds' struggle emerged under conditions of extreme political violence. Hence, in the 1990s massive state violence intersected with the Kurdish national revolutionary struggle as Kurds risked their lives in demanding recognition of their existence and their dignity. This was the time when Kurdish masses reconstructed a sense of self and collective unity, becoming in the process *the Kurdish people*. Even those who preferred to distance themselves from the national liberation struggle had to face their Kurdishness and assume a position in relation to the civil war. *Yurtsevers* were among the new actors who redefined "the Kurdish question" from their newly constituted positions. The PKK's fight with the Turkish state in the 1990s provided a condition for possibility for the formation of *yurtsever* subjectivity. However, this form of political subjectivity was not an automatic production of the given conditions, but it was, like any other revolutionary subject formation, a result of human will and dedication. The Kurds, who carried the burden of the situation they faced, formed this subjectivity as a historical possibility.

The struggle of the *yurtsever* drew upon the moral construction of a Kurdish revolutionary self against state violence. My respondent Nevzat, for example, implying the rage that he felt as response to the sate violence that he observed, told me that "the state wanted us to be killing machines, but we resisted and did not become one; we [instead] became *yurtsever*." *Yurtsevers*, as Nevzat understood the movement, emerged as moral subjects with values instead of mere killing machines fighting the security forces. My other respondents also stressed the role of human will and dedication in *yurtsever* mobilization. One, for example, defined her position in the 1990s Kurdish struggle as one *drop* in one huge river, enriching the river while flowing through it. Another narrated the example of the Prophet Abraham, who was thrown into the fire by Nimrod, and compared his own position to that of the *ant* in the story, carrying water in its small mouth to help extinguish the fire. These examples reveal a particular understanding of one's subject position within a complex set of relationships that are at once constructive and destructive. This subject is humble but confident, genuinely believing in his or her power to enrich the river (the Kurdish struggle) as well as to extinguish the fire (Turkish state violence). In summary, then, in the 1990s the revolutionary will to participate in the Kurdish struggle overlapped with the moral duty to stand against Turkish state violence and created *yurtsever* subjectivity at the intersection of *the political* and *the ethical*.

My field research in Diyarbakir with former ZGL students revealed that in their struggle the *yurtsever* youth not only risked their lives but also created an alternative imaginary of the self and alternative forms of connecting to each other, thereby uniting against the physical and symbolic state violence. When I queried about the impact of *yurtsever* mobilization at the school, one of my respondents replied, "Suddenly the air we breathed changed, the emotions we felt changed." It was a new beginning more than anything else as the students contested the school as a disciplinary state institution, changing it instead into "a shared social space" (Willis 2006) for students to form new aspirations, imaginaries, and utopias in opposition to the divisive, discriminatory, and marginalizing practices of the state. Their class and ethnic differences no longer segmented them but instead provided them with the energy to help them heal each other's injuries stemming from those differences. *Yurtsever* students united in a position that the state considered "inferior"—that is, being Kurdish and poor, not speaking proper Turkish, and having "messy hair" and "shabby gym clothes."

Between 1992 and 1995, the *yurtsever* youth became the "dominant popular"[8] group of the school. They were so influential that even students outside their group asked them to settle the personal problems they had

---

8. I borrow this term from Paul Willis (1977).

with each other. They organized numerous protests at the school, openly and publicly supporting the PKK. They also intimidated the teachers and *subay çocuğu*s, sabotaged the rituals of singing the national anthem and reciting the national student oath, destroyed the bust of Atatürk, and set fire to the school archives. They also confronted brutal attacks by the radical-right secret party the Kurdish Hizbullah,[9] many of them receiving deadly injuries. Many were tortured at police stations, and some were imprisoned. And hundreds of ZGL students lost their lives after they joined the PKK guerrilla forces. By 1995, the *yurtsever* youth mobilization at the ZGL was brutally suppressed by Hizbullah on the one side and police violence on the other.

Conclusion

My ethnographic analysis demonstrates that the exclusion of Kurdishness from the space of the state with its specific ethnic and class elements was constitutive in the formation of *yurtsever* subjectivity. Understanding how political subjectivity is formed through critical engagements with the state opens a fruitful dialogue between the political and the marginalized; Jacques Rancière, Davide Panagia, and Rachel Bowlby (2001) frame the political as the creation of a new space for the excluded and the marginalized, and Philip Corrigan and Derek Sayer (1985) analyze state-formation processes where "alternative forms of thinking and acting" become marginalized. *Yurtsever* subjectivity was formed as the mobilization of those who were excluded and marginalized within state space; what they formed was "the political" in that it shattered existing meanings and significations, bringing new relations into existence. In fact, during the 1990s, the period when *yurtsever* subjectivity crystallized, the relationship between Kurdish society and the Turkish state fundamentally changed, undergirding the very possibility of a Kurdish movement today.

9. Hizbullah in Turkey is mainly a Kurdish Sunni Islamist militant organization and is different from the Hizbullah based in Lebanon. In the early 1990s, the Kurdish Hizbullah acted as an effective oppositional force against the PKK. For an ethnographic analysis of this group, see Kurt 2017.

Yurtsever youth mobilization took shape on the ground as a struggle for recognition—recognition in the sense of "the acknowledgment of one's existence in the world as a valuable life" (Aretxaga 1995, 132). It was the uprising of those who had "messy hair," "shabby gym clothes," and a Kurdish accent. And their uprising was not formed solely in reaction to what the state wanted to dictate. This was a new beginning for them. They took the path of crafting a new self while struggling for a revolution that would create a new social reality. In my opinion, their experience conveys that resistance against state power is not only a reaction to violence but also a practice of community building where one can start to imagine and produce revolutionary possibilities.

References

Aretxaga, Begoña. 1995. "Dirty Protest: Symbolic Overdetermination and Gender in Northern Ireland Ethnic Violence." *Ethos* 23, no. 2: 123–48.
Avar, Sıdıka. 1999. *Dağ çiçeklerim*. Ankara, Turkey: Öğretmen Dünyası Press.
Ayhan, Ece. 2014. "Meçhul öğrenci anıtı" / "Monument of the Unknown Student." Translated by Turkey Page Roundup Media editors. *Jadalliya*, 13 May. At http://www.jadaliyya.com/Details/30372/Monument of-the-Unknown-Student.
Corrigan, Philip, and Derek Sayer. 1985. *The Great Arch: English State Formation as Cultural Revolution*. Oxford: Blackwell.
Das, Veena. 1995. *Critical Events: An Anthropological Perspective on Contemporary India*. Oxford: Oxford Univ. Press.
Ellis, Carolyn S., and Arthur P. Bochner. 2006. "Analyzing Analytic Autoethnography: An Autopsy." *Journal of Contemporary Ethnography* 35, no. 4: 429–49.
Fanon, Frantz. [2004] 2007. *The Wretched of the Earth*. Translated by Richard Philcox. New York: Grove Press.
Gökalp, Ziya. 2011. "Red Apple" (Kızılelma). In Uğur Ümit Üngör, *The Making of Modern Turkey: Nation and State in Eastern Anatolia 1913–1950*, 35. New York: Oxford Univ. Press.
Göral, Özgür Sevgi, Ayhan Işık, and Özlem Kaya. 2013. *The Unspoken Truth: Enforced Disappearances*. Istanbul: Truth Justice Memory Center (Hafıza Merkezi).
Gupta, Akhil. 1995. "Blurred Boundaries: The Discourse of Corruption, the Culture of Politics, and the Imagined State." *American Ethnologist* 22:375–402.

Kaplan, İsmail. 2002. "Milli eğitim ideolojisi." In *Modern Türkiye'de siyasi düşünce, milliyetcilik, cilt*, 4. Istanbul: İletisim.

King, Vanessa. 2017. "Race, Stigma, and the Politics of Black Girls' Hair." PhD diss., Minnesota State Univ., Mankato.

Kurt, Mehmet. 2017. *Kurdish Hizbullah in Turkey: Islamism, Violence, and the State*. London: Pluto Press.

Navaro-Yashin, Yael. 2002. *Faces of the State: Secularism and Public Life in Turkey*. Princeton, NJ: Princeton Univ. Press.

Özgönül, Emin. 1998. "Ersever iç hesaplaşma kurbanı." 21 Jan. At http://arsiv.sabah.com.tr/1998/01/21/r04.html.

Rancière, Jacques, Davide Panagia, and Rachel Bowlby. 2001. "Ten Theses on Politics." *Theory & Event* 5, no. 3: 1–16.

Savaş, Kutlu. 1998. *Susurluk raporu* (The Susurluk report). At https://tr.wikisource.org/wiki/Susurluk_Raporu_(Kutlu_Sava%C5%9F.

Türkiye Büyük Millet Meclisi, İnsan Hakları İnceleme Komisyonu (Grand National Assembly of Turkey, Committee on Human Rights). 2013. *Terör ve şiddet olayları kapsamında yaşam hakkı ihlallerini İnceleme raporu* (Investigation report on violations of the right to life within the scope of terrorism and violence). Ankara: Türkiye Büyük Millet Meclisi.

Türkiye İnsan Hakları Vakfı (Turkish Human Rights Association). 1991. *Turkiye Insan Haklari Vakfi 1991 raporu* (Turkish Human Rights Association 1991 report). Ankara: Türkiye İnsan Hakları Vakfı.

Üngör, Uğur Ümit. 2011. *The Making of Modern Turkey: Nation and State in Eastern Anatolia 1913–1950*. New York: Oxford Univ. Press.

Willis, Paul E. 1977. *Learning to Labour: How Working Class Kids Get Working Class Jobs*. New York: Columbia Univ. Press.

———. 2006. "Foot Soldiers of Modernity: The Dialectics of Cultural Consumption and the Twenty-First-Century School." In *Education, Globalization, and Social Change*, edited by Hugh Lauder, Phillip Brown, Jo-Anne Dillabough, and A. H. Halsey, 507–23. Oxford: Oxford Univ. Press.

10

Far from Separatist Violence

The Kurdish Political Prisoners' Hunger Strike of 2012 in Turkey

Amy Bartholomew and Ruşen Fırat Güllüoğlu

Self-sacrificial political acts have long been a staple in the repertoires of emancipatory movements around the world. Among these forms of action, mass hunger strikes and death fasts constitute an important form of resistance for Kurdish political movements in Turkey.[1] A recent episode in the long history of mass hunger strikes in Turkey was set in motion by Kurdish political prisoners on 12 September 2012, the anniversary of the military coup of 1980.[2] This hunger strike took place in the shadow of the failure of peace talks between the Kurdish movement's representatives and the Turkish state. The result of that failure was a return to mass violence, with

---

We dedicate this chapter to the hunger strikers and to their supporters, and we thank those who met with us despite the risks in doing so. We also thank Emre Şahin, who helped with interviews in 2017.

1. Most famous were the hunger strikes and death fasts in the notorious Amed (Diyarbakir in Turkish) Prison in the early 1980s. Julia Harte quotes Koray Çalışkan: "In the last decade, I don't know of any place that's had more hunger strikes, and deaths from hunger strikes, than Turkey" (Harte 2012). Also see Firat News Agency 2013; Sevinç 2008; Yılmaz 2012; Zana 1997.

2. As Welat Zeydanlıoğlu argues, the coup d'etat and the Constitution of 1982 that followed "were significant in launching a violent political and cultural programme for the sake of 'national unity and integrity' in order to suppress dissident leftist/Kurdish movements" (2010, 71).

dramatic increases in military and other state violence against the Kurds; mass arrests of Kurdish mayors, activists, and anyone said to be associated with the Union of Kurdistan Communities (Koma Civakên Kurdistanê, KCK) or the Kurdistan Workers' Party (Partîya Karkerên Kurdistanê, PKK); and the continuing isolation of Abdullah Öcalan, the founder of the PKK, in prison.[3] We argue that the 2012 hunger strike was important for the Kurds for contesting the injustices and violence with which the Turkish state confronted the Kurdish movement. We also contend that the strike illustrates how social groups such as the Kurds—groups that are targeted by the state and forcibly excluded from the formal sphere of politics—engage in resistance against the state through sheer determination, political agency, and organizational capacity.

Despite having denied the existence of the hunger strike for seven weeks (Butler 2012; *T24* 2012), officials were no longer able to downplay it when it entered its eighth week. Official recognition came, albeit in the form of a condemnation, when Prime Minister (as he then was) Recep Tayyip Erdoğan claimed that the hunger strikers were engaging in "blackmail," insisting that "a hunger strike is not an appropriate method

---

3. The KCK was formed as part of the PKK's reorganization in keeping with the framework of democratic confederalism. The origin of the concept lies in Abdullah Öcalan's book *Bir halkı savunmak* (Defending a People, 2004), in which he argued the PKK's orientation toward establishing a nation-state should be replaced with a "nonstatist . . . Democratic Kurdistan," a goal he further substantiated in his book *Democratic Confederalism* (2011, an English translation). In the former, Öcalan argues that a certain "KOMA GEL [People's Group] initiative" will play a crucial role in the restructuring of the movement within different parts of Kurdistan along the nonstatist and nonnationalist lines" (2004, 257). In this manner, the KCK is the concretization of the KOMA-GEL, and its main goal is to coordinate all political organizations and movements related to the PKK in Turkish, Syrian, Iraqi, and Iranian parts of Kurdistan under a unified representative and decision-making body. Officially, it came into being as a result of the Fifth Congress of the Kongra Gel (People's Congress) held by the PKK in the Qandil Mountains in May 2007. On the conceptual development and history of the KCK, see *Bia haber merkezi* 2011 and Öcalan 2004, 2011. On the state's repression of those associated with the KCK, see, for example, Hess 2012 and İlkiz 2014. Jake Hess (2012) maintains that Öcalan had not seen his lawyers since July 2011.

of claiming one's right in a democracy" (*Bia haber merkezi* 2012; *Hürriyet Daily News* 2012a).⁴ His position on what constitutes legitimate political action in a "democracy" echoed that of Ria Oomen-Rujiten, the European Parliament's rapporteur on Turkey. When she was in Ankara a day before Erdoğan made his statement, she denounced the hunger strikers' actions as "oppression and force" that is "unacceptable in a democracy."⁵

These vulgar interpretations of democratic acts that are aimed at the repressive status quo also reveal a wider strain both in democratic theory and politics and in reactions to Kurdish struggles in Turkey. Democratic theory sometimes suggests that formal democracies can neither accommodate nor require radical protest politics.⁶ Nor has democratic theory, until quite recently, seriously addressed the role of bodily suffering or sacrifice as a mode of democratic agency (Feola 2018). And like the European rapporteur, mainstream media in both Turkey and the West and even some scholars interpret Kurdish struggles in Turkey along the lines drawn by the official apparatuses of the Turkish state: as strictly "separatist" in aims and "violent" in means.⁷ At the level of public discourse and law in

---

4. Arrested BDP member of Parliament Selma Irmak said at the time that Erdoğan's statements on the hunger strike were "invitations to death, not to solutions" (Irmak 2012, 4).

5. Given the importance of Oomen-Rujiten's claims for our chapter, it is worth quoting her in full: "[Conducting a] hunger strike is *an unacceptable method in a democracy*. If you have an *aim*, you should get involved in politics and try to *convince* people. If you conduct a hunger strike for something today, you'll do the same for something else tomorrow. This is unacceptable. There's no place for *oppression and force* in democracies. I demand officials prevent any possible deaths from happening" (quoted in *Hürriyet Daily News* 2012, emphases added).

6. For example, both John Rawls (1993) and Jürgen Habermas (1996) have been criticized for emphasizing a disembodied public reason that narrowly constrains legitimate protest to entirely communicative, nonstrategic action. For such readings of Rawls and Habermas, see, most famously, the one given by Chantal Mouffe, who argues, "The rationalist longing for undistorted rational communication and for a social unity based on rational consensus is profoundly anti-political because it ignores the crucial place of passions, contestation, and affect in politics" (1993, 115).

7. Onur Günay analyzes the ways liberal theory typically overlooks the constitutive and ongoing violence of states and as a consequence of this oversight "perpetuates and

Turkey, this alleged combination of Kurdish separatism and a penchant for political violence has rendered much Kurdish political activity de facto illegitimate. Consequently, Erdoğan's employment of the term *blackmail* and his and Oomen-Rujiten's criticism of the hunger strike in 2012 as "unacceptable" "oppression and force" literally delegitimized all Kurdish political movements by attributing separatism and violence to them.

In this chapter,[8] we interrogate these claims of separatism and violence, including the "illegitimacy" of the Kurdish hunger strike in 2012, by drawing on interviews we conducted with the hunger strikers and their supporters in June 2014 and June to October 2016. In conducting the interviews, we employed a critical interpretive methodology for two reasons. First, it pays special attention to the lived experiences of injustice (Honneth 2004), and, second, it brings to the forefront the narratives of the participants themselves with the aim of uncovering their judgments and reflections.

Our analysis thus contributes to this volume by studying one instance of the Kurdish struggle in Turkey. We make four main points. First, the Kurdish hunger strikers, who were largely excluded from the formal sphere of politics, undertook an extraordinary if by now common form of political action. Second, the hunger strike started in prisons with the concerted aim of initiating constitutional revision and the renewal of peace negotiations, publicizing in the process the everyday suffering of Kurds through corporeal struggle. Third, the official Turkish state politics of violent repression and the state's aggressive and unconstitutional use of

---

justifies the continuum of state violence by producing and reproducing a violent image of the other" (2013, 174).

8. With an interest in both democratic theory and Kurdish progressive politics in Turkey and elsewhere, Bartholomew considers in a previous, companion paper (Bartholomew 2017) whether indefinite hunger striking may count as a legitimate mode of democratic action by viewing it through the lens of Jürgen Habermas's work. She argues there that Habermas's conception of deliberative democracy, despite the many criticisms of it for endorsing merely "consensual politics" or even for being an "antipolitical" conception of democracy, is sufficiently capacious to justify hunger striking in contexts of deep injustice.

law and the corporeal resistance against them were mutually constitutive. Finally, fourth, our analysis of the hunger strike contrasts sharply with the conservative stands taken by the Turkish state and the European rapporteur. Both from the hunger strikers' perspective and from our own, the hunger strike was a legitimate mode of democratic action and was, indeed, far from violent or separatist.

We interviewed fourteen former prison hunger strikers, three in Urfa and four in Istanbul in the summer of 2014 as well as five in Amed and two in Istanbul in 2016.[9] Most of the interviewees had been members of the Peace and Democracy Party (Barış ve Demokrasi Partisi, BDP, the forerunner of the People's Democratic Party [Halkların Demokratik Partisi, HDP]), and many held party positions in local politics at the time they were arrested. We also met with other former prisoners, lawyers for the hunger strikers, representatives of human rights organizations, translators for the KCK trials, and journalists. The interviews were structured around a set of open-ended questions, the answers to which were recorded in Turkish, translated and transcribed into English, and analyzed both as empirical information on the hunger strike and as narratives of experience.[10]

We analyzed the hunger strikers' responses according to three criteria: first, the strikers' views of the context of injustice[11] against which the

---

9. One interviewee (number 02) did not go on the hunger strike but was actively involved in its support from the outside. We include his comments in this chapter but do not include him in the figure of fourteen interviewees. We interviewed more hunger strikers in 2017, but these interviews are not included in this chapter.

10. We have anonymized sources to protect them. The sort of questions we asked include: How does a hunger striker decide her act of self-sacrifice is warranted and legitimate? What process of reflection and what considerations are important to him? How do the hunger strikers respond to the claim that the hunger strike is an unacceptable method of protest in a democracy, that it is more like "blackmail," or that it is political violence rather than a legitimate form of political action in pursuit of democratic aims? How do they describe the injustices they perceived, and how did they frame their aims or demands?

11. Shane O'Neill describes a situation of injustice as one where "a dominant group excludes others completely from access to political power and uses state violence in brutal ways to repress all non-violent resistance" (2010, 136). This seems an apt description of the context in which the hunger strike occurred in Turkey.

hunger strike was deployed and justified; second, the particular means the strikers employed; and third, the way the strikers understood and defined the aims of the hunger strike. Based on our analysis, we argue that the hunger strike was a justifiable, legitimate act of nonviolent democratic protest against a state that has continually and systematically perpetrated deep-seated injustices and widespread violence against the Kurds (and other dissidents) in their fight for their legal, political, and cultural rights. Put more broadly, the hunger strikers insisted on the nonviolent quality of the means they chose and demanded not separatism but rather an "equal right to coexistence" within Turkey.[12] In fact, they specifically aimed to restart the peace talks with the state, demanding democratic citizenship and a pluralistic conception of radical democracy within Turkey.

Attending to the opinions of the hunger strikers not only includes their political positions within scholarly analysis but also addresses the gap between their interpretations, on the one hand, and the viewpoints expressed by the dominant public opinion, on the other, which is manipulated largely by political elites. In addition, the hunger strikers' demands were crucial to the development of a more pluralistic, egalitarian, and democratic Turkey grounded in constitutional revision. From the current vantage point, the hunger strikers' demands remain fundamental to restarting any prospective peace talks, to achieving a just peace, and, indeed, to developing democracy in Turkey. Yet the Turkish state led by the Justice and Development Party (Adalet ve Kalkınma Partisi, AKP) has squandered such an opportunity; it has instead aggressively paved the way for further violence and deepened authoritarianism.

In the first section, we describe the hunger strike to convey the larger context of injustice against which the hunger strikers decided to engage in corporeal protest. We then turn to the reasons the hunger strikers gave to describe their understandings of how the Turkish state exercises its powers in unjust, violent, and other ways that are antithetical to democratic norms. The second section focuses on the means the hunger strikers deployed and the justifications they gave for viewing the hunger strike

---

12. On an "equal right to coexistence," see Habermas 1994.

as a democratic act. In the third section, we analyze the hunger strikers' demands and aims to reveal the connection between the seemingly limited and immediate demands, such as the right to a legal defense in Kurdish and an end to Öcalan's isolation, and their broader demands, such as restarting the PKK–government negotiations, undertaking constitutional reform to grant Kurds legal status, and pursuing the democratization of the Turkish state and society, including achieving local autonomy, democratic autonomy, and democratic confederalism within Turkey (Akkaya and Jongerden 2014; O'Connor 2017).

The Hunger Strike and the Context of Injustice

For decades, the Turkish state has been in a violent struggle against Kurdish dissidents, movements, and forces (including against the People's Defense Force [Hêzên Parastina Gel, HPG], the PKK's military wing). It is widely estimated that since the early 1980s at least forty thousand people, mostly Kurds, have died in the struggle. Since coming to power in 2002, the AKP government has been engaged in a complex and brutal dance with the "Kurdish issue." In late 2009, the government banned the Democratic Society Party (Demokratik Toplum Partisi, DTP), then the largest Kurdish party in Turkey and the only one represented in Parliament. Between 2009 and 2012, well more than eight thousand Kurdish journalists, lawyers, politicians, and "sympathizers" were imprisoned, most of them accused of being tied to an outlawed Kurdish group, the KCK (Hess 2012; Mouradian 2012).[13] Alongside these repressive moves,

---

13. Michael Gunter reports that in 2009 the Turkish "government took 4000 children to court and had 400 of them imprisoned for participating in [pro-Kurdish] demonstrations." The mayor of Amed, too, was "scheduled to go to court on charges of 'membership in a terror organization,'" while Muharrem Erbey, the vice chairman of Turkey's largest human rights organization, the Human Rights Association (IHD), had already been imprisoned. [Meanwhile,] [t]he Turkish government had deported Jess Hess, an American freelance journalist, for reporting critically on human rights abuses against the Kurds" (2012). Human Rights Watch has characterized the arrests of members of the BDP, the KCK, and suspected supporters as attacks on "legal pro-Kurdish politics" (2011) rather than as responses to terrorism. The Turkish public first became aware of the KCK

the AKP government also appeared to display some constructive ones. For two years, between 2009 and 2011, it claimed to address the "Kurdish problem" of the Turkish state and society with a "Kurdish Opening" (Kurban 2013), in which government members engaged in (officially) secret negotiations with Öcalan, an attempt also known as "the Oslo talks" (Ünal 2016, 103).[14] Yet when the AKP government abandoned the talks, it once again resumed widespread attacks on the PKK, its guerrilla forces, as well as Kurdish citizens of Turkey whom the government suspected of supporting the PKK (Hess 2013). In addition to increased military violence and atrocities against the Kurds, as in the Roboskî massacre of late 2011,[15] the AKP government also cut off all access to Öcalan.

---

through the simultaneous arrests of 53 people on 14 April 2009 in twelve different cities. From this date on, the arrests continued in waves, and by July 2012 more than 7,000 had been detained, and the total number of arrestees rose to 1,951 (Bianet 2011; Yağmur 2012).

14. It has been widely reported that the AKP was in officially secret negotiations with Öcalan at least since 2009.

15. The Roboskî massacre refers to the aerial bombardment of thirty-eight Kurds, mostly children, from the border village of Roboskî in Bakur based on US Predator and Turkish Heron drones' false identification of the group as PKK operatives on 28 December 2011. From a Kurdish perspective, this event showed that when the Turkish state claims to be at war only against the PKK, the innocence and the civilian status of Kurdish victims simply did not matter. The atrocity gave Kurds the sense that so long as the victims were Kurdish, not only were their deaths merely collateral damage, but also the attacks on them deserved neither public scrutiny nor meaningful legal accountability.

The attitudes displayed by state officials contributed to the cementing of this perspective. First, there was no first-responder support immediately after the massacre and, as a result, the victims' families had to carry the charred and dismembered bodies in makeshift blankets. Second, although the chief public prosecutor's office opened an investigation into the massacre, it was done under a press ban. Furthermore, the investigation concluded that the massacre was a mere mistake by the armed forces, and the public prosecutor concluded therefore that those who were culpable deserved no punishment. As such, he decided not to prosecute. Finally, when the families and the general public gathered at the site of the massacre to protest the prosecutor's decision on the one hundredth day after the massacre and then again on the five hundredth day, they were met with tear gas, police brutality, and heavy fines. (See *Evrensel* 2018; Green and Karaka 2014; and chapter 8 in this volume).

By September 2012, neither his lawyers nor his family members nor the general public had heard from him for more than a year.[16]

This escalation of mass arrests, state violence, and Öcalan's isolation led sixty-four Kurdish prisoners across six Turkish prisons to commence on 12 September 2012 what was represented by the hunger strikers as a nonrotational and "indefinite hunger strike" (Demirtaş and Kışanak 2012, 2–3).[17] According to contemporaneous Turkish media coverage, the hunger strikers made two immediate, basic demands: end Öcalan's isolation and grant Kurds the right to use Kurdish in legal proceedings (including the hunger strikers' own trials) and in public schools. When the demands were not met and the strike continued, the number of hunger strikers escalated to include 782 Kurdish prisoners in sixty-seven prisons in a mass, indefinite hunger strike.[18] Toward the strike's end, Kurdish media sources and our interviewees maintained that more than ten thousand people joined the hunger strike both inside and outside of prisons, including BDP parliamentary representatives. The hunger strike dragged on for more than sixty-eight days, entering the "death zone" around the forty-fifth day. It was called off by the imprisoned Öcalan and thus ended on 18 November 2012. By its conclusion, the hunger strike of 2012 was reported to be one of the largest of such strikes in Turkish history (Kurban 2013).

Only some of the hunger strikers' demands reached the public, and media accounts often overlooked the larger context of injustice that had

---

16. With respect to the significance of Öcalan's isolation for the hunger strikers, many interviewees told us that the Turkish government's treatment of Öcalan is a tell-tale sign of both their fates as political captives and the government's approach to the Kurdish issue on the whole. For them, it is no coincidence that when the government allows Öcalan to see his lawyers and lets his insights reach the general public, there are fewer arrests and a more tolerant attitude toward Kurdish demands. For this reason, the hunger strikers believe that Öcalan's freedom is inextricably tied both to their freedom as captives and to the freedom of Kurds in Turkey in general.

17. These figures come from the BDP's contemporaneous report. The BDP cochairs at the time, Selahattin Demirtaş and Gültan Kışanak, also referred to the protest as an "indefinite hunger strike" (Demirtaş and Kışanak 2012, 2–3). Also see Harte 2012 and Hess 2012.

18. These figures are provided by the Turkish Ministry of Justice according to Amnesty International (2012). Also see Hess 2012.

led the Kurdish prisoners to action in the first place. Especially silenced in Turkish mainstream media reports and public debate was the way the hunger strikers had been initially arrested and prosecuted; neither the flagrant abuses of state power they experienced nor the state's intent to annihilate Kurdish "existence" in public life were often mentioned.[19] Yet it is crucial to understand the Kurds' violent experiences with and repression by the Turkish state because only then does their decision to engage in a hunger strike become clear.

The hunger strikers articulated two fundamental injustices that they had experienced at the hands of the state: first, the unlawfulness surrounding their own arrests and imprisonment; second, the state's persistence in violently suppressing or destroying "Kurdishness" in public life, including in politics, law, and culture. About their arrest and imprisonment, most hunger strikers revealed that the state had willfully misinterpreted their entirely legal activities as criminal evidence against them. In fact, only two had declared PKK membership, and those two stressed that they had been working within the legal/democratic (nonarmed) division of the organization (12, 14).[20] Yet their willingness to work within the

---

19. Given the all-encompassing connotations of the phrase "Kurdish existence," it may be necessary to clarify what our interviewees meant by it. They recognized the fact that there are many ethnic Kurdish citizens of Turkey who do not consider their existence under threat and even adopt the same attitude as that of the Turkish state toward the HDP/BDP's demands. A Kurdishness of the latter ethnocultural type is entirely consistent with and even encouraged by the Turkish nationalism that is imbued in the Constitution. As such, it does not constitute a point of political tension. So long as a Kurd does not make political demands on the basis of Kurdishness, including demands for constitutional recognition, education in the mother language, and local autonomy, he or she is no different from the myriad ethnocultural groups melted in the pot of Turkishness. Since the so-called Kurdish issue is precisely about these political demands, however, the Kurdish existence that is claimed to be under threat is the existence of Kurds who are not only ethnoculturally Kurdish but also politically Kurdish—that is, the biological, cultural, and political existence of Kurds who make these very demands. For one consideration of this Kurdish existence, see Bayır 2014.

20. In line with our anonymization of sources to protect them, we cite our interviewees parenthetically by number throughout the chapter.

constitutionally established boundaries of "legal" politics did not prevent the de facto criminalization of their activities by the state. For instance, media workers who publish in Kurdish were prosecuted because the state wrongly insisted that the KCK had instructed them to publish in Kurdish; the state used their publications and professional contacts as proof against them (02, 09). Furthermore, state authorities delegitimized and criminalized their legal activities by employing "specially authorized courts and prosecutors"[21] that deployed what in other contexts scholars often call "faux" law or "implausible legality."[22] Put another way, the state used such "special" apparatuses to bypass the legal system (01).

Many of the hunger strikers described similar criminalization in their arrest, detention, and prosecution. For instance, in the case of some BDP members, the state unlawfully used their visits to party headquarters, the manifestos they published, their participation in lawful protests, and their phone conversations as evidence against them (04, 05, 06, 07). Furthermore, prosecutors argued that their campaign work for the general elections in 2011 was, in fact, illegal KCK activity (13). As one hunger striker put it, "The prosecutor put together a bill of indictment against us using our party work and campaigning. He argued that what we were doing here at BDP was actually KCK activity. The argument was that because the KCK is illegal, everything we did at BDP, regardless of the fact

---

21. On special courts, see International Commission of Jurists, "Turkey: The Judicial System in Peril—a Briefing Paper" (2016). In this report, the ICJ states that State Security Courts were abolished in 2005, but "criminal courts with special powers (Specially Empowered Courts), the heirs of State Security Courts," were not abolished until 2014. In both cases, it concludes that the Special or Security Courts failed to uphold the right to a fair trial. Also see İlkiz 2014. According to Luca Perilli, an "independent expert" agreed to by the European Commission and the government of Turkey to review reforms in the Turkish judicial system, "special courts have been at the center of controversy since their establishment. Criticism has focused on the wide interpretation of their special powers, imposition of a strict pre-trial detention regime, limitations on the rights of the defense, excessively long indictments, the role of the police in launching investigations and handling arrest decisions, the slow pace of judicial proceedings linked to the very large number of individuals tried by the courts" (Perilli 2015).

22. On "faux" law, see Cohen 2013; on "implausible legality," see Sanders 2011.

that our activities were constitutionally protected, was also illegal. What the prosecutor was really doing was criminalizing our legitimate political endeavors" (04). The state charged others under the pretext that their involvement with trade unions and other civil society organizations was criminal. In one case, the only piece of evidence of "crime" brought against a person was that person's membership in a teachers' union (11). Another person was arrested for participating in "Friday prayers for human rights" and for possessing Kurdish media, such as newspapers and music mp3 files (01). In yet another case, the prosecutor used a photograph of the participant holding a beer bottle, claiming that he was preparing a Molotov cocktail. He was charged with preparing to launch a terrorist attack and was detained for two and a half years before being acquitted (03). In addition to employing such trumped-up charges, the Turkish state also charged one person by using the testimony of a "secret" witness whose identity was never revealed (03).

Many strikers commented that the injustices they personally experienced were part of the Turkish state's much larger political agenda to undermine the Kurdish movement by continuously and systematically blocking and thereby silencing Kurds' legal political engagement and representation in formal politics (04, 07). The same unjust official stand also extended to the trials of Kurds, which many of the interviewees denounced as being "shams" employing "dirty tactics" (03, 05, 06, 09, 11). Some Kurdish prisoners connected their imprisonment to the Turkish state's overall violent and discriminatory policy against the Kurds, which they expressed as "political genocide" or "politicide" of Kurds and Kurdishness (04, 05, 07). One prisoner in particular argued that Erdoğan's strategy of marginalizing Kurdish political activity, thereby rendering it inoperable, was predicated on his belief that he could "liquidate the entire Kurdish political movement in Turkish Kurdistan" (05).[23] Another pointed out that the

---

23. The hunger strikers we met echoed another hunger striker interviewed by the journalist Jake Hess at the time of the strike. That striker insisted that "thousands of people are in prison for no good reason. Everyone feels like I do: These sentences are given because we're Kurds, not because we're good PKK activists. The goal is to scare and

hunger strikers of 2012 referred to themselves and other hunger strikers as "captives" rather than as "prisoners," thereby calling attention to the lawless, warlike conditions that confront the Kurdish struggle. The striker we interviewed in Amed in 2016 maintained that by the time of his arrest in 2011, "a period of intensified warfare had already started." He continued:

> We knew that our arrests were entirely due to our political activity on the outside. We were imprisoned because of a political shift in the way the government wants to deal with the Kurds—[it is therefore] not due to any type of legal wrongdoing on our part. We were kept inside indefinitely; we did not know when we were going to get out. Our trials kept getting prolonged. Proceedings were comical; they were a sham. . . . We saw that if we could make the government change its course of action, we might eventually be free. So our struggle inside was directly related to and was a consequence of what was happening on the outside. Therefore, finding a solution process directly concerned us on many different levels. (09)

Aside from these themes, which were present in many of our interviews, some strikers highlighted the loathing they felt toward particular instances of injustice. Three emphasized their humiliation when their microphones were cut off and their words were transcribed as an "inaudible language" when they spoke in Kurdish in their court proceedings (09, 12, 15). Two referred to the Roboskî massacre, explaining how they used their trials as a platform to draw further attention to it (04, 13). Such passionate resentment of injustices by the state at every turn was key in the strikers' mobilization of the hunger strike. Many cited among such iconic injustices the Turkish state's isolation and mistreatment of Öcalan, the breakdown of the "peace process," and the Turkish state's escalating violence against the Kurds. One noted that "at the time the [peace] process was alarmingly paralyzed. Dear Öcalan couldn't speak to his lawyers,

---

suppress us with prisons, but this has had the exact opposite effect—it increased their [sic] resolve" (Murat Çiftçi, quoted in Hess 2012). Also see Hakyemez 2017.

and the armed conflict between the two parties was deepening at an ever-increasing speed" (06). Another insisted that "our struggle was certainly directed toward reigniting the [peace] process. This was our first goal. Many villages were being emptied; our people had to migrate to metropolises, and they were in bad shape. The people of Turkey were waking up daily to the news of gunfights and martyrs. The same went for the guerillas. So, for us, it was imperative that both parties go back to the negotiation table" (10).

In summary, the significance of the hunger strike becomes more evident when the strike is placed within the larger context of persistent injustice enacted by the state against Kurds in Turkey. This injustice made it clear to the hunger strikers that the AKP government, despite having initiated the Kurdish Opening, was engaging in widespread illegal repression and was reverting to its violent methods of dealing with the Kurds, an approach that was unfortunately all too familiar to them.

The Legitimacy of Means

We asked the hunger strikers not only why they went on strike but also how they decided to do so and how they reacted to official claims that the strike was presumptively illegitimate in a "democracy" as "an act of blackmail" or a use of "oppression and force," as Erdoğan and Oomen-Rujiten characterized it. We thus wanted to understand the strikers' justifications for their actions. In all our conversations, the strikers depicted the hunger strike as a political act that was justly and deliberatively decided upon; they regarded it as a legitimate and democratic form of action given the context of injustice, the limitations on other forms of protest that they faced as prisoners, their principled decision-making, and their decision to refuse acts of violence in favor of something more like civil disobedience. In making the decision, the strikers also invoked radical conceptions of citizenship and reflected deeply on life and death and on the course of democratic, pluralistic, and egalitarian politics.

Refuting Erdoğan's official claims that the BDP and PKK had manipulated the hunger strike (Saktanber 2012), the strikers emphasized that they had made their own decision based on deliberations with those close to them both inside and outside the prisons.[24] Two acknowledged the role of "the party" in the decision (07, 02), with one arguing that the BDP communiqué to the cities suggested such resistance (02). But many others emphasized the fullness of their discussions, including how to carry out the strike and the processes they used to communicate about it with each other, including yelling from cell to cell (01), organizing meetings in communal spaces (11, 12, 13), and discussing it during the "countless hours of going to court" (09). They also noted that they discussed the hunger strike with their lawyers (05), family members, and friends (05, 11) through letters and visits (09). Several described the rich and extensive pre-hunger-strike discussions, such as the possibility of having shorter hunger strikes to warn the state (09); instead, the plan to start a longer, indefinite hunger strike "solidified through debate" (10). Another striker stressed the significance of the Kurdish community in prison; because their relatives, lawyers, and friends were arrested en masse, there was a significant degree of "organization of communal life in prison . . . with its own discipline" (05). Still another hunger striker underlined that they considered their prison experience to be a "part of the political process" because so many Kurds were incarcerated by a state that did not respect freedom of thought and expression; hence, imprisonment was defined as the cost of "practicing freedom of thought politically" (03).

More details emerged as they discussed the decision-making process. One pointed out that they faced opposition even from within the Kurdish community in that "the [Kurdish] movement" outside was "firmly against it. They wanted to stop us from doing it" (13). Several hunger strikers described their attempts to dissuade the elderly, infirm, youthful, and other vulnerable inmates from joining the hunger strike. The great concern to protect these vulnerable comrades from risky behavior prompted some of the latter to protest the intervention, arguing that their

---

24. One striker, however, refused to address this question: "Unfortunately, I cannot tell you how we communicated and decided to start the hunger strike. We have our own system of doing things I cannot disclose here. . . . [O]ur party [the BDP] had its own mechanisms of decision-making. That being said, nothing was imposed; if anything, we were trying to stop people from joining the hunger strike" (07).

autonomous decision to participate was being undermined (12). Indeed, the hunger strikers tried to convince a cancer survivor to stay off the strike, yet he vehemently refused, stating, "You are trying to convince me to undertake *political suicide* [by not joining the strike], and I refuse to [abstain]" (07). In all, then, the process of deciding on this form of corporeal resistance was robustly deliberative, arrived at collectively, and undertaken autonomously. One participant eloquently summarized the decision-making process:

> Before the hunger strike, there was discussion across prisons through letters and visitations regarding the general principles of our resistance.... [Then] individual groups in different prisons started the hunger strike and/or decided to join it. Hence, it grew across prisons.... Of course, ten thousand people can't come to a decision at the same time and unanimously while in prison. As such, it was crucial for the first [striking] group to ignite the resistance... to build accord with the rest of the movement. After it [the strike] caught on, our organizations on the outside also demonstrated their solidarity. (04)

Outside support was certainly important in that it demonstrated that the Kurdish public agreed with the prisoners' decision to strike, strengthening their belief in their chosen method of action. The Kurdish public then turned into another front of the battle with protests and marches, media presence, and collaborations with nongovernmental organizations. The interviewees repeatedly expressed the mutuality of the struggle both inside and outside prison walls. One participant, for example, maintained the hunger strike was a "continuation of our politics inside" (05); another stressed that "prisons became part of the political process" (03); while a third emphasized that "outside support was important, perhaps especially the hunger strike started by party members in Parliament" (07).

In interpreting the hunger strike, many linked it to civil disobedience, with one referring to the Gandhi and Irish Republican Army hunger strikes and concluding, "So I think its democratic legitimacy was established long before us" (05). They contrasted the nonviolent character of the act with the Turkish state and society's relentless, overarching violence against the Kurdish political movement and those suspected of supporting it. They emphasized, as Onur Günay has said, that "violence is inscribed into the very fabric of everyday life" (2013, 181) of Turkish society and that in the context of extreme state violence against the Kurdish minority it was important that *they, the Kurds*, were the ones to choose to engage in nonviolence for both tactical and principled reasons. One striker gave expression to tactical reasons:

> It was important for us that the hunger strike was a purely "civil initiative." Especially for our prison [Silivri], we juxtaposed our nonviolence with the violence of the state. We didn't have weapons, not even sticks and stones. Yet the state had guards, prisons' weapons, and cameras. At least in our prison, they had cameras everywhere. They were recording us twenty-four/seven. It was like a zoo.... So we wanted to contradict these conditions with pacifism. We were aware of the [significance] of the media ... [and also that] the public's support ... was absolutely crucial. ... [Our method of protest] was also important for [its] legitimacy [to] the people outside. It gave them visibility and a method of action to follow. [The public] played an important part in preventing deaths by way of forcing the opposition to the negotiation table. Their protests somehow resonated with the authorities. Otherwise, the authorities could take this [hunger strike] to the worst place possible, and there could have been many deaths. (06)

Yet principled reasons predominated over tactical ones. For instance, the mayor of Amed, who also went on the hunger strike, reported that "all of my life I have stayed away from violence and the instruments of violence and have viewed a legal, democratic struggle as the only means to achieve change" (Osman Baydemir, quoted in Yeğinsu 2012). Another hunger striker summed up the principled position of the prisoners' rejection of violence: "We thought long and hard about the hunger strike. In the past, we have taken hostages and the like. But for us, life is sacred on all levels, from women to ecology. Because of this, violent means have lost their appeal when assessed from the rules and ethics that our party cherishes. There were two parameters of action for us: avoiding loss of life and achieving political results" (07).

To depict the hunger strike as a legitimate democratic act, hunger strikers would sometimes emphasize the larger context of injustice that the Turkish state had single-handedly created. One who had been on the strike for sixty-eight days expressed this position succinctly:

> It is comical to question the legitimacy of our hunger strike when the Turkish state can't even tolerate the mother language of its citizens, when it resorts to violence in dealing with democratic demands.... Our hunger strike did not destroy thousands of lives or violate anybody's rights.... For this reason, I do not [think] it makes sense for Erdoğan to school us in democracy. We are not the ones bombing people with planes, nor are we denying the cultural and political existence of others. We are not the ones imprisoning political dissidents.... So I do not see how this is "blackmail." (09)

The hunger strikers, thus, seemed genuinely intent on "flipping the script"—that is, illuminating Turkish state violence by withstanding its humiliations, assaults, and deprivations through nonviolent corporeal protest. In fact, one striker made this strategy explicit, stating that "we wanted to show the regime and the rest of the world that the 'Kurdish issue' cannot be resolved by coercion and war. We wanted people to say, 'a country like this cannot be a democracy'" (03). Another stressed that Turkey's lack of serious commitment to the peace process would push Kurds to "look for alternative avenues, let it be known." He then continued, "They cannot pacify us. They cannot expect us to disappear, go away, or get drowned out in the whole process. They must understand that they are bringing Afghanistan, Iraq, Syria to Turkey. If this happens, it will haunt them. We are trying to do everything we can to prevent this. We are fighting for a more democratic Turkey for all" (06).

Others reflected on harm to the body committed in indefinite hunger striking (03, 08, 11). Jake Hess reports that one hunger striker wrote in a letter from Amed Prison that "by melting our bodies, we're trying to intervene in the situation, to shape our future.... Between these four walls, there's nothing else we can do in the face of tyrannical repression" (Mazlum Tekdağ, quoted in Hess 2012). One hunger striker we spoke with poetically connected the body to the fullness of a good life, noting that "the cultural and linguistic fullness is much more important to us than the fullness of our stomachs. Our [physical] hunger was symbolic of our hunger for self-determination" (03). Others spoke of sacrificing their health in the process; nevertheless, they poignantly spoke of taking back control over their own bodies and using them against those (the Turkish state and society) who had abused them through rape, torture, execution (15). But many also focused on life and death more than on the body itself. For instance, one striker argued the hunger strike was "a choice of death, if necessary, for life. . . . Death . . . for life is contradictory." But he went on to maintain that this "contradiction underlines the voicelessness of the Kurdish people at the time" (04; also 02).

One might argue that the talk of possible death in this hunger strike was exaggerated because no one died and because many of the hunger strikers we spoke with were on the strike for less than three weeks. Yet by hunger striking, the prisoners were building upon the memory of many earlier, deadly hunger strikes. One reflected on this history: "You know, hunger striking is not something new to the Kurdish movement. Since '82, we have been using it as a means of protesting injustices in varying degrees. In fact, many people lost their lives in '82; it was a heroic struggle" (09). Another insisted, "We were determined to get what we wanted even if it meant certain death" (05). And a third reflected on the stakes of this hunger strike: "We had a lot of difficult days where we were waiting for news of deaths across prisons. . . . It was a difficult atmosphere to bear, seeing your comrades slowly die right next to you. . . . We all were worried that we were going to hear news of martyrdom, but, like I said, we were extremely lucky" (13). When asked about their view of the success or failure of the hunger strike, many responded that the first or greatest victory was that no one died (a "miracle" [10]); any death, one said, "would be a catastrophe" (08).

Using life and risking death were not motivated by the wish to end an unbearable individual life by an act of suicide. The strike was not a "negation of life" (Bargu 2014, 272) or an escape from unbearable life. Rather, it resisted, as Hannah Arendt puts it, "a life without speech and action," which the hunger strikers intimated may, indeed, be a state of being "dead to the world; it has ceased to be a human life because it is no longer lived among men" (Arendt 1958, 176). They also, however, resisted "bare life" (Agamben 1998; Bargu 2014, 81) by acting—by living "among men" in political ways even in prison, undertaking an indefinite hunger strike while also both enacting and demanding a right *to* politics. Hence, hunger striking drew upon life—upon sacrifice, pain, hunger, self-inflicted degradation—and upon possible death, but only of one's cramped corporeal self in resisting "civil death," or death "in law" (Dayan 2014), and political/public death, or "politicide." They were using and risking life in an attempt to generate legal, political, and cultural life, understanding themselves as citizens, indeed as radical democratic citizens seeking fundamental democratic transformation.

The Legitimacy of Ends

To understand the form of citizenship and democracy that the hunger strikers attempted to advance, it is necessary to analyze their aims and demands. The woman who narrated the most searing story of the torture that she, her father, and others who spoke Kurdish suffered at the hands of the Turkish state noted that the act of hunger striking itself made life honorable so that one did not continue living enslaved (15). Others also defined engaging in political life or life in common, even in prison, as the reestablishment of a dignified life in both the individual and social senses. But an honorable, dignified life in common outside prison was the hunger strikers' primary aim. In making this case, the strikers identified different strands of what constitutes a dignified life, all of which are hallmarks of radical democratic citizenship. This conception of citizenship is not only constituted of the familiar concepts of the rule of law and the recognition and extension of civil, political, and cultural rights to all but also, more radically, infused with the intent to establish local autonomy, direct democracy, democratic autonomy, and democratic confederalism. Let us briefly unpack these elements.

Dignified common life, the hunger strikers argued, requires, first, the protection of legal and political life through commitment to the rule of law and democracy. One said, "In a country where you can imprison thousands of people in an instant without any legal reasoning, you can't speak of a democracy" (08; also 12). Another recognized that "where rights are denied, there is no democracy, despite elections" (03).

Democracy and with it a dignified common life also require the protection of the Kurdish community's cultural life (which in this case was identified as the recognition of minority or national language rights), an end to Öcalan's isolation, reignition of the peace process, and negotiation with the state over the terms of "local" or "democratic autonomy." The hunger strikers argued that it was necessary to end Öcalan's isolation because he is viewed as the necessary interlocutor for the resumption of peace negotiations (05). He had to be a part of the "public dialogue" (08). His inclusion in the process, it was emphasized, "concerns the fate of an entire nation" (09), and this is so not just in terms of his status within the Kurdish movement. Rather, when the Turkish state talks to Öcalan, the communication leads to political negotiations, but when he is isolated, the state acts much more aggressively. In fact, one striker pointed out that "bringing Öcalan back into the political picture would also mean the end of this violent process that the state has started. This is part of the reason why all BDP/HDP components point to Öcalan as the relevant interlocutor" (09). They thus identified the hunger strike itself as a "preventative measure against the death of the peace process" (06; also 04, 07) and, more broadly, a political act that demanded the end of the "political genocide" of the Kurds (04, 05, 07).

Importantly, the hunger strikers and their supporters aimed for the establishment of equal rights of citizenship within Turkey. We can "never speak of democracy in Turkey," one maintained, "until they [those in power] consider Kurds as equal citizens, who deserve to have a say in how they are governed" (08). Many emphasized that equal citizenship necessitates constitutional revision that specifically recognizes Kurdishness. They deemed such recognition to be necessary for two reasons. First, they mistrusted the Turkish state to stay true to its word, so they wanted textual revisions of the Constitution; second, such recognition would acknowledge the Kurds' equal right to coexistence, which, following Öcalan, would prepare the groundwork for the new political structure of "local autonomy" (08, 09, 10, 11), "democratic autonomy" (08, 13), and "democratic confederation" (08, 12). Yet they were also clear that the change would be oriented toward establishing radically egalitarian and pluralistic citizenship that applied not just to Kurds but also *to everyone* living in Turkey (06, 07, 08, 11, 13, 14).

One hunger striker, for example, said that the strike aimed to "steer the contemporary [political] agenda toward the overall democratization of Turkey, starting from the Kurdish issue" (14). Another put the matter similarly: "I was in the Diyarbakir D-type prison as a political prisoner. There we made a decision . . . that both Kurdish and Turkish people should be able to benefit from the insights and ideas of our leader and that we as political prisoners have to take an active part in destroying the barriers that hamper the flourishing of democracy, like a 'bulldozer'" (08). Striking for a pluralistic conception of citizenship and radical democracy was a central aim that the strikers repeatedly contrasted to an undemocratic Turkey. One pointed out that "Turkey is not a democracy—because there is torture, unlawful imprisonment, and all-around political repression. . . . I would define it as a capitalist nation-state with an ultranationalist bent. If Kurds pushed for a political system of this sort, one with the singularizing logic of vulgar nationalism, to enjoy our nationhood at the expense of others, I would rise against it as well" (12). Hence, the ultimate vision of the hunger strikers also included ensuring that all people living in Turkey would be as free and equal as the Kurds were to become. One hunger striker articulated their demands especially well:

> Ending Öcalan's isolation, restarting the negotiations, establishing the right to legal defense in Kurdish, and introducing a system of local autonomy are all interconnected. Öcalan has been the main political actor in devising these negotiations. Since the late '90s, he has been saying that we must strengthen democracy in Turkey[;] . . . strengthening democracy means, first, going back to the negotiation table to discuss our demands of local autonomy. Obviously, the concept of local autonomy is much more comprehensive than just language rights. We are talking about a form of direct democracy, where local peoples get to decide on matters without feeling the weight of top-down pressures of the central government in Ankara on their shoulders. . . . We do not want this [these legal and political reforms] just for Diyarbakir. . . . This is why the idea of strengthening local autonomy is directly tied to democratizing Turkey as a whole. (11)

He then pointed out that Öcalan had to be visible and accessible during this process, maybe just under house arrest. The legal reforms that would be formulated would apply to all minorities in Turkey so that "if somebody wants to be educated in Arabic or Armenian in Hatay, they should be able to do so as well." Getting an education in one's native tongue is a basic human right. He concluded, "Whereas in Turkey there is a certain way of 'being Turkish' that is imposed on every citizen through oppressive laws and state mechanisms, . . . we are proposing [something quite similar to] what is happening in Rojava [in Syria] with the canton system" (11).

The radical implications of the view of citizenship and democratic politics imagined and endorsed by many of the hunger strikers and their supporters should not be underestimated. They reject a homogenous conceptualization of the nation with brutally ruthless assimilation policies deployed by the state, which they want replaced with the rule of law, free political participation, cultural and language rights, and the resumption of the peace process. Their political commitment to local autonomy and democratic confederalism, if accepted or successful, *would* indeed alter Turkish society and governance in a far more directly democratic direction; their inclusive standpoint also gives their demands for equal rights to coexistence a more radical "bite." But the radicalism of their aims is suffused with liberal democratic demands for rights as well as with a flexibility that made the hunger strikers self-consciously experimental, oriented to learning over time, and always open to negotiations. As such, the vision they expressed is consistent with the HDP's stated position of not just representing the Kurds but also democratizing Turkey as a whole in newly imagined ways. As articulated in the HDP's platform for the parliamentary elections in 2015, such a vision, in addition to opposing oppression, exploitation, and discrimination, also aims at creating "a democratic popular government in which all obstacles against the labour struggle are removed[,] . . . [one that is] against the imposition of 'a uniform Turkish nation in terms of ethnic identity, culture, language and religion' [and instead defends] a pluralistic social life based on equal and voluntary togetherness of differences [to achieve the] goal of an emancipated and democratic Turkey" (Öcalan, quoted in Heinrich Böll Stiftung 2015). This vision is certainly radically democratic, but the hunger strikers' commitment to this vision signals neither separatism nor violence. On the contrary, the hunger strikers, like the party, demand nonviolence, democratization, and radically democratic citizenship premised on rights and constitutional reform for the entire country.

Conclusion

The hunger strikers thus did not argue for a separatist politics grounded in ethnic nationalism, territory, or statehood; instead, they viewed their actions in relation to Öcalan's vision of democratic confederalism and democratic autonomy. They argued for democratic, local, relatively autonomous political structures that would guarantee an equal right to coexistence within the Turkish nation as equal citizens of Turkey. They did so hoping that the hunger strike, a nonviolent democratic act itself, could elicit political negotiations to this end.[25]

Ten years have passed since the hunger strike in 2012. Is it too late now for a return to peace negotiations and to hope for constitutional revisions aimed at democratization of the Turkish state that would satisfy Kurdish demands? During this time, the Turkish military has carried out systematic attacks on the Kurdish Southeast, established violent curfews, and declared a state of emergency over the entire country after the attempted coup d'etat in July 2016. In September 2016 the Turkish state fired eleven thousand teachers with impunity and replaced twenty-four mayors in the Southeast with trustees (Craine 2016; Demirtaş and Yüksekdağ n.d.). It also arrested and imprisoned HDP's lawfully elected parliamentary representatives, including the party's co-mayors in Amed as well as its co-leaders, Selahattin Demirtaş and Figen Yüksekdağ, who remain in prison. In April 2019 the AKP refused to respect and accept municipal-election results in cities such as Istanbul and to accept newly elected Kurdish mayors in Amed and elsewhere. As of 2020, the majority of mayors belonging to the HDP were imprisoned, and sixty of the sixty-five mayoral positions held by HDP members had been transferred to trustees appointed by the Ministry of Internal Affairs, thus leaving

---

25. For one evaluation of the possibilities of peace after 2015, see Gunter 2016.

more than four million people without democratic representation at the mayoral level (BBC Türkçe 2020).

What would it take to achieve a return to peace negotiations and an "equal right to coexistence" today? It would depend on the actions of the AKP government. In 2016 Michael M. Gunter argued optimistically that "despite the current impasse, official Turkish talks with Öcalan, the PKK, and the legal pro-Kurdish Peoples' Democratic Party (HDP) have given the Kurdish issue in general and the PKK specifically a permanent legitimacy that would have been inconceivable even a decade ago" (2016, 79). And on 11 September 2016, after another, shorter hunger strike by HDP members, Öcalan told his brother Mehmet that "if the [Turkish] state is ready, it can send two people to the island [where I am imprisoned], and we can start negotiations" (quoted in *Kurdish Question* 2016). Yet the Turkish state's massive violence against the Southeast since 2015 (Koefoed 2017, 184) and its wider attacks bode ill for future peace negotiations, as does its ongoing penchant for depicting legal HDP politics, protests, and resistance as violent separatism or terrorism. These state acts, as in the hunger strikers' description of earlier machinations, constitute politicide.

It appears extremely unlikely that Öcalan's isolation will come to an end any time soon. In fact, between the hunger strike in 2012 and the publishing of this chapter in 2022 the Turkish state was confronted by another indefinite hunger strike protesting Öcalan's isolation, first started by HDP Hakkari member of Parliament Leyla Güven on 6 November 2018. Güven was joined by seven thousand prisoners in Turkey (Kayar 2019), and the strike spread to Europe and North America. What was more worrisome about this hunger strike in comparison to the one in 2012 is that there were *eight deaths* in the form of protest-suicides. The political prisoners Ayten Beçet, Zehra Sağlam, Zülküf Gezen, Medya Çınar, Yonca Akıcı, Sıraç Yüksek, and Mahsum Pamay all took their own lives in prison "to end the isolation of Öcalan" (Mezopotamya Ajansi 2019; see also Bianet English 2019). In Germany, Uğur Şakar immolated himself in front of the Krefeld court building, declaring the same goal.[26] Güven ended the hunger

---

26. Earlier, in September 2016, HDP members were also on a hunger strike. See Cupolo 2016; *Deutsche Welle* 2016; and *T24* 2016.

strike on its two hundredth day, declaring that the strike had "achieved its goal" in terms of bringing attention to the isolation of Öcalan and his call for a political solution to the Kurdish issue (Bianet English 2019). But, of course, Öcalan's isolation has not been ended, and no political solution process has commenced.

In all, the hunger strikers we interviewed and those who supported them, including PKK party members, lawyers, journalists, translators, and BDP leaders, maintained a continuing willingness to return to peace negotiations with the Turkish state, explicitly aware that the window for productive negotiations is exceedingly narrow. Without wishing to sanitize the violence that has been and remains a part of Kurdish politics in Turkey, it is crucial to grasp that Öcalan, much of the Kurdish movement, and certainly the HDP (as well as the BDP and Democratic Regions Party [Demokratik Bölgeler Partisi, DBP] before it) view violence as a last resort and have instead been committed to nonviolence where possible. Politically, they have rejected the "one nation–one state" principle in favor of equal citizenship and an equal right to coexistence within the Turkish Republic, predicated on the development of a democratic Turkish state, local autonomy, and democratic confederation. It is, therefore, a cause for concern that several participants interviewed in 2016 expressed a rapidly growing skepticism about the possibility of democracy in Turkey and questioned whether they ought to continue to pursue democratic autonomy within Turkey (06). A woman hunger striker who had been in Bakırköy Prison seemed to capture the mood of the hunger strikers by 2016 when she told us:

> Now we have a completely different picture. The Suruç, Ankara, and Antep bombings as well as the massacres in Cizre, Sur, and other places make me cynical about the state of democracy in Turkey. Therefore, many of us have come to the point of seriously reevaluating our stance toward the state: Do we want to live with this state or not? Because they are truly untrustworthy. So now it is really difficult to convince people when it comes to ideas of democratic autonomy since they do not trust the state anymore. [Given that] many massacres took place since then, ... can you really blame them? So I don't know if we are as persistent about democratic confederalism as before. (13)

References

Agamben, Giorgio. 1998. *Homo Sacer: Sovereign Power and Bare Life*. Translated by Daniel Heller-Roazen. Stanford, CA: Stanford Univ. Press.

Akkaya, Ahmet Hamdi, and Joost Jongerden. 2014. "Confederalism and Autonomy in Turkey: The Kurdistan Workers' Party and the Reinvention of Democracy." In *The Kurdish Question in Turkey: New Perspectives on Violence, Representation, and Reconciliation*, edited by Cengiz Gunes and Welat Zeydanlıoğlu, 186–204. London: Routledge.

Amnesty International. 2012. "Turkey: Hunger Strikers Denied Medical Care." 9 Nov. At https://www.amnesty.org/en/documents/eur44/022/2012/en/.

Arendt, Hannah. 1958. *The Human Condition*. Chicago: Univ. of Chicago Press.

Bargu, Banu. 2014. *Starve and Immolate: The Politics of Human Weapons*. New York: Columbia Univ. Press.

Bartholomew, Amy. 2017. "Does Habermasian Theory Exclude Self-Sacrifice as Legitimate Political Action?" Paper presented at the Philosophy and Social Science Colloquium in Critical Theory, Prague, Czech Republic, May.

Bayır, Derya. 2014. "The Role of the Judicial System in the Politicide of the Kurdish Opposition." In *The Kurdish Question in Turkey: New Perspectives on Violence, Representation, and Reconciliation*, edited by Cengiz Gunes and Welat Zeydanlıoğlu, 21–47. London: Routledge.

BBC Türkçe. 2020. "Kars Belediyesi'ne kayyum atanmasıyla HDP'nin il belediyesi kalmadı." 2 Oct. At https://www.bbc.com/turkce/haberler-turkiye-54386357.

Bia haber merkezi. 2011. "İki buçuk yıldır gündemdeki 'KCK' nedir?" 11 June. At https://bianet.org/bianet/siyaset/131077-iki-bucuk-yildir-gundemdeki-kck-nedir.

———. 2012. "Erdoğan'ın gündemi idam." 2012. 11 Nov. At https://m.bianet.org/bianet/siyaset/142003-erdogan-in-gundemi-idam.

Bianet. 2011. "Otuz ayda KCK'den 7748 gözaltı,3895 tutuklama." 6 Oct. At http://bianet.org/bianet/siyaset/133216-30-ayda-kckden-7748-gozalti-3895-tutuklama.

Bianet English. 2019. "Leyla Güven: I End My Hunger Strike." 26 May. At https://m.bianet.org/bianet/human-rights/208860-leyla-guven-i-end-my-hunger-strike.

Butler, Daren. 2012. "Risk of Death Close for Turkish Hunger Strike: Doctors." Reuters, 1 Nov. At http://www.reuters.com/article/us-turkey-kurds-idUSBRE8A00SZ20121101.

Cohen, Jean L. 2013. "Sovereign Equality v. Imperial Right: The Battle over the 'New World Order.'" *Constellations* 13, no. 4: 485–505.

Craine, Naomi. 2016. "Ankara Escalates Attacks on Turkey/Syria." *Militant* 80, no. 3. At http://www.themilitant.com/2016/8038/803855.html.

Cupolo, Diego. 2016. "Kurdish Politicians Declare Hunger Strike to Protest Öcalan Communication Ban." *Deutsche Welle*, 31 Aug. At http://www.dw.com/en/kurdish-politicians-declare-hunger-strike-to-protest-ocalan-communication-ban/a-19517299.

Dayan, Colin. 2014. "With Law at the Edge of Life." *South Atlantic Quarterly* 113, no. 3: 629–39.

Demirtaş, Selahattin, and Gültan Kışanak. 2012. "Letter from BDP Co-chairs, Mr. Selahattin Demirtaş and Ms. Gültan Kışanak." In *Special File: Hunger Strike in Prisons of Turkey*, 2–7. Ankara, Turkey: Foreign Affairs Commission of the Peace and Democracy Party, 14 Nov. At https://peaceinkurdistancampaign.files.wordpress.com/2011/11/special-file-for-hunger-strike-14-11-2012.pdf.

Demirtaş, Selahattin, and Figen Yüksekdağ. n.d. "Letter by HDP Co-chairs on Recent Purges against Peace Academics and School Teachers." At https://hdp.org.tr/en/letter-by-hdp-s-co-chairs-on-recent-purges-against-peace-academics-and-schoolteachers/8794/.

Deutsche Welle. 2016. "Jailed Kurdish Leader Urges Turkey to Revive Peace Talks." 12 Sept. At http://www.dw.com/en/jailed-kurdish-leader-urges-turkey-to-revive-peace-talks/a-19546420.

Evrensel. 2018. "Roboski Katliamı: 7 yıl önce bugün ve sonrasında yaşananlar." 28 Dec. At https://www.evrensel.net/haber/369544/roboski-katliami-7-yil-once-bugun-ve-sonrasinda-yasananlar.

Feola, Michael. 2018. "The Body Politic: Bodily Spectacle and Democratic Agency." *Political Theory* 46, no. 2: 197–217.

Firat News Agency. 2013. "Martyrs of the 14 July Death Fast Remembered." 15 July. At https://anfenglish.com/news/martyrs-of the-14-july-death-fast-remembered-7573.

Green, Penny, and Saniye Karaka. 2014. "State Crime in Turkey: The Roboski Massacre." *Open Democracy*, 12 May. At https://www.opendemocracy.net/penny-green-saniye-karakas/state-crime-in-turkey-roboski-massacre.

Günay, Onur. 2013. "Toward a Critique of Nonviolence." *Dialectical Anthropology* 37:171–82.

Gunter, Michael. 2012. "The Closing of Turkey's Kurdish Opening." *Columbia Journal of International Affairs*, 20 Sept. At https://jia.sipa.columbia.edu/online-articles/closing-turkey's-kurdish-opening.

———. 2016. "The Kurdish Issue in Turkey: Back to Square One?" *Turkish Policy Quarterly* 14, no. 4: 77–86. At http://turkishpolicy.com/article/786/the-kurdish-issue-in-turkey-back-to-square-one.

Habermas, Jürgen. 1994. "Struggles for Recognition in the Democratic Constitutional State." In *Multiculturalism: Examining the Politics of Recognition*, edited by Amy Gutmann, 107–48. Princeton, NJ: Princeton Univ. Press.

———. 1996. *Between Facts and Norms: Contributions to a Discourse Theory of Law and Democracy*. Translated by William Rehg. Cambridge, MA: MIT Press.

Hakyemez, Serra. 2017. "Margins of the Archive: Torture, Heroism, and the Ordinary in Prison No. 5, Turkey." *Anthropological Quarterly* 90, no. 1: 107–38.

Harte, Julia. 2012. "Turkey's Critical Hunger Strike." *Foreign Policy*, 6 Nov. At https://foreignpolicy.com/2013/01/08/turkeys-pkk-talks/.

Heinrich Böll Stiftung. 2015. "Turkey's Newest Party: Understanding the HDP." 27 Oct. At https://www.boell.de/en/2015/10/27/turkeys-newest-party-understanding-hdp.

Hess, Jake. 2012. "Behind the Kurdish Hunger Strike in Turkey." *Middle East Report Online*, 8 Nov. At www.merip.org/mero/mero110812.

———. 2013. "Turkey's PKK Talks." *Foreign Policy*, 8 Jan. At http://foreignpolicy.com/2013/01/08/turkeys-pkk-talks/.

Honneth, Axel. 2004. "Recognition and Justice: Outline of a Plural Theory of Justice." *Acta sociologica* 47, no. 4: 351–64.

Human Rights Watch. 2011. "Turkey: Arrests Expose Flawed Justice System." 1 Nov. At http://www.hrw.org/news/2011/11/01/turkey-arrests-expose-flawed-justice-system.

Hürriyet Daily News. 2012a. "Hunger Strikes Unacceptable in Democracies: Rapporteur." 17 Nov. At http://www.hurriyetdailynews.com/hunger-strikes-unacceptable-in-democracies-rapporteur-34846.

İlkiz, Fikret. 2014. "KCK Cases and the Judiciary Mechanism." Heinrich Boll Foundation, Istanbul, 16 June. At https://tr.boell.org/en/2014/06/16/kck-cases-and-judiciary-mechanism.

International Commission of Jurists. 2016. "Turkey: The Judicial System in Peril—a Briefing Paper." July. At https://www.icj.org/wp-content/uploads

/2016/07/Turkey-Judiciary-in-Peril-Publications-Reports-Fact-Findings-Mission-Reports-2016-ENG.pdf.

Irmak, Selma. 2012. "Letter from Arrested MP, Ms. Selma Irmak." *Peace and Democracy Party: International E-Bulletin*, Nov., 4–6. At https://peaceinkurdistancampaign.files.wordpress.com/2011/11/bdp-bulletin-november-2012.pdf.

Kayar, Sertaç. 2019. "HDP'den cezaevlerindeki açlık grevleriyle ilgili uyarı: Toplu ölumler yaşanabilir." *Sputnik Türkiye*, 13 Apr. At https://tr.sputniknews.com/turkiye/201904131038748646-hdpden-cezaevlerindeki-aclik-grevleriyle-ilgili-uyari-toplu-olumler-yasanabilir/.

Koefoed, Minoo. 2017. "Martyrdom and Resistance in the Case of Northern Kurdistan: Hidden and Public Emotional Resistance." *Journal of Political Power* 10, no. 2: 184–99.

Kurban, Dilek. 2013. "To Europe and Back: The Three Decades of Kurdish Struggle in Turkey," Policy Brief no. 7, Istanbul Policy Centre, Sabancı Univ., Istanbul, Mar. At https://opus4.kobv.de/opus4-hsog/frontdoor/deliver/index/docId/1643/file/GTE_Policy_Briefs_07-+DK.pdf.

Kurdish Question. 2016. "'I Am a Democrat and Revolutionary': Important Messages from Abdullah Öcalan." 30 Sept. At http://kurdishquestion.com/article/3480-039-i-am-a-democrat-and-revolutionary-039-important-messages-from-abdullah-ocalan.

Mezopotamya Ajansi. 2019. "Leyla Güven'in eylemi 150'inci gününde." 6 Apr. At http://mezopotamyaajansi16.com/tum-haberler/content/view/53413.

Mouffe, Chantal. 1993. *The Return of the Political*. London: Verso.

Mouradian, Khatchig. 2012. "Of Hunger Strikes and Role Models: An Interview with Bilgin Ayata." *Armenian Weekly*, 5 Nov. At https://armenianweekly.com/2012/11/05/of-hunger-strikes-and-role-models-an-interviewwith-bilgin-ayata/.

Öcalan, Abdullah. 2004. *Bir halkı savunmak*. Istanbul: Amara Yayincilik.

———. 2011. *Democratic Confederalism*. Translated by International Initiative Edition. London: Transmedia.

O'Connor, Francis. 2017. "The Kurdish Movement in Turkey: Between Political Differentiation and Violent Confrontation." *PRIF Reports* 147:1–33. At https://www.hsfk.de/fileadmin/HSFK/hsfk_publikationen/prif147.pdf.

O'Neill, Shane. 2010. "Struggles against Injustice: Contemporary Critical Theory and Political Violence." *Journal of Global Ethics* 6, no. 2: 127–39.

Perilli, Luca. 2015. "Report on the Findings and Recommendations of the Peer Review Mission on Criminal Justice (Istanbul and Ankara, May 19–23, 2014)." 2 Feb. At https://www.avrupa.info.tr/sites/default/files/2016-11/Criminal _Justice_report_final_January_2015.pdf.

Rawls, John. 1993. *Political Liberalism*. New York: Columbia Univ. Press.

Saktanber, Binnaz. 2012. "Will Erdogan Do Nothing to Save the Lives of Kurdish Hunger Strikers?" *Guardian*, 8 Nov. At https://www.theguardian.com /commentisfree/2012/nov/08/erdogan-kurdish-hunger-strikers.

Sanders, Rebecca. 2011. "Implausible Legality." *International Journal of Human Rights* 15, no. 4: 605–26.

Sevinç, Murat. 2008. "Hunger Strikes in Turkey." *Human Rights Quarterly* 30, no. 3: 655–79.

T24. 2012. "Erdoğan: Ölüm orucu yok, bu tamamen şov!" 31 Oct. At http://t24 .com.tr/haber/erdogan-olum-orucu-yoktur-bu-tamamen-sovdur,21635.

———. 2016. "Elli kişiyle başlayan açlık grevi büyüyor; 7 hapishaneden 35 tutuklu açlık grevine başlıyor!" 8 Sept. At http://t24.com.tr/haber/50-kisiyle -baslayan-aclik-grevi-buyuyor-7-hapishaneden-35-tutuklu-15-eylulde-aclik -grevine-basliyor,358945.

Ünal, Mustafa Coşar. 2016. "Is It Ripe Yet? Resolving Turkey's 30 Years of Conflict with the PKK." *Turkish Studies* 4, no. 1: 91–125.

Yağmur, Fatih. 2012. "KCK'da 2000 tutuklu." *Radikal*, 1 July. At http://www .radikal.com.tr/turkiye/kckda-2000-tutuklu-1092791/.

Yeğinsu, Ceylan. 2012. "Hunger Strike Exposes Turkey's Festering Kurdish Problem." *International Business Times*, 15 Nov. At http://www.ibtimes.com /hunger-strike-exposes-turkeys-festering-kurdish-problem-883414.

Yılmaz, Ismail Guney. 2012. "Türkiye'de ölüm oruçları." Bianet, 3 Nov. At https://m.bianet.org/biamag/diger/141828-turkiye-de-olum-oruclari.

Zana, Mehdi. 1997. *Prison No. 5: Eleven Years in Turkish Jails*. As told to André Vauquelin. Translated by Sarah Hughes. Preface by Elie Wiesel, postscript by Kendal Nezan. Watertown, MA: Blue Crane Books.

Zeydanlıoğlu, Welat. 2010. "The Period of Barbarity: Turkification, State Violence, and Torture in Modern Turkey." In *State Power and the Legal Regulation of Evil*, edited by Francesca Dominello, 67–78. Oxford: Inter-Disciplinary Press.

11

Silencing Historical Traumas versus Constructing Resistance Narratives

The Saturday Mothers and Peace Mothers in Turkey

Emine Rezzan Karaman

One of the greatest tragedies in Turkey's history is happening now. Our Kurdish brothers are being slaughtered, and apart from a couple of hesitant voices, no one is demanding to know what the government is doing. No one is saying, "You are riding towards doomsday, leaving the earth scorched in your wake. What will come of this?" ... Already over 1,700 people have been murdered. The houses of nearly 2,000 villages have been burned. People and animals have been burned inside them. The government has burned almost all the forests of eastern Anatolia to find the guerrillas hiding out in them. Not much that could be called forest is left. Turkey is disappearing in flames along with its forests—anonymous acts of genocide—and 2.5 million people have been exiled from their homes, in desperate poverty, forced to take to the road.

—Yaşar Kemal, "Turkey's War of Words" (1995)

They want to scare us: Kurds, Alevis, leftists. They don't give us our bones as a warning. They actually tell us: "Hey, be careful, you may be one of them in the future!" Yes, the state tells us: "Look, if you challenge me, I'll give you intolerable sufferings. I'll kidnap you. I'll keep you in custody with no records! Then I'll put you in prison if you are lucky. If not, I'll humiliate you in a long interrogation where you stand in front of me naked. I'll keep you naked in a cold cell, which is full of mice and bugs. Then, I'll torture you. I'll disable you. When I am done, I'll shoot you in the head. I'll leave your body in the middle of nowhere. I'll bury you somewhere that I want. I won't even give your remnants to your family." It would be easier if they shoot you in the head. Instead, they want to keep you in a constant

state of fear and anxiety. They do all this to make you give up . . . but you don't give up! No, we'll never give up!
—a Saturday Mother

On 12 September 1980, the Turkish Armed Forces took over the "democratically elected government." Following this military coup, the generals led by Kenan Evren ruled the country for three years, which witnessed a systematic destruction of oppositional groups. Torture, extrajudicial killings, and enforced disappearances became common methods of state violence (Arifcan 1997, 268). In the following decade, the 1990s, human rights violations became intensive as the conflict between the Kurdish Workers Party (Partîya Karkerên Kurdistanê, PKK) and the Turkish army escalated dramatically. Although extrajudicial killings and enforced disappearances took place more frequently in the majority-Kurdish cities and targeted Kurdish citizens, the members of various leftist organizations, such as the Communist Party of Turkey/Marxist-Leninist (Türkiye Komünist Partisi/Marksist-Leninist, TKP/ML) founded by Ibrahim Kalpakkaya in the early 1970s, also went through systematic torture and disappearance in prisons and military headquarters and torture centers (Şanlı 2018, 156).

The escalating everyday violence gradually brought about a pervasive and comprehensive erasure of the rule of law. The failure of judicial institutions to combat human rights violations in the country led the European Court of Human Rights to allow applications from Turkey even before applicants exhausted domestic judicial channels.[1] The violence created a society of fear in Turkey in the 1990s. However, there was also a social mobilization

---

1. Although the rule is that domestic remedies must be exhausted before an application is made to the European Court of Human Rights, the rising number of unacknowledged killings, the widespread circulation of rumors about mass graves in the Kurdish regions, and the domestic system's failure (or refusal) to deal with this violence has led the court to accept applications from Turkey without demanding the applicants exhaust domestic judiciary channels. See European Court of Human Rights 2016, Art. 47-b and 35.

against state violence. The Saturday Mothers (Cumartesi Anneleri) and the Peace Mothers (Barış Anneleri) became the prominent actors of this mobilization. This chapter focuses on the Kurdish cases to analyze how the Mothers have effectively used their suffering to build a social movement against the extrajudicial practices and violence since the 1980s.

Mothers' Mobilization

The Saturday Mothers emerged as the earliest mother organization in Turkey and is the most prolonged civil disobedience movement in the country (Ahıska 2014). The roots of the organization go back to a group of human rights activists that formed to find Hasan Ocak, a Kurdish member of the Marxist-Leninist Communist Party (Marksist-Leninist Komünist Partisi, MLKP) who was kidnapped in Istanbul in 1995. After a fifty-seven-day search, his body was found in a cemetery for the nameless.

The group continued their demonstrations after finding Hasan's tortured body. As the Saturday Mothers, they met for the first time on Saturday, 27 May 1995, at Galatasaray Square in the Beyoğlu district of Istanbul. Hasan Ocak's mother, Emine Ocak, his father, Baba Ocak, and his siblings also started to attend the weekly vigils and became the symbolic figures of the group (Can 2014).

The Saturday Mothers announced with a press release that they would meet at the same time and the same place until they learned the fate of their loved ones. The group was initially optimistic about finding the disappeared alive. This hope gradually increased the number of families that appeared at the square. With the growing participation of other mothers and families of the forcibly disappeared, the group quickly expanded within a few weeks. The Mothers also demanded that the authorities guarantee a fair trial for those accused of crimes against the state and that new administrative and legal changes be put in place to ensure the violence and enforced disappearances would discontinue.[2]

---

2. The drafting of the International Convention for the Protection of All Persons from Enforced Disappearance had begun four years earlier, in 1992, and it was hoped that

The Peace Mothers emerged in 1996 as a group of mothers of PKK fighters, who lost their children in the armed conflict between the state forces and the PKK. The Peace Mothers organize demonstrations to increase the level of awareness for the fatal outcomes of the ongoing conflict between the PKK and the Turkish army. They work to receive public support for a peaceful solution to the armed conflict. They also demand the improvement of the imprisonment conditions of Abdullah Öcalan (leader of the PKK), the end of military operations, education and publication in the mother tongue (Kurdish), the abolishment of the village guard system in Kurdish regions, indemnity for burned villages, amnesty for political convicts and guerrillas in the mountains, and the trial of war criminals, such as murderers of Kurdish civilians and rapists of Kurdish women and children (Aslan 2007).

The Saturday Mothers' meeting at Galatasaray Square has become the longest civil disobedience action in Turkey. As their number increased dramatically over time, the police started to attack the Saturday Mothers by beating them, dragging them on the ground, taking them into custody, and spraying pepper gas into the vehicles that took the Mothers from the square to the police stations (Koçali 2004). The Mothers had to suspend their meetings in 1999, but they never gave up looking for their children. Some maintained judicial struggles on domestic and international platforms. Some attended national and international panels, conferences, and TV programs on oppositional TV channels to tell the public what was happening. Years passed, and some mothers died without finding their children.

In 2009 the Saturday Mothers restarted their silent vigils with the beginning of the Ergenekon trials, in which many military officials, lawmakers, and journalists were charged and given lengthy prison sentences for unlawful activities and plotting against the Turkish government. The mothers saw this as an opportunity to demand justice. They claimed that some of the military officers who had been arrested during the trials were

---

Turkey would be signing it. The draft wasn't completed until 2006, but Turkey has still not signed the convention.

also related to cases of enforced disappearance and extrajudicial killing. In the meantime, confessions by some military figures enabled the legal authorities to find many mass graves in the Kurdish region. However, in general, the trials did not end with the desired outcomes for the Mothers. Thus, the Mothers continued sitting together in silence at Galatasaray Square on Saturdays and maintained the longest civil disobedience action in Turkey. In 2018 government authorities enacted a ban on the Mothers' gathering to prevent the seven hundredth meeting, arguing that the sit-in had been hijacked by the PKK. The Mothers and other participants of the gathering were faced with police violence, including tear gas, plastic bullets, and water cannons (Gall 2018).

Despite the ban and violent interventions, the Mothers have kept waiting in Taksim to demand truth, justice, and peace not only for their children but also for all citizens of Turkey. The Mothers' appearance in the masculine and restricted Turkish public sphere introduced new ways in which the marginalized can appear and ask for justice in the public space.

Forms of Enforced Disappearance

As the Saturday Mothers started to share their stories at the regular meetings at the square and in other platforms, it became more apparent that the relatives of most of the forcibly disappeared were not as "lucky" as a few of those who found their loved ones in mass graves or in the cemeteries for the nameless (Kural 2013a, 2013b). One of my interviewees explains this feeling: "Can you imagine that you feel happy for the family because they found their relatives' dead body, but at the same time you envy them because yours has not been found? How can you be jealous of a dead body? I could! I kept telling myself: 'I wish I could find his dead body!'"[3]

The stories of the Mothers and the families of the disappeared people brought to light not only their suffering but also the extensive unlawfulness, extrajudicial abductions, and forced disappearances conducted by

---

3. I conducted interviews with members of Saturday Mothers and Peace Mothers in Istanbul from 2009 to 2022.

state security and the official unwillingness to bring the culprits to justice. The Mothers' narratives address three basic patterns of disappearance in the country.

The Case of Kenan Bilgin and Disappearance under Custody

Kenan Bilgin was a thirty-five-year-old Kurdish leader of a workers' union. He was accused of being a member of an illegal left-wing organization, the Revolutionary Communist Party of Turkey (Türkiye Devrimci Komünist Partisi, TDKP). Plainclothes police officers from the Antiterrorism Bureau in Ankara detained him while he was waiting at a bus stop in Dikmen, a neighborhood in Ankara, on 12 September 1994. His family was not informed about his arrest, but his brother, İrfan Bilgin, received three anonymous telephone calls telling him that Kenan was in the Gölbaşı district of Ankara with three prisoners. He was told that his brother's life was at risk. During the last conversation, which took place on 15 November 1994, the caller said that his brother had been moved elsewhere (Göral 2014). That was the last information the family received about Kenan. His lawyer contacted the Human Rights Commission of the Turkish National Assembly and issued a press release about her client's situation on 3 October 1994, while İrfan Bilgin requested information from the principal public prosecutor at the Ankara National Security Court, Selahattin Kemaloğlu, about his brother's whereabouts. On 10 October 1994, the prosecutor reported that there had been no one by the name of Kenan Bilgin under detention, and there had been no warrant for his arrest. The following day, Kenan's lawyer informed the prosecutor that she had in her possession written statements by ten detainees who claimed that they had seen Kenan Bilgin at Ankara Security Directorate. According to the statements, the witnesses saw him at the headquarters, and he was having difficulty walking and bore heavy marks of torture. One of these witnesses, Cavit Nacitarhan, stated to the public prosecutor:

> I was arrested on 12 September 1994 and remained in custody for twenty-four days. I did not know Kenan Bilgin. However, after my second day in custody I saw him every day. He would cry out: "My name is

Kenan Bilgin, I have been in custody since 12 September, and my name has not been entered on the records; if anyone is released, please inform the press, lawyers, and human rights [associations] about my case." I do not know why he was arrested, but I saw him over twenty-one days. He was dressed only in his underpants. He did not have the strength to stand unaided and had to be supported by two people. After my release, I saw his photograph in newspaper articles about his disappearance, and that is how I recognized him.[4]

Another witness, Salman Mazı, gave a very similar statement to the public prosecutor:

I certify that I signed the written statement dated 11 October 1994. When I was in custody at the offices of the antiterrorist branch at the Security Directorate between 12 and 25 September 1994, I saw Kenan Bilgin on several occasions. At one stage, I noticed that he was being dragged by his arm to the toilets in his underpants. He was often taken for interrogation and was severely tortured. He was in cell number 8. On the eighth day, I saw him in the toilets. He said to me in a weak voice: "My name is Kenan Bilgin; I was arrested on 12 September in Dikmen. My name has still not been entered on the records. They are probably going to make me disappear. If you get out of here, contact the public prosecutor's office and inform the press." The warder then appeared and reprimanded him for having spoken to me, before taking him away. Later I recognized his photograph in the newspapers.[5]

Finally, Murat Demir also stated to the public prosecutor that he had seen Kenan Bilgin several times during his own thirteen days under detention:

I was taken into custody on 10 September 1994 and was put in cell number 11. Kenan Bilgin was in number 13 or 14. I did not know him. We

---

4. *İrfan Bilgin v. Turkey*, Application no. 25659/94, European Court of Human Rights (ECHR), Strasbourg, 17 July 2001, para. 26-a, at http://hudoc.echr.coe.int/app/conversion/pdf/?library=ECHR&id=001-59592&filename=001-59592.pdf&TID=ihgdqbxnfi.

5. *İrfan Bilgin v. Turkey*, para. 26-c.

were severely tortured. The remanded prisoner in number 13 stopped me and, as I was known as "the lawyer," asked me if I really was a lawyer. He gave me his name and continued: "I have been here for twenty-two days. My name has not been entered on the records. I will probably not get out of here alive.... If you are brought before a judge, tell the lawyers that I am here." He, too, was tortured. I heard the sounds of torture and groans. I certify that the signature on the written statement is mine and confirm the content. I saw his photograph in the newspapers later. However, he seemed far more exhausted and tired [in custody].[6]

The names of these witnesses were in Prosecutor Selahattin Kemaloğlu's records, but he found no evidence of the existence of Kenan Bilgin in custody because the police did not record his name when he was first detained. Bilgin spent a long time in detention, went through torture, and tried many times to make his voice heard. In 1996 the family took his case to the European Court of Human Rights (ECHR), where, besides the witnesses quoted earlier, a witness for the defendant—the Turkish state—also acknowledged that Bilgin had been forcibly disappeared in custody. Based on these testimonies, the ECHR found the Turkish government responsible for the disappearance of Bilgin and required the state to pay retribution to Bilgin's family. However, the body of Kenan Bilgin was never found, nor were the offenders brought to justice.

The Case Mass Killings by Security Forces in Güçlükonak

The second type of enforced disappearance takes the form of mass killing outside of a torture center, police station, or gendarmerie headquarters. This is what happened in the Kurdish district Güçlükonak in the city of Şırnak. Turkish military forces raided Kurdish villages in Şırnak on 12 January 1996. They detained six citizens—Abdullah İlhan, Ahmet Kaya, Ali Nas, Neytullah İlhan, Halit Kaya, and Ramazan Oruç—for supporting the PKK. While these six detainees were being transferred from Taşkonak Village to Koçyurdu Gendarmerie Station on 15 January 1996,

---

6. *İrfan Bilgin v. Turkey*, para. 26-d.

their minibus was attacked in Güçlükonak. When villagers came to the spot to see what had happened, they found the destroyed minibus and ten bodies burned to ashes (Özvarış 2013). Soon after the incident, the Turkish General Staff announced that the PKK had attacked the minibus and killed villagers. The announcement did not mention that the villagers in the minibus were under detention, and newspapers and TV programs featured the event as a massacre by the PKK (Özvarış 2013).

However, after conducting investigations in the region, a human rights organization built a case showing that the tragic event had been carried out by state security forces, not by the PKK (Hafıza Merkezi 2016). According to local witnesses who spoke to investigators, the detained villagers had already been dead when they were put into the vehicle. Some villagers from Koçyurdu testified seeing a helicopter firing rockets on the road when the minibus left the village. Security forces ordered a quick burial of the bodies' remains without conducting any religious rituals and without making any identification or further investigation of the killings (Saturday Mothers 2016).

Because there had been no trial in the Turkish courts about the incident in Güçlükonak, the relatives of victims were able to take the case directly to the ECHR in July 1996 without exhausting the domestic Options (*Bianet News* 2015). The court acknowledged the difficult situation in Southeastern Turkey, where a state of emergency had been in force at the time that the incident happened. According to the ECHR, the risk of such incidents was higher in that region than in the rest of the country. Thus, the court concluded that the authorities could not be blamed for failing to protect the transportation of the detainees in Güçlükonak due to the existence of unforeseeable risk. However, the court found the Turkish state guilty of the violation of Article 2 of the European Convention of Human Rights (Council of Europe 1952) by not conducting an adequate and effective investigation or full autopsy.[7]

7. *Affaire Belkıza Kaya Et Autres C. Turquie*, 33420/96 and 36206/97, ECHR, 22 Feb. 2006, para. 87–89.

No statements were taken from the gendarme who had been responsible for escorting the minibus until 2002, six years after the incident.[8] In 2010 former gendarmerie lieutenant commander Özcan Tozlu, who had been dismissed from his position in 2000, stated that the six detained men in Taşkonak village had been Kurdish village guards. These local men had been working with the Turkish security forces earlier. According to Tozlu, Lieutenant General Selahattin Uğurlu first gave the order for their arrest. Later, General Uğurlu commanded their massacre. A team of local village guards massacred their colleagues in return for $50,000 under the observation of Combat Search and Rescue Teams. Finally, they blamed the PKK for the massacre (*Evrensel* 2010).

The Case of Fehmi Tosun and Kidnapping by Security Agents

The third most common form of enforced disappearance is through the kidnapping of an individual by unknown people. This is what happened to Fehmi Tosun. Unlike Kenan Bilgin, who was seen at police headquarters several times, nobody heard of or saw Tosun after he was kidnapped in his neighborhood in Istanbul on 19 October 1995. Tosun, the father of four, was originally from a village in Diyarbakir, from which he and his family were forcibly evacuated in the early 1990s. On the day of the kidnapping, his wife, Hanım (Mrs.) Tosun, saw a couple of men with walkie-talkies bring him to the neighborhood where the family lived. Hanım Tosun never forgot that moment. She saw her husband with those men outside of their building before he was forced into a white car when the men accompanying him noticed her looking out of the window. She rushed into the street with her children and started to run barefoot after the car until it disappeared. Memorizing the plate of the car, she went to the nearest police station to report the incident and to find the name of her husband on the custody list. However, she was told that there was no one on the list by his name.

---

8. *Affaire Belkıza Kaya Et Autres C. Turquie*, para. 87–89.

Hanım Tosun never heard of him again except in a call she received a few months after the kidnapping. The caller uttered a single word, "Listen!," before a gunshot could be heard. Hanım Tosun believes it was at that moment that they killed her husband.[9] The daughter of Fehmi Tosun, Besna, narrates her memory of her father's disappearance as follows:

> I saw everything that day. They dragged my father from the door of our building . . . in the middle of a busy quarter in Istanbul. . . . Passing through the silence of a big crowd . . . I remember. . . . This crowd was silent again when we moved into this building, this neighborhood, this city running away from a burned house in a destroyed Kurdish city. . . . They disappeared my father when this crowd chose to be silent again. And my father was looking at my eyes when they took him away somewhere beyond this heavy silence. . . . Who knows how many children's dreams they smashed that cruelly so far. . . . Back then, I was only 12. "They will kill me!" My father's voice echoed in my ears as I started to run on the street behind the car that took him away. Today, I am still on the same street running. (Tosun 2017, 66–67, ellipses indicate pauses)

Years after the kidnapping, when the police took Hanım Tosun into custody for her political activities, they told her that Fehmi Tosun had been blacklisted as a member of the PKK and that they had escorted him to his home that day to find the weapons he had been hiding in his garden. The family took the case to the ECHR. Like Kenan Bilgin's, Fehmi Tosun's body was not found.

Transforming Personal Loss into a Counterhistory of State Violence

The stories of the Saturday Mothers and Peace Mothers provided the public with a counterhistory of state oppression and violence, which government

---

9. The information from the beginning of this section up to this point comes from my interview with Hanım Tosun, the wife of forcefully disappeared Fehmi Tosun, 18 July 2009, Istanbul. From here on in telling Fehmi Tosun's story, I rely on the article written by Besna Tosun, his daughter (Tosun 2017).

authorities continued to deny. Their witness testimonies turned into stories told and shared at demonstrations, bringing different people together through the power of sharing and empathy. Magical words such as "I saw," "I heard," "I felt," and "I knew" connected the families of the disappeared to each other and to other sections of the society as daring witnesses of unspoken violence in Turkey. Besna Tosun explains the power, solidarity, and mobilization that the Saturday Mothers generated in Galatasaray Square:

> One day, my mother held my hands tight and said: "We're going to look for your father, Besna!" . . . I was only twelve. Others started to join us one. . . . I became more confident as we got crowded. I was so young. I thought everyone was there for my father. . . . I thought that if I tell all I know to these many people, it would be enough to find my father. After all, I was there as a witness. . . . The crowd got bigger by noon. Then, my mother took a photo out of her handbag. The other hands were raised one by one holding photos. I saw the faces of Hasan Ocak, Rıdvan Karakoç, Kenan Bilgin, Düzgün Tekin, Hasan Gülünay and others, being raised in the hands of their relatives. I was puzzled. . . . I was there to find my father. Instead, what I found was a bunch of photos. . . . I looked at my mother . . ."Haven't we come here to find my father? Who are the people in these photos?" I clenched my teeth. . . . That was the first time I realized the truth: My father was one of the hundreds of missing people. That's how I met the Saturday Mothers. . . . A cry broke my silence. . . . That day I cried for the first time after the loss of my father. . . . But I am not alone now. I am holding the pictures of thousands of disappeared people. I know that we will be here, running behind my father. (Tosun 2017, 67, ellipses indicate omissions)

As Besna Tosun explains it, her father was one of the hundreds of missing people. Their mothers and families drew strength from sharing that pain. The weekly gathering at Galatasaray Square allowed them to see their pain as a collective feeling and experience. One interviewee explained this feeling:

> This pain was very destructive and constructive at the same time. On the one hand, it is impossible to explain how painful it is to wait for someone you love in the way we have been doing for years . . . I mean

waiting for your lover, your brother, your father or mother. . . . It is impossible, really impossible, to tell you how much you go back and forth between patience and impatience, between hope and disappointment, between anger and wisdom while waiting for them to come back home . . . to come back to you . . . in one piece, as healthy as they were in the past. . . . You cannot imagine how painful it is. *But we know it. We feel it. This is the most important natural connection between us.* We, the relatives of the disappeared, traveled between patience and impatience altogether. . . . Our travel, our dilemmas, our pain are the same. [. . .] After my husband was disappeared, they took me to the Anti-Terrorist Branch of Istanbul Police Headquarters. It was my first time there. They told me that he might have been kidnapped by the TKP-ML, which he was a member of. Or what if he got tired of me and ran away with another woman? Maybe he left the country? Or he became a guerilla fighting on the mountains of Tunceli? Yeah, I should have checked the mountains instead of checking headquarters, they recommended. Later, as we started to share our initial experiences at [Galatasaray] Square, I learned that I was not alone. They did the same thing to everyone who looked for their disappeared. Can you believe it, they even tried to make us believe that they disappeared by themselves like insane people? *But we all knew it. We knew that our relatives were revolutionary, open-minded, communist people who loved their country. We all knew it that the state officers took them into custody. We all knew that the police killed them because of their oppositional political identity.* [. . .] He was not there when his children grew up, got married, and had children. We know that they not only killed our beloved ones but also killed part of us. That's what we all are looking for now. This is a social trauma. And I know that I did not go through it alone. You and I, we all shared it. At different levels, though. . . . I mean, we are all survivors of what happened in the bloody past of this country. [. . .] After the disappearance of my husband, I was also involved in politics. I did my best to improve myself. Actually, getting closer to the state, seeing its real face—[as I did when I was detained] under torture myself—[is] the best opportunity to see for yourself and raise your political awareness. You cannot learn it from books. You experience it in person what may the state do to you if you are oppositional. This encounter teaches you. This encounter relieves you. You get closer to the state, and you tell: "Look, you took him alive. . . . You took him alive. . . . And you will not give him [back] alive. . . . I know you killed him. You killed them all. But you will tell me what happened to his bones. You will give me his bones! You will give us our bones! We know you did it, and we will get our beloved ones from you altogether![10]

The Mothers adopted various ways to support each other and reach out to others in society who had experienced the same loss. They turned their individual sufferings into a narrative of social trauma. In this way, they strengthened their cause by inviting as many people as possible to the square to support their voice and search for justice. What these people saw, witnessed, felt, and learned throughout their own individual journeys led them to understand that their loss was a part of collective trauma. One of my interviewees explained how by bridging the personal and the collective, the Mothers formed coalitions in different realms of Turkish society:

> To be in the same space with those who have gone through the same painful process is definitely a relief. [. . .] First of all, you know that you bleed in the same way. Also, whenever you see them, you understand better that it is all real. I mean, all those things really happened. They happened; they happened to us, and we went through it. This realization fires your fight to prevent this from happening again to anyone as it happened to us. Thus, whenever we see each other, we understand it better: It is "we" who went through this painful process, should prevent others from experiencing the same pain.

This bridge between personal and collective trauma built by the Mothers allowed those protesting state violence to travel from the sense of individual loss to social loss and memory, thus triggering communal hope for a possibility of social peace in the future, helping to write a counterhistory of violence of Turkey's recent past, and telling the public about what happened in the 1990s from the perspective of the victims and survivors.

10. In quotations from the interviews I conducted, all ellipses except those inside square brackets indicate pauses in speech; emphasis has been added.

The Transformative Power of Mobilization in the Mothers' Lives

The Mothers' notion of motherhood has gradually transformed throughout their decades-long struggle from its being something sociobiological into its being something political. The Saturday Mothers and the Peace Mothers consider themselves not only the mothers of their own lost children but also the mothers of all marked citizens in Turkey. Thus, they have raised their voice not only to recover the history and the remains of their dead children but also to help create a peaceful and just society for survivors, as one of my interviewees explained:

> Can you take our motherhood from our hands by killing our children? You may take our children treacherously, as your equals have done in Chile, Argentina, Iran, or other countries where lawlessness is accepted as normal. Yes, you may kill our children on behalf of the state, which, ideally, has to be there to protect its citizens. What an irony! You stole our children, and you believed that you could also steal our motherhood. No, you were wrong! You couldn't take our motherhood from us! Our children multiplied each Saturday when we met here. [...] History will write about us. History will write about what happened here. We will always remind everyone of what has happened here!

With this motivation to write their loss into the country's history, the Mothers have been gathering at Galatasaray Square for decades. They want not only justice for their children but also the truth for the rest of society. In the process, they have also transformed their own lives, challenging the meanings attached to what is considered appropriate womanhood and motherhood. In a country where women's physical mobility and actions are regulated by patriarchal norms and relations, some mothers' struggle has begun at home in their effort to convince their family members that they should be able to attend the demonstrations regularly. For some mothers, both as the new heads of their families (because the male heads have been disappeared) and as the new political figures in the Turkish public sphere, survival in large cities such as Istanbul after being forcefully moved from their Kurdish villages was itself already a big challenge. They had to fight patriarchal, language-related, and financial obstacles to carry out their lives and political activities. For some, their political struggle brought about other new experiences, such as attendance at international conferences to construct new solidarities with various human rights organizations all around the world (Arslan 2013). That is to say, the mobilization also transformed the Mothers' lives in significant ways. Breaking gender-based family restrictions was an important part of this transformation, as was politicization. One mother summarized this transformation:

> In general, we have a feudal family model in Turkey. After the disappearance of our loved ones, we, the spouses, mothers, lovers, siblings, and children of revolutionary activists, left our ordinary lives and met with the others at a point where our pain could unite us with one another. This process, as a whole, politicized us. Here, you may put it in a way that some "appropriate women" had to break some rules. I was luckier because I was coming from an open-minded socialist family. But, in general, we have reached this point by breaking many rules. So don't think that this has been a smooth process for us. It's also very ironic and sad that our politicization and political identities rose over our dead. I believe that none of the Mothers received this political education from their disappeared relatives. They learned it in person while breaking the rules during this painful experience. No, don't think that it was a smooth process. We had to fight with our relatives, neighbors, acquaintances to reach here. I mean, going to the streets for demonstrations was not as easy as going to the parks for promenades.

For Kurdish women whose children and husbands have been brutally disappeared, the long-term ethnic discrimination and violence intersect with grave maternal suffering. According to the Mothers, the Kurds have citizenship rights on paper, but in practice they do not have equal rights with the rest of society. Most Kurds do not trust state institutions, the courts, the hospitals, the police, or the army to respect their citizenship and protect their citizenship rights. The following narrative of a Peace

Mother illustrates the everyday discrimination and insult that the Kurdish women face, which overlaps with grave maternal suffering:

> When we moved to Izmir [that is, were forced to relocate to a city in non-Kurdish western Turkey], we warned our children not to tell anyone that we were Kurds. Our children grew up with such fear all the time.... One day I was sick and went to the public hospital. The doctors, actually everyone, initially paid attention to me. Then, they asked me where I was from. As soon as I said I was from Batman [a Kurdish-majority city in southeastern Turkey], I noticed that all of them stopped paying attention to me. I knew it was only because ... they thought that I was ... just because I was a Kurd. I knew that they did not care if we died like a dog. They did not like the idea that we were going to their hospitals.... Some told me that the Kurds were dirty.... I was looking at myself. I was very clean. I was a Kurd, and I was clean. I mean, I was young at that time. I mean, I even changed my dressing style, my appearance, to keep up with them. I looked like you; I resembled them. I changed my appearance just because I want to avoid them understand[ing] that I was a Kurd so that I could live with them in the same district. However, unfortunately, it was apparent from our accent.... Whenever I went to the hospital, I observed the way they dealt with me.... [When] they ... asked me where I was from, ... I always hesitated to answer.... I waited for a few minutes to make up an answer.... I would tell them that I was from Erzurum [an eastern city populated by Turks]. I developed a strategy: I used to keep candy in my mouth to make them think that it was not my Kurdish accent but the candy that made me speak that way.... I mean, it was extraordinarily humiliating. If I did not put those candies in my mouth, if I did not lie that I was from Erzurum, I mean, if I directly told them that I was a Kurd from Batman, I would have been treated in much more insulting ways. I was young at that time.... I looked like them, dressed like them, was clean like them.... Nobody could be as clean as I was. But ... I was still the dirty Kurd, everywhere.... Wasn't my grandfather a soldier in your army? Would not he die to protect this country with your grandfathers? When it came to taking our children to the army, they did not discriminate against us.... I kept asking, "Why? Why? Why?"... These pains taught me a lot. I started to ask why the Kurds do not have their own Atatürk? I had a five-year-old daughter

at that time. My daughter was like you . . . beautiful. . . . She was very successful [in school]. She was the one who sang the Turkish National Anthem every morning at the school . . . but, on the other hand, she had to listen to the stories about the Kurds. They told us without any shame that they should have poured gasoline and burned all the Kurds. . . . We always lived in fear. . . . Whenever they insulted us . . . *the state, the doctors, my neighbors* . . . we remained silent, . . . but from inside, we were dreaming of salvation. . . . They did not give my husband a job. They expelled my daughter from school. She could be a teacher. She could be a doctor . . . but unfortunately they did not let her. . . . Just because we were Kurds. . . . Then she went to the mountains . . . and my husband went, too. . . . And starting from their leaving, I understood, in time, that as long as we don't have an official identity, as long as our identity, our language, our culture are not officially recognized, we will not have any place in this country. (speaker's emphasis)

Becoming Peace Mothers allowed women like this one new ways of making sense of the racial/ethnic discrimination and violence that as Kurds they have been subjected to. While crying for their lost children in public, they also brought their experiences to the public's attention. By telling their stories, they transformed the language of ethnic, political, and masculinized violence into the language of maternal suffering. The Mothers believed in their own healing power against the destructive power of the state's war with the PKK. They stood against the discourse of terrorism employed by the states to justify violence against Kurds and promoted a peaceful and constitutional solution for the armed conflict between the PKK and the Turkish state.

Neither Dead nor Alive

The majority of families of PKK members are unable retrieve the dead bodies of their loved ones from the state institutions to organize a proper funeral for them. When the bodies are given back to the families, they are often incomplete. One Peace Mother tells of the years-long systematic persecution of her husband and her family and their inability to prove their innocence to the state as well as of her ensuing struggle for survival, the agony of loss, and the recovery of the remains of her brother in a mass grave.

> We knew very well that it was impossible for my husband to prove his innocence. We tried. . . . We talked to a lawyer to tell the state that my husband was innocent, but he [the lawyer] was killed, too. Afterward, whenever an event happened in the village, the state came to our place. Whenever an armed conflict happened . . . whenever a bus was burned . . . they always accused my husband . . . because now they had a name to accuse and an address to go to . . . The state raided our house every two months when we were in the village. They were asking for my husband and wanted us to tell them his place. He hid for a while. Then in 1994 they burned down our villages. They took all the male family members into custody to make my husband surrender himself to the state. We left Bitlis in this way. For nothing. . . . He was not guilty. . . . They made him guilty. . . . We went to Van first. We stayed there for three months. Once they start observing you, once they took you into custody, it never ends. So violence continued there, too. My husband knew that there was nowhere else to go except the mountains. We ran away to Istanbul, and he went to the mountains. He never planned to fight against the state as a guerrilla. He just wanted to save his family by being far from us. My brother went to the mountains after him. After all the tortures . . . he [the brother] was found in a mass grave. My world was sunk with this news. We had received the news of his death years ago, but we did not know where he was until recently. I learned his place on that day. When he and his twenty-six comrades were found in a mass grave—six women and twenty men guerrillas. . . . Imagine, none of them had their heads. Most likely, somebody killed them for money: they cut off their heads to give them to the state. In return, they might get their money. We did DNA tests. In this way, we figured out that he was my brother. . . . My husband stayed in the mountains for three years. [. . .] He told me that he would return in the summer. We didn't know that it was the last time that I saw him. He became a martyr in Tatvan . . . in June 1997. I was very young at that time. I was twenty-six. It was my first time in Istanbul. I had two daughters. Even though he [her husband] was not with us anymore, oppressions continued because wherever we went, the state was the same state. It was the same violence

that showed itself in the village burnings. I had to work. I had to take care of my children. I had to escape from the state.

The Turkish state's politics over Kurdish corpses have informed the Kurds' strategies and rituals of resistance. From the start, the Peace Mothers undertook several forms of resistance to draw attention to the secret burials and the mass graves of PKK fighters. But most of the families could not receive the bodies of their relatives. Since that is the case, as Hişyar Özsoy observes, the separation of the dead from the living cannot take place in the family's imagination properly (2010, 30). The lack of a proper farewell by means of a burial prevents the transition of the dead to the afterlife, which means that even after decades the relatives of the deceased cannot believe that their loved ones are dead. The liminal position between life and death turns the missing corpse into an uncanny entity—"dead yet not really, not fully, not properly, unless it goes through the symbolic process of initiation into the Hereafter" (Özsoy 2010, 30). But the symbolic process of a funeral does not happen until the retrieval of the missing body. Thus, the missing people remain neither alive nor dead for their mothers.

The International Humanitarian Law (IIIL) provides several rules to regulate the treatment of the dead in the context of armed conflict. The regulation against despoiling or mutilating the dead derives from the principle of "respect for every dead [person]" (rule 112; rules 112–16 are given in International Committee of the Red Cross 2005). Moreover, the IHL characterizes the dead as family members and requires the return of remains to the family for a decent burial (rule 112). The proper treatment of the dead also overlaps with respect for family life (rule 116). The IHL also regulates that the dead must be identified before their disposal (rule 116) and that the authorities have to guarantee their burial individually, not in mass graves, according to rites prescribed by the person's religion (rule 115).

When the bodies are missing and the graves are unknown, the Galatasaray Square where the mothers meet every week becomes not only a place of sharing and solidarity but also a place where families symbolically visit their lost ones. İkbal Eren, the sister of the forcibly disappeared

Hayrettin Eren, describes the square as a place of meeting with his disappeared brother: "I feel that this Square is like a graveyard in which my brother is lying. That's why I feel very unhappy when I don't come here every Saturday. I feel that I don't fulfill my duties to him. I feel relieved when I carry and kiss his photo here. Don't I have his photo at home? Of course, I do. But here it is different. I feel that he remains alone when I don't come here" (in Kural 2013b).

The Last Letter

My dear comrades,

    I came to Galatasaray Square for many years with excitement as if I was coming there to meet with my dear son, Hüseyin. I was beaten there, dragged on the ground, taken into custody when they wanted to keep us away from Galatasaray. However, I never gave up. I believed that defending the square was like taking care of my dear son, Hüseyin. You know, I am old and sick now. I can't join you anymore, but my children and grandchildren are there. Now, I'll tell you one more time what happened to my son. My son, Hüseyin Morsümbül, was disappeared in custody by the junta under Kenan Evren thirty-six years ago. It was Lieutenant Durmuş Coşkun Kıvrak who took my son into custody in Bingöl. Durmuş Kıvrak gave pain to many people back then. I've been waiting for the trial of the perpetrators for thirty-six years. I demand a real trial, not a show. I had six children, and we were a simple family. On 18 September, a few days after the 1980 coup, soldiers and police officers raided our house. My son was a high school student back then. They took him, tying his eyes and his hands. "We'll get his statement and leave him in five minutes," they said. I've never heard from my Hüseyin anymore after that moment. Hüseyin was my oldest son, my first love, my sweetheart, my first experience with motherhood. . . . I actually couldn't perform my motherhood for my other children after Hüseyin. After Hüseyin, my mind was occupied with him all the time. After Hüseyin, my children raised one another.

After Hüseyin, there was no celebration at our place neither for Bairams nor for weddings. After Hüseyin, tears, pain, and longing dominated our family. The marriage of my other children reminded me that I could not see Hüseyin growing up and getting married. Each of my grandchildren joined us, making me think that Hüseyin could not be a father. My son Ekin grew up in such a heavy atmosphere. Finally, he rebelled and went to the mountains to fight on behalf of his brother. He was killed after long years of fighting as a guerilla. They even tortured his dead body. They delivered my Ekin to me after letting his body decompose in an unplugged freezer in the morgue. I'm a mother who gave two of her babies to this dirty war. My liver burned with pain. I know what the pain of a lost child is. It never diminishes. No, it gradually penetrates deeper and deeper into you. For this reason, I demand peace. I demand peace to [prevent] other mothers [from] going through the same pain. I'm calling you, oh mothers! Where are you? Where are you? Why are you staying quiet? Why don't you rush into the streets and demand peace for everyone? Why don't you go to the streets and demand justice for the mothers who are looking for the bones of their children? Don't you know that the pain of a child is the same for all mothers? I've been waiting for the trial of my son's killers for thirty-six years. I've been waiting to get my son's bones for thirty-six years! If one day I get his bones, I won't bury them. I'll carry them with me everywhere I go until I die. Then, I'll be buried with them. This is my biggest dream.[11]

Fatma Morsümbül sent this letter to the Saturday Mothers from her sickbed. Her letter not only summarizes what the Mothers have gone through with the systematization of enforced disappearance in the country but also contains their strong demand for justice and peace. She

11. Fatma Morsümbül sent this letter to Galatasaray Square for the 545th meeting on 5 September 2015; copy in the author's files.

maintained this demand even after her numerous pleas could not trigger any official action to find her beloved Hüseyin, who was forcibly disappeared when he was a high school student. Fatma Morsümbül did not lose her motivation to find Hüseyin. Indeed, she and her husband, Hanefi, were detained by security officials just for looking for their son, and Hanefi was severely tortured. This enduring search to find Hüseyin alive was replaced by the hope to find his bones after the family received a call from a former soldier who had witnessed Hüseyin's death by torture at the Bingöl Military Brigade Command (Söylemez 2011). Ironically, the authorities, which had never acknowledged Hüseyin's enforced disappearance, took away his citizenship in 2003 because he had not done his military service. The Human Rights Association's criminal complaint in 2011 initiated a new investigation. In 2015, however, the case was closed because there was not sufficient evidence for further litigation. Fatma Morsümbül passed away in 2016 before finding her son Hüseyin's bones.

This letter delivers her last will: she invites all mothers of the country to understand, protect, and strengthen the Saturday Mothers' enduring search for justice for their forcibly disappeared children as well as for peace for living. By sharing their stories to form bridges of empathy and solidarity in society on the basis of "tears, pain, and longing," both the Saturday Mothers and the Peace Mothers have provided a counterdiscourse that delegitimizes the state's discourse of terrorism. In this way, they have opened up a counterpublic sphere, as Nancy Fraser puts it: a "parallel discursive arena[] where members of subordinated social groups invent and circulate counter-discourses to formulate oppositional interpretations of their identities, and needs" (1992, 124). Like mothers in Chile and Argentina, the Saturday and Peace Mothers in Turkey have sought to create a social memory of the state violence by telling their individual stories in public (Karaman 2016). They have effectively used their maternal suffering to create consciousness and solidarity against the extrajudicial state policies involving enforced disappearance and escalating violence toward the living in the country. The Mothers' determination was clearly evinced in their 820th meeting, held online amid the COVID-19 quarantine measures, indicating that they are determined not to give up until their demands are met.

Acknowledgements

I thank the Research Lab team that worked on constitutional politics in Turkey under the supervision of Silvia von Steinsdorff and Ece Göztepe for supporting this project during my postdoctoral research in the program Blickwechsel: Contemporary Turkey Studies at Humboldt-Universität zu Berlin in 2018 and 2019.

References

Ahıska, Meltem. 2014. "Counter-Movement, Space, and Politics: How the Saturday Mothers of Turkey Make Enforced Disappearances Visible." In *Space and the Memories of Violence: Landscapes of Erasure, Disappearance, and Exception*, edited by Estela Schindel and Pamela Colombo, 162–75. London: Palgrave Macmillan.
Arifcan, Umut. 1997. "The Saturday Mothers of Turkey." *Peace Review* 9, no. 2: 265–72. At https://doi.org/10.1080/10402659708426062.
Arslan, Rengin. 2013. "100 Kadın: Cumartesi Anneleri." *BBC News*, 21 Oct. At http://www.bbc.com/turkce/haberler/2013/10/131020_cumartesi_anneleri _rengin.
Aslan, Özlem. 2007. "Politics of Motherhood and the Experience of the Mothers of Peace in Turkey." Master's thesis, Boğaziçi Univ.
Bianet News. 2015. "What Happened in Güçlükonak?" 15 Jan. At http://m.bianet .org/english/human-rights/161577-what-happened-in-guclukonak.
Can, Başak. 2014. "State-Making, Evidence-Making, and Claim-Making: The Cases of Torture and Enforced Disappearances in Post-1980 Turkey." PhD diss., Univ. of Pennsylvania.
Council of Europe. 1952. *The European Convention on Human Rights*. Strasbourg, Germany: Directorate of Information.
European Court of Human Rights. 2016. "Rules of Court. Rule 47—Contents of an Individual Application." At https://www.echr.coe.int/Documents/Rule _47_ENG.pdf.
Evrensel. 2010. "A Terrible Claim about Güçlükonak!" 10 Jan. At https://www .evrensel.net/haber/193535/guclukonak-ta-korkunc-iddia.
Fraser, Nancy. 1992. "Rethinking the Public Sphere: A Contribution to the Critique of Actually Existing Democracy." In *Habermas and the Public Sphere*, edited by Craig Calhoun, 109–42. Cambridge, MA: MIT Press.

Gall, Carlotta. 2018. "Turkey Clamps Down on a Group Erdogan Once Championed: Grieving Mothers." *New York Times*, 29 Sept.
Göral, Özgür Sevgi. 2014. "Three Questions for Mehmet Ağar's Investigation." *Hafıza Merkezi*, 11 July. At http://hakikatadalethafiza.org/en/3-questions-for-mehmet-agars-interrogation-2/.
Hafiza Merkezi. 2017. "Hafiza Merkezi Co-director Murat Celikkan's Defence in Court: 'Propaganda Can Only Be Bad Journalism'—the Güçlükonak Massacre." 16 May. At https://hakikatadalethafiza.org/en/hafiza-merkezi-co-director-murat-celikkans-defence-in-court/.
International Committee of the Red Cross (ICRC). 2005. *Customary International Humanitarian Law*. Vol. 1: *Rules 112–16*. Geneva: ICRC. At https://www.refworld.org/docid/5305e3de4.html.
Karaman, Emine Rezzan. 2016. "Remember, S/he Was Here Once: Mothers Call for Justice and Peace in Turkey." *Journal of Middle East Women's Studies* 12, no. 3: 382–410.
Kemal, Yaşar. 1995. "Turkey's War of Words." *New York Times*, 6 May. At https://www.nytimes.com/1995/05/06/nyregion/news-summary-743195.html.
Koçali, Filiz. 2004. "Cumartesi Annelerinin inadı." In *Kamusal alan*, edited by Meral Camcı, 357–60. Istanbul: Hil Yayın.
Kural, Beyza. 2013a. "I Have an Uncle, Who Doesn't Exist." Interview with Setenay Yarıcı. *BİA Haber Merkezi*, 20 May. At https://bianet.org/bianet/insan-haklari/146726-bir-dayim-var-o-dayim-yok.
———. 2013b. Interview with İkbal Eren. *BİA Haber Merkezi*, 20 May. At https://bianet.org/bianet/insan-haklari/146726-bir-dayim-var-o-dayim-yok.
Özsoy, Hişyar. 2010. "Between Gift and Taboo: Death and the Negotiation of National Identity and Sovereignty in the Kurdish Conflict in Turkey." PhD diss., Univ. of Texas, Austin.
Özvarış, Hazal. 2013. "The Former Governor of Şırnak: 'Soldiers Killed Many People; I Informed Ankara about This, but Nobody Cared!'" *T24*, 16 Dec. At http://t24.com.tr/haber/eski-sirnak-valisi-asker-cok-insan-oldurdu-ankaraya-anlattim-ilgilenmedi,246146.
Şanlı, Ayşem Sezer. 2018. "Gündelik hayatın dönüşümünde bir imkan olarak toplumsal muhalefetin değerlendirilmesi: Cumartesi Anneleri üzerine bir araştırma." PhD diss., Hacettepe Univ., Ankara.
Saturday Mothers. 2016. "Week 615." Press release, 7 Jan. At http://cumartesianneleri.tumblr.com/post/155617738178/cumartesi-anneleri-615hafta.

Söylemez, Ayça. 2011. "Morsümbül için suç duyurusu." Bianet, 16 Nov. At https://m.bianet.org/bianet/insan-haklari/134060-morsumbul-icin-suc-duyurusu.

Tosun, Besna. 2017. "Besna's Story: 'They Will Kill Me!'" In *Women against War System*, edited by Nadja Furlan Štante, Anja Zalta, and Maja Lamberger Khatib, 65–70. Zurich: Lit Verlag.

12

Institutionalizing Kurdish Women's Political Engagements

Party Politics and Affirmative-Action Measures

Hazal Atay

This chapter critically analyzes the pro-feminist and pro-gender stand of Kurdish politics within the larger male-dominated political landscape in the world in general and in Turkey in particular. Globally, even though the number of women in national parliaments has nearly doubled over the past two decades (Inter-Parliamentary Union 2016), politics systematically excludes women, thereby reproducing male hegemony.[1] There is also significant variation in women's political representation across regions. Whereas women's presence in the parliaments of Nordic countries has reached 42 percent, thus approximating parity (equal representation), the Arab states and the Pacific lag behind dramatically, with women comprising only 18 percent and 16 percent of the legislatures in these areas (Inter-Parliamentary Union 2016). These figures also reflect the political participation of women in the Turkish Parliament, where women constituted only 17 percent of the members in 2018. In the absence of comprehensive efforts, political parties vary dramatically in their strategies with

---

1. Today, women still occupy less than a quarter of the seats in the world's legislative assemblies and remain underrepresented in world political leadership positions (Dahlerup 2018). As of November 2018, per the statistics of the Inter-Parliamentary Union (2018), women constitute only 24 percent of representatives in parliaments across the world.

respect to gender equity. It is this larger context that makes the gender approach of pro-Kurdish parties in Turkey even more dramatic: whereas males politically hegemonize the Turkish political landscape, pro-Kurdish politics fosters the participation of large female cadres, thereby approximating parity, and articulates feminist claims on the political landscape, hence altering the political narrative in favor of women.

Over the years, gender equity has become a major political problem across the globe (Walby 2005). As gender politics have formally penetrated international organizations, governments, and other institutions, women's movements have generated new paradigms and strategies.[2] Hence, the "new politics of gender equity" has two equally significant components: one is the generation of new resources and actors, and the other is the creation of new strategies. The experiences of Kurdish women within the Turkish political landscape reflect this transformation. Across the years, pro-Kurdish party politics in Turkey has been increasingly feminized, with Kurdish women's political engagement within parties becoming steadily institutionalized.

Women's representation in Turkish politics has been studied in depth over the years. Most recently, feminist historiography has challenged official accounts of state feminism, shedding light on the complex relationship between women's groups and the state (Çakır 1994; Davaz 2014; Zihnioğlu 2003) as well as on the interplay of gender, religion, and ethnicity (Ekmekçioğlu and Bilal 2006; Mojab 2001). In terms of women's engagement in pro-Kurdish politics, many studies have focused on the images of Kurdish women and the women's individual trajectories. For instance, Lale Yalçın-Heckmann (1999) contrasts the political imagery of Turkish and Kurdish women, underlining how the images of the two groups developed in similar and distinct ways. Martin van Bruinessen (2001) concentrates specifically on Kurdish women, highlighting how they have managed over the years to obtain political power and authority over their communities despite the omnipresent patriarch. Finally, Handan

---

2. In this respect, "the new politics of gender equality" is distinguished from the earlier forms of informal activism, entailing a different relationship with both formal and informal institutions (Squires 2007, 20).

Çağlayan (2007) examines the different political roles of Kurdish women, which have transformed from the symbolic (as sisters, mothers, and goddesses of the nation) to the highly autonomous (as comrades and political counterparts). In analyzing Kurdish women's political engagement, this chapter employs an institutionalist perspective, scrutinizing in particular affirmative-action measures that enable women's representation and participation in pro-Kurdish politics. As such, it argues that when the discursive tinkering around gender equity was recast as pro-Kurdish claims, these affirmative-action measures led to the institutionalization of women's political engagement within party politics.

I present my argument in three parts. In the first section, I provide a brief historical overview of women's political participation in Turkey, thereby contextualizing the Kurdish exception within the highly masculinized Turkish political landscape. In the second section, I tackle extant political discourses on gender quota and parity, analyzing how they were legitimated and incorporated into the pro-Kurdish agenda in line with the stance taken by the People's Democratic Party (Halkların Demokratik Partisi, HDP) on autonomy and freedom of identity. I conclude in the third section by studying various affirmative-action measures adopted by the pro-Kurdish HDP, especially in relation to how they enabled and encouraged women's political engagement at different levels of policy and decision making.

Mustachioed Politics and Women's Underrepresentation in Turkey

The Republic of Turkey was among the few pioneering countries that granted women's suffrage early on, within about a decade of its establishment, in 1930 for regional elections and 1934 for national elections. Although the Turkish official narrative contends that women's suffrage was granted because of the wisdom of Turkey's Founding Father, Mustafa Kemal Atatürk, recent feminist historiography has demonstrated that women's suffrage had already been advocated by a small but well-organized and internationally connected group of women suffragettes since the late Ottoman Empire (Çakır 1994; Ötüş-Baskett and Baykan

1999; Zihnioğlu 2003). However, the Ottoman suffragette movement was soon co-opted by the new republican political leadership, and the suffragists disappeared into the emerging "state feminism."[3] Already in 1935, the only Turkish political party at the time, the Republican People's Party (Cumhuriyet Halk Partisi, CHP), dominated by Atatürk, stated that because women's suffrage was already granted by the state, there was no need for an autonomous women's movement—those women who wanted to be active in politics could join the CHP's women's branch. Hence, the state and society expected women to participate only in the established republican state institutions (Zihnioğlu 2003).

Within this political framework, women first participated in the national elections of 1935, resulting in a 4.6 percent representation in Parliament by eighteen women deputies. This minimal representation dropped further to 3.7 percent in the national elections of 1943. In 1950, as the country transitioned to a multiparty system with the establishment of the Democrat Party (Demokrat Parti, DP), women's representation was drastically lowered to 0.6 percent. This pattern did not change in the succeeding half century; up until 2007, women's representation remained marginal as they constituted less than 5 percent of the Turkish Parliament.[4] Today, the portion of women in the Parliament barely comes to 17 percent, with even less representation in executive positions and local governance.[5] In summary, women in Turkey were recognized as citizens with electoral rights as early as the 1930s, but their chronic underrepresentation continues to this day (see table 12.1). As feminists put it, politics still

---

3. Under state feminism, women are exclusively seen as attributes of the national ideal. Reforms are implemented under the flagship of the state and target primarily the public sphere. For more on state feminism, see White 2003.

4. The initial high gender-participation record of 4.6 percent in the elections of 1935 wasn't beaten until seventy-two years later, in 2007, with 9.1 percent (Turkish Statistical Institute 2020).

5. From 1935 to 2010, only fourteen women occupied ministerial positions in Turkey, and women's representation in local governance remained less than 3 percent (Sancar 2008). Following regional elections of 2014, only 2.93 percent of elected mayors were women (Kadın Koalisyonu 2014).

Table 12.1

Women's Representation in the Turkish Parliament, 1935–2018

Election Year	Total Number of Deputies	Number of Women Deputies	Percentage of Women in Parliament
1935	395	18	4.6
1943	435	16	3.7
1950	487	3	0.6
1957	610	8	1.3
1965	450	8	1.8
1973	450	6	1.3
1991	450	8	1.8
1999	550	22	4.2
2002	550	24	4.4
2007	550	50	9.1
2011	550	79	14.3
2015 (June)	550	97	17.6
2015 (November)	550	81	14.7
2018	595	104	17.4

Source: TBMM 2018.

wears a mustache in Turkey, with women unequivocally excluded from equitable participation.[6]

Despite such gender underrepresentation in practice, the state and society made very few efforts to increase women's political participation nationally. International efforts to increase gender participation failed to gain the support of political actors at the national and local levels. It was only in 1996, seventy-three years after the establishment of the Turkish Republic, that Turkey published its first National Plan on Gender Equality

---

6. The expression "moustachioed politics" (*bıyıklı siyaset*) was coined by the Association for Support and Training of Women Candidates (Kadın Adayları Destekleme Derneği). In 2007, on the eve of elections, the association asked whether having a moustache is a prerequisite of being elected to office and then disseminated campaign visuals with photoshopped images of women with moustaches.

following the Fourth World Congress on Women held in Beijing in 1995.[7] Then, in 2000, the Turkish state defined its millennium development goals for women's representation to reach 17 percent by 2015 ("National Action Plan" 2008),[8] a target that has been reached not as a result of an extensive national reform but thanks largely and ironically to the electoral success of pro-Kurdish politics. In the same spirit, only a few constitutional amendments have incorporated gender equality into the Turkish political agenda. In 2004 the legislature added to Article 10 of the Constitution a paragraph explicitly stating that "men and women have equal rights." In 2005, within the scope of the Turkey–European Union Pre-Accession Financial Assistance Program, the state started to prepare the Promoting Gender Equality project. One of the project's outputs was the Second National Action Plan on Gender Equality, prepared for the 2008–13 term. In 2010 Article 10 was amended again, with the following two sentences added: "The State has the obligation to ensure that this [gender] equality exists in practice. Measures taken for such a purpose should not be interpreted as contrary to the principle of equality." In all, although the Turkish Constitution has acknowledged women's de jure equality and opened the way for affirmative-action measures, there is no real comprehensive effort nationally; the pursuit of gender equity in Turkey is left largely to political parties and the few civil society organizations.

How has women's representation in the Turkish Parliament varied across political parties? Today, women provide the following representation

---

7. As discussed, international organizations have a significant role in setting the agenda for gender equality. The Beijing conference of 1995 was important because it shifted the quota debates to equal participation (parity) and promoted parity in power and decision making "not only [as] a demand for simple justice or democracy" but also "as a necessary condition for women's interests to be taken into account." The declaration concluded that "without the active participation of women and the incorporation of women's perspective at all levels of decision-making, the goals of equality, development and peace cannot be achieved" (United Nations 1995).

8. Herein, it is important to note that this objective has been achieved due not to national and comprehensive efforts by the government but to efforts by political parties, most remarkably the pro-Kurdish HDP.

of deputies in Parliament in ascending order: 7 percent of deputies for the Good Party (İyi Parti, IP), 8 percent for the Nationalist Movement Party (Milliyetçi Hareket Partisi, MHP), and 18 percent each for the (ruling) Justice and Development Party (Adalet ve Kalkınma Partisi, AKP) and the (main opposition) CHP. What is most striking is the proportion among the pro-Kurdish HDP deputies. With 39 percent representation, this pro-Kurdish party has more than twice the number of women representing the main ruling and opposition Turkish parties at 18 percent each (Türkiye Büyük Millet Meclisi [TBMM] 2018). Also, among the major political parties that are represented in the Turkish Parliament, only the main opposition party, the CHP, and the pro-Kurdish HDP have introduced candidate quotas for women to sustain women's political representation; the conservative-right parties, the AKP, MHP, and IP, have not made such structural adjustments.

Historically, the center-left CHP was the first to implement a gender quota of 25 percent as early as 1989. Likewise, HDP's predecessor, the Democratic Society Party (Demokratik Toplum Partisi, DTP), had started in 2005 to apply a 40 percent gender quota, promising gender parity for all candidates since 2014 (HDP 2014). As for the CHP, the party increased in 2012 its gender quota for candidates nominated by the party's headquarters to 33 percent (CHP 2020). The CHP bylaws state that candidates nominated by the headquarters cannot exceed 15 percent of the party's total allowed candidacies, so the overall CHP gender quota applies to the very narrow rate of 4.95 percent of the entire list of CHP candidates. Hence, the CHP gender quota barely makes a lasting societal impact.

The efficacy of using quotas as a measure of gender participation is still contentious.[9] Nevertheless, empirical research has been able to

---

9. Although gender quotas are employed globally, their usage has remained controversial, and their success questionable. Studying quotas and affirmative-action measures, Mona Krook (2006) contends that these strategies have simply not been in operation long enough for anyone to reach a definite conclusion regarding their impact. Drude Dahlerup (2006) in turn recommends a shift in focus from the adoption of quotas to their implementation, thus building a large empirical database. In addition, quotas are also criticized on the basis that they only ameliorate gender inequity rather than eliminate it by its roots;

establish that affirmative-action measures do work as a "fast-track" strategy (Norris and Dahlerup 2015) in increasing the number of women in politics (Dahlerup 2006; Krook 2006). Such increases do not immediately translate to an increased number of women delegates, however, and so quotas remain a mere political gesture. Not supported sufficiently by the party, women candidates are relegated to the lower ranks of electoral candidate lists, where they have close to zero chance of getting elected. Indeed, quotas can be effective only if and when they are accompanied by two changes in the larger political context: a favorable general political will and the necessary institutional structure. If such changes do not occur, as in the case of Turkey until very recently, gender quotas serve to strengthen the party rather than women due to the centralized structure of Turkish politics (Kılıç 2000). Indeed, the lack of gender power in the CHP exemplifies this observation. On the other side of the spectrum, the pro-Kurdish HDP comes to the fore in defying women's chronic underrepresentation in Turkish politics. The next two sections discuss how the HDP ideologically generated and then institutionalized gender representation.

Gender Equity and Pro-Kurdish Party Politics: Toward "Ideological Tinkering"?

Turkey had long experienced "state feminism," whereby the state-controlled and state-shaped women's participation in society at large suppressed the emergence of a women's movement there. It was only toward the 1980s that women's autonomous advocacy and organization emerged once again, leading to the second wave of feminism in Turkey (Diner and Toktaş 2010). In the 1990s, when Kurdish conflict and political Islam were on the rise, Turkish feminists had to take a stand about the state

---

put another way, research on quotas "do not address the norms and rules that generated discrimination directly, but rather seek to redress the inequalities that result from them" (Squires 2007, 94). Despite the ongoing debates around the quota measure, today 47 percent of countries worldwide apply some sort of quota based on gender or ethnicity or class (Dahlerup 2018).

oppression of Kurdish and Muslim women. Similarly faced with a double oppression, ethnocentrism with respect to the Turkish feminist movement and gender-blindness with respect to the Kurdish nationalist movement, Kurdish women themselves had to take on the challenge of gender equity (Al-Ali and Taş 2018). This challenge set the grounds for a new social space for both collaboration and conflict within the Turkish political landscape in general and pro-Kurdish party politics in particular.[10]

Women's representation and participation in pro-Kurdish politics was also challenging given the tenuous trajectory of pro-Kurdish political parties. First of all, the majority of these parties were accused of having a separatist agenda, an accusation that led to frequent party closures by the Turkish Supreme Court.[11] Second, even when such parties were allowed to operate, the candidates had to run either as independent candidates or as candidates on the list of other parties due to the election barrier of a minimum of 10 percent of the general vote per Article 33 of Electoral Law 2839. This was the only means available to Kurdish politicians to bypass the threshold and acquire parliamentary representation. Third, such parties were challenged to create malleable organizations, ones "robust enough to structure goals but at the same time . . . flexible enough to reach informal networks and activist communities that connect people to each other" (Meyer and Tarrow 1998, 24). To accomplish this aim, the Kurdish movement had to transform its main principles, norms, and values regarding gender into party politics. In doing so, it had to tinker with its ideology on the one side and its institutional design on the other.

---

10. Naomi Watts (2010) insists that the institutionalization of the Kurdish movement and Kurds' engagement in party politics enabled the Kurdish opinion leaders with new resources, access, and legitimacy to shape and advance a pro-Kurdish agenda in conventional politics.

11. The accusation of a separatist propaganda and the decision to close a party were often grounded on Political Parties Law 2820, which asserts that political parties cannot act against "the indivisible integrity of the state with its territory and nation." It was claimed that pro-Kurdish political parties divide the nation by creating minority groups and have the ultimate aim to declare independence from Turkey and thus violate territorial integrity.

It was in 1990 that the first pro-Kurdish party, the People's Labor Party (Halkın Emek Partisi, HEP), was initially formed by seven members of the Turkish Parliament who had been expelled from the Social Democratic Populist Party (Sosyaldemokrat Halkçı Parti, SHP) for participating in a pro-Kurdish conference in France.[12] In the ensuing elections of 1991, the HEP was able to get twenty-one deputies elected to Parliament, with political activist Leyla Zana the only woman among them. Because Zana was also the first Kurdish woman to acquire parliamentary representation, she soon became a symbolic yet controversial figure in Turkish politics for her attempts to introduce Kurdish culture and language into the body politic in Turkey.[13] In studying the political imagery of women, Lale Yalçın-Heckmann compares the political image of Leyla Zana to that of the first Turkish woman prime minister, Tansu Çiller.[14] Whereas Çiller represented a westernized image of Turkish modernity, Zana stood for rural, oppressed, yet resilient Kurdish women. Indeed, Zana's life and political trajectory were often narrated as being parallel to the struggle and awakening of the Kurdish people. Zana was the "symbolic village girl" as well as "the mirror" and "micro-cosmos" of the Kurdish political struggle (1999, 19–22).

Mirroring the experiences of most pro-Kurdish political parties and politicians, Zana's political career was also violently interrupted. She was

---

12. The conference was organized by the Kurdish Institute of Paris and France-Libertés on 14–15 October 1989 under the theme "The Kurds: Cultural Identity and Human Rights." Hosted with the financial and political support of the French government, the conference accused the Turkish government of severe human rights violations vis-à-vis its Kurdish citizens (Kurdish Institute of Paris n.d.). The Turkish state considered the participation of SHP deputies in the conference a disciplinary breach constituting a threat from Kurdish nationalism (Watts 2010).

13. On the day of her parliamentary oath, Zana wore a headband with the three colors of the Kurdish flag—green, red, and yellow—which immediately triggered protest. Zana also concluded her oath in Kurdish, which resulted in her arrest in the Parliament's backyard (Çağlayan 2007).

14. Tansu Çiller served as prime minister from 1993 to 1996 and as minister of foreign affairs in 1996–97. She was associated with the True Path Party (Doğru Yol Partisi, DYP) at center-right.

arrested in 1991, the same year she got elected, for conspiring against the unity of the Turkish Republic. Two years later, in 1993, her party, the HEP, was banned but reemerged under a different name, the Democracy Party (Demokrasi Partisi, DEP). A year later in 1994, the DEP was also banned on the same ground of having an allegedly separatist agenda, which led to the party's reestablishment with yet another name, the People's Democracy Party (Halkın Demokrasi Partisi, HADEP). HADEP encouraged women's participation, considering it crucial for electoral success; it valued such participation as "an extension of its liberation doctrine and [considered] women's activism outside the home . . . important as a mobilizing mechanism toward electoral victory" (Narlı 2007, 87). HADEP's program stated that women had to be emancipated from feudalism and patriarchy and that women's status had to be improved through the specific implementation of two feminist principles: the elimination of gender discrimination and the escalation of women's political representation. HADEP then had to put these principles into practice in a way that appealed to all Kurdish women, progressive and conservative alike. For example, Nilüfer Narlı notes that women in HADEP were able to attract religiously conservative Shafi Kurds through the slogan "Revolt against an oppressive state in the name of Islam" (2007, 87). It was assumed that religious appeal and ethnic unity would jointly lead to electoral success and that Kurdish women would serve as both the constituents and the recipients of this strategy. HADEP tinkered women's emancipation with pro-Kurdish claims. However, despite its gender-sensitive agenda, it was not able to surpass the 10 percent vote threshold to acquire parliamentary representation in the national elections. Yet it had outstanding success in local elections as it obtained municipal representation in the eastern and southeastern provinces (Watts 2010). HADEP's electoral success at the mayoral level had a significant impact on the trajectory of the Kurdish movement, paving the way to claims of local autonomy. This ideological stand was then further developed and advocated by other pro-Kurdish parties: the Democratic People's Party (Demokratik Halk Partisi, DEHAP) from 1997 to 2005, the DTP from 2005 to 2009, the Peace and Democracy Party (Barış ve Demokrasi Partisi, BDP) from 2008 to 2014, and finally the HDP beginning in 2012.

Today, the HDP is the only prominent pro-Kurdish political party represented in the Turkish Parliament. Continuing with the tradition of previous pro-Kurdish political parties' tinkering of gender equity with pro-Kurdish claims, the HDP embraces a feminist ideology in the articulation of direct democracy through autonomy in governance. Through women's *direct* participation, the HDP aims to "transform and democratize the political arena, which was long conceptualized as a monopolist competitive landscape." As such, HDP is committed to developing "mechanisms and tools that enable women to exercise their *agency* by having a say regarding decision-making authority in their lives" (HDP 2016, emphasis added). Within the HDP's ideology, women's direct participation is seen as a fundamental component and requirement for autonomy in governance. This autonomy will then extend to women's agency over their lives:

> Recognizing that male domination (patriarchy) has deep systematic roots in all areas of social life, our party acknowledges the fact that in addition to other types of domination and exploitation (class, ethnicity, religion), male domination and oppression have a specific type of operation. Faced with all kinds of oppression and exploitation that women suffer, our party takes women's side. We support the emancipation (liberation) of women and commit to fighting for it. Our party is fighting against all types of sexism in gender relations and gender discourse. (HDP 2015)

In addition to declaring a fight against sexism and male domination, HDP's program also addresses other prominent feminist concerns, such as sexual violence, abortion, and domestic work. The program states that "against male control over the body and female sexuality, the party acknowledges abortion as a woman's right."[15] Moreover, the HDP condemns all types of violence, including state violence and male violence, reiterating its intent to implement policies that protect women. Concerning

---

15. Among the four political parties represented in the Turkish Parliament, only the HDP mentions abortion in its party program.

the exploitation of women domestic workers, the party first recognizes and respects the production value of domestic work; it then reiterates that it will continue its fight for the social rights of domestic workers and will do so in solidarity with the women's movement (HDP 2015).

On paper, then, the HDP commits to fostering women's agency and freedom of identity through enabling their direct political participation as well as through advancing a feminist agenda. This particular conceptualization of gender equity comes in line with the main pro-Kurdish claims over agency, autonomy, and freedom to express identity.

Yet how well does this textual, narrative commitment translate into action? The ideological tinkering[16] of gender equality within pro-Kurdish party politics has not always been straightforward. For the HDP's predecessors, gender-equality claims came in many different forms. Women's empowerment initially had a merely symbolic and instrumental meaning in the Kurdish movement; it was sufficient for Kurdish women to self-identify as a Kurd and to engage in pro-Kurdish politics (Çağlayan 2007). This initial step then led to the feminization of party cadres on the one side and to the consolidation of gender-equality claims within pro-Kurdish politics on the other. As a consequence, the feminization of Kurdish politics not only has led to a numerical increase of women in the political arena but has also articulated and advanced a feminist agenda that propounds "women's interests."[17]

---

16. I borrow the phrase "ideological tinkering" from Réjane Sénac-Slawinski to refer to a context where different reforms are not necessarily "conceptualized specifically, but rather made consistent with party lines" (2008, 251).

17. Given the diversity of women's groups, it is difficult to talk about a unified set of "women's interests." Acknowledging this difficulty, feminist scholarship has come up with some useful categorizations of what constitutes "women's interests." Within this framework, Karen Beckwith (2011) has introduced distinctions among interests, issues, and preferences. According to Beckwith, women's interests are the most fundamental, and they derive from women's shared experiences, which differ from men's. "Interests" are constructed in specific instances of political, economic, and social arrangements. In contrast, "issues" refer to immediate events women encounter, and as such they are more focused and limited. Finally, "preferences" are the strategic alternatives that women's groups from different ideological background can put forth in remedying an issue in question.

Women in Pro-Kurdish Politics: From Discourse to Institutional Change

Kurdish women's participation in politics transformed from narrative to action through institutionalization. A burgeoning literature in feminist institutionalism articulates well how "women work within, through and against institutions" (Mackay 2011, 184). Feminist institutionalism commences by proclaiming that institutions are not unpretentious and neutral structures but rather "the result of political compromise" (Waylen 2013, 216). Because institutions are unequivocally gendered, it is imperative to transform them to achieve gender equity (Waylen 2013, 212). Such a gendered analysis of institutions needs to include the systemic examination of gendered aspects of norms, rules, and practices as well as their effect on political outcomes (Mackay 2011). The adoption of such an institutionalist perspective to Kurdish women's political engagement reveals how such measures embedded in practice enable women's participation to continue over time.

Today, Kurdish women participate in politics in large numbers, and their participation constitutes a distinguishing feature of pro-Kurdish politics in Turkey. During the general elections of November 2015, the HDP nominated 232 female candidates, which constituted almost half (42 percent) of total nominees. During the eighty-one city elections throughout the country, HDP had 29 first-row female candidates (35.8 percent), and the number of female candidates was greater than the number of male candidates in sixteen cities (Bianet 2015). After the elections, women constituted 14.5 percent of the Parliament with a total of eighty-one women legislators. The HDP took fifty-nine seats in the Parliament, of which twenty-three (39 percent) were occupied by women. In the general elections of 2018, although the HDP nominated 230 women candidates, which once again constituted 38 percent of all of its candidates, only 18 women were first-row candidates with the highest possibility of being elected. Today, the HDP's women representatives in Parliament constitute 40 percent of the total number of women in Parliament.

Although the HDP has failed so far to fulfill its promise of exact parity among its legislative members, it nevertheless has the largest proportion of women deputies in the Parliament. This impressive outcome resulted from the effective implementation of a woman's quota across the party—as explained earlier—and from the institutionalization of affirmative-action measures.

Women's Assemblies

Historically, political parties worldwide utilized their women's branches to reach female electorates and identify women candidates. In Turkey, women's branches were finally reestablished after the constitutional reform of 1995, which lifted the ban prohibiting political parties from establishing women's or youth branches. Currently, all political parties represented in the Turkish Parliament have some sort of operating women's branches. The HDP likewise publicly advocates the establishment of women's assemblies at all policy-making levels, with the intent to directly involve women in local governance. Women's assemblies are autonomous organizations that work across a variety of issues and at different levels. The party program states that "in this model women's assemblies are organized at municipal, regional, and all other local government levels to ensure the development of urban services concerning gender equality and women's claims. Women's assemblies supervise the implementation of these decisions" (HDP 2015).

Women's Co-presidency

The organization of all women's assemblies parallels the co-presidency system, whereby a female president is assigned along with a male president at every level of decision making, including party leadership (HDP 2015). This co-presidency aims to secure gender equity in decision making as well as the sharing and distributing of power at the highest presidential level. This practice is put in place to ensure that women not only participate in policy making but do so as women leaders equal in position to men.[18] The HDP's strategic decision to include women as co-presidents

---

18. In her study of women's political participation in West Africa, Dzodzi Tsikata (2001) notes that women's branches of political parties have rarely provided the breeding

complements the activities of women's assemblies as a parity measure at the decision-making level. Hence, the co-presidency system "was designed to function as a preventive measure to transform the male-dominant structure of power relations and to enable women to execute politics on their own behalf" (TBMM 2015).

The co-presidency strategy that helped institutionalize women's position was inspired by the German Green Party, which applied the same measure to its party leadership. Within the Turkish context, the DTP first applied the co-presidency model for party leadership in 2005 when Aysel Tuğluk was elected as the party's first woman co-president (Bianet 2009). The party later explained its practice:

> The co-presidency system of the DTP enables women to participate more effectively in decision-making processes, to produce and implement policies. In this sense, the enlargement of the co-presidency system and its implementation in municipalities will be a step to[ward] widen[ing] the political space for women. As far as is known, there is no country that implements a co-presidency system at the municipal level. In this context, Turkey will also have the opportunity to make a pioneering change in opportunity structures that will serve as a model to the rest of the world. (TBMM 2015)

Yet only a year later, in 2006, the Turkish Supreme Court ruled against the co-presidency on the grounds that it violated Article 15 of the Political Parties Law, which states that only one person may be elected for party presidency. As a consequence, the DTP was forced to withdraw from the implementation of co-presidency in 2007. Nonetheless, in 2008 the DTP's Diyarbakir deputy, Sevahir Bayındır, sponsored a bill before the Parliament to amend three laws (the Political Parties Law, the Law on Basic Provisions on Elections and Voter Registers, and the Parliamentary Elections Law) with the intent to implement parity by guaranteeing a minimum 40 percent of representation by women on all electoral lists and to ascertain co-presidency across all political positions (TBMM 2008). The bill was

---

ground for solidarity on feminist issues, nor have they promoted any women to leadership positions.

partially accepted, and Article 15 of the Political Parties Law was amended in 2014, allowing political parties to have a maximum of two presidents.

The HDP has continued to apply co-presidency at both the presidential and the municipal levels. Although the co-presidency measure ensures parity in decision making, one could also argue that the measure conforms to heteronormative standards with the image of women and men coupled in the office. Women having a seat "next to men" is much less defiant than women taking executive leadership positions alone. However, the HDP claims to conceptualize co-presidents less as executive leaders than as political leaders sharing equal power. Hence, the HDP's co-presidency aims to promote women's participation in decision making on the one side and to destabilize, democratize, and decentralize the hegemonic male power structure within political parties on the other. As such, the HDP precisely aims at transforming the concept of executive leadership by assigning shared decision-making power to male and female co-presidents while ensuring parity in power sharing.

Women's Co-mayorship

When the BDP succeeded the DTP, it reincorporated the co-presidency principle, extending it to the municipal level during the local elections of 2014. After the elections, the co-presidency of mayors in the form of co-mayorship was applied to all the municipalities that the BDP won. Co-mayorship was an important innovation for women's representation at the local level, enabling them to establish the necessary networks to mobilize women into politics from the ground up. Women's co-mayorship in Kurdish municipalities is significant for both the Turkish context and beyond it. Co-mayorship is significant for Turkey because it is a unique measure to challenge the long-lasting "Turkish paradox" of "lower representation of women in municipal councils as compared to in parliament" (Drechselová 2000, 42). Moreover, it is also significant for the world because it constitutes one of the few examples of the extension of the co-leadership model to local governance (TBMM 2015).

Yet just as with the practice of co-presidency, co-mayorship was also legally challenged by the Turkish judiciary. In October 2014 the Diyarbakir

Third Administrative Court ruled against the co-mayorship practice on the grounds that it had no legal basis per the Law on Municipalities. Notwithstanding this ruling, the HDP did not give up the practice, announcing that it would continue co-mayorship (M. Bozarslan 2014). The HDP group deputy chairwoman Pervin Buldan addressed this court decision at the Turkish Parliament plenary session, noting that "the Diyarbakir Third Administrative Court has declared co-mayorship inconsistent with the law, deciding to stop its execution. As a party, we [will continue to] implement this principle in practice. Laws lump behind as society moves ahead" (quoted in in M. Bozarslan 2014). Indeed, when Berrin Koyuncu and Ahu Sumbas analyzed the practice of female mayorship in pro-Kurdish politics, they concluded that it "opens up spatial and political accessibility for women" and "leads to a better expression of women's interests" (2016, 48). Although the practice does indeed empower women, it is too soon to tell what its long-term impact will be.

Going beyond a simple quota measure, the HDP has taken a very progender stand in politics, committing to the institutionalization of gender equality and parity across its party institutions and among its elected representatives. The establishment and practice of women's assemblies and co-presidency enable women's equal representation and participation in both policy making and decision making. Moreover, the HDP sets precedent in Turkey as the first political party promising and practicing gender parity as well as other affirmative-action measures to remedy women's chronic underrepresentation in politics. In the past two general elections, although the party did not reach 50 percent parity in its legislative candidate list and elected deputies, per its promise, it did nevertheless manage in 2014 to consolidate parity in its leadership through its practice of co-presidency in the Parliament and co-mayorship in its local governance. Given the sad state of affairs in Turkey regarding gender parity in politics, the HDP thus can serve as a model that other political parties need to follow in the future.

Conclusion

The Turkish political landscape continues to remain under male domination to this day, with women consistently excluded from equal participation.

The pro-Kurdish politics challenges this misogynous pattern. Focusing on Kurdish women's engagement in party politics, this chapter has argued that the politicization of Kurdish women and the feminization of Kurdish politics emerged as a result of an ideological tinkering of gender equity with pro-Kurdish claims on the one side and the institutionalization of gender parity across all pro-Kurdish party organizations on the other. I specifically have demonstrated how women's empowerment and gender equity have been articulated by various pro-Kurdish political parties in relation to the practice of agency, autonomy, and freedom to express identity. By appealing to and successfully engaging more women, pro-Kurdish politics has been able to put these ideological premises into practice through the institutionalization of measures affirming gender equality and parity across the party. I have further argued that these measures work together to ensure women's political participation at different levels, both at policy making in women's assemblies and at decision making in co-presidency and co-mayorship. Given that most of the literature on the Kurdish women's movement almost exclusively focuses on (and therefore stereotypes) women guerrilla fighters, this chapter has aimed to portray the role of pro-Kurdish politics in challenging and reshaping politics in Turkey to extend parity to women.

References

Al-Ali, Nadje, and Latif Taş. 2018. "Reconsidering Nationalism and Feminism: The Kurdish Political Movement in Turkey." *Nations and Nationalism* 24, no. 2: 453–73.

Beckwith, Karen. 2011. "Interests, Issues, and Preferences: Women's Interests and Epiphenomena of Activism—ERRATUM." *Politics & Gender* 8, no. 4: 554–55.

Bianet. 2009. "DTP'nin kısa tarihi." 12 Dec. At https://bianet.org/biamag/siyaset/118826-dtp-nin-kisa-tarihi.

———. 2015. "HDP kadın seçim bildirgesi: Özgürlük ve eşitlik için kadınlar kazanacak." 4 Oct. At https://bianet.org/bianet/toplum/168014-hdp-kadin-secim-bildirgesi-ozgurluk-ve-esitlik-icin-kadinlar-kazanacak.

Bozarslan, Mahmut. 2014. "Eşbaşkanlık hukuka aykırı." *Al Jazeera*, 2 Oct. At http://www.aljazeera.com.tr/al-jazeera-ozel/esbaskanlik-hukuka-aykiri.

Çağlayan, Handan. 2007. *Analar, yoldaşlar, tanrıçalar: Kürt hareketinde kadınlar ve kadın kimliğinin oluşumu*. Istanbul: İletişim Yayınları, 2007.

Çakır, Serpil. 1994. *Osmanlı kadın hareketi*. Istanbul: İletişim Yayınları.

Cumhuriyet Halk Partisi (CHP). 2020. "CHP parti tüzüğü." 5–6 Sept. At https://www.chp.org.tr/sayfalar/chp-yonetmelikleri.

Dahlerup, Drude. 2006. "The Story of the Theory of Critical Mass." *Politics & Gender* 2, no. 4 (Dec.): 511–22.

———. 2018. *Has Democracy Failed Women?* Cambridge: Polity Press.

Davaz, Aslı. 2014. *Eşitsiz kız kardeşlik: Uluslararası ve ortodoğu kadın hareketleri, 1935 kongresi ve Türk Kadın Birliği*. Istanbul: Türkiye İş Bankası Yayınları.

Diner, Çağla, and Şule Toktaş. 2010. "Waves of Feminism in Turkey: Kemalist, Islamist, and Kurdish Women's Movements in an Era of Globalization." *Journal of Balkan and Near Eastern Studies* 12, no. 1 (Mar.): 41–57.

Drechselová, Lucie G. 2020. "Contextualizing the 'Turkish Paradox.'" In *Local Power and Female Political Pathways in Turkey: Cycles of Exclusion*, 41–92. London: Palgrave Macmillan.

Ekmekçioğlu, Lerna, and Melisa Bilal. 2006. *Bir adalet feryadı: Osmanlı'dan Türkiye'ye beş feminist yazar*. Istanbul: Aras Yayınları.

Halkların Demokratik Partisi (HDP). 2014. "HDP parti tüzüğü." 22 June. At https://www.hdp.org.tr/tr/parti-tuzugu/10/.

———. 2015. "HDP parti programı." At http://www.hdp.org.tr/parti/parti-programi/8.

———. 2016. "HDP kadın meclisi toplantısı sonuç bildirgesi." 10 Feb. At https://www.hdp.org.tr/tr/kadin-meclisi-toplantisi-sonuc-bildirgesi/6522/.

Inter-Parliamentary Union. 2016. "Women in Parliaments: 2015-Year in Review." At https://www.ipu.org/resources/publications/reports/2016-07/women-in-parliament-in-2015-year-in-review.

———. 2018. "National Parliaments." At https://www.ipu.org/national-parliaments.

Kadın Koalisyonu. 2014. "2014 yerel yönetim seçim sonuçları." 15 Mar. At https://kadinkoalisyonu.org/2014-yerel-secimleri-aday-analizi/.

Kılıç, Zeynep. 2000. *Eşitlik için kota politikaları*. Ankara, Turkey: Ankara Üniv. Kadın Sorunları Araştırma ve Uygulama Merkezi.

Koyuncu, Berrin L., and Ahu Sumbas. 2016. "Discussing Women's Representation in Local Politics in Turkey: The Case of Female Mayorship." *Women's Studies International Forum* 58 (Sept.): 41–50.

Krook, Mona. 2006. "Reforming Representation: The Diffusion of Candidate Gender Quotas Worldwide." *Politics & Gender* 2, no. 3 (Sept.): 303–27.

Kurdish Institute of Paris. N.d. "The Defense of Human Rights." At https://www.institutkurde.org/en/institute/hrights.php.

Mackay, Fiona. 2011. "Conclusion: Towards a Feminist Institutionalism?" In *Gender, Politics, and Institutions: Towards a Feminist Institutionalism*, edited by Mona Lena Krook and Fiona Mackay, 181–96. Houndmills, UK: Palgrave Macmillan.

Meyer, David S., and Sidney Tarrow. 1998. *The Social Movement Society: Contentious Politics for a New Century*. Oxford: Rowman & Littlefield.

Mojab, Shahrzad. 2001. *Women of a Non-state Nation: The Kurds*. Costa Mesa, CA: Mazda.

Narlı, Nilüfer. 2007. "Women in Political Parties in Turkey: Emerging Spaces for Islamic Women." In *From Patriarchy to Empowerment: Participation, Movements, and Rights in the Middle East, North Africa, and South Asia*, edited by Valentine Moghadam, 78–96. Syracuse, NY: Syracuse Univ. Press.

"National Action Plan Gender Equality (NAPGE) 2008–2013." 2008. In *The Republic of Turkey Prime Ministry General Directorate on the Status of Women*. Ankara: Republic of Turkey. At http://www.huksam.hacettepe.edu.tr/English/Files/NAP_GE.pdf.

Norris, Pippa, and Drude Dahlerup. 2015. "On the Fast Track: The Spread of Gender Quota Policies for Elected Office." HKS Faculty Research Working Paper Series no. 15-041. At https://papers.ssrn.com/sol3/papers.cfm?abstract_id=2662112.

Ötüş-Baskett, Belma, and Ayşegül Baykan. 1999. *Nezihe Muhittin ve Türk kadını 1931*. Istanbul: İletişim Yayınları.

Sancar, Serpil. 2008. "Türkiye'de kadınların siyasal kararlara eşit katılımı." *Toplum ve demokrasi* 2, no. 4 (Sept.–Dec.): 173–84.

Sénac-Slawinski, Réjane. 2008. "Justifying Parity in France after the Passage of the So-Called Parity Laws and the Electoral Application of Them: The 'Ideological Tinkering' of Political Party Officials (UMP and PS) and Women's NGOs." *French Politics* 6, no. 3 (Sept.): 234–56.

Squires, Judith. 2007. *The New Politics of Gender Equality*. Houndmills, UK: Palgrave Macmillan.

Tsikata, Dzodzi. 2001. "National Machineries for the Advancement of Women in Africa: Are they Transforming Gender Relations?" Third World Network–Africa. At http://old.socialwatch.org/en/informesTematicos/29.html.

Turkish Statistical Institute. 2020. "İstatistiklerde kadın, 2019." 17 Sept. At https://tuikweb.tuik.gov.tr/PreHaberBultenleri.do?id=33732.

Türkiye Büyük Millet Meclisi (TBMM, Grand National Assembly of Turkey). 2008. "TBMM Bill No. 2/342." At https://www.tbmm.gov.tr/develop/owa/tasari_teklif_sd.onerge_bilgileri?kanunlar_sira_no=69775.

———. 2015. "TBMM Bill No. 2/584." At https://www.tbmm.gov.tr/develop/owa/tasari_teklif_sd.onerge_bilgileri?kanunlar_sira_no=194084.

———. 2018. "TBMM milletvekillerimiz dağılım." At https://www.tbmm.gov.tr/develop/owa/milletvekillerimiz_sd.dagilim.

United Nations. 1995. "The Beijing Declaration and the Platform for Action: Fourth World Conference on Women." 4–15 Sept. At https://www.un.org/en/events/pastevents/pdfs/Beijing_Declaration_and_Platform_for_Action.pdf.

Van Bruinessen, Martin. 2001. "From Adela Khanum to Leyla Zana: Women as Political Leaders in Kurdish History." In *Women of a Non-state Nation: The Kurds*, edited by Shahrazad Mojab, 95–112. Costa Mesa, CA: Mazda.

Walby, Sylvia. 2005. "Gender Mainstreaming: Productive Tensions in Theory and Practice." *Social Politics* 12, no. 3: 321–43.

Watts, Naomi. 2010. *Activists in Office: Kurdish Politics and Protest in Turkey*. Seattle: Univ. of Washington Press.

Waylen, Georgina. 2013. "Informal Institutions, Institutional Change, and Gender Equality." *Political Research Quarterly* 67, no. 1: 212–23.

White, Jenny B. 2003. "State Feminism, Modernization, and the Turkish Republican Women." *NWSA Journal* 15:145–59.

Yalçın-Heckmann, Lale. 1999. "Kürt kadınlarının imajı: Bazı eleştirel değerlendirmeler." *Birikim dergisi* 119:17–30.

Zihnioğlu, Yaprak. 2003. *Kadınsız inkılap: Nezihe Muhittin, Kadınlar Halk Fırkası*. Istanbul: Metis Kitap.

13

A Displaced, Unsettled Political Subject

Kurdish Women's Struggles in Europe

Nisa Göksel

Being away from the place where you are born is hard. Kurds came here [to Europe] for several reasons, but the common cause was the conditions of living and surviving back there [in Turkey]. It might be poverty, the bad economy, or political pressures, or war, . . . but the reason for migration is never important. Whatever the reason, our migration is an exile. We are displaced, de-territorialized, and stateless. If you burn our village, we have to go somewhere else to live. If you are poor, you have to go somewhere to earn money to support your family. [Yet] wherever we go, we [Kurds] come together and act together. (Sema, 2013, German)

Sema,[1] whom I met during my fieldwork in Germany, had to move there as part of a wave of political migration in the wake of the military coup in Turkey in 1980. She was one of many political refugees criminalized by the Turkish state when their leftist activities and views were seen as a threat. Many Kurdish women activists I interviewed in Germany and France echoed Sema's statement: they claimed that living in exile was their de

---

This chapter develops some of the discussions that appeared in my article "Ulus-Ötesinde *öteki* politik özneler: Avrupa'da Kürt kadınlarının siyasi, toplumsal ve kültürel mücadeleleri" [Other Political Subjectivities in a Transnational Space: Kurdish Women's Political, Social, and Cultural Struggles in Europe], *Modus Operandi* 3 (2015): 11–45.

1. The names of all interviewees are pseudonyms, except in the case of public persons such as Feleknas Uca.

facto condition of existence, as much a part of their everyday struggles as their political mobilization. Sema raised another striking point: regardless of the reasons for which Kurds migrate, she considers them to be living in *exile*, a condition marked by displacement, de-territorialization, and statelessness. In the case of the Kurds, then, it becomes harder to differentiate the conditions of migration from displacement and exile because these conditions become for many Kurdish women at once never-ending and quotidian.

This chapter examines the subject formations and political engagements that politically active Kurdish women develop in exile by asking: How do the conditions of displacement and the ongoing war in Turkey's Kurdistan region affect the struggle of Kurdish women in Europe as migrants and political subjects? Given that the lives of Kurdish activist women take shape at the intersection of migration and exile, this chapter examines the political subjectivities and activities of Kurdish women from a transnational perspective by considering the question of how they strive to sustain their political ties and agency despite the daily difficulties of migrant/exile life. Whenever women are forced to migrate, their political attachments become displaced as well. What happens to Kurdish women's political identities when they are thus displaced?

On the one hand, war, displacement, and statelessness have forced members of the Kurdish community to maintain their political struggle beyond the states where they lived in the Middle East. In both Europe and the Middle East, the dispersed Kurdish body politic has been seen as a major threat to the sovereignty of states. On the other hand, with politically active Kurds from Turkey moving to Europe for reasons ranging from political repression to economic deprivation, living in Europe has long seemed to open up a new realm of politics for Kurds. Kurds have formed the Kurdish movement[2] across borders, against the transnational regimes of war and violence that have constituted the very foundations of their displacement and de-territorialization. The Kurdish movement

---

2. The Kurdish movement encompasses a broad range of Kurdish organizations, including the armed organization the PKK and the legal pro-Kurdish political parties.

not only generates transnational solidarity through its advocacy activities but also ideologically challenges the centrality and hegemony of the nation-state structure. The movement has thus established itself beyond the borders of Turkey and Kurdistan and across Europe. At the peak of the war between the Turkish state and the Kurdistan Workers' Party (Partîya Karkerên Kurdistanê, PKK) in the 1990s, Europe became one of the "arteries" of the Kurdish movement, defined as the movement's "third space" (after Kurdistan and Turkey, respectively).

Like the Kurdish movement as a whole, Kurdish women face a political struggle with this transnational character. To illuminate the intersection of women's political and daily struggles in Europe, I conducted forty in-depth interviews and participant observations with Kurdish women living in Germany and France who are affiliated with the Kurdish movement and/or the Kurdish women's movement in Turkey and currently in Europe. To supplement interviews and observations, I analyzed written and visual materials about the lives of Kurdish women. Based on my analysis of the data I gathered, I argue that the political identities and acts of Kurdish women in the diaspora are shaped in a liminal space and the tenuous terrain of politics.

Following Cecilia Menjívar's (2006) conceptualization of uncertain and liminal legality, I approach the position and identities of women in the diaspora as liminal in that they lie between their past and present political experiences as well between their revolutionary ideals[3] and their family life in the context of migration/exile. This liminality derives not only from the multiple subject positions these women inhabit but also from the constant strife between the legal and illegal regimes, a tension that leads to the widespread stigmatization of Kurdish political activities. To explore this liminality, I further discuss how Kurdish women's political attachments and identities are likely to be under threat due primarily to the following issues: (1) the stigma around "terrorism" and the fear of imprisonment; (2)

---

3. Being a revolutionary in this context dictates a certain mode of existence, examined later in the chapter (for further discussion, see also Göksel 2019). The revolutionary ideals of Kurdish politics are centered on women's freedom and expected to be embraced by guerrillas as well as by activists.

the transformation of Kurdish political agendas regarding local democracy and, in turn, the decreasing significance of transnational politics in Europe; (3) the struggles women encounter in everyday life as migrants and refugees in Europe; and (4) the conflict between familial and political obligations as well as women's "return" to the site of the home and family in the face of the uncertainties of migrant life.

In the first section, I briefly lay out the scholarly conceptualizations of displacement and migration as well as the dynamics of transnational forms of existence and mobilization. In the second, I provide background on the history of Kurdish migration and the transnational formation of the Kurdish movement in Europe. In the third, I summarize the findings of my fieldwork with activist Kurdish women in Germany and France and examine their experiences of and responses to exile in Europe.

Gender, Mobility, and Politics at the Juncture of Displacement, Exile, and Migration

Much of the scholarship on migration relies on drawing categorical distinctions between forced and voluntary migration, home and host countries, and national and transnational (for exceptions, see Ayata 2011; Başer 2015; Castles 2003; Van Hear 2006). However, under conditions of pervasive violence, when migration becomes a never-ending, daily reality (as in the case of Kurdish women), such categories and narratives collapse. Following Bilgin Ayata (2011, 4), I view displacement and exile through a broader, more transnational lens that perceives displaced, stateless, and exiled communities as "political entrepreneurs" and, indeed, agents who mobilize and craft political agency across borders. This characterization does not deny the violent experiences these groups have undergone and continue to undergo; rather, it gives a voice to refugees and exiles so that they can share those violent processes of displacement and exile. Although transnational political relations endow displaced and stateless groups with a certain amount of political leverage, they also come with their own predicaments.

In light of the scholarship on displacement, exile, and migration, I suggest that a transnational political landscape can be both empowering and disempowering for political subjects because the experience of war as embedded in the narratives of migration and displacement impedes certain modes of political existence while also breaking new ground for alternative forms of political being and mobility. In this respect, I contribute to the existing scholarship by giving an account of the gendered aspects of transnational politics, asking how women relate to politics and sustain their political selves under conditions of exile, displacement, and migration.

The political relations and activities of transnational communities are generally discussed within the scope of citizenship, incorporation, and other matters related to the political and social participation of migrants (Adamson 2002). As Fiona Adamson demonstrates, transnational communities' political relationship to their home countries is "as likely to be defined by a desire for transformation, contestation and political change as it is by nostalgia, continuity, and tradition" (2002, 155). Many scholars have also studied transnational advocacy networks formed in the fields of human rights, environmental issues, and women's rights (Ferree and Tripp 2006; Keck and Sikkink 1998; Risse-Kappen, Ropp, and Sikkink 1999). Within this broad body of scholarship, two main trends are dominant in works addressing the gendered dimensions of transnational mobility: (1) the discussions around home and belonging as well as the interactions between women's participation in the global labor force and care work (e.g., Parreñas 2000; Salih 2013; Spitzer et al. 2003); and (2) the formation of transnational networks and women's activism (e.g., Desai 2005; Ferree and Tripp 2006; Moghadam 2005).

However, few of these studies examine the gendered aspects of mobility with regard to the changing political experiences in the context of migration and displacement (among the few, see Hardy-Fanta 1993 and Jones-Correa 1998). Carol Hardy-Fanta (1993), for instance, notes the gendered nature of Latina/Latino politics and political participation in Boston. She underlines that for Latina women political participation is connected with the formation of the political self, a crucial part of migrant women's personal development (1993, 127). *Politics* and *political* take on different meanings during different stages of women's lives (137). Like Hardy-Fanta, I focus on the adult resocialization processes and their difficulties for Kurdish women by examining how women migrants navigate their political and familial relations in a state of liminality.

To examine Kurdish women's experiences in the diaspora, I employ Cecilia Menjívar's term *liminal legality*, which she defines as a gray zone in citizenship categories that traps immigrants between legality and illegality and creates uncertainty that directly affects the everyday life of migrants as well as of their families and communities (2006, 1000). This uncertain legality threatens women migrants' political selves, producing a sense of fear, insecurity, and precarity and turning politics into a "dangerous occupation" for women. The political action of the women in this study is shaped in such a zone of uncertain legality.

I next elaborate on how the Kurdish movement has become a transnational one as the condition of liminal legality is formed through the transnational politics of war and terrorism. This transnationality creates intersecting positions for Kurdish women as refugees, migrants, "terrorists," "criminals," and/or victims of war. As a result, women's political agency is undermined, and they are socially and politically marginalized through regimes of security/migration, and life in exile becomes, for them, a liminal state of political existence.

Transnationalization of the Kurdish Movement: "Guest Workers" of the Past, "Terrorists" of the Present

Detailing the transnationalization of the Kurdish movement as well as the history of Kurdish migration and displacement to Europe is crucial for any exploration of the political subjectivities and attachments of Kurdish women. Kurdish migration to Europe from Turkey first gained momentum in the 1960s and 1970s. During this period, Kurds migrated to Europe for both economic and political reasons.[4] Labor migration was a key factor throughout the 1960s and 1970s. However, as my interviewees explained, even if the apparent reason for their migration was economic, most Kurds

---

4. For further elaboration on the general characteristics of the Kurdish diaspora across European countries, see Akkaya 2013; Ayata 2011; Başer 2013, 2015; Demir 2012.

were also escaping from Turkey's assimilationist and discriminatory politics against Kurds, such as the nonacknowledgment of Kurdish identity and the ban on the Kurdish language.[5]

In the aftermath of the military intervention in 1971 and the coup d'etat in 1980, the political pressure on Kurds intensified. As the war broke out between Turkish military forces and the PKK in Turkey's Kurdistan region in 1984, Kurds began to seek asylum in European countries, which increased the number of Kurdish immigrants there (Ayata 2011, 141). Meanwhile, the PKK began to play a crucial role in politicizing and mobilizing Kurds living in Europe (Başer 2015), who have come to be seen as the most politically active migrant group on the continent (Grojean 2011). As Olivier Grojean observes, "Since 1982, not a month has gone by without a pro-Kurdish demonstration in a European country, and the average number of these events annually could be several hundred" (2011, 182). Thus, Kurds have become, according to Grojean, "the most 'demonstrative' group in Europe, and undoubtedly the most 'Europeanized' group" (182). This has meant existing as a political group working actively to transform repressive conditions in Turkey and Kurdistan, while also using the "European way" of conducting politics as a baseline for their political agendas.[6] Therefore, during the 1980s and 1990s Europe held a

---

5. Although Germany and France have different histories of migration, most of the PKK-affiliated organizations in different countries have similar structures. According to various unofficial records of the number of Kurds living in Germany and France, Germany has a larger Kurdish population than France (Ayata 2011; Başer 2015; Khayati 2008). Germany, as one of the first settlement destinations for Kurds, has historically played a central role in the Kurdish mobilization in Europe. Nevertheless, as many interviewees expressed, due to the strong economic and political agreements between the German and Turkish governments, since the 1990s Germany has increasingly implemented strict antiterrorism and criminalization measures against organizations affiliated with the PKK. This policy differs from the policy in France. The interviews demonstrate that France more often hides politically marginalized Kurds and runaways due to the geographical dispersion of Kurds in France.

6. Many structural, historical, and contextual features differentiate the way of conducting politics in different countries in Europe. It is therefore difficult to talk about a homogenous way of doing politics in Europe. When I refer to "European politics," "life in Europe,"

unique place in the transnational political mobilization of the Kurdish movement.

An early instance of the formation and dispersion of transnational Kurdish political activities in Europe was the establishment of the Kurdish Parliament in Exile, a political organization founded in 1995 with the participation of fifty-nine men and six women (van Bruinessen 1998, 46), eventually including approximately four hundred delegates from a variety of Kurdish groups in Turkey, Europe, and parts of Kurdistan (Keles 2015; van Bruinessen 2000). At a time when Kurdish political participation and representation were limited in Turkey and Kurdistan, Europe served as an alternative political arena for the pursuit of Kurdish political agendas through stateless diplomatic alliances. Martin van Bruinessen states that the Kurdish Parliament in Exile exemplified the kind of transnational politics that Kurds conducted: it was formed primarily by the Kurdish diaspora but also had a "trans-state" character (2000, 15). It brought together Kurds not only from the part of Turkey that is Kurdistan but also from the Kurdish parts of Iran, Iraq, and Syria (2000, 15). Van Bruinessen also notes that members of this parliament "have political asylum in different European states and that, although [the Parliament in Exile] has permanent offices in Brussels, it has held its plenary sessions each time in a different European country, including the Netherlands, Austria, Denmark,

---

and "European conduct of politics," I refer to the perception of a homogeneous Europe among the activist Kurdish women I interviewed. When I asked women about their distinct experiences of living in Germany and France, they generally conceived of "Europe" as one homogenous space, as if no difference exists between the two countries with respect to modes of living and politics. As Olivier Grojean also claims, "The dimensions of the pro-Kurdish mobilizations in Europe (emergence, strategies, forms of the protest, temporalities, rhythms, individual engagements, commitment to the cause, etc.) have to be understood not within the political structures of the countries where these mobilizations take place, but within the whole, interdependent complex of the Kurdish movement: they vary according to several interacting systems (relationships with the authorities, media and other mobilized groups, and internal relationships) that are not limited to the objectively present actors in a given interaction site" (2011, 182). In line with Grojean, I observed that the Kurdish movement functions similarly in Germany and France; accordingly, women with relationships to the PKK expressed similar political experiences in the two countries.

Russia, and Italy" (2000, 15). Although the Parliament is transnational in that it forms political alliances in multiple states to pressure the Turkish state, it initially had a national motivation insofar as it was defined as "a first step towards the creation of a National parliament," according to a PKK representative in Europe (Chris Kutschera, 1995, quoted in Keles 2015). In this respect, the Kurdish Parliament in Exile was a significant attempt to create a nonstate political structure to bring Kurds together across Europe and the Middle East. However, Kurdish women's participation and representation in Kurdish politics were limited at that time in both Turkey and Europe; less than 10 percent of the founding Kurdish Parliament members were women.

Besides the Kurdish Parliament in Exile, Kurds also began to form PKK-affiliated political associations (*dernekler* in Turkish) across Europe beginning in the early 1990s. These associations have provided spaces of community building and political mobilization for Kurdish migrants and refugees by organizing activities, such as courses in Kurdish, to strengthen political and communal ties. The associations have also enabled some Kurdish women to regularly leave their homes to form political alliances and social ties. For instance, Ayten, who has long been part of the diaspora political scene and worked recently in a leftist party in Germany, pointed to the role of Kurdish political associations in women's socialization as political activists:

> In the 1990s, the number of Kurds arriving in Europe increased significantly. In this period, the associations were important sources of socialization and politicization for women. People were coming to the Kurdish associations in huge numbers to get news about Turkey, but now they get news about the country from social media outlets. Now, these have also been replaced by social media outlets and the local assemblies.... And those people who were identified as *guest workers* in the past have started to be defined as *terrorists* since the events of 9/11. (emphasis added; ellipses indicate an omission)

Ayten identifies two major shifts in Kurds' mobilization in Europe. First, in the early 1990s, forced migration, village evacuations, and extrajudicial killings across the Kurdistan region left many Kurds with no choice but to migrate. Throughout this period, political associations significantly mobilized Kurdish women yet later lost their importance with the growth of virtual political activities through social media in the 2000s. Second, with the war on terror ongoing since 11 September 2001, Kurds' political activities in Europe have reinforced the perceptions of Kurds as a security issue there. In the early 1990s already, Turkey pushed Germany and France to ban the PKK as a terrorist organization; both countries also prosecuted many Kurdish political activists. Plus, the ban on the PKK has been used not only to criminalize pro-Kurdish political activities but also to stigmatize Kurds and control their mobility and political activities. Although European states grant refugee status to Kurds fleeing from oppression in Turkey, the PKK's "terrorist" status effectively restricts these same Kurds' political activities. In May 2002 the European Union also added the PKK to its list of terrorist organizations and individuals, citing the organization's "potential" to carry out violent actions, even though the PKK had officially renounced violence in 1999 (Ayata 2011, 148). The European Union's move caused Kurds living in European countries to be seen as "potential terrorism suspects" even if they were not affiliated with the PKK (Ayata 2011).

Ayata argues that the PKK's designation as a "terrorist" organization, first by Turkey and later by many European states, also affects scholarship on transnational Kurdish politics (2011, 150). She asserts that some works on the subject (e.g., Østergaard-Nielsen 2003) consciously omit the PKK within their discussions of Kurds' transnational advocacy networks because of its use of violent means to achieve its goals. Ayata critiques this silence, pointing out that "neither ethnically-based advocacy networks nor networks that incorporate organizations that use violence are treated as transnational advocacy networks" (2011, 150). Transnational advocacy networks are viewed as a category often restricted to organizations that do "good" policy work, particularly in the areas of the environment, women, and human rights (Ayata 2011, 150). Yet the tendency to write about "good" transnational advocacy networks leads to the invisibility of the political mobilization and agendas of those movements that pursue both violent and nonviolent means "as part of a larger grand strategy that seeks to effect political change by drawing on resources and opportunities at the level of the international system" (Adamson 2005, 37). Also central to counterterrorism discourses is the treatment of stateless and nomadic groups (particularly because of their mobility) potentially as terrorists and vice versa (see Porras 1994). It is therefore not only the employment of violence by the PKK but also the Kurds' very conditions of displacement and statelessness that render their political identity a "borderless threat" under the category of "terrorism." Nevertheless, many European states' ban on the PKK does not prevent Kurdish transnational political mobilization in Europe. Ayata observes that "the arrival of Kurdish refugees in Europe in the 1990s instigated a transnational mobilization that not only actively supported the Kurdish struggle in Turkey but also created a new space of political contestation in Europe" (2011, 6). This mobilization generated a new political space that she calls "Euro-Kurdistan" (6).

During a meeting I attended in Istanbul in 2014, the Kurdish activist Zeynep declared, "Kurdistan is a space where multiple ethnic, cultural, and religious identities exist. Kurdistan has not just been divided into four countries; in fact, the region has been divided into four parts—and even five and six parts with the diaspora." Zeynep imagines Kurdistan as a larger space, bridging the Middle East and Europe and bringing together Kurds living across borders. What connects Kurds living in these spaces is not merely their shared ethnic background but also their Kurdishness, a collective political identity that dissolves the differences between diaspora Kurds and those in Turkey and Kurdistan. This image of "Euro-Kurdistan" describes the two spaces as one geographical entity and reimagines Europe itself as part of Kurdistan in the Middle East, crossing the boundaries that historically, geographically, and epistemologically separate Europe and the Middle East and including diaspora Kurds in political struggle (Ayata 2011). Kurdistan, therefore, is not described solely as a geographical homeland for Kurds because it is not imagined in territorial terms. Its borders are continuously contested politically and epistemologically and are formed by political and nonpolitical groups in and beyond the Middle East.

The transnationalization of Kurds through their movement has created its own limitations and antinomies, however. Because the Kurdish movement has operated through transnational ties and networks, its political activities across territories have posed a perceived "transnational threat" to state structures, leading to increased control and regulation of movement activists' activities. For instance, Leyla from Germany indicated that although Europe was one of the main "arteries" for the Kurdish movement throughout the 1990s, its importance for Kurdish mobilization declined significantly after that. Kurdish activities in Europe were increasingly criminalized, whereas in Turkey the political environment became relatively peaceful in the mid-2000s. At this time, Kurdish local mobilization in Turkey's Kurdistan region has developed in line with Abdullah Öcalan's ideas of radical democracy.[7] However, although the Kurdish political imagination remains transnational, its demands and activities are shaped by the dynamics of local politics as well as of the national and global politics of counterterrorism.

Europe's shrinking role for the Kurdish movement has had a crucial effect on Kurdish women's political subjectivities and collective identity in Europe. These women feel themselves to be at the margins of Kurdish transnational politics, while their mobility is bounded by nation-states that constantly dictate what activity is forbidden and criminal. European authorities often limit and penalize Kurdish political activities, creating a major predicament for activist Kurdish women. Their political identity is an important part of who they are, yet their very survival in Europe is conditional on leaving their political identities behind. The next section examines the effects of this conundrum on women activists.

Exiles, Migrants, Refugees:
Kurdish Activist Women in Europe

My analysis in this section relies on nine months of multisited ethnographic research, including life-story interviews and participant observation in Germany and France. Both countries have hosted hundreds of thousands

---

7. According to the Kurdish movement, radical democracy as an idea could be practiced only through democratic autonomy, one of the main demands of the Kurdish movement during the peace process (2013–15). For further elaboration, see Akkaya and Jongerden 2012, 2013.

of Kurds,[8] from waves of migration mainly as workers in the 1960s and as political refugees in the 1970s and 1980s. I interviewed forty women political activists—twenty in Germany and twenty in France—who self-identify as Kurdish, are originally from Turkey's Kurdistan region, and are currently or were previously affiliated with the Kurdish movement. These women come from a range of class and family backgrounds.

There also exist politically active Kurdish women in Europe who work for different socialist and leftist groups but are not necessarily part of the Kurdish movement. However, for two reasons I chose to interview only women who are politically close to the PKK's ideology. First, that ideology has gone through a significant gender transformation (especially after the mid-1990s) because women have participated in the movement in large numbers as guerrillas, local and transnational activists, and politicians. The gender aspect of this particular ideology differentiates the Kurdish movement from other leftist organizations in Turkey and the diaspora. Second, when I searched for Kurdish women's organizations across Europe, I found that most of them were already affiliated with the Kurdish movement. Whenever I asked Kurdish women how they became politicized in Europe, they emphasized the PKK's significance as a mobilizing force, even when they did not personally identify with its ideology. Most characterized the transformation and increasing political visibility of Kurdish women as starting with the advent of the PKK.

During my nine months of research carried out over multiple trips to France and Germany between 2013 and 2015, in addition to the one-on-one interviews I held, I conducted ethnographic observations by dividing my time between women's associations and conferences and meetings organized by Kurdish women. I made regular visits to Kurdish associations and to women's associations in particular. I also spent time with Kurdish women in cafés and their homes and observed them and talked with them at conferences, protests, meetings, rallies, and marches. Based on these observations, I divide the political activities of Kurdish activist women

8. The Kurdish Institute of Paris has estimated the Kurdish population to be around 13,700,000 in Turkey, about 500,000 in Germany, and 100,000–120,000 in France (cited in Hassanpour and Mojab 2005, 214).

in Europe into two main categories. The first includes protests, demonstrations, and rallies organized by Kurdish women in various European countries. These activities often aim to create transnational solidarity networks to address issues of political violence and human rights violations toward Kurds. The second category includes events and meetings organized to provide language education, find employment, and improve living conditions and socialization. These activities aim at community development and well-being as well as at supporting Kurdish women with respect to everyday domestic issues, including sexual and gender-based violence within the family. Although Kurdish women's associations in Europe are fewer and more scattered geographically than those in Turkey and the Kurdistan region, they are modeled on the latter's organizational structures.

In analyzing the data, I am interested in the conditions under which the activist—the political subject—emerges and evolves in time and across space. To address this question, I focus on the particular moments, events, and turning points in Kurdish women's lives that have shaped their engagement or disengagement with politics. In the following subsections, I draw on the detailed stories of Kurdish women to examine the difficulties that politically active women encounter and the development of distinct, more liminal political subjectivities and activities in exile.

The Struggle of Being an Activist and a Revolutionary in Germany

PKK guerrillas hold an important place in the political socialization of Kurdish women I interviewed. Some activists had one or more guerrilla family members who were deceased, imprisoned, or alive in the mountains.[9] Many activist women expressed that they view the guerrilla woman as a political role model, the highest standard of being a revolutionary, and a model for a new, transformed form of existence (see also Göksel 2019). I

---

9. Being alive in the mountains means sustaining one's life as a guerrilla. "Going to the mountains" is generally used as an idiom for becoming a guerrilla.

would like to exemplify this form of existence through the story of Berivan, a political activist I met in one of the Kurdish women's associations in Germany. Berivan was a guerrilla from the late 1980s until the early 2000s. When she came to Germany, her life changed dramatically. The association where she worked was located in a small, secluded village and had been founded as a women's shelter to host women facing family and communal violence. The association's primary purpose was to provide women with temporary accommodation as well as legal and psychological counseling. On the weekends, feminist groups from various European countries came to visit the association and held meetings and workshops with the activists. Berivan was not only an ordinary activist of the women's movement but a member of the PKK political cadre, responsible for the control and regulation of party work in Germany. Berivan's transition from being a PKK guerrilla when she started her political journey in Kurdistan to being an activist and a member of the political cadre in Germany illustrates how her political subjectivity changed and multiplied over time. How did this change from guerrilla to activist alter Berivan's way of being and acting?

Berivan's experience as a guerrilla unearths all the contradictions involved in living up to the standard of the Kurdish movement. As a guerrilla, she had many conflicts with men and women comrades, and many times she questioned her decision to lead a militant life. However, as she narrated, despite all the difficulties she experienced throughout her guerrilla life, she never questioned the PKK's ideology. She committed herself to the party and to the standard life of a professional revolutionary. As part of this life, she first had to transform herself by breaking her ties with her family because the primary condition of being a revolutionary is detachment from family. For this reason, she did not see her family for long periods. Her way of being in the world was shaped by the code of conduct implemented by the party (see Çağlayan [2007] 2020 and Grojean 2011, 2014). She openly expressed that she did not know any other way of existing because she had been socialized as a revolutionary. In the process of transitioning to an activist lifestyle, Berivan had to adapt to the new codes of the activist world and juggled being a revolutionary and being an activist. One can say that in this process she entered into a phase of *resocialization*[10] through which she had to learn and adapt both to everyday life in Germany and to activism.

Few of the women I interviewed critiqued the revolutionary subjectivity that the PKK seeks to create. Meral was one of the few who did. I interviewed her as she sat under the large photo of her sister hanging on the wall in her Berlin residence. Her sister was a guerrilla and was killed in 2005. Unlike Berivan and Meral's sister, Meral never became a guerrilla, yet she had what she called "unbreakable" ties to the PKK through the memory of her fallen guerrilla sister. Although Meral might be considered less "ideologically committed" than Berivan, her narrative is embedded in a long family history of militancy. She said that she was a "full-time revolutionary" from the age of sixteen to twenty-one, engaging in Kurdish political activism by leaving her family home to work at one of the party associations in Germany. However, during those five years of activism, Meral was frequently subject to her comrades' critiques for lacking a "real" political and ideological attachment to the PKK. They thought she was in the PKK only because of her family connection to the organization. Meral also found difficult the conditions of being a political activist—that is, being away from her family and not having a stable home. A political activist is expected to cut all familial ties, refrain from marriage and love relationships (which potentially impede the activist's full-time commitment), as well as discipline himself or herself to keep healthy by abstaining from drinking and smoking (Grojean 2011, 188). Meral moved from place to place and worked in various Kurdish associations across Germany; she could not bear the lifestyle of an activist and was hospitalized for six months when she was twenty-one:

> I was sixteen years old, and I left my family behind. I did not have a stable home for a long time. I was far from my family. I stopped going to school. I had just finished tenth grade. . . . I was at the party [associations] twenty-four hours a day. I had many responsibilities. I became a *professional revolutionary*. At the age of sixteen, one is very young, . . . and I cannot stand for any injustices people did at the party. . . . Over

---

10. I borrow the concept of "resocialization" from Hamit Bozarslan, professor at L'école des hautes études en sciences sociales, personal communication to the author, May 2013.

time, I became more conscious about what was going on around me. . . . I began to question where I was and what I wanted to do in my life and where I wanted to live. I asked myself: What could an individual succeed at in five years [the duration of her activism from age sixteen to age twenty-one]? One could finish a university education in those five years. One could find a job, . . . right? (emphasis added; all ellipses except the first one indicate pauses in speech)

After leaving the hospital, Meral broke her ties with the PKK and started university. Even as she critiqued the requirements of the revolutionary lifestyle, she said that she still believed in the possibility of different political existences. She later reengaged with political activism by distancing herself from the baggage of her family's militancy. She expressed that this time she better understood the PKK's political agenda: "The PKK is a political party, but it is not just a party for us [Kurds]; it creates life. The word *party* is so narrow, then, and this word does not explain anything." Other interviewees also indicated that the PKK symbolizes many things about home, collectivity, and resistance. For many women, it provides meaning and resources for life—a framework to make sense of the world and function in it as well as a way to survive.

Berivan's and Meral's stories exemplify different stages and aspects of political socialization through which Kurdish women pass. Guerrillas and activists are socialized in particular ways as they relearn how to become revolutionaries in Europe. Even though the revolutionary code of conduct remains the same in Europe (including the strict regulations concerning alcohol consumption, romantic relationships, and dress codes) (Grojean 2011, 188), the life in exile indicates a new phase of "resocialization." I next discuss the resocialization processes that await politically active Kurdish women in Europe and how they navigate them in politics, family, and everyday life as migrants and exiles.

Two Women, Two Stories of "Return"

In terms of their migration and political histories, I had two main groups of interviewees in France and Germany. First, there were women belonging to the second generation of Kurds in Europe who have various family histories of migration and links to Kurdish and European politics and who can easily take action based on local and transnational ties thanks to their language skills and citizenship rights; and, second, there were Kurdish women with a long history of involvement in politics in Turkey and the Kurdistan region and who migrated to Europe as political refugees or took up a role in PKK organization. The stories of two politically well-known women illustrate the subject positions of these two groups.

Feleknas Uca, one of the most notable examples of the first group of Kurdish women, was born in Germany to a migrant Yezidi (Ezidi) family from Turkey's Kurdistan region. She became active in the Kurdish movement from a young age, acquired significant political experience, and became an elected representative of Germany at the European Parliament at the age of twenty-two before her election to the Turkish Parliament with the People's Democratic Party (Halkların Demokratik Partisi, HDP) in 2015.[11] Uca described herself as she first entered the European Parliament:

> I was wearing sneakers when I was first elected to Parliament. I was also wearing comfortable clothes. I couldn't even imagine the Parliament building before I saw it. Suddenly, I found myself in this huge building, encircled by large windows. I just stood inside the building. I looked like a child next to my colleagues; most of them were male and relatively older than me. After that, a group of parliamentary representatives came to me and said, "We may come from different political backgrounds, but we can help you with anything." The experience of working with these people was very nice because although we have

---

11. Immediately after the elections in June 2015, the situation changed in Turkey, and the "relatively democratic" environment and peace process gave way to war, violence, and the political repression of Kurds and all oppositional groups by the Turkish state. Not only did violence and war intensify, but many women parliamentarians, cochairs of municipalities in the Kurdish cities, and activists were prosecuted under terrorism charges. Uca is among those parliamentarians who was taken into custody and put on trial for terrorism. Although she was released after being arrested in 2017, her trial is ongoing.

different political opinions, we approached each other politely. (interview in Doğan and Güzel 2015)

Uca felt like a "foreigner" in European politics and the European Parliament owing not only to her young age and lack of experience but also to her appearance and ethnic origin. Although her multiple identities of being German, Kurdish, and Yezidi made Uca a foreigner in the European Parliament, she still had political leverage there to voice the atrocities and violence Kurds had experienced for decades. As Ayata notes, Kurds in Europe function as "the paradigmatic Other" of the Turkish state in that diasporas in general are seen as the most typical, visible others of nation-states (2011, 31–32), yet Kurds still have the political tools to critique and challenge the nation-state structure (see Tölölyan 1991). In this respect, although Kurds have been the others of nation-states in many ways, their involvement in European politics provides them a space to enable the recognition of the long-standing atrocities against them and to raise the profile of the Kurdish struggle in Europe. For instance, Feleknas Uca was one of the first speakers in the European Parliament to note the violence, war, displacement, and other atrocities against Kurds and to promote the public recognition of Kurdish identity. Although most Kurdish women I interviewed have had only limited involvement with the French and German political spheres, the second-generation, politically active Kurdish women such as Uca are the ones most likely to be participants in those spheres as they confront the European public with the violence and war in Turkey.

Uca's experience illustrates the changes that Kurdish politics underwent in the 2000s. First, in the years following the capture of Abdullah Öcalan in 1999, the Kurdish movement's political goals shifted toward the ideal of democratic autonomy in the Middle East. This change catalyzed the localization and decentralization of Kurdish politics. The relative democratization in Turkey in the 2010s helped reduce the amount of direct state repression of Kurdish political expression,[12] allowed Kurds

---

12. The 1990s in Kurdistan were marked by intense conditions of war and human rights violations, including forced displacements, political assassinations, state-perpetrated sexual violence, torture, enforced disappearances, village evacuations, and

in Turkey and Kurdistan to mobilize in local and national politics, and instigated a "reverse" migration. This relative democratization in Turkey in the 2010s and the temporary peace process between the Turkish state and the PKK led Kurdish women born and raised in Europe, Uca among them, to relocate to Turkey to participate in local and electoral politics. Uca's return to Turkey was not technically a "return" to her homeland but rather a risky journey to the unknown. In fact, immediately after the elections of June 2015, the political situation abruptly changed for the worse in Turkey. Many Kurdish politicians, including parliamentarians such as Uca, cochairs of municipalities, and activists were prosecuted and imprisoned under terrorism charges.

Kurdish women in exile in Europe often occupy a fragile position unless they were born and raised there. Life in exile brings many constraints to their everyday mobility and political activities. The story of Sozdar, a PKK guerrilla, exemplifies the sense of entrapment and *illegal*

---

more. Whenever the Turkish state felt that legal repression of Kurds was not enough, it turned to more coercive measures. In this context, as Hamit Bozarslan states, human rights violations "became a part of the state's everyday coercive praxis" (2001, 50). According to some members of human rights organizations I talked to in Istanbul and Diyarbakir, the visible and directly violent techniques of the 1990s saw a relative decline in the mid-2000s and gave way to more subtle and psychological forms of violence. In the summer of 2004, the PKK declared a unilateral cease-fire, and then in 2007 democratic autonomy was defined as its main political goal (Ercan 2013). In 2005 the Justice and Development Party (Adalet ve Kalkınma Partisi, AKP), the ruling party in Turkey, hesitantly accepted the existence of a Kurdish issue and initiated the process of "democratic opening." Along with this move, the AKP government allocated limited cultural rights, such as TV broadcasts in Kurdish in 2004 (Ercan 2013, 116). However, no constitutional or legal framework formally supported these changes. They were followed by the "peace" or "reconciliation" process from 2013 to 2015, which created a relatively "democratic" environment. Even during that time, though, Kurdish political activities were still the target of the Turkish state's "terrorism" measures. It is worth noting that immediately after I finished my research in 2015, there was a return to war conditions in Turkey and a dramatic increase in human rights violations. The temporary period of peace suddenly gave way to antidemocratic measures, an escalation of state violence, conditions of war, and the declaration of curfews and states of emergency both in the Kurdistan region and across Turkey.

liminality experienced by Kurdish women in Europe, as vividly captured in the documentary *Sozdar, She Who Lives Her Promise* (Annegriet Wietsma, 2007).[13] Sozdar had first migrated to Germany with her family when she was twelve. As her mother explains in the documentary, the family had to abandon their land and property in Kurdistan due to pressures from the Turkish state authorities. When Sozdar arrived in Germany, her life changed dramatically. Two incidents in particular fundamentally shaped her future self. First, her family wanted her to enter into an arranged marriage. Rejecting her family's wishes for the first time was not easy, but it became an important turning point for Sozdar's subject formation, indicating to her the possibility and value of autonomy.[14] Second, Sozdar witnessed the Halabja massacre on TV, when thousands of Kurds were killed with chemical weapons by Iraqi forces as part of the ongoing genocidal campaign in Iraqi Kurdistan in 1988. This massacre prompted Sozdar to become conscious of her Kurdish identity and of the violence against Kurds in their homeland and eventually to become a PKK guerrilla. Witnessing violence was a prime instigator of the politicization of many of the Kurdish women I interviewed.

In the opening scene of the documentary, we see Sozdar leave the mountains of Kurdistan to travel to the Netherlands in 2001, soon after 11 September, to communicate the PKK's new political agendas regarding many topics, from women's emancipation to the political conditions of Kurds living in Europe. Upon setting foot in the Netherlands, however, Sozdar is captured at the Schiphol Airport and arrested as an "undesirable alien" because she is holding a fake passport. Turkey requests her immediate extradition, which the Netherlands denies at the behest of the United

---

13. This documentary is available to view at https://vimeo.com/104315712.

14. As also laid out in note 15, most of the interviewees expressed that their families, as feudal and traditional structures, controlled and regulated their behaviors as women. For many Kurdish women, their political mobilization is a route to liberate themselves from family obligations such as marriage. For the PKK as well, it has been fundamental to cut youths' ties with these feudal and traditional relations, a tactic that would in turn enlarge the ground of revolutionary mobilization. For further discussion, see Çağlayan [2007] 2020.

Nations. After spending three years in prison, Sozdar is released with a "temporary exception order with a duty to report [to the police] every fortnight." However, she has no legal status or identification papers or residence rights because her asylum request is rejected by the Dutch government. Thus, the obligation of judicial control makes it impossible for her either to stay legally in the Netherlands or to leave the country. Later, as a result of a Dutch investigation, she is declared to be "persona non grata," an *unwelcome person*, in all Schengen countries until 2016.

In the documentary, Sozdar identifies herself as a "freedom fighter for women's rights." She finds it unbelievable that she has been labeled "the most dangerous woman in Europe." Kurds see her as a revolutionary, the Turkish state calls her a terrorist, and the Dutch state sees her as a criminal and an exile. Her situation epitomizes the liminal existence of migrants living in "uncertain legality," which turns them into "transitional beings" (Menjívar 2006), who are, in Victor Turner's eloquent words, "neither one thing or another; or maybe both; or neither here nor there; or maybe nowhere . . . and are at the very least 'betwixt and between' all the recognized fixed points in space–time of structural classification" (1967, 96, quoted in Menjívar 2006, 1007). This transitional and in-between existence is imbued with the potential for social and political transformation as well as for uncertainty and loss of power (Menjívar 2006, 1007). In the case of Sozdar, she lives on an uncertain (il)legal ground marked by the intertwined definitions of terrorist, criminal, and exile. Sozdar's exile in the Netherlands also brings back all of the memories of her youth in Germany, and she feels stifled with a stark sense of alienation and vulnerability. As Sozdar repeatedly stresses in the documentary, she does not want to stay in Europe, where her life has turned into an existential and political crisis.

Whereas Uca's transnational and transborder mobility gives her a political advantage, Sozdar's transnational mobility is constrained by her condition of exile. For Sozdar and many other exiled women, the Kurdish movement's political imagination is centered on Kurdistan. This political imagination necessarily involves a desire for "return." But, for them, Kurdistan is not just a geographic region populated by Kurds, nor is it simply where the ideal of home exists somewhere far away. Rather, it is a political and social imaginary that could include one's residence in Europe. For Sozdar, exile in Europe is not a matter of detachment from home; as she notes, neither Turkey nor Europe nor even the geographical location of Kurdistan (until it is "liberated") can be seen as her homeland. Her main concern is her feeling of being uprooted from her political and collective ties in her exile life. In this vein, Sozdar's narrative shows that the ideal of returning home is focused not just on the existence and acknowledgment of Kurdish identity and Kurdistan but also on a desire to exist and to act politically.

The Threat of Depoliticization and Cultural Assimilation

Despite the ban on the PKK, Europe provided a relatively "safe" space for Kurds in the 1990s. Living in Europe opened up new political avenues for Kurdish women to participate in both European and Kurdish politics. However, for some refugee women who moved to Europe as political exiles later in life, Europe has also imposed constraints on their physical mobility and political actions. In Europe, refugee women experience ongoing strife between their past and present lives and subjectivities. This strife can result in crises and conflicts that ultimately alienate and marginalize these women in the Kurdish movement.

The everyday struggles of Kurdish women as migrants and refugees in Europe go hand in hand with their struggles to become the revolutionary subjects they hope to be. As documented earlier, living in Europe produces a constant state of liminality for activist Kurdish women, between being migrants/exiles and being political agents. The label *terrorism* in particular functions as a social and political stigma, creating a sense of liminality because it produces a state of precariousness for Kurdish women faced with the risk of deportation or imprisonment. Like Sozdar, many activist women operate within this tenuous realm of being deemed terrorists or criminals and/or migrants or exiles. Although both Kurdish men and women might experience this sense of liminality, women experience it differently. In Turkey and Kurdistan, the collective support provided by other Kurdish women often gives women the strength to handle conflicts with men inside and outside the home and facilitates their political participation. In Europe, in the absence of such support from other women, Kurdish women in Europe may feel constrained to the domestic sphere. Relying on men in their families for survival in a foreign country, they are devoid of the collectivity and bonding among Kurdish women that have been at the core of their political activities and subjectivities.

Most Kurdish women I interviewed in Germany and France said that because they were struggling to survive as migrants and refugees in Europe, they felt they were falling behind Kurdish women activists and guerrillas in Kurdistan, for whom they expressed admiration. They felt "insufficient" and "belated" in comparison to their counterparts back home. Many women acknowledged that these feelings of "lacking" and "insufficiency" might result in self-questioning or total separation from politics. The Kurdish activist women with whom I talked (especially those who had not been politically active in Turkey and/or Kurdistan) said that the most obvious threats to women's politicization in Europe are assimilation and depoliticization. For them, assimilation into European culture threatens their political identity and leads to political demobilization. Serpil, who migrated to France at a young age, explained this threat:

> We live in *a capitalist system* in Europe. So the degree of freedom is different here, and how the pressures and events in Kurdistan have affected Kurds here are significant questions because there are newly formed identities in Europe, like French Kurdish and French Turkish identities. . . . For instance, in the 1960s the atmosphere in France was very political. Later on, French people went through a serious process of depoliticization, and this atmosphere has affected French Kurdish people, too. We can say that we need to do something about Kurdistan, but this need isn't that pressing here, . . . [and] *this struggle in Kurdistan is also a struggle for our freedom in Europe.* But Kurds here don't really realize this, and the younger generations don't understand this urgency, I think. (emphasis added; ellipses indicate omissions)

As Serpil stated, everyday life in Europe is more intensely encircled by the capitalist system and its relations than it is in Turkey—thus bringing a higher risk of assimilation and a decline in Kurdish collective identity and political mobilization. Serpil raised issues of the emergence of hybrid identities, such as "French Kurdish," and Kurds' growing detachment from the Kurdish struggle for freedom. Abdullah Öcalan also discusses this process in many accounts (including Öcalan 2020), addressing "Western" modernity and the capitalist subject it produces (seen as apolitical, marginalized, and "corrupt") as major obstacles to the PKK's revolutionary goals. According to him, the capitalist subject prioritizes individual desires and freedom over the collective will and in so doing conflicts with the Kurdish movement's framing of freedom as a collective will. Moreover, the idea of "sexual freedom" and sexual liberation, perceived as the core characteristic of European capitalist, modernist society, is defined as a "false sense of freedom" in many of Öcalan's writings (see, e.g., Öcalan 2020, 294–30). For Öcalan, women's freedom lies in their commitment to and participation in the political struggle. Many Kurdish women I talked to echoed this belief that they can attain freedom only through their work for the PKK, and so they subsume their individual will to the collective will of the Kurdish political movement (see also Hakyemez 2016; Özcan 2006). In their view, following Öcalan's accounts, freedom—the foundation of an equal and peaceful society—is possible only if the society is divorced from patriarchal, capitalist relationships of power and from the centralized state power.

For Kurdish refugee women, especially former PKK members, life in Europe carries the risk of not only depoliticization but also a loss of status. The admiration and respect that their political commitment won them—especially as they risked imprisonment and death in Turkey and Kurdistan—are often replaced in Europe by pity, if not criminalization, precipitating a crushing sense of worthlessness. However, the women refugees who had higher-level status in the PKK, such as Sozdar, maintain a certain level of recognition and political leverage among Kurds in Europe, which helps them establish political connections with Kurds across borders and with transnational women's and political organizations in Europe. For many former PKK members and other activist women, though, this rupture between their past experiences and present lives often results in life crises, which I examine in the following subsection.

Subjectivity in Crisis: "Return" to the Family

Squeezed between the past and present, many women refugees have a hard time finding a place in European politics. They experience a deep existential crisis, questioning not only the condition of their lives in Europe but also their past commitments. "Staying at home" and "returning to the family" are among the main factors that distance women from political engagement in Europe. As shown by the story of the former guerrilla and now activist Berivan, severing one's ties with one's family is an essential part of becoming a revolutionary subject. When the women members of the PKK come to Europe as refugees, they might in the absence of their political community embrace familial roles by marrying and having children—even though they consider this a "step backward" in their political and personal development. However, this return to familial life under the harsh conditions of exile and migration ironically creates isolation and loneliness. As one of my interviewees, Rojda, explains, "I think that no women here would want to remain outside the political atmosphere consciously. When they stay outside of politics, they get lonelier, and they're stuck in their homes. They then become really weak and defenseless."

In an interview, the former guerrilla Nalîn described the experience of becoming a mother as a loss of the sense of collectivity (Bingöl 2016, 34). She felt that family life displaced the greater and sacred meaning of her life as a guerrilla and replaced it with the "smaller" goal of raising a family (Bingöl 2016, 34). For many interviewees, marriage and children provide an escape from the daily loneliness of refugee and migrant life but also deepen their alienation from politics and can involve feelings of oppression. In her study of the Kurdish diaspora in Sweden, Minoo Alinia similarly states: "Women construct home and homeland communities as familiar places that offer security and stability, yet they are aware of the gender oppression that makes up 'home'" (2004, 621). Although my interviewees often view the home as a secure site against the insecurities of migrant and exile life, they also talked about the relations of domination in the family. For instance, one interviewee said that because the Kurdish women's movement is more dispersed, less visible, and less effective in the diaspora than in Turkey and Kurdistan, feudal[15] and patriarchal inequalities predominantly shape the relations among Kurds in the diaspora, contributing to the major differences between men's and women's experiences of migrant and refugee life. Further, politically active Kurdish men in Europe are more able and likely to constrain the behaviors of their daughters, wives, and sisters than they were in Turkey and Kurdistan. As my interviewees explained, these men find the outside world and its unfamiliarity particularly threatening to the integrity of the family. Women, spending most of their time on domestic duties, find it difficult to defy men's rule in the family. I also observed during fieldwork that most PKK meeting sites and cafés are located in the central parts of cities, far from the neighborhoods where most Kurdish women live. These parts of cities are populated mostly by men and are not welcoming to women. Some women complained that even men who embrace the PKK ideology do not allow their wives to visit those spaces due to the overriding male presence there. This male dominance, as Alinia explains, is related to how some men and women see those party spaces as "public spaces for men" (2004, 300). But women's absence from those spaces does not necessarily mean that women are less politically engaged than men (304). Many women raise this issue to critique the PKK's organizational structure.

The issue here concerns more than the demobilization and political marginalization of Kurdish women. As Rojda and many other women I interviewed noted, women who lose their political attachments may also lose their ties with the Kurdish community. Feelings of loneliness and despair become prevalent in their lives. Rojda added that women in Turkey and Kurdistan are more likely to have other support networks outside

---

15. The term *feudal* refers to a system of land ownership and distribution, a form of land economy prevalent in the Kurdistan region. Those feudal relations produce a particular gender regime that relies on the regulation and control of women's bodies and lives through a code of honor. That is to say, whenever women refer to "feudal" relations, they are not referring to land ownership but to the masculine domination that the system produces. When Kurdish men migrate to Europe, as expressed by many interviewees, they may hold on to those feudal values to control women in their lives.

of their political networks, so they can establish relationships easily with family members and neighbors there. In Europe, where these women have no preexisting familial or community relations, maintaining their connection with the Kurdish political community may be the only way to maintain ties with Kurdistan. But as my interviewees emphasized, preserving both relations with the Kurdish community as well as a revolutionary identity is difficult to achieve in the diaspora.

In this context, some women have chosen to detach from their political engagements completely and return to the family. Fears of living a "bourgeois life" and of being assimilated into European culture are prevalent among many. Although some said they have been able to strike a balance between their migrant lives and their political activities, they also described their life in Europe as one of precarity and despair.

Conclusion

In this chapter, I have examined how activist Kurdish women constitute and negotiate their political subjectivities and actions within a transnational social and political setting; how they navigate their daily lives and family relations; and how they engage in politics while struggling with the economic, social, and political effects of migration and exile. Examining these questions led me to conclude that for Kurdish women in Europe, politics is not just a way to create international support and advocacy networks. It is also a form of everyday sociability, connecting women with the Kurdish community across Europe and in Kurdistan. I have shown that politically active Kurdish women experience two fundamental tensions within the context of migrant/exile life.

The first tension is the impossibility of living in line with the Kurdish revolutionary imagination and mobilization while away from the people of Kurdistan, whom the movement seeks to emancipate. Moreover, Kurdish women also see living in Europe as a challenge to their politics because of the risks of "assimilation" into mainstream society and "criminalization" by European states. The social and political setting in Europe generates a state of "liminal legality" (Menjívar 2006) for Kurdish women.

Although many Kurdish women take refuge on the continent to escape imprisonment based on terrorism charges in Turkey, they are also vulnerable to similar charges in Europe if they act on their political engagement with the PKK. Their legality in exile is contingent on their breaking ties with the organization.

Second, Kurdish women face an ongoing tension between political and familial spheres. Although there has always been a tension between women's familial and political identities and obligations, and even though the family has been a major source of mobilization for the Kurds in the diaspora, the lack of communal ties in Europe leaves women more engulfed in the familial space, which creates further tension between their political ambitions and family constraints. For women Kurdish activists, being a migrant, getting married, and having children seem like steps backward in their political lives because they see the family as the locus of the very patriarchal and feudal relations that they seek to transform through their politics. Nevertheless, in the diaspora, marrying and having children become means of survival and protection from the uncertainty of exiled and migrant lives.

In conclusion, some Kurdish women respond to the conditions of migration and exile by holding onto their politics. Many others feel the limitations that their liminal situation imposes on their political activities. Although Europe opens up new ground for Kurdish women to become politicized, it also subjects them to different politics and codes of living that can fundamentally challenge their existing political subjectivities. Kurdish women in Europe strive to transgress the national borders of both European and Turkish politics, yet their mobility is constrained by the sovereignty of nation-states, the surveillance and criminalization of Kurdish political identity across borders, and the restrictions created by the following of patriarchal norms. In turn, Kurdish women's political positionalities in Europe become displaced and reconfigured, and sustaining their political affiliations becomes an existential battle. Therefore, at a time when conditions are uncertain for these and other migrant women in Europe, this chapter sheds light on the ways that women living within the liminal legality of migrant life nevertheless constitute political selves.

Acknowledgments

I thank the editors of this volume, Ayça Alemdaroğlu and Fatma Müge Göçek, as well as all the participants in the Historical and Comparative Perspectives on Kurdish Politics conference at Northwestern University in 2016 for a very lively and insightful discussion. I also thank Héctor Carrillo, Imge Oranlı, Nurseli Yeşim Sünbüloğlu, Caroline McKusick, and Serra Hakyemez for commenting on earlier drafts of this chapter and offering their very valuable feedback. I am thankful to Ann Shola Orloff for her support and insightful comments and for organizing the feminist/gender writing group and to my colleagues in that group—Natalia Forrat, Elizabeth Onasch, Savina Balasubramanian, Jane Pryma, Talia Shiff, and Marie Laperriere—for their valuable feedback on the chapter. This work was supported by the Sciences Po–Northwestern University Visiting and Research Fellowship and Northwestern University Graduate Research Grant.

References

Adamson, Fiona. 2002. "Mobilizing for the Transformation of Home: Politicized Identities and Transnational Practices." In *New Approaches to Migration? Transnational Communities and the Transformation of Home*, edited by Nadje Al-Ali and Khalid Koser, 155–69. London: Routledge.

———. 2005. "Globalisation, Transnational Political Mobilisation, and Networks of Violence." *Cambridge Review of International Affairs* 18, no. 1: 31–49.

Akkaya, Ahmet Hamdi. 2013. "Kurdish Diaspora: A New Subject Formation in Transnational Space." In *Perspectives on Kurdistan's Economy and Society in Transition*, edited by Alan Dilani and Serwan M. J. Baban, 109–21. Newcastle, UK: Cambridge Scholars.

Akkaya, Ahmet Hamdi, and Joost Jongerden. 2012. "Reassembling the Political: The PKK and the Project of Radical Democracy." *European Journal of Turkish Studies* 14:1–18.

———. 2013. "Confederalism and Autonomy in Turkey: The Kurdistan Workers' Party and the Reinvention of Democracy." In *The Kurdish Question in Turkey: New Perspectives on Violence, Representation, and Reconciliation*, edited by Cengiz Gunes and Welat Zeydanlıoğlu, 186–205. London: Routledge.

Alinia, Minoo. 2004. "Spaces of Diasporas: Kurdish Identities, Experiences of Otherness, and Politics of Belonging." PhD diss., Göteborg Univ.

Ayata, Bilgin. 2011. "The Politics of Displacement: A Transnational Analysis of the Forced Migration of Kurds in Turkey and Europe." PhD diss., Johns Hopkins Univ.

Başer, Bahar. 2013. *Diasporada Türk-Kürt sorunu: Almanya ve İsveç'te ıkinci kuşak göçmenler* [The Turkish-Kurdish Question in Diaspora: Second-Generation Migrants in Germany and Sweden]. Istanbul: Iletişim Yayınları.

———. 2015. *Diasporas and Homeland Conflicts: A Comparative Perspective.* New York: Routledge.

Bingöl, Berivan. 2016. *Bizim gizli bir hikayemiz var: Dağdan anneliğe kadınlar* [We Have a Hidden Story: Women from the Mountains to Motherhood]. Istanbul: Iletişim Yayınları.

Bozarslan, Hamit. 2001. "Human Rights and the Kurdish Issue in Turkey: 1984–1999." *Human Rights Review* 3, no. 1: 45–54.

Çağlayan, Handan. [2007] 2020. *Women in the Kurdish Movement: Mothers, Comrades, Goddesses.* Translated by Simten Coşar. Houndmills, UK: Palgrave Macmillan.

Castles, Stephen. 2003. "Towards a Sociology of Forced Migration and Social Transformation." *Sociology* 37, no. 1: 13–34.

Demir, Ipek. 2012. "Battling with Memleket in London: The Kurdish Diaspora's Engagement with Turkey." *Journal of Ethnic and Migration Studies* 38, no. 5: 815–31.

Desai, Manisha. 2005. "Transnationalism: The Face of Feminist Politics Post-Beijing." *International Social Science Journal* 184:319–30.

Doğan, Zehra, and Şeyma Güzel. 2015. "Feleknas Uca: Meclis'tekilere Kürtçeyi öğreteceğiz" [Feleknas Uca: We Will Teach Kurdish to Those in Parliament]. Interview. *Jinha*, 5 May.

Ercan, Harun. 2013. "Talking to the Ontological Other: Armed Struggle and the Negotiations between the Turkish State and the PKK." *Dialectical Anthropology* 37, no. 1: 113–22.

Ferree, Myra M., and Aili M. Tripp, eds. 2006. *Global Feminism: Transnational Women's Activism, Organizing, and Human Rights.* New York: New York Univ. Press.

Göksel, Nisa. 2015. "Ulus-Ötesinde *öteki* politik özneler: Avrupa'da Kürt kadınlarının siyasi, toplumsal ve kültürel mücadeleleri" [Other Political

Subjectivities in a Transnational Space: Kurdish Women's Political, Social, and Cultural Struggles in Europe]. *Modus Operandi* 3:11–45.

———. 2019. "Gendering Resistance: Multiple Faces of the Kurdish Women's Struggle." *Sociological Forum* 34, no. 1: 1112–31.

Grojean, Olivier. 2011. "Bringing the Organization Back In: Pro-Kurdish Protest in Europe." In *Nationalisms and Politics in Turkey: Political Islam, Kemalism, and the Kurdish Issue*, edited by Marlies Casier and Joost Jongerden, 182–97. London: Routledge.

———. 2014. "The Production of the New Man within the PKK." *European Journal of Turkish Studies* (online only). At https://journals.openedition.org/ejts/4925. A translation of "La production de l'Homme nouveau au sein du PKK." *European Journal of Turkish Studies* 8 (2008).

Hakyemez, M. Serra. 2016. "Lives and Times of Militancy: Terrorism Trials, State Violence, and Kurdish Political Prisoners in Post-1980 Turkey." PhD diss., Johns Hopkins Univ.

Hardy-Fanta, Carol. 1993. *Latina Politics, Latino Politics: Gender, Culture, and Political Participation in Boston*. Philadelphia: Temple Univ. Press.

Hassanpour, Amir, and Shahrzad Mojab. 2005. "Kurdish Diaspora." In *Encyclopedia of Diasporas: Immigrant and Refugee Cultures around the World*, edited by Melvin Ember, Carol R. Ember, and Ian Skoggard, 214–24. New York: Springer.

Jones-Correa, Michael. 1998. "Different Paths: Gender, Immigration, and Political Participation." *International Migration Review* 32, no. 2: 326–49.

Keck, Margaret, and Kathryn Sikkink. 1998. *Activists beyond Borders: Advocacy Networks in International Politics*. Ithaca, NY: Cornell Univ. Press.

Keles, Janroj Y. 2015. *Media, Diaspora, and Conflict: Nationalism and Identity amongst Turkish and Kurdish Migrants in Europe*. London: I. B. Tauris.

Khayati, Khalid. 2008. "From Victim Diaspora to Transborder Citizenship? Diaspora Formation and Transnational Relations among Kurds in France and Sweden." PhD diss., Linköping Univ.

Menjívar, Cecilia. 2006. "Liminal Legality: Salvadoran and Guatemalan Immigrants' Lives in the United States." *AJS* 111, no. 4: 999–1037.

Moghadam, M. Valentine. 2005. *Globalizing Women: Transnational Feminist Networks*. Baltimore: Johns Hopkins Univ. Press.

Öcalan, Abdullah. 2020. *The Sociology of Freedom: Manifesto of the Democratic Civilization*. Vol. 3. Oakland, CA: PM Press.

Østergaard-Nielsen, Eva. 2003. *Transnational Politics: Turks and Kurds in Germany*. London: Routledge.

Özcan, Ali Kemal. 2006. *Turkey's Kurds: A Theoretical Analysis of the PKK and Abdullah Öcalan*. London: Routledge.

Parreñas, Rhacel S. 2000. "Migrant Filipina Domestic Workers and the International Division of Reproductive Labor." *Gender & Society* 14, no. 4: 560–80.

Porras, Ileana. 1994. "On Terrorism: Reflections on Violence and the Outlaw." *Utah Law Review* 119:119–46.

Risse-Kappen, Thomas, Steve C. Ropp, and Kathryn Sikkink. 1999. *The Power of Human Rights: International Norms and Domestic Change*. Cambridge: Cambridge Univ. Press.

Salih, Ruba. 2013. *Gender in Transnationalism: Home, Longing, and Belonging among Moroccan Migrant Women*. London: Routledge.

Spitzer, Denise, Anne Neufeld, Margaret Harrison, Karen Hughes, and Miriam Stewart. 2003. "Caregiving in Transnational Context: 'My Wings Have Been Cut; Where Can I Fly?'" *Gender & Society* 17, no. 2: 267–86.

Tölölyan, Khachig. 1991. "The Nation and Its Others: In Lieu of a Preface." *Diaspora* 1, no. 1: 3–7.

Turner, Victor. 1967. *The Forest of Symbols: Aspects of Ndembu Ritual*. Ithaca, NY: Cornell Univ. Press.

Van Bruinessen, Martin. 1998. "Shifting National and Ethnic Identities: The Kurds in Turkey and the European Diaspora." *Journal of Muslim Minority Affairs* 18, no. 1: 39–52.

———. 2000. "Transnational Aspects of the Kurdish Question." Working paper, Robert Schuman Centre for Advanced Studies, European Univ. Institute, Florence, Italy.

Van Hear, Nicholas. 2006. "'I Went as Far as My Money Would Take Me': Conflict, Forced Migration, and Class." In *Forced Migration and Global Processes: A View from Forced Migration Studies*, edited by François Crépeau, Delphine Nakache, Michael Collyer, Nathaniel H. Goetz, Art Hansen, Renu Modi, Aninia Nadig, et al., 125–59. Lanham, MD: Lexington Books.

Afterword

Hamit Bozarslan

The ambition of this edited volume is to come to a deeper understanding of the lives of Kurds, of the very conditions of being, surviving, struggling, and dreaming oneself as a Kurd. Beyond its strictly social scientific goals, however, the volume also launches an invitation; put more strongly, it formulates an imperative that conditions the very existence of both the "agora" and academia: thought. Thinking about and thinking of something or someone do not formulate the ultimate Cartesian proof of the existence of someone as a human being, however. Still: in a country such as Turkey, being able to think has become a precondition for preserving one's cognitive faculties and being a member of the res publica.

For many years, in fact, one observes in Turkey an Orwellian style of destruction of the very capacity of making sense of life and the world. No one in Turkey can do this across time and space: no one is able to read her/his past, consider the present as a meaningful time–space framework, and project her/himself in the future. This process of annihilation goes so far that the regime ultimately ends up destroying the internal memory as well as the decisional rationality it needs to stabilize itself. Like some totalitarian experiences of the past, what could be termed "Erdoganism" (named after Turkey's current president, Recep Tayyip Erdoğan) is a regime of perpetual movement, surviving thanks to a vertiginous succession of internal and external, often artificial or deliberately unleashed but unmastered crises. Although largely nonreflexive, this "social engineering" developed by Erdoganism throughout the past couple of years makes it impossible to build a shared memory on the basis of a limited but meaningful number of events, with continuity of some dynamics in some and advent of ruptures in others.

In a country where the members and partisans of Fethullah Gülen are officially named FETÖ, the Fethullah Terrorist Organization (Fetullahçı Terör Örgütü), who still remembers that only a couple of years ago criticism of this Muslim Opus Dei leader would have cost years of prison to any dissident intellectual? Under a regime where the themes of war, "terrorism," and "national survival" were constantly chanted, who still remembers which country was a foe and which a friend? And who could predict which one of the former foes (Israel, Iran, Iraq, Syria, Russia, Saudi Arabia, United Arab Emirates, United States, Germany, Netherlands, Austria, Greece, Armenia, France ...) would turn into a friend or "enemy number 1" in the foreseeable future? Who still remembers that only a couple of years ago in Turkey, Numan Kurtuluş and Süleyman Soylu, who today constantly express their readiness to die for Erdoğan, once proffered unpronounceable insults against him? Who will still dare quote Erdoğan's official discourse of peace on the Kurdish issue in 2013–14 without the risk of spending years in jail? As Hannah Arendt argued and as Viktor Klemperer, Theodor Adorno, Ernst Bloch, Karl Kraus, and the like then underlined, under some historical conditions, interpreting and criticizing decisions and orientations that a government or a society takes become an imperative of survival and an imperative to preserve one's cognitive faculties—that is, the very capacity of making sense of the world.

As the volume editors, Ayça Alemdaroğlu and Fatma Müge Göçek, note, to preserve one's capacity to make sense of what is happening in Turkey in these dark times, it is imperative to take the responsibility to "think" about the Kurds as a defense against the darkness of their oppression, torture, killing, and constant experiences of discrimination and stigmatization. It is imperative to document and communicate their struggle, dreams, hopes, experiences, narratives, subjectivities transmitted temporally and spatially from one generation to another, from Kurdish-inhabited areas in the East to the Kurdish neighborhoods in Istanbul and in diaspora. Whether by peaceful means of resistance or by violence, the Kurdish struggle has always aimed at the abrogation of the "Kurdish *question*" by achieving equal rights of citizenship and/or local autonomy or autonomies in the Kurdish regions of Turkey. The very existence of the Kurdish *question* as a *question* has always been intrinsically linked to the status of the Kurds as a de facto (but not a de jure) minority—that is, as a group that has been reduced to the status of a "minority" as a consequence of the power-building processes in Turkey.

Defining Kurds as a "minority" group has indeed nothing to do with their demographic weight: as Kurdish activists constantly underline (sometimes vehemently), they are not a minority group but an overwhelming majority in their own territory. Nevertheless, Kurds in Turkey constitute a "minority" in the Kantian sense in three ways. First, they are deprived of the juridical and political equality that would allow them access to majority status to act as subjects in control of their own destiny, take their decisions freely, and feel responsible for their deeds. Second, they are deprived of the right to "punish themselves[,] their own criminals," as "other nations" do[1]—in other words to have sovereign authority. Third, it is a truism that for Kurds, as for any other "national minority," becoming "a major force" means having the right to and developing the capacity of reading *their* past, evaluating *their* present time and the constraints it imposes and the opportunities it offers, as well as elaborating their own imaginary concerning *their* future. This Kantian emancipation from minority status also means overcoming the status of "the object" that has been imposed upon them by the majority as well as disabling the symbolic violence entailed in how they are defined as "feudal," "terrorist," "separatist," "agents of imperialism," and the like (Vali 1998).

The processes of moving from the condition of being the "object" to being the "subject" has tremendous impact in the Kurdish case as well as in the case of any minoritized and/or reified group, including slaves and their descendants, women, sectarian groups such Baha'is and Yazidis, and LGBTQ communities. The incredible vivacity with which Kurdish studies and, more astonishingly, *critical* Kurdish studies—in other words, *also* critical of internal strife for control within Kurdish society and its internal

---

1. Sheikh Ubeydullah (1826–83), leader of the Kurdish rebellion of 1881 bearing his name, quoted in Jwadieh 2006, 169.

relations of domination—have developed fully in only three decades attests to the pace with which praxis transforms academia. Kurdish as well as non-Kurdish—almost all American and European—scholars have played a significant role in the advent of a golden age in Kurdish studies. Notwithstanding the role of individual scholars, Kurdish studies has won undeniable legitimacy as a specific branch of Middle Eastern studies.

The acquisition of this legitimation has increased scholarly production; before the period in which this legitimacy was attained, however, during the 1980s and the 1990s, scholars of the Middle East were either— at least publicly—totally blind to the "sensitive" issues of the region, such as the Kurdish problem or the Armenian Genocide, or were simply executing censorship orders from Ankara and other Middle Eastern capitals. The one incredible exception was the famous sociologist İsmail Beşikçi: his pioneering academic work in the 1970s not only documented the violence extremely well but also proposed an entirely new research agenda. However, as he rightfully conjectured, realizing this agenda was impossible without shaking the very foundations of Turkish academia. Introducing the Kurdish issue to the academic study of Turkey would undermine and destabilize the official, nationalist Turkish History Thesis (all nations descend from Turks) and the Sun Language Theory (all languages descend from Turkish). Such an intervention would inevitably bring down the entire edifice of Kemalist social sciences as well as the worldwide practice of Turcology. "History, and particularly modern history will be re-written," stated Beşikci, "but who will rewrite them? Undoubtedly those who have suffered from their falsification" ([1977] 1991, 247).

This volume provides yet another proof of the vitality of Kurdish studies as well as the enterprise of rewriting history by those who have suffered from the Turkish official historical narrative and its endless falsifications or by a new generation of non-Kurdish scholars who reject the official narrative that diminishes, stereotypes, and criminalizes Kurds as separatists or terrorists. I remember that during the long *dark* 1980s, which cost the lives of some two hundred thousand Kurds, there were hardly a total of twenty-five to thirty books on the Kurds in the three main European languages—English, French, and German. Today, what could be defined as the "Kurdish library" or "la bibliothèque kurde" contains hundreds of books in these three languages, not to mention many unpublished academic theses as well as specialized periodicals, peer-reviewed articles, and internet publications.

It is because of this wealth of information that there was no need for the volume editors to propose a macrolevel analysis to study the Kurdish issue; such analyses emerged and evolved during the past century or were reconfigured throughout the past two decades. What scholars emphasize instead are *mezzo-* and *micro*level studies. This choice is indeed a judicious one because separating these two levels reveals not only their internal dynamics but also how deeply these dynamics are affected by Turkish macrolevel power relations, by mechanisms of domination, segregation, marginalization, state coercion, as well as by the symbolic violence committed by the state and nonstate actors. To be sure, the constraints that Kurdish actors face, be they mothers whose daughters and sons have "disappeared" or seasonal workers, necessitate the inclusion of macrolevel processes. But these "secondary" if not invisible actors create, through their everyday resistance or through their capacity to win some agency, valuable symbolic and mobilization resources, discourses of legitimization, behavioral codes, new aesthetic forms of expression, and the like. Needless to say, all of these things themselves thereby attain the capacity to change macrolevel process.

The historian Ibn Khaldun (1332–1406) suggested, based on his observations of his times, which were also extremely dark, that dominated ethnic groups do not have a history of their own; their history is simply a part of the history of their masters (Martinez-Gros 2006, 143–44). What holds for the past also holds for the future: the destiny of dominated groups is determined not by themselves but by their lords. This does not of course imply that Kurds cannot be a part of the nation-states of Turkey, Iran, Iraq, and Syria. Kurds can co-read the past and co-build the future, but such participation would be meaningful and emancipatory for the Kurds only if it takes the same form as Basque and Catalan integration into post-Franco Spain. Such integration, in its own plurality, accepted these national groups for what they were and what they wanted to be in the new era—namely, free Basques and free Catalans in a democratic Spain.

Likewise, Kurds can live as equals in Turkey only if there is democracy in Turkey and if the Turkish state and society treat all social groups, including marginalized ones, as equals.

Yet this is not at all the case at the moment. As Barış Ünlü demonstrates both in his book published in Turkish (Ünlü 2018) as well as in chapter 3 in this volume, what Kemalist Turkey and later post-Kemalist regimes proposed to the Kurds in Turkey was always the same: deny your "Kurdishness" so that you can enjoy the rights and privileges of the Turkish majority. Scholars trace the origins of the Kemalist regimes to the decade of war (1912–22), when Turkey lost hundreds of thousands of inhabitants mostly in the Balkans and Asia Minor. The Ottoman Unionist and early Kemalist regimes further exterminated or expelled from the country yet another three million people. The Kemalist regime was subsequently established in a country of barely thirteen million. These secular Kemalist Turks could instrumentalize the Muslim Kurds only as "raw human material" with which to demographically "produce" the Turkish nation. Yet at the same time the Kurds ethnically emerged as a threat to Turkishness. For instance, internal reports prepared during the early republic by Abdülhalik Renda (1881–1957)—brother-in-law of Ottoman grand vizier Talaat Pacha and one of the architects of the Armenian Genocide—leave no doubt that the Kemalist regime was a social Darwinist one, considering the Kurds a potential biological threat to Turkishness. For Renda, who also prepared the official Turkish state Plan for Reforming the East (Şark İslahat Planı), there were dual priorities: prevent the "Kurdification" to the west of the Euphrates and develop a long-term strategy to "Turkify" the East Bank of the Euphrates (Bayrak 1993, 1994, 2009). The Kemalist elite thus used three violent means—repression, deportation, and assimilation—to resolve the Kurdish issue. Its violence may have been rooted in time and in space; this elite was born mostly in the Balkans or had worked or fought there only to become further traumatized by the loss of the Ottoman Macedonia (Bozarslan 2013).

The "Contract of Turkishness" that Ankara proposed to the Kurds was not the end result of negotiations between equal partners who have different positions, interests, and projections concerning their respective futures. It was instead a "pact." According to the French philosopher Jean

Baudrillard (2002a, 2002b), a *pact*, in contrast to a contract, is imposed by force, signed by blood, and can be dissolved only through bloodshed. In the Turkish case, the submission to this pact— which explicitly stipulated that under any condition Kurds *would not* have equal political, cultural, judicial status to the Turkish majority—was the sine qua non of Kurds to survive, which they thus could do only as individuals. It is therefore not an accident that the Kurds reacted to this blatant and violent exclusion with proactive violence. Moreover, as demonstrated by the quite large number of "assimilated" Kurds who have discovered their "identity" since the 1980s, some people also choose the discomfort of being a Kurd in Turkey, thus sharing the negative condition and fate of the Kurds rather than enjoy the theoretical—that is, imagined but not actualized—happiness offered by the Turks.

The first part of this volume delves into history. Barış Ünlü's chapter identifies the Unionist–Kemalist venture as a radical rupture in the *longue durée* of both Kurdish–Turkish state relations as well as Kurdish–Armenian–Turkish state relations. Metin Atmaca's reading of the Kurdish condition(s) under the Ottoman Empire reveals the sharp contrasts between the leaders of the Ottoman Empire and the future Turkish nation-state. As the founder of the Turkish Republic, Mustafa Kemal not only had a radical Turkish nationalist vision based on denial of the Kurds but also wanted the neighboring countries—that is, Iran, Iraq, and Syria— to refuse to give them any political rights.[2] As the struggling leader of the Ottoman Empire, the sultan at his palace, be it Topkapı, Dolmabahçe, or Yıldız, had no denial policy vis-à-vis the Kurds. Until the period of the Nizam-i Cedid (New Order) initiated by Sultan Selim III between 1789 and 1807, the Ottoman state considered the Kurds as Muslim partners who were attached to the empire by a contract dating back to the Ottoman–Persian war fought at Chaldiran in 1514, a contract that had been honored and renewed over time. In spite of brutal Ottoman state suppression

---

2. See, for example, H. Dobbs, "Note on Conversation with R. Rushtu Bey at Cinner at Angora on 23rd Novembre 1926," enclosure in Sir G. Clerck to O. Lancelot, Constantinople, 20 Dec. 1926 (Private), 7086/6677/44, Foreign Office–East, London, and R. Lindsay to A. Chamberlain'e, Constantinople, 21 Nov. 1926, 6635/32/65, Foreign Office.

of contemporaneous Kurdish revolts thereafter—that is, during both the Tanzimat (Reforms or Reorganization of 1839–76) and the Hamidian rule (1876–1908/9)—the Ottoman state did not deny the existence of Kurds and did not attempt to violently co-opt the Kurdish elite.

The Ottoman Empire was indeed not a *fabrique de citoyens*, as modern states are now and as the Roman Empire was to some extent. Nevertheless, I believe that the Ottoman dynasty was clearly aware that it had a triple identity. First, it was the "Third Rome," fulfilling the universal goal of empire building inherited from the Roman and Byzantine Empires. Second, it was a Muslim entity in Europe, very different in both its geography and its imaginary from the Arab empires of the past, which were mainly eastern or at best Mediterranean. Third, it was ruled by a *Turkish* dynasty, which, even after the elimination of the Turkic bureaucracy by Mehmed II (1432–81), never forgot that it was Turkish and that it would remain so in the future. The Ottoman state initially preserved the tribal structures or derogatory power structures in Kurdistan and the Arab provinces. It was only during the nineteenth century that the Kurdish political structures were brutally destroyed by the Ottoman state. For the Turks, the situation was different: already by the conquest of Constantinople, they were reduced to subjects of the sultan alone, without any internal, infrastate solidarities across imperial ethnicities. It was the sultan's own ethnic group that directly and exclusively depended on his authority. In contrast, the Kurds had been recognized qua Kurds, and their *hükûmet*s (governments or hereditary dynasties) enjoyed exclusive rights on some delineated albeit fragmented territories of the empire. Unlike the Turkish urban notables (*ayan*s), who emerged in the seventeenth century and had a very weak social basis, the rights of Kurdish notables were recognized by the Ottoman state, so they did not obtain their privileges against the will of the sultan or Bab-ı Ali, as was the case for *ayan*s. Nevertheless, such recognition was based on the Kurds' submission to the Ottomans. Indeed, the well-known poetry of Ehmedê Xanî quoted by Metin Atmaca in his chapter attests that at least some Kurds were perfectly aware of their subordinated position. They kept asking themselves the unbearably heavy question: "Why are we the losers of an imperial history, whose winners are Ottoman and Persian?"

Janet Klein analyzes the Armenian challenge that emerged after the uprisings of Christian communities in the Balkans from the early nineteenth century on. She argues that the Armenian case presented a triple threat to the Ottoman Empire. The first threat was to the imperial structure; in an era of awakening nationalities (*réveil des nationalités*) after Ottoman subjects were transformed into citizens, the Ottoman imperial identity was proving not to be sufficient. The second threat was to the imperial Muslim identity; the empire could not entirely accept and put into practice either the full emancipation of its non-Muslim subjects or full equality between Muslims and non-Muslims. The third threat was to the imperial Turkish identity; as attested by the discourse of Sultan Abdülhamid II, the imperial ruler was aware of the significance of establishing religious networks with Muslims outside the empire to politically contain the wild expansion of Christian Europe. Even though Ottoman policy thus connected with Muslims elsewhere, the state still denied the legitimacy of other national communities on its soil (Dündar 2015, 51).

The Armenian challenge was in fact quite heuristic in terms of imperial analysis: first, it demonstrated that the Ottoman Empire was, before anything else, a system of domination and subordination; this system ensured the survival of non-Muslims alone but did so only insofar as they did not claim equality to Turks in status. It is important to underline here that the late Ottoman Empire, compared even to its Austrian-Hungarian and Russian neighbors, was not actually an "empire" in the strict sense of the word except for with respect to its accommodation of ethnic and confessional plurality. It also contained the seeds of a nation-state in that it was inhabited by strong Turkish nationalist aspirations and put these aspirations to practice by adopting social Darwinism as its main ideology and practical roadmap. One can thus argue that the Ottoman Empire was behind its time as an empire but also to a large extent ahead of its time as a budding nation-state. Undeniably, the empire was archaic, underdeveloped, and quite sterile in its public social and cultural life, but it still made its own contributions to European history, especially in generating the secret paramilitary organizations that enacted significant changes on contemporaneous states and societies. The Russian Revolution of 1905 had a clear social base; the Persian Revolution of 1906 possessed constitutionalist and some anti-imperialist aspirations. Yet the Ottoman "revolution" of 1908 occurred only due to the intervention of a secret, largely military organization, the Committee of Union and Progress (İttihat ve Terakki Cemiyeti) and its secret paramilitary branch of destruction that would take the name "Special Organization" (Teşkilat-ı Mahsusa) later on. The post-1913 Committee of Union and Progress, the first example of a party–state in world history, was largely ahead of its time because other party–states were not constructed, especially in Europe, until the 1920s. Thus, the so-called Young Turk Revolution of 1908, enacted to reform the empire, would end up adopting an aggressive and exclusive Turkish nationalism that systematically targeted non-Turks (the Kurds) and Christian communities. When the Unionist and pro-Unionist authors compared the so-called Young Turk Revolution to the French Revolution, they explained that the Christians constituted the "first" and "second" state—that is, the oppressive aristocracy and clergy—while the Turks represented the "third" state (*tiers état*), the oppressed "people."

The dramatic loss of the Balkans in 1912 within a month and the almost total annihilation of the Ottoman Armenians in 1915 not only put a de facto end to the Ottoman Empire but also accelerated the process of Islamization of the remaining heartland in Asia Minor. For the first time, Muslims became a solid majority. After the forced population exchange with Greece in 1923, the new Turkey founded by an agnostic if not atheistic elite was initially proud of "being Muslim at 99 percent." The Turkification process, however, was extremely challenging due to the presence of a substantial Kurdish community. Turkish state coercion during the 1920s and 1930s went hand in hand with heavy symbolic violence to silently eliminate the Kurds; the new régime either denied the existence of the Kurds or described them only as a retrograde ethnofeudal class (Bozarslan 2015).

The contributions to this volume by Michel Ferguson, Güllistan Yarkın, Deniz Duruiz, and Şefika Kumral reveal that the coercion, discrimination, and stigmatization practiced against the Kurds went well beyond the foundational period, covering in the following decades not only Kurdistan but also all Kurdish communities across time and space.

Michael Ferguson's article on the Kadifekale district in Izmir demonstrates the significance of the *mahalle* (neighborhood) both spatially and ethnically, especially as a system of classification, stratification, and stigmatization of the Kurds and other non-Turkish groups. Whereas Turkishness is located in the upscale "high-class" neighborhood formerly known as Gavur İzmir (Smyrna the Infidel), Kurdishness can be found in the "low-class" neighborhood on the outskirts of the city. Indeed, Turkish authorities study and analyze Kurdishness through the framework of Cesare Lombroso's (1838–1909) criminal anthropology, finding its ultimate justification for their treatment of Kurds in the theory of atavism. Güllistan Yarkın's reading of "coloniality" as a continuous process also examines how the Turkish state's discourse on the Kurds is reappropriated historically, symbolically, practically, and locally in everyday interactions in an Istanbul district. Hence, the Turkish state's irresponsibility, immunity, and impunity are replicated largely at the local level within the *mahalle* framework, producing thus a systemic violence against the Kurds.

Deniz Duruiz's contribution, predicated on a comparison of Kurdish and Syrian seasonal workers, focuses on the experiences of Kurdish seasonal workers and their double construction by the Turkish locals as the "other" in terms of both class and ethnicity. Even though harvesting and conditioning fruits and vegetables depend on the low-waged Kurdish workers, Turkish locals continue to refer to them as "invaders," "separatists," and "terrorists." The narrow social confines imposed by the perceptions of otherness and enmity leave migrant Kurdish workers little alternative other than either silence—that is, submission—or resistance—that is, the rejection of their marginalization.

Şefika Kumral's chapter also allows a comparison in the context of *komshuluk* (intraneighborhood relations) and violence, studied also by other scholars—for instance, in the case of Bosnia (Bougarel 1996)—by a mapping of the Kurdish conflict, which although deepening in time is getting narrowed in space. Kumral demonstrates the degree to which "intimate" forms of violence against the Kurds can be brought on by Turkish state and society in the sharing of everyday spaces. The Turkish state and its various regimes not only observe and tolerate this "intimate violence" but even encourage it by refusing to punish the perpetrators of it. Amid this violence, the particular Turkish "regime" ceases to be a Leviathan and transforms itself instead into a Behemoth, the second well-known

Hobbesian maritime monster. In political theory, whereas the advent of the Leviathan signifies the emergence of an impersonal and even potentially coercive authority that delivers security to all, the Behemoth marks a radical return to the state of nature and civil war. One could therefore argue that the increasingly controlled media in Erdoğan's Turkey today is an organ of Behemoth, propagating its violence through calls for hate and then covering up and legitimizing its evil deeds.

Ali Eşref Keleş's chapter on the Roboskî massacre reveals how the Turkish state can deny a crime not only that it has committed but that has also been perfectly documented. The pro-Turkish state press covers the event extensively, but only for the rhetorical act of blaming the victims and exonerating the killers. The "narrative" or symbolic violence deployed by the Turkish state and its media before, during, and after this massacre not only prepared the ground and accompanied the physical coercion but post facto legitimized it as well. More importantly, while sacralizing the borders and consequently an entire territory as national, this symbolic violence enacted by the Turkish state and media defines the inhabitants of the border areas merely as "bare lives."

According to the official Turkish state discourse, the "Turk" is defined as civilized, historically significant, and proud, the ideal citizen who has to be protected by the borders that belong to him and him alone. In comparison, the same discourse portrays the Kurd inhabiting the borderland as "uncivilized" and "historically insignificant," ashamed of his identity. To be sure, past empires also had borders, but (except in periods of war) they were neither militarized nor portrayed as barriers of national honor and national economy. National borders that were either created or militarized after the Great War (1914–18) not only divided the Kurds as a national group but also separated tribes and families, as geographers showed in their maps of villages on the Syrian–Turkish and Iraqi–Turkish borders (Société des nations 1924).[3] As Yunus Nadi (1879–1945), who was first a Unionist and then a Kemalist journalist with close ties to Mustafa Kemal, stated, already by the 1930s the Turkish state had stigmatized the Kurds;

---

3. For the maps, see Clergé 1938.

first, they were officially defined as "bad citizens," and then they were referred to with the equally denigrating term *smugglers*—that is, "those traitors to the nation's economy and honor" (see Nadi 1931). It is therefore not at all surprising that the transitivity of the borders has always been one of the Kurds' main demands, a demand turned down by the Turkish state along with every other demand Kurds had made through the years. Having no means of communication with the Turkish state except through violence, Kurds in Turkey gradually militarized the borders, turning them into areas of armed resistance (Fleming 1992; van Bruinessen 1992).

The third part of this volume focuses on the relationships between life and death, coercion and resistance, through the contributions by Delal Aydın, Amy Bartholomew and Ruşen Fırat Güllüoğlu, Emine Rezzan Karaman, Hazal Atay, and Nisa Göksel. Debates on civilization in Turkey took an unexpected turn during the transition from Kemalism (1923-47) to post-Kemalism (1948-2002) to Erdoganism (2003-). The former Kemalist discourse had portrayed the "Kurd" as "feudal," "primitive," and oppressive to "his" girls and women, so the Turkish Republic took upon itself the mission to educate the "female gender" in order to transform all Kurdish women into "civilized" Turks. Yet the terms of this debate have been reversed in the past couple of decades. Nowadays, it is the Kurds who define the emancipation of women as part of their social vision following their participation in public life. In opposition, "Turkishness" is defined as more and more macho, "reactionary," "obscurantist," and repressive of *its* "female gender." Indeed, in Turkey's Erdoganism, whereas "mustachioed politics" appears to be a Turkish political trait, it is now Kurds who publicly promote unveiled (and some veiled) women, cochairing positions with "cool" and progressive men. In addition, "Kurdishness" is no more a source of shame, a secret "illness" one has to bear hidden away, but a source of pride, a foundation upon which new interclass, intergender, and intergenerational subjectivities are constantly built. In terms of the reversibility of these positive developments in the future, I would argue that unlike the demobilization of women in the Algerian War of Independence (1954-61) and the Palestinian struggles (the First Intifada, 1987-91), the participation of Kurdish women in society is supported by the majority of Kurdish society.

The history of sufferings has also become a field in which the terms of the debate related to civilization have been transformed: the suffering of mothers whose loved ones have disappeared gives birth to an act of indictment designating the state not as a father with his strong muscles who imposes the superiority of the Turkishness but as a criminal and barbarian male whose unjust authority oppresses and stigmatizes the Kurds. Amy Bartholomew and Ruşen Fırat Güllüoğlu's contribution also documents this stigmatization and oppression. The Turkish state confines the body of Kurdish prisoners into a narrowed space; its "stateness" necessitates that the Turkish state alone has the monopoly of violence over the individual body; concerning the prisoners, however, the violence incarnates a collective struggle and sustains it as long as necessary. One could even argue that the hunger strikes and acts of self-immolation that occur among Kurdish prisoners deprive the Turkish state of having monopoly over violence, thereby destabilizing its hold. Also, these acts of violence transform the Kurdish victims who are objects of the Turkish state into subjects in control of their own bodies and their own fate, albeit a violent one. There are, hence, complex relationships among coercion, violence, and self-sacrifice; domination through reification; and emancipation through action.

In conclusion, then, it is necessary to insist on a syntax that never remains at the level of words but produces concrete outcomes. Nisa Göksel's contribution demonstrates the manner in which the Turkish state was able to impose its category of "terrorism" onto how Kurdish militancy in Europe was and has been dealt with, especially in the 1990s. There is no doubt that Kurdish activism in Europe still occurs in a marginal space determined by a "liminal legality." But today, in relation to the murder of twelve at the offices of the periodical *Charlie Hebdo* in Paris in 2015, it is Turkey's president who accuses the *cartoonists* of terrorism for caricaturing the Prophet Mohammad. In the context of preadolescent children parading in uniforms with wooden Kalashnikovs and of the past experience of the paramilitary organization the Grey Wolves' mundane violence against the Kurds and the Armenians in European cities, one ought to ask: Who is a terrorist?

"You shall think..." is the motto of this book. Let us start that process by thinking about this question on the terrorist.

References

Baudrillard, Jean. 2002a. *Esprit du terrorisme*. Paris: Galilée.
———. 2002b. *Power Inferno*. Paris: Galilée.
Bayrak, Mehmet. 1993. *Kürtler ve ulusal demokratik mücadeleleri: Gizli belgeler—araştırmalar—notlar*. Ankara, Turkey: Öz-Ge.
———. 1994. *Açık-gizli / resmi-gayriresmi Kürdoloji belgeleri*. Ankara, Turkey: Öz-Ge.
———. 2009. *Kürtlere vurulan kelepçe: Şark islahat planı*. Ankara, Turkey: Öz-Ge Yayınları.
Beşikçi, İsmail. [1977] 1991. *Cumhuriyet Halk Fırkası'nın tüzüğü (1927) ve Kürt sorunu*. Ankara, Turkey: Yurt.
Bougarel, Xavier. 1996. *Bosnie: Anatomie d'un conflit*. Paris: La Découverte.
Bozarslan, Hamit. 2013. "Söyleyenler ve söylenenler: Kemalist Türkiye'de tarihyazımı, tarih söylemi ve Kürdlerin varlığı." In *Cumhuriyet tarihinin tartışmalı konuları*, edited by Bülent Bilmez, 120–39. Istanbul: Tarih Vakfı.
———. 2015. "Sosyal Darwinizm, 'ötekileştirme' ve Kürtlerin diyabolizasyonu." In *Öteki'nin var olma sancısı: Türk politik kültüründe seytanlaştırma eğilimleri*, edited by İsmet Parlak, 123–49. Istanbul: Dora Basım-Yayın.
Clergé, Marcel. 1938. *La Turquie, passé et présent*. Paris: A. Collin.
Dündar, Fuat. 2015. *İttihat ve Terakki'nin Müslümanları iskân politikası (1913–1918)*. Istanbul: İletişim Yayınları.
Fleming, Glenn, Jr. 1992. "L'écologie et l'économie des villages kurdes." In *Les Kurdes par-delà l'exode*, edited by Hawkat Hakim, 157–81. Paris: L'Harmattan.
Jwaideh, Wadie. 2006. *The Kurdish Nationalist Movement: Its Origins and Development*. Syracuse, NY: Syracuse Univ. Press.
Martinez-Gros, Gabriel. 2006. *Ibn Khaldûn et les sept vies de l'Islam*. Arles, France: Actes-Sud.
Nadi, Yunus. 1931. "Une plaie saignante: La frontière syrienne." *La République* 17, no. 12: page nos. unavailable.
Société des nations. 1924. *Frontières entre la Turquie et l'Irak*. Geneva: Société des nations.

Ünlü, Barış. 2018. *Türklük sözleşmesi: Oluşumu, işleyişi ve krizi*. Ankara, Turkey: Dipnot.

Vali, Abbas. 1998. "The Kurds and Their 'Others': Fragmented Identities and Fragmented Politics." *South Asia, Africa, and Middle East* 18, no. 2: 82–95.

Van Bruinessen, Martin. 1992. *Agha, Cheikh, and the State: The Social and Political Structures of Kurdistan*. London: Zed.

Contributor Biographies

Index

Contributor Biographies

Ayça Alemdaroğlu is research scholar and associate director of the Program on Turkey at the Center for Democracy, Development, and the Rule of Law at Stanford University. She completed her PhD at Cambridge University. Her work focuses on political constructions of culture and identity and on social inequalities and how they are produced and reproduced through bodies, places, and institutions. She has published in *Foreign Policy*, *Social and Cultural Geography*, *Women's International Forum*, *Review of Middle East Studies*, *Middle East Report*, and *Turkish Studies*. She coedited *Confronting the New Turkey* (Middle East Report no. 288) and *Kurdistan: One and Many* (Middle East Report no. 295). She previously worked as assistant professor of research in sociology and the director of the Keyman Modern Turkish Studies Program at Northwestern University.

Hazal Atay is a PhD candidate in comparative politics at Sciences Po Paris. She is an INSPIRE Marie Skłodowska-Curie Fellow and affiliated with the Centre for Political Research at Sciences Po. Her research interests include biopolitics, gender and sexuality, democratic theory, and institutions, with a focus on the Middle East, North Africa, and Turkey. Her recent publications concern abortion rights and access in restrictive settings and Muslim-majority countries as well as women's political representation.

Metin Atmaca is associate professor in the Department of History at the Social Sciences University of Ankara and associate member at Center d'etudes Turques, Ottomanes, Balkaniques et Centrasiatiques at École des hautes études en sciences sociales in Paris. He completed his MA degree at the University of Texas at Austin in 2006 and his PhD at the University of Freiburg in 2013. In the 2021–22 academic year, he taught at Rowan University in New Jersey as Fulbright scholar-in-residence. He has published several articles and book reviews on Ottoman Arab historiography, microhistory in Ottoman studies, the Kurdish emirates, and the perception of the Kurds in the Middle Eastern historiography in major scholarly journals such as *Middle Eastern Studies, Insight Turkey, Oxford Bibliographies Online, Journal of World History, Ab Imperio,* and *Kurdish Studies.*

Delal Aydın is a Philipp Schwartz Initiative Fellow in the Institute for Turkey Studies at the University of Duisburg-Essen. Before Germany, she was a postdoctoral researcher in the Faculty of Political and Social Sciences and a research fellow at the Center of Social Movement Studies at the Scuola Normale Superiore. She received her PhD in sociology from the State University of New York at Binghamton. Her work focuses on the forms of community making in the Kurdish national struggle against the Turkish state's symbolic and physical violence. Aydın's research interests span political sociology, theories of the state, subject formation, social movement theories, youth studies, standpoint epistemology, race, and ethnicity.

Amy Bartholomew is associate professor in the Department of Law and Legal Studies at Carleton University in Ottawa, Canada. Her current research is on Habermasian legal and political theory; borders, camps, and prefigurative politics; and hunger striking as necroresistance or act of natality. Recent publications include *Justice without Guarantees: Habermasian Theory and Radical Politics* (2007) and "Beyond the 'Barbed-Wire Labyrinth': Migrant Spaces of Radical Democracy in Greece" (with Hilary Wainwright, 2020). She is coauthoring "Natality, Necroresistance, Life Politics: Kurdish Political Prisoners' Hunger Strikes" with Ruşen Fırat Güllüoğlu.

Hamit Bozarslan is director of studies at École des hautes études en sciences sociales in Paris. He is the author of a series books on the Kurdish issue and Middle Eastern politics, including *Histoire de la Turquie: De l'empire à nos jours* (2013), *Le luxe et la violence: Domination et contestation chez Ibn Khaldûn* (2014), and *Révolutions et état de violence: Moyen-Orient, 2011–2015* (2015). He is currently researching antidemocracy in the twenty-first century.

Deniz Duruiz is assistant professor at Concordia University (Montreal). She received her PhD in anthropology from Columbia University. Her work focuses on migration through the lens of labor. She conducted ethnographic research with Kurdish migrant farmworkers and Syrian refugees in Kurdistan and on the farms of western Turkey. She is working on a book that examines the relationship between racialization, political violence, and capitalist production in Turkey. Her current research project is a comparative ethnography of the Syrian experience of migration to France and Canada with a focus on labor both as a category of political economy and as an embodied everyday practice.

Michael Ferguson is assistant professor of history at Concordia University (Montreal). He completed his PhD in history at McGill University. His work focuses broadly on the history of forced labor, slavery, displacement, and migration in the late Ottoman Empire and the Turkish Republic. His recent publications include "Abolitionism and the African Slave Trade in the Ottoman Empire (1857–1922)," in *The Palgrave Handbook of Bondage and Human Rights in Africa and Asia* (2020), and, with Ehud R. Toledano, "Slavery and Emancipation in the late Ottoman Empire," in *The Cambridge World History of Slavery*, vol. 4 (2017).

Fatma Müge Göçek is professor of sociology and women's studies at the University of Michigan. Her recent research critically analyzes the impact of processes such as development, nationalism, religious movement, and collective violence on minorities. Her publications include her monographs *Denial of Violence: Ottoman Past, Turkish Present, and Collective Violence against the Armenians, 1789–2009* (2014); *The Transformation of Turkey: Redefining State and Society from the Ottoman Empire to the Modern Era* (2011); *Rise of the Bourgeoisie, Demise of Empire: Ottoman Westernization and Social Change* (1996); and *East Encounters West: France and the Ottoman Empire in the 18th Century* (1987). She has also edited *Reconstructing Gender in the Middle East: Tradition, Identity, Power* (with Shiv Balahghi, 1994) and *Political Cartoons in the Middle East* (1998).

Nisa Göksel is assistant professor of sociology in the New College of Interdisciplinary Arts and Sciences at Arizona State University. She completed her PhD in sociology at Northwestern University, with a graduate certificate in gender and sexuality studies. She was a visiting research fellow at the Kroc Institute for International Peace Studies at the University of Notre Dame in 2017–18; a visiting researcher at the Center for Middle Eastern Studies at Lund University in the fall of 2018; and a lecturer at MEF University in Istanbul in the spring of 2019. Her publications appear in *Social Sciences*, *Critical Times: Interventions in Global Critical Theory*, and *Sociological Forum*. Her areas of research are gender and sexuality; feminist and women's movements in the Middle East; war, violence, and peacemaking; as well as migration, displacement, and diaspora studies.

Ruşen Fırat Güllüoğlu is a PhD student in the Political Studies Department at the University of Ottawa, specializing in political philosophy and international relations. His doctoral research concerns the potential merits of teleological thinking in mitigating the effects of postpolitical governance and political apathy. He is coauthoring "Natality, Necroresistance, Life Politics: Kurdish Political Prisoners' Hunger Strikes" with Amy Bartholomew.

Emine Rezzan Karaman is a lawyer in Istanbul, Turkey. She completed law school at Istanbul Bilgi University in 2021. She was a postdoctoral research fellow at Humboldt University in 2018–19. She studied sociology and history at Boğaziçi University from 2000 to 2005. She received her PhD in history from the University of California, Los Angeles, in 2016. Her academic work is in dialogue with various disciplines, including history, gender studies, anthropology, sociology, and law. Her chapter in this volume is an outcome of her recent research on the Saturday and Peace Mothers' struggle to find justice at the Turkish courts and the European Court of Human Rights. She has published various articles on the Mothers, including "Remember, S/he Was Here Once: Mothers Call for Justice and Peace in Turkey" (2016) and "The Saturday Mothers and Their Politics of Motherhood in Turkey," in *Women against War System* (2018).

Ali Eşref Keleş is an instructor at Ardahan University. He completed his PhD and MA in sociology at the University of Essex. His dissertation focuses on Turkish media, the Kurdish question, and the peace process (2009–15) in Turkey. His research takes a multidisciplinary approach to the Kurdish issue and encompasses the fields of media, discourse, political theories, nationalism, identity, and representation.

Janet Klein is associate professor of history at the University of Akron. She completed her BA at the University of Montana and PhD at Princeton University. Her work focuses on mass violence and the ways in which constructions of minorities and majorities have contributed to structural and mass violence. She is the author of *The Margins of Empire: Kurdish Militias in the Tribal Zone* (2011) and of many articles related to themes of mass violence and late Ottoman, Kurdish, and Armenian histories.

Şefika Kumral is assistant professor of sociology at the University of North Carolina at Greensboro. Her research interests lie in the fields of political, comparative-historical, and development sociology. She has published articles and book chapters on ethnic relations and nationalist violence in Turkey, the extreme Right and fascism, waves of global social protest since the eighteenth century, and transformation of global income inequality. She is currently working on a book project, "Democracy and Violence: Origins of Anti-Kurdish Riots in Turkey."

Barış Ünlü completed his PhD in sociology at the State University of New York at Binghamton in 2008. He has a BA in economics and an MA in political science from Ankara University. His books include *Bir siyasal düşünür olarak Mehmet Ali Aybar* (Mehmet Ali Aybar as a Political Thinker, 2002); *İsmail Beşikçi* (with Ozan Değer, 2011); *Osmanlı: Bir dünya-imparatorluğu'nun soykütüğü* (The Ottoman: A Geneology of a World Empire, 2011); *Türklük sözleşmesi: Oluşumu, işleyişi ve krizi* (The Turkishness Contract: Formation, Operation, and Crisis, 2018). In February 2017, with a State of Emergency decree, he was expelled from Ankara University, where he had been employed for seventeen years, for signing the Academics for Peace Petition. He is currently a Philipp Schwartz Research Fellow at the University of Duisburg-Essen.

Güllistan Yarkın is an independent researcher living in Istanbul. She completed her PhD in sociology at the State University of New York at Binghamton in 2017. Her research interests include racism, antiracism, social movements, colonialism, coloniality, labor history, and Kurdish studies. In 2018 she applied to the Interuniversity Board in Turkey for her doctoral diploma equivalency. In 2020 the board sent her a rejection letter, arguing that some of the statements in her dissertation may commit the crime of propaganda for a terrorist organization banned by the Antiterror Law and the crime of insulting the Turkish nation, the State of the Republic of Turkey, and the government of the Republic of Turkey, as regulated in the Turkish Penal Code.

Index

Abdülhamid II, 73–74, 397
Abdullah Cevdet, 73–74, 80–81
Abdurrahim Rahmi, 82–83
Abdurrahman Baban, 57
Abdurrahman Bedir Khan, 73, 74
abortion, 345
academic freedom, 3–6
actors and strategy, 102–3
Adalet ve Kalkınma Partisi (AKP). *See* AKP (Adalet ve Kalkınma Partisi)
Adamson, Fiona, 360
affect: and embodiment, 168–69, 171; and racialization, 168–69, 171, 184–85; and Turkishness contract, 105
affirmative action and political mobilization by women, 334–52
Afghan refugees in Izmir, 134
Africans and displacement, 123–24, 134–35
Afro-Turks, 124, 134–35
Agamben, Giorgio, 245, 296
Agnew, John, 233
Ahmed, Sara, 246, 247
Akçam, Taner, 76
Akçay, Faik, 150
Akıcı, Yonca, 301
AKP (Adalet ve Kalkınma Partisi): authoritarian shift of, 215, 220–21, 282; and coup attempt (2016), 15; and media ties, 228–29; peace negotiations with PKK, 2–3, 13–15, 220, 284, 375; reform period (Kurdish Opening), 13, 214–15, 284, 374n12; and Roboskî massacre, 246; women's participation in Parliament, 340
Akyol, Taha, 240–41
Albanian migrant workers, 148–49, 150n6
Albayrak, Berat, 229
Alemdaroğlu, Ayça, 1–25, 390
Alevi Kurds: and communal violence, 195; and Dêrsim massacre, 14, 152, 153, 195n1, 233, 237; as migrant workers, 21, 150, 154–57; racialization of, 154–56
Alinia, Minoo, 381
Alkan, Zekiye, 131
Anderson, Benedict, 98
Anter, Musa, 270n7
Antiterror Law and academics, 4–5, 6
appearance and clothes, 261–64, 275, 324
Arendt, Hannah, 1, 7, 295, 390
Aretxaga, Begoña, 257
Armenian Genocide: denial of, 95; and Kurds, 84, 143n1; and minoritization, 76, 78, 80, 84, 398; and Muslimness contract, 94–95, 96
Armenians: Armenian reforms, 69–70, 71–72, 76; displacement of, 233, 258;

Armenians (*cont.*)
    and geography/location of Kurdistan, 35, 36, 41, 149n3; as migrant workers in Istanbul, 149, 150n6; minoritization of, 19, 63, 65, 67–80, 83–84, 86–87; and minoritization of Kurds, 83–84; and Muslimness contract, 94–95; and Sasun rebellion, 72; as threat to national identity, 114–15, 397
assassinations, 12, 270n7
assimilation: and displaced women in Europe, 378–80; and education, 146, 257, 259–67; and minoritization, 82; and political mobilization, 9; and Turkishness contract, 98, 174, 233; and youth mobilization, 23, 256
Atatürk. *See* Mustafa Kemal/Atatürk
Atay, Hazal, 24–25, 334–52
athletics and class, 264–66
Atmaca, Metin, 18–19, 33–58, 395, 396
authoritarianism: AKP shift to, 215, 220–21, 282; and communal violence, 213–21, 399–400
autonomy: democratic, 283, 296–97, 300, 302, 367n7, 374; and hunger strikes, 297–99; Kurdish semi-autonomy in past, 96, 145; and women's political participation, 345
autopsies, 316
Avar, Sıdıka, 263
Ayata, Bilgin, 359, 365, 366, 374
Aydın, Delal, 23, 255–75
Aydın, Felat, 268
Aydın, Vedat, 268–69
Ayn Ali, 39–40

Baban Sancak name, 35, 50, 52. *See also* Kurdistan, geography/location of

Babanzâde İsmail Hakkı, 81–82
backwardness: and colonialism, 145–47; in early accounts of Kurdistan, 47n13; and media, 234; and minoritization of Kurds, 19, 80, 82; and racialization of Alevi Kurds, 155; and racialization of Kurds, 21, 152–55, 173, 175, 401; and schools, 259, 262, 263–64; and skin color, 178–79; and violence, 152, 155
Bakur. *See* Northern Kurdistan
Bakurê Kurdistanê. *See* Northern Kurdistan
Balibar, Étienne, 174–75
Balkans: loss of, for Ottoman Empire, 398; migrant workers in Istanbul, 148–50, 156; support for Bulgarian Turks, 206; Turkish settlement in, 149n4
bare life, 227, 245, 296
Bargu, Banu, 295, 296
Barış Anneleri. *See* Peace Mothers
Barış ve Demokrasi Partisi. *See* BDP (Barış ve Demokrasi Partisi)
Bartholomew, Amy, 23–24, 277–302, 402
Barzani, Mustafa, 10, 12
Barzincizade Abdulvahid, 83
Baudrillard, Jean, 394–95
Bayındır, Sevahir, 349
Bayır, Derya, 66
BDP (Barış ve Demokrasi Partisi): and hunger strikes, 281, 285–86, 287, 290–91; and Roboskî massacre, 244; and women's political participation, 345, 350
Beçet, Ayten, 301
Beckwith, Karen, 346n17
Bedirxan, 53
Behemoth, 399–400
Berg, Ulla D., 171

Berkan, İsmet, 244
Beşikçi, İsmail, 3–5, 392
bey, as title, 56
Bhabha, Homi, 184
Bilgin, İrfan, 313
Bilgin, Kenan, 313–15
Birgün and Roboskî massacre, 22–23, 226–30, 241–42, 244, 246–49
Bir Kürd. *See* Abdullah Cevdet
blackness. *See* racialization; skin color
blaming the victim: and Roboskî massacre, 22, 227, 234, 235, 237, 242–44, 248, 400; and state violence, 279n7
blue as skin color, 178–79
body and embodiment: and affect, 168–69, 171; and hunger strikes, 294–95; and racialization, 169, 171, 176, 177–79, 184–85; and Turkishness contract, 112, 113, 114
Bourdieu, Pierre, 92, 102–3, 113n7
Bowlby, Rachel, 274
Bozarslan, Hamit, 25, 375, 389–403
Brown, Malcolm, 171
Brubaker, Roger, 207
Buldan, Pervin, 351
Bulgarian Turks and migration, 206

Çağlayan, Handan, 336
Çalık Holding, 228
Campanile, Giuseppe, 51, 54–55
capitalism: and depoliticalization, 379–80; and use of racism to control labor, 144, 157
censorship, 2, 3–6, 236
Charlie Hebdo attacks (2015), 402
Chatty, Dawn, 120
children, imprisonment of, 283n13
CHP (Cumhuriyet Halk Partisi), 337, 340, 341

Christians: decline in population, 97; in millet system, 155; and minoritization, 70, 74; and minority concept, 66; and Muslimness contract, 93–94, 96
Çiller, Tansu, 343
citizenship, inequities in; and hunger strikes, 297–300, 302; and media, 239–40; and migrant workers, 147; and mothers' groups, 323
civil death, 296
civil servants and 2016 coup, 15
Çınar, Medya, 301
class: and displacement, 121, 399; and education, 259–60, 261, 264–67, 273; and *kıro* figure, 177; and nation-building, 266–67; and odor/smell, 165–66, 167, 168; and racialization, 21, 143–58, 164–87; and sports, 264–66; and youth mobilization, 270, 271, 273
clothes, 261, 264, 275, 324
coexistence, equal right to, 282, 297, 299, 300–302
colonialism and coloniality: and backwardness, 145–47; colonialism term, 144; coloniality term, 144; and compartmentalization, 267; and education, 263–64; and political mobilization, 9–10; and racialization, 143–58, 399; and racialization scholarship, 172–73; racism as legitimizing, 144, 172–73, 176, 184, 186–87; and youth mobilization, 263–64, 269
co-mayorships, 350–51
Committee of Union and Progress, 94, 95, 258, 398
communal violence: and authoritarianism, 213–21, 399–400; defined, 200; and democratization, 22, 193–94, 197, 199, 213–19, 221; forms of, 200;

communal violence (*cont.*)
   increase in, 22, 192, 193, 195, 211, 219; locations of, 194–95; and media, 212, 400; and non-Muslims, 195; overview of, 22, 192–94; and political mobilization, 22, 193–94, 197, 198, 199, 204, 205, 208–10, 213–19, 221; qualitative analysis of, 201–19; quantitative data, 196–201; and retributive violence, 207n5, 210n6, 211; and security fear, 194, 207, 210–13, 219; and socioeconomics, 193, 194, 201–7, 219; and state capacity, 193, 207–13; triggers for, 192, 218
communists and disappearances, 309, 310, 313
compartmentalization, 267
competition and communal violence, 201–7, 216, 219
Constitution: and autonomy of Kurds, 96; and gender equity, 339; and minoritization in Ottoman Empire, 68
contested democratization, 22, 193–94
co-presidencies, 348–52
corpses: autopsies, 316; and remains of disappeared, 310, 312, 325–28, 329, 330
Corrigan, Philip, 258n1, 266, 274
coup (1980): and communal violence, 195n1; and disappearances, 309; and hunger strikes, 277–78; and split in regimes, 10; trials, 14
coup (2016), 4, 5, 15
Crimean War, 74, 124
Criminal Law and academics, 6
critical discourse analysis, 229–30
critical events, 268–69
culture and racialization, 174–76

Cumartesi Anneleri. *See* Saturday Mothers
Cumhuriyet Halk Partisi. *See* CHP (Cumhuriyet Halk Partisi)

Dahlerup, Drude, 340n9
dams, 12–13
darkness, thinking as defense against, 1–2, 7, 25, 389–90, 402
Das, Veena, 268
Davud Pasha, 52
death and hunger strikes, 295–96
decolonization and racialization, 174–75, 186
DEHAP (Demokratik Halk Partisi), 344
dehumanization: and colonialism, 143–44, 153; and racialization, 178–79
deliberative democracy, 280n8
Demir, Murat, 314–15
Demirel, Emine, 132
Demirel, Rahşan, 130–32
Demirören Holding, 228n1
Demirtaş, Selahattin, 15, 285n17, 300
Demirtaş-Milz, Neslihan, 121–23, 133
democracy and democratization: and communal violence, 22, 193–94, 197, 199, 213–19, 221; de-democratization and violence, 220; deliberative, 280n8; HDP's focus on for all, 299–300; radical, 282, 296, 298, 367
Democracy Party. *See* DEP (Demokrasi Partisi)
democratic autonomy, 283, 296–97, 300, 302, 367n7, 374
democratic confederation, 297, 302
Democratic Party. *See* HDP (Halkların Demokratik Partisi)

Democratic People's Party. *See* DEHAP (Demokratik Halk Partisi)
Democratic Society Party. *See* DTP (Demokratik Toplum Partisi)
Democrat Party. *See* DP (Demokrat Parti)
Demokrasi Partisi. *See* DEP (Demokrasi Partisi)
Demokratik Toplum Partisi. *See* DTP (Demokratik Toplum Partisi)
Demokrat Parti. *See* DP (Demokrat Parti)
denial: of Armenian genocide, 95; and Roboskî massacre, 22, 227, 235–36, 238–42, 244, 248; state's denial of ethnicity, 8, 9, 10, 398
DEP (Demokrasi Partisi), 344
depoliticization, 378–80, 383
Deringil, Selim, 145
Dêrsim massacre, 14, 152, 153, 195n1, 233, 237
differentialist racism, 174–75
dignified life, 296–97
Dink, Hrant, 114
disappearances: and coup (1980), 309; under custody, 313–15; forms of, 312–18; and kidnappings, 317–18; and mass killings, 315–17; and remains, 310, 312, 325–28, 329, 330; trials for perpetrators of, 14, 310, 311–12. *See also* mothers' groups and disappearances
displacement: and accuracy of population figures, 8; and class, 121, 399; and colonialism, 146, 147; and communal violence, 195; effects of, 130–32; in Izmir, 20, 119–36, 398–99; and nationalism, 258; and PKK, 12, 127–30, 131, 133, 147; and protests, 130–32; scholarship on, 120–23, 359–61; trials for perpetrators of,

14; and urban renewal, 122, 132–33. *See also* women and displacement in Europe
Diyarbakır, youth mobilization in, 23, 255–56, 268–75
Doğan, Avni, 147
Doğan Holding, 228, 229
domestic work, 345–46
double consciousness, 113
DP (Demokrat Parti), 337
dress. *See* clothes
Drouville, Gaspard, 49–54
DTP (Demokratik Toplum Partisi), 234, 283, 340, 349
Dupre, Adrien, 50
Duruiz, Deniz, 21, 164–87, 399

Eastern Reform Plan, 146–47
Ebussuud, 39
economic development, 12–13, 38
education and schools: and assimilation, 146, 257, 259–67; mass firings of teachers, 300; and national identity, 99; and officer's kids (*subay çocuğu*), 259–68; and social class, 259–60, 261, 264–67, 273
Ehmedê Xanî, 42–43, 396
Eichmann, Adolf, 1–2
Eldem, Edhem, 145–46
election laws, 342, 349–51
embodiment. *See* body and embodiment
emirates: Baban, 49–54; origins of, 40–41; under Ottoman Empire, 39–40; titles for, 56–57
emotions. *See* affect
empathy, 246
ENViT. *See* Ethnic and Nationalist Violence in Turkey (ENViT)

Erbey, Muharrem, 283n13
Erdoğan, Recep Tayyip: and authoritarianism and totalitarianism, 220–21, 389–90; and communal violence, 220–21; and hunger strikes, 278–79, 280, 290, 294; and Peace Petition, 4; and Roboskî massacre, 236, 238, 239, 244, 245
Eren, Hayrettin, 328
Eren, İkbal, 327–28
Ergenekon trials, 311
Ergin, Murat, 175, 177
Ersever, Ahmet Cem, 270n7
Esmer, 177n7
Ethnic and Nationalist Violence in Turkey (ENViT), 22, 194, 196–201, 204–5, 211, 217–18
ethnicity: as constructed, 171; denial of by state, 8, 9, 10, 398; lack of state data on, 8, 144; race and racialization vs. ethnicization, 170–71; in Roboskî massacre coverage, 22–23, 241–42, 247, 248–49; as term, 170–71; Turkishness as umbrella ethnicity, 10. *See also* minoritization; racialization; Turkishness contract
Europe: and geography/location of Kurdistan, 34–35, 44, 45, 50, 51, 54–57; Kurdish associations in, 368, 369, 370; migrant workers in, 361–62; and minoritization of Armenians, 69–70, 72–75; numbers of Kurds in, 8; PKK in, 362, 364, 365, 368–83; protests in, 362. *See also* women and displacement in Europe
European Convention of Human Rights, 316
European Court of Human Rights: and disappearances, 309, 315, 316, 318; and Roboskî massacre, 248

European Union (EU): accession to and peace negotiations, 3, 13–14; ban on PKK, 365; EU-Turkey migration agreement, 134; and judicial reforms, 287n21; women in European Parliament, 373–74
evil, 1–2
Evliya Çelebi, 46–48
Evrensel, 237
exile: and displaced women in Europe, 356–57, 377–78; and Turkishness contract, 100. *See also* displacement
expression, freedom of, 3–6, 11n1

Fairclough, Norman, 229–30
families and displaced women in Europe, 359, 360–61, 370, 371, 376, 381–83, 384
Fanon, Frantz, 153, 267
farmworkers: and communal violence, 204; and racialization of, 21, 164–87, 399
Fearon, James, 193
feminism: feminist institutionalism, 347; and oppression of Kurdish women, 342; state, 337, 341; and women's political mobilization, 24–25, 334–52
Feraizi-zade, 44
Ferguson, Michael, 20, 119–36, 398–99
First Treaty of Erzurum, 51
Fourteen Points, 82–83, 84–85
Fourth World Congress on Women (1995), 339
France: ban on PKK, 365; *Charlie Hebdo* attacks (2015), 402; displaced women in, 25, 363n6, 367–83; and minoritization of Armenians, 72; numbers of Kurds in, 362n5, 368n8
Frankenberg, Ruth, 91

Fraser, Nancy, 330
freedom, academic, 3–6
freedom of expression, 3–6, 11n1
Fuzuli, 41–42

Garzoni, P. Maurizio, 54
gecekondus, 148
Geerdink, Fréderike, 236
Gellner, Ernest, 98
gender: displaced women in Europe and gender control, 379, 381–83; equity in politics, 24–25, 334–52; equity policy, national, 338–39; quotas in politics, 24, 339n7, 340–41, 348; and institutions, 347; and *kıro* figure, 177; mothers' groups and gender roles, 322–23; and racism, 91–92; and skin color, 177–78; and transnational mobility, 360
genocide/politicide. *See* Armenian Genocide; Dêrsim massacre; Roboskî massacre and narrative violence; state violence
Germany: ban on PKK, 365; displaced women in, 25, 363n6, 367–83; numbers of Kurds in, 8, 362n5, 368n8; protest suicides in, 301
Gezen, Zülküf, 301
Göçek, Fatma Müge, 1–25, 390
Goffman, Erving, 93
Gökalp, Ziya, 258–59
Göksel, Nisa, 25, 356–85, 402
Gönen, Zeynep, 175–76
Good Party. *See* IP (İyi Parti)
Great Powers. *See* Russia; United Kingdom/Great Britain
Greece and Greeks: displaced in Turkey, 122, 126, 150n6, 258; exclusion from Turkey, 233; and Muslimness contract, 95; population exchange with Turkey, 97, 126–27, 398; and Turkishness contract, 97; in Zeytinburnu, 149, 150n6
Grojean, Olivier, 362
Güçlükonak, mass killings in, 315–17
Gülen movement, 247
Gulf War, 11, 12
Güllüoğlu, Ruşen Fırat, 23–24, 277–302, 402
Günay, Onur, 279n7, 293
Güneydoğu Anadolu Projesi, 12–13
Gunter, Michael M., 283n13, 301
Güven, Leyla, 301–2
"Gypsies." *See* Roma

Habermas, Jürgen, 279n6, 280n8
habitus, 92–93, 103, 104
HADEP (Halkın Demokrasi Partisi), 344
hair, 261, 262–63, 264, 275
Halabja massacre, 376
Halil Hayali, 83
Halkın Demokrasi Partisi. *See* HADEP (Halkın Demokrasi Partisi)
Halkın Emek Partisi. *See* HEP (Halkın Emek Partisi)
Halkların Demokratik Partisi. *See* HDP (Halkların Demokratik Partisi)
Hardy-Fanta, Carol, 360
Hasan Fehmi Paşa, 124
HDP (Halkların Demokratik Partisi): arrests and detentions of, 15, 300; election gains by, 2, 14–15; focus on democratization for all, 299–300; and hunger strikes, 281, 297, 299–300, 301; and women's political participation, 336, 339n8, 340, 341, 345–51
Hearth of Idealists, 212n7

HEP (Halkın Emek Partisi), 343
Herman, Judith Lewis, 243–44
Hess, Jess, 283n13, 288n23, 294
Heude, William, 56
Hiçdurmaz, Muzaffer, 157n9
Hizbullah, 274
Hobbes, Thomas, 104
Hobsbawm, Eric, 98
homo sacer concept, 227, 235, 245–48
housing and home ownership, 148, 176
hükûmets, 38
Human Rights Association, 330
hunger strikes: and injustice, 281–90; legitimacy of, 278–80, 290–300; in 1982, 295; organization of, 290–92; overview of, 23–24, 277–79; risks of, 291–92, 295; study methodology, 281–82; in 2012, 23–24, 277–302, 402; in 2016, 301
Hürriyet and Roboskî massacre, 22, 226–30, 238–49
hygiene: and farmworkers, 21, 165–66, 167, 168, 185; and women in mothers' groups, 324

Ibn Khaldun, 393
identity, national. *See* national identity and nation-building
identity, personal: and displaced women in Europe, 357, 358, 367–68; hybrid, 380; and place of origin, 181–82; and racialization, 168–70, 171, 183–85, 186; and Turkishness contract, 104; and youth mobilization, 23, 255–56, 257, 269–75. *See also* subjectivity
İdris-i Bidlisi, 36, 37
ignorance and Turkishness contract, 106–7, 174
İlhan, Abdullah, 315–17

İlhan, Neytullah, 315–17
Imad al-din al-Isfahani, 35
implicit signs, 104
imprisonment. *See* prisoners and imprisonment
infrastructure development, 12–13
injustice. *See* justice/injustice
İnönü, İsmet, 146–47, 260–61
institutionalism, feminist, 347
International Convention for the Protection of All Persons from Enforced Disappearance, 310n2
International Humanitarian Law, 327
international organizations: and pressure for Kurdish rights, 343n14; and pressure on gender equity, 338n7; Turkish monitoring of events in, 11
IP (İyi Parti), 340
Iran: and geography/location of Kurdistan, 36, 44, 47, 51–52, 53; post-WWI borders, 86
Iraq: campaign in (2015–16), 3; and geography/location of Kurdistan, 36, 47; and Halabja massacre, 376; Iraqi refugees in Izmir, 134; and PKK support, 12, 13
Irmak, Selma, 279n4
ISIS (Islamic States of Iraq), 2, 15
Islam: and Muslimness contract, 93–96, 99, 108, 173–74; in 17th c. accounts of Kurdistan, 47–48; Sunni vs. Shi'i tensions in Safavid/Ottoman rivalry, 38–39; and Turkishness contract, 97–98
Ismail I, 37
Istanbul and racialization of Kurds, 21, 143–45, 147–58
İyi Parti (IP). *See* IP (İyi Parti)
Izmir, displacement in: historical, 120–27; and Kurds since 1980, 127–36;

overview of, 20, 119; population of, 128; and refugees, 134; urban renewal in, 122, 132–33

Jews: in Izmir, 122; in Kurdistan geography, 41; in millet system, 155; and minority concept, 66; and Turkishness contract, 109
Jiyan, Agirê, 131
Justice and Development Party. *See* AKP (Adalet ve Kalkınma Partisi)
justice/injustice: and hunger strikes, 281–90; and mothers' groups, 311, 322

Kadifekale, displacement in: historical, 120–27; and Kurds since 1980, 127–36; overview of, 20, 119; population of, 128; and refugees, 134; urban renewal in, 122, 132–33
Kafadar, Cemal, 41
Kalyoncu, Cemal, 229
Kalyon Holding, 229
Kamuran Ali Bedir Khan, 85
Kapılar, 135
Karaman, Emine Rezzan, 24, 308–30
Karayılan, Murat, 241
Katib Çelebi, 44–46
Kaya, Ahmet, 315–17
Kaya, Halit, 315–17
KCK (Koma Civakên Kurdistanê), 278, 283n13, 287–88
KDP (Partiya Demokrat a Kurdistanê), 12
Keleş, Ali Eşref, 22, 226–49, 400
Kemal, Yaşar, 308
Kemaloğlu, Selahattin, 313, 315
Kemalpaşazade, 39
kidnappings, 317–18

kıro figure, 177
Kışanak, Gültan, 285n17
Kıvrak, Durmuş Coşkun, 328
Klein, Janet, 19, 63–87, 397
Koğacıoğlu, Dicle, 174
Koma Civakên Kurdistanê. *See* KCK (Koma Civakên Kurdistanê)
KOMA-GEL, 278n3
Kordestan name, 35. *See also* Kurdistan, geography/location of
Kourdistan name, 49. *See also* Kurdistan, geography/location of
Koyuncu, Berrin, 351
Krook, Mona, 340n9
Kumral, Şefika, 22, 192–221, 399
Kurdish Democratic Society Party. *See* DTP (Demokratik Toplum Partisi)
Kurdish Federated State, 12
Kurdish identity: and Armenian genocide, 84; and displaced women in Europe, 379–80; and minoritization, 80–82, 83; PKK's use of, 11; post-WWI, 85
Kurdish language: and AKP policy reforms, 13, 215; banning of, 9; and body, 112; and hunger strikes, 297, 299; and migrant workers, 150; and Peace Mothers, 311; as term, 7–8
Kurdish Opening, 13, 214–15, 284, 374n12
Kurdish Parliament in Exile, 363–64
Kurdish Peace and Democracy Party. *See* BDP (Barış ve Demokrasi Partisi)
Kurdish Socialist Youth, 2
Kurdistan, geography/location of: and Baban emirate, 49–54; as borderland or frontier, 34, 38, 39, 52, 54, 400–401; and borderland smuggling, 232–33, 242–43, 400–401; and boundary negotiations in 19th c., 44;

Kurdistan, geography/location of (*cont.*) and displaced women in Europe, 366, 377–78; and Europe, 34–35, 44, 45, 50, 51, 54–57; as fluid, 18–19, 33–35, 41–44; maps, 45, 55; in medieval sources, 34, 35–37; names for, 8, 35–37, 49–50, 84, 146, 149n3, 164n2, 237; and Ottoman Empire, 18–19, 34–35, 37–54, 149n3; as political entity, 37, 49, 54, 58, 377–78; as unknown, 18, 34, 46

Kurdistan Democratic Party. *See* KDP (Partiya Demokrat a Kurdistanê)

Kurdistan Workers. *See* PKK (Partîya Karkerên Kurdistanê)

Kurds: claims to land, 78, 79; Kurd term, 9; names for, 146; numbers of in Turkey, 7–8; origin myths and stories, 40–41, 46; state's denial of ethnicity, 8, 9, 10, 398; use of by Kemal, 96

labor: and communal violence, 204–6; hierarchies of, 21, 146, 154, 156–58, 205–6; mobility of, 147; and racialization of farmworkers, 21, 164–87, 399; and racialization of Kurds in Istanbul, 21, 143–58. *See also* migration and migrant workers

Laitin, David, 193, 207

Lake, David, 211

legality, liminal, 360, 383–84

life, dignified, 296–97

liminality of displaced women in Europe, 358–59, 361, 376, 383–84

literacy, 132

Lombroso, Cesare, 399

loyalty: and Kurdish migrant workers, 151–52; and minoritization of Armenians, 69, 70, 72, 77, 78–79, 84; and minoritization of Kurds, 63, 75, 80; and nationalism, 152; and Ottoman Empire, 19; and social contract, 100

lynchings. *See* communal violence

Malik, Sarita, 247

Mardin province and displacement to Izmir, 128–30, 133

marriage and displaced women in Europe, 371, 376, 381

mass killings and disappearances, 315–17

mayorships, co-, 350–51

Mazı, Salman, 314

Mazzarella, William, 168

McIntosh, Peggy, 91

media: and communal violence, 212, 400; and critical discourse analysis, 229–30; and Dêrsim massacre, 237; and hunger strikes, 285, 292, 293; imprisonment of media workers, 287; and minoritization of Kurds, 80–82; and othering of Kurds, 234; relationship to state, 227, 234, 236, 241, 245, 246; and Roboskî massacre, 284n15; self-censorship by, 236; shutdown during 2016 coup, 15; social media, 236, 365. *See also* narrative violence

Melayê Cizîrî, 42

Menjívar, Cecilia, 358, 361

MHP (Milliyetçi Hareket Partisi), 205, 208, 340

migration and migrant workers: and accuracy of Kurdish population figures, 8; and communal violence, 195, 204–5; and displacement, 147; in

Europe, 361–62; EU-Turkey migration agreement, 134; hierarchies of, 21, 146, 154, 156–58; and housing, 148; and Kurdish movement as transnational, 361–62; non-Kurdish, 148–49, 150, 180–83; and racialization of farmworkers, 21, 164–87, 399; and racialization of Kurds in Istanbul, 21, 143–58; and rise in tensions, 9; scholarship on, 359–61; struggles of migrant life, 359, 369, 378; Syrian, 165, 180–83, 399. *See also* displacement; refugees; women and displacement in Europe

Miles, Robert, 171

military: and assimilation, 146; campaign (2015–16), 2–3; and mass killings, 315–17; deaths and communal violence, 194, 197, 198, 209, 210n6, 211–13; and national identity, 99; officer's kids (*subay çocuğu*), 259–68; and racialization of Kurds, 153–54. *See also* Dêrsim massacre; mothers' groups and disappearances; Roboskî massacre

millet system, 66, 68, 145, 146, 155

Milliyetçi Hareket Partisi. *See* MHP (Milliyetçi Hareket Partisi)

Mills, Charles W., 20, 92

minorities: as constructed, 65; intergroup relations among, 67; and millet system, 66, 68, 145, 146, 155; minority term, 19, 64, 65, 66, 70, 71, 78; non-Muslims as, 19; problems with designation, 65–68

minoritization: of Armenians, 19, 63, 65, 67–80, 83–84, 86–87; of Kurds, 19, 63–65, 67–68, 79–87, 390–91; and national identity and nation-building, 69, 80–82, 83, 398; and nationalism, 19, 69, 77–78, 398; overview of, 19, 63–65; and sovereignty, 19, 64, 69, 82–83, 84–85; and territorial integrity, 19, 64, 68–69, 71; and threat to state, 70–71, 76–78, 79–80; and Turkishness, 67–68, 76–78; and violence, 64, 69, 72, 73–78, 84

Mirê Kor, 51, 53

morality: and ignorance, 106; moral ethos and state, 258; and Turkishness contract, 105, 106; and youth mobilization, 271–73

Morsümbül, Ekin, 329

Morsümbül, Fatma, 328–30

Morsümbül, Hanefi, 330

Morsümbül, Hüseyin, 328–30

mothers' groups and disappearances: as counter-narrative to state violence, 24, 319–21, 330; effect on mothers' lives, 322–25; and forms of disappearance, 312–18; origins of, 310–12; overview of, 308–10; and remains of disappeared, 310, 312, 325–28, 329, 330

Mouffe, Chantal, 279n6

muhajir term, 149–50

Muhammad Ali Mirza, 49, 56

Muslimness contract, 93–96, 99, 108, 173–74

Mustafa Kemal/Atatürk, 96, 336, 395

Mustafa Naima Efendi, 44, 48

Nacitarhan, Cavit, 313–14

Nadi, Yunus, 400–401

names: for Kurdistan, 8, 35–37, 49–50, 84, 146, 149n3, 164n2, 237; renaming people in Turkish, 9, 109; renaming places in Turkish, 9, 231

Narlı, Nilüfer, 344
narrative violence: and blaming the victim, 22, 227, 234, 235, 237, 242–44, 248, 400; defined, 226–27; and denial, 22, 227, 235–36, 238–42, 244, 248, 400; overview of, 22–23, 226–27; and silencing/erasure of Kurds, 227, 235, 241–42, 245–48; study analysis, 235–49; study methodology, 227–30
Nas, Ali, 315–17
National Action Plan on Gender Equality, 339
national identity and nation-building: and Armenian problem, 114–15, 397; and borders, 232–33; and class, 266–67; and institutions, 99; and media, 234; and minoritization, 69, 80–82, 83, 398; and suffering, 96–97; and Turkishness contract, 92, 96–99, 114–15, 173–74; and youth mobilization, 256
nationalism: and communal violence, 208; and education, 260–67; as focus in Kurdish studies, 16; and Gökalp, 258–59; and loyalty, 152; and media, 234; and minoritization, 19, 69, 77–78, 398; and political mobilization of Kurds, 210; and state violence, 258; and suppression of ethnicity in early Republic, 8–9; and Turkishness contract, 96–99, 115; and youth groups (*ülkücü*), 212–13
Nationalist Movement Party. *See* MHP (Milliyetçi Hareket Partisi)
National Party (Ulusal Parti), 129
National Plan on Gender Equality, 338–39
Nizam al-Din Shamsi, 36
non-Muslims: and communal violence, 195; millet system, 66, 68, 145, 146, 155; and minority term, 19; numbers of, 108; purging of, 97; and Turkishness contract, 97, 108–10
Northern Kurdistan: colonialism in, 143–45, 153, 158; and displacement to Izmir, 127; military campaign in (2015–16), 3; as name, 143, 165n2, 237. *See also* Kurdistan, geography/location of
nostalgia, 151

Ocak, Baba, 310
Ocak, Emine, 310
Ocak, Hasan, 310
Ocaklık, 38
Öcalan, Abdullah: and academic censorship, 4; capture and imprisonment of, 13, 208, 284–85; and Demirel, 131; on depoliticalization, 380; flight of, 11; as focus in Kurdish studies, 16; and hunger strikes, 23, 278, 285, 289–90, 297, 298–99, 301–2; on KCK, 278n3; and Peace Mothers, 311; peace negotiations with AKP, 2, 284; and radical democracy, 367
odor/smell, 21, 165–66, 167, 168, 185
officer's kids (*subay çocuğu*), 259–68
Öncü, Ayşe, 172n4
O'Neill, Shane, 281n11
Oomen-Rujiten, Ria, 279, 280
Oruç, Ramazan, 315–17
Oslo talks, 284
othering: of Kurds in Europe, 374; by media, 234; and minoritization, 76–77, 82, 86–87
Ottoman Empire: boundaries of, 34; conflicts with Russia, 124–25; and displacement in Izmir, 123–25, 127; and geography/location of Kurdistan,

18–19, 34–35, 37–54, 149n3; and minoritization, 19, 63–87; and minority term use, 19, 71; as nation-state, 397–98; Ottoman as term, 33n1; Ottoman identity, 34, 397; regional policy in Kurdistan, 38–40, 53, 145–46, 395–96; rivalry with Safavids, 18–19, 34, 37–44; settlement policy, 149n4; and slavery, 123–24; social standing of Kurds in, 8–9, 395–96; and women's suffrage, 336–37

Özgür gündem, 237–38

Özsoy, Hişyar, 327

pacts, 395
Pamay, Mahsum, 301
Panagia, Davide, 274
Pandey, Gyanendra, 65, 76–78
Parliament: and hunger strikes, 292, 301–2; women's participation in, 337, 338, 339–40, 343, 347, 373
Partîya Demokrat a Kurdistanê. *See* KDP (Partiya Demokrat a Kurdistanê)
Partîya Karkerên Kurdistanê. *See* PKK (Partîya Karkerên Kurdistanê)
pasha, as title, 56
Pateman, Carol, 92
patriarchy: and displaced women in Europe, 382, 384; effects of mothers' groups on, 322–23; and social contract, 92; and women's participation in politics, 24–25, 335, 344, 345
Patriotic Revolutionary Youth Movement. *See yurtsevers*
Patriotic Union of Kurdistan. *See* PUK (Yekîtiya Nîştimanî ya Kurdistanê)
patriotism: and minoritization, 81–82; and PKK, 11; and youth mobilization, 23, 255

peace: and displaced women in Europe, 375; and EU membership, 3, 13–14; and hunger strikes, 277, 280, 282, 283, 289, 297; and media coverage, 247; negotiations between AKP and PKK, 2–3, 13–15, 220, 284, 375; Peace Petition, 4–5, 6; potential negotiations post-2012, 300, 301, 302
Peace Mothers, 24, 308–12, 318–30
Peace Petition, 4–5, 6
People's Democracy Party. *See* HADEP (Halkın Demokrasi Partisi)
People's Labor Party. *See* HEP (Halkın Emek Partisi)
performance and Turkishness contract, 102, 103–5, 109, 110–13
Perilli, Luca, 287n21
PKK (Partîya Karkerên Kurdistanê): appeal of, 11–12; blame for disappearances and, 316, 317; blame for Roboskî massacre and, 22–23, 237, 240, 243, 245, 246; and communal violence, 208–13, 217; as crisis of state, 10–11, 173, 174; and displacement, 12, 127–30, 131, 133, 147; in Europe, 362, 364, 365, 368–83; as focus in Kurdish studies, 16; funding of, 11–12; listing of as terrorist organization, 10–11; peace negotiations with AKP, 2–3, 13–15, 220, 284, 375; rise of, 10; violence by, 10; women guerrillas, 369–72, 375–78; and youth mobilization, 2, 3, 255–56, 257, 268–75. *See also* Peace Mothers
police: and mothers' groups, 311, 312; murders of in Ceylanpınar, 2; and racialization, 175–76; and repression after 2016 coup attempt, 15; and youth mobilization, 270–71

political mobilization: and assimilation, 9; and bans on Kurdish parties, 14; and colonialism, 9–10; and communal violence, 22, 193–94, 197, 198, 199, 204, 205, 208–10, 213–19, 221; and displacement in Izmir, 135; and election laws, 342, 349–51; and feminization of politics, 24–25, 334–52, 401; and hunger strikes, 23–24, 277–302, 402; and identity, 23; Kurdish movement as transnational, 357–58, 361–67; and perception of Kurds as threat, 111; and resistance to Turkishness contract, 101, 111, 114–15, 174, 233; state's claim of Kurds as pawns, 8; state's response to, 288–90; youth mobilization, 3, 23, 255–56, 268–75. *See also* mothers' groups and disappearances; separatism and independence; women and political mobilization

politicide/genocide. *See* Armenian genocide; Dêrsim massacre; Roboskî massacre and narrative violence; state violence

Poole, Elizabeth, 241

popular violence. *See* communal violence

Posen, Barry, 211

presidencies, co-, 348–52

prisoners and imprisonment: child prisoners, 283n13; and displaced women in Europe, 358; and hunger strikes, 23–24, 277–302, 402; and PKK recruitment, 11; and protest suicides, 301

privilege: and Turkishness contract, 92, 100, 101, 102, 106–7, 174, 394; and whiteness, 92, 106

Promoting Gender Equality, 339

protests: and displacement, 130–32; in Europe, 301, 362; hunger strikes, 23–24, 277–302, 402; radical protests and democratic theory, 279; and Roboskî massacre, 284n15; suicides and self-immolations, 130–32, 301, 402. *See also* mothers' groups and disappearances

PUK (Yekîtiya Nîştimanî ya Kurdistanê), 12

quotas in politics, gender, 339n7, 340–41, 348

race: as constructed, 90, 91–92, 171; as term, 170–71

racialization: and culture, 174–76; and education, 262–63; vs. ethnicization, 170–71; of farmworkers, 21, 164–87, 399; of Kurds in Istanbul, 21, 143–58, 399; and minoritization of Kurds, 83–84; and odor and smell, 165–66, 167, 168; racial learning, 169; resistance to, 183; scholarship on, 170–77; and skin color, 21, 177–79; and social contract, 92; of Syrians, 180–83; third element in, 179–83, 184; and Turkishness contract, 20, 174; and violence, 152, 155–56, 176, 399

racism: as constructed, 91–92; differentialist, 174–75; and displacement, 121; and ignorance of privilege, 106; involuntary participation in, 104–5, 169; and labor control, 144, 157; as legitimizing colonialism, 144, 172–73, 176, 184, 186–87; and sexism, 91–92; without races, 174–75

radical democracy, 282, 296, 298, 367

Ramos-Zayas, Ana Yolanda, 169, 171, 183
Rancière, Jacques, 274
Rauf Pasha, 52
Rawls, John, 279n6
refugees: and displacement in Izmir, 122, 125, 133, 134, 135; and *muhajir* term, 149–50; racialization of, 180–83, 186; as third element in racialization, 179–83, 184, 186. *See also* women and displacement in Europe
remains of the disappeared, 310, 312, 325–28, 329, 330
Renan, Ernest, 96
Renda, Abdülhalik, 394
Republican People's Party. *See* CHP (Cumhuriyet Halk Partisi)
retributive violence, 207n5, 210n6, 211
Revanduzlu Mehmed Bey, 53
Revolutionary Communist Party of Turkey. *See* TDKP (Türkiye Devrimci Komünist Partisi)
Rewandiz, 50, 51
Rich, James C., 55
rights: and AKP policy reforms, 13, 214, 215; and *homo sacer* concept, 227, 235, 245–48; and hunger strikes, 297–300; and Turkishness contract, 100; and uprisings, 233
Roboskî massacre and narrative violence: analysis of, 235–49; and blaming the victim, 22, 227, 234, 235, 237, 242–44, 248, 400; and denial, 22, 227, 235–36, 238–42, 244, 248, 400; events of, 230–31, 284; and hunger strikers, 289; overview of, 22–23, 226–27; and silencing/erasure of Kurds, 227, 235, 241–42, 245–48; study methodology, 227–30; terms for, 231; trials, 232, 247–48, 284n15

Robson, Laura, 65–66
Rojava, 15, 221, 299
Roma: and displacement in Izmir, 122; and racialization, 170, 176, 178, 179, 183, 184, 186
Rothchild, Donald, 211
Rousseau, Jean-Jacques, 99, 100
Rueschemeyer, Dietrich, 220
Russia: boundary negotiations with, 44; displacement from conflicts with, 124–25; and minoritization of Armenians, 69–70, 72, 74n9
Russo-Turkish War, 124

Sabah and Roboskî massacre, 22, 226–30, 238–49
Sadettin Pasha, 71–75, 78–79
Safavids, 18–19, 34, 37–44
Sağlam, Zehra, 301
Şakar, Uğur, 301
Şanizade, 50
Saraçoğlu, Cenk, 121–23, 128, 129, 133, 175
Sarı Abdullah Efendi, 44
Sarıgörez, 39
Sasun rebellion, 72
Saturday Mothers, 24, 308–12, 318–30
Sayer, Derek, 258n1, 266, 274
scholarship: academic freedom and freedom of expression, 3–6, 11n1; dismissals after 2016 coup, 4, 5; and Peace Petition, 4–5, 6; rise of scholarship on Kurdish studies, 16–17, 391–93
Second Treaty of Erzurum, 51
security fear and communal violence, 194, 207, 210–13, 219
self-censorship by media, 236
self-immolations, 130–32, 301, 402

Selim I, 37
separatism and independence: Kurdish autonomy and hunger strikes, 297–99, 300; Kurdish autonomy in early republic, 96; Kurdish semi-autonomy in Ottoman Empire, 145; media focus on, 279–80; and political parties, 9, 342n11, 344; post-WWI, 85; and women's political participation, 342
Şeref Xân, 40–41, 58
Serres, Michel, 179
sexism. *See* gender
sexuality and racialization, 21, 166, 167, 168, 180, 185
şeyhülislam, 38–39
shame, 112–13
Sheikh Said Rebellion, 8, 101, 195n1, 233
Sheikh Ubeydullah movement, 75, 391n1
Silêmanî, 35, 44–45, 51, 52, 55–57. *See also* Kurdistan, geography/location of
Sincar, Mehmet, 270n7
Şırnak, airstrike in, 14
situational knowledge, 270n7
skin color, 21, 177–79, 180, 184
slaves and slavery, 123–24, 135, 179
smell. *See* odor/smell
Smith, Anthony D., 99
smuggling, 231–32, 240, 242–43, 401
social contract, 92, 99, 100. *See also* Muslimness contract; Turkishness contract
socialization: of displaced women in Europe, 364–65, 371–78; and Turkishness contract, 103–4
social media, 236, 365
socioeconomics: and communal violence, 193, 194, 201–7, 219; in critical discourse analysis, 230; cross-border trade and smuggling, 232–33, 242–43; and development projects, 12–13; economic crises, 220; effects of colonialism on Kurdistan, 146; and Muslimness contract, 94; state's focus on, 8; and Turkishness contract, 100
Soran, 38, 47, 50–51, 54
Southeast Anatolia Dam Project, 12–13
sovereignty: and displacement, 357; of Kurds post-WWI, 84–86; and minoritization, 19, 64, 69, 82–83, 84–85
Sözcü, 237
special courts, 287
sports and class, 264–66
state capacity and communal violence, 193, 207–13
state feminism, 337, 341
state violence: and backwardness, 152; and blaming the victim, 279n7; and coup (1980), 277–78; and hunger strikes, 280–81, 283–86, 292–94; increase in, 195n1, 300–301; against mothers' groups, 311, 312; mothers' groups as counter-narrative to, 24, 319–21, 330; and nationalism, 258; and Peace Petition, 4–5, 6; and secrecy, 243–44; and Turkishness contract, 394; and youth mobilization, 268–78. *See also* Dêrsim massacre; disappearances; displacement; narrative violence; Roboskî massacre and narrative violence; Sheikh Said Rebellion
Stephens, Evelyne Huber, 220
Stephens, John, 220
Steyn, Melissa, 105, 106

stigmatization. *See* minoritization; racialization
Stoler, Ann Laura, 175, 185
strategy and actors, 102–3
subay çocuğu (officer's kids), 259–68
subjectivity: and displaced women in Europe, 23, 357, 358, 361, 367–84; and racialization, 168–69, 171; and Turkishness contract, 104; and youth mobilization, 23, 257, 272–75
suffering and Turkishness contract, 96–97
suffrage, women's, 336–37
suicides, 5, 130–32, 301
Süleyman I, 39
Süleymaniyeli Tevfik, 83
Süleyman Nazif, 83
Süleyman Pasha, 56
Sumbas, Ahu, 351
Sümer, Tuncer, 129–30, 136
Sun Language Theory, 392
Susurluk Report, 270n7
Syria: ISIS in, 2; military campaigns in (2015–16), 3; Öcalan in, 11; and PKK support, 11, 12, 13, 15; political mobilization in, 132, 221; post-WWI borders, 86
Syriacs: displacement of, 258; in Kurdistan geography, 35; migrant workers, 165, 180–83, 399; Syrian refugees as third element in racialization, 179–83, 184, 186; Syrian refugees to Izmir, 134

Tadiar, Neferti X. M., 169–70, 183, 186
tails, 153, 158, 173
Talabani, Celal, 12
Tamer, Rauf, 246
Tamerlane, 36

Taraf, 237
TBMM (Türkiye Büyük Millet Meclisi), 340
TDKP (Türkiye Devrimci Komünist Partisi), 313
Temizöz, Cemal, 14
territorial integrity: and communal violence, 208; and minoritization, 19, 64, 68–69, 71
terrorism: and academic persecution, 4–5, 6; and Gülen movement, 247; and minority status, 391; and repression after 2016 coup attempt, 15
terrorism, Kurds as linked with: and displaced women in Europe, 364–67, 378, 402; and displacement in Izmir, 130; and election gains by pro-Kurdish parties, 2; and media, 152, 234; and minoritization, 76–78, 79–80; and PKK listing as terrorist organization, 10–11; and racialization, 173; and repression, 15, 152
Tezcan, Baki, 35–36
thinking: as defense against totalitarianism, 1–2, 7, 25, 389–90, 402; hunger strikes and freedom of thought, 291; and Turkishness contract, 102
tımars (fiefdoms), 19, 38
Tıraş, Mehmet Fatih, 5
toilets and racialization, 164, 168, 185
Tosun, Besna, 318, 319
Tosun, Fehmi, 317–18
Tosun, Hanım, 317–18, 319
totalitarianism, thinking as defense against, 1–2, 7, 25, 389–90, 402
Tozlu, Özcan, 317
transnational political relations scholarship, 359–61, 365–66
trauma of disappearances, 320–21

Treaties of Erzurum, 44, 51
Treaty of Berlin, 70, 74
Treaty of Lausanne, 86, 233
Treaty of San Stefano, 70
Treaty of Sèvres, 86
tribal-settlement programs, 127
Tsikata, Dzodzi, 348n18
Tuğluk, Aysel, 349
Turkey: Kurdish population in, 7–8; lack of state data on ethnicity, 8, 144; population exchange with Greece, 97, 126–27, 398
Turkish History Thesis, 392
Turkish language, 102, 108, 109, 111–12, 122, 392
Turkishness: compared to whiteness, 91–93; as created, 97; and education, 260–67; as habitu, 92; and minoritization of Kurds and Armenians, 67–68, 76–78; and racialization of farmworkers, 168–70; structures of, 101–7; as umbrella ethnicity, 10
Turkishness contract: historical framework, 93–101; as interaction order, 93, 107–14; and Kurds, 101, 108, 110–15, 233, 394–95; and Muslimness contract, 93–96, 99, 108, 173–74; and national identity, 92, 96–99, 114–15, 173–74; overview of, 20, 92–93; and performance, 102, 103–5, 109, 110–13; and privilege, 92, 100, 101, 102, 106–7, 174, 394; and punishments, 99–101, 106, 108; and racialization, 20, 174; resistance to, 101, 111, 114–15, 174, 233; structures of, 101–7; and violence, 109–10, 174
Türkiye Büyük Millet Meclisi. *See* TBMM (Türkiye Büyük Millet Meclisi)

Türkiye Devrimci Komünist Partisi. *See* TDKP (Türkiye Devrimci Komünist Partisi)
Turkuvaz Media Group, 228

Uca, Feleknas, 373–75
Uğurlu, Selahattin, 317
ülkücü (youth groups), 212–13
Ulusal Parti (National Party), 129
unemployment: and communal violence, 197, 198, 200, 202, 204; and development projects, 13
Üngör, Uğur Ümit, 78
United Kingdom/Great Britain: and boundary negotiations, 44; and minoritization of Armenians, 69–70, 72
United Nations High Commissioner for Human Rights, 3
United States: and capture of Öcalan, 13; and Kurdish Federated State, 12
Ünlü, Barış, 4, 20, 90–115, 173, 394, 395
urban renewal, 122, 132–33, 151

van Bruinessen, Martin, 335, 363–64
violence: and backwardness, 152, 155; and de-democratization, 220; and education, 261; as focus of Kurdish studies, 17; and minoritization, 64, 69, 72, 73–78, 84; and Muslimness contract, 94–95; perception of all Kurds as violent, 279–80; by PKK, 10; and racialization of Kurds, 152, 155–56, 176, 399; retributive, 207n5, 210n6, 211; and secrecy, 243–44; of transition to democracy, 213; and Turkishness contract, 109–10, 174; against women,

3, 345–46; and youth mobilization, 268. *See also* communal violence; narrative violence; state violence

von Hammer, Joseph, 45n10

wages and communal violence, 197, 198, 202

Watts, Naomi, 342n10

Watts, Nicole, 16

Weheliye, Alexander, 178–79

welfare support and communal violence, 206–7

White, Benjamin, 65, 68

whiteness: compared to Turkishness, 91–93; and ignorance, 106; involuntary participation, 104–5, 169; and privilege, 92, 106; studies, 20, 90–92, 105, 106

Wilkinson, Steven, 202n2

Wilson, Woodrow, 82–83, 84–85

women: guerrillas, 369–72; participation in politics globally, 334; participation in politics in Turkey, 334–35, 347; removal of Alevi Kurd girls, 153; violence against, 3, 345–46; women's interests term, 346; women's suffrage, 336–37. *See also* mothers' groups and disappearances

women and displacement in Europe: and depoliticization, 378–80, 383; and liminality, 358–59, 361, 376, 383–84; overview of, 25, 356–59; and political activity in Europe, 357, 359, 367–84, 402; and scholarship on displacement, 359–61; and struggles of migrant life, 359, 369, 378; and transnationalism of Kurdish movement, 361–67

women and political mobilization: and co-mayorships, 350–51; and co-presidencies, 348–50; and displaced women in Europe, 357, 359, 367–84; and election laws, 342, 349–51; and feminization of politics, 24–25, 334–52, 401; in Ottoman Empire and early Republic, 337–41; overview of, 24–25, 333–35; and participation in Parliament, 337, 338, 339–40, 343, 347, 373; participation in politics globally, 334; participation in politics in Turkey, 334–35, 347; scholarship on, 335–36; and suffrage, 336–37; women's assemblies, 24, 348–50. *See also* mothers' groups and disappearances

Xane Pasha, 51

Yahya Ibn Fadlallah, 36

Yalçın-Heckmann, Lale, 335, 343

Yanık, Yalçın, 134–35, 136

Yaqut al-Hamawi, 42

Yarkın, Güllistan, 5–6, 21, 143–58, 176, 399

Yeğen, Mesut, 80n18

Yekîtiya Nîştimanî ya Kurdistanê. *See* PUK (Yekîtiya Nîştimanî ya Kurdistanê)

Yeni şafak, 237

Yeşil, 270

Yezidis, 48, 373

Yıldırım, Mahmut, 270

Yılmaz, Mesut, 270n7

youth groups, nationalistic (*ülkücü*), 212–13

youth mobilization: and military campaign (2015-16), 2-3; *yurtsevers* in Diyarbakır, 23, 255-56, 268-75
Yüksek, Sıraç, 301
Yüksekdağ, Figen, 15, 300
yurtluk, 38
yurtsevers and political mobilization, 3, 23, 255-56, 268-75

Zaman, 236-37
Zana, Leyla, 343-44
Zeydanlıoğlu, Welat, 277n2
Zeynep (activist), 366
Zeytinburnu district (Istanbul) and racialization of Kurds, 21, 143-45, 147-58
Ziya Gökalp High School, 256-60

www.ingramcontent.com/pod-product-compliance
Lightning Source LLC
Chambersburg PA
CBHW032136010526
44111CB00035B/589